POLAMALU

THE INSPIRATIONAL STORY OF PITTSBURGH STEELERS STRONG SAFETY TROY POLAMALU

BY JIM WEXELL

TRIUMPH
B O O K S

The Library of Congress has catalogued the previous edition as follows:

Names: Jim Wexell, 2020-author.
Title: POLAMALU
First edition | Wisconsin: Worzalla Publishing Company, 2020.
ISBN 13: 978-0-9820225-1-1

This book is available in quantity at special discounts for your group or organization. For further information, contact:
  Triumph Books LLC
  814 North Franklin Street
  Chicago, Illinois 60610
  (312) 337-0747
  www.triumphbooks.com

Printed in U.S.A.
ISBN: 978-1-63727-253-4

Editor: Alan Paul
Designer: Pamela Diana

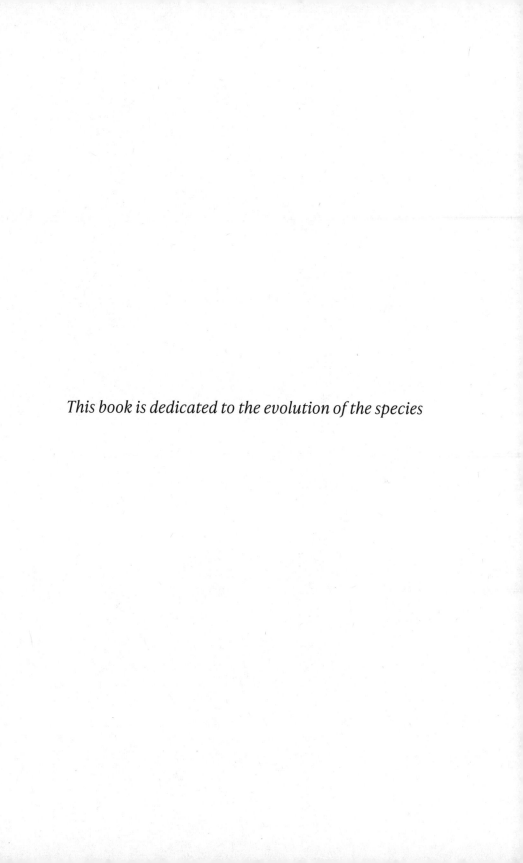

This book is dedicated to the evolution of the species

INTRODUCTION

It was a sticky August morning and I was finishing a brutal jog around the St. Vincent College campus.

Of course, all of my jogs are brutal, but I remember thinking that hot, humid and sweaty was no way to go through life as I turned off the road and up the school's main driveway for the final tenth of a mile.

I had stretched my usual two miles into three miles that day, and was awfully proud of myself as I reached the finish line – just as Troy Polamalu was coming out of breakfast at a 90-degree angle to my right.

I stopped and stood there, soaked, hoping he would notice my tremendous athleticism.

"Did you just jog up from the road?" Troy asked.

It was a jab.

"The road" was a tenth of a mile back. The drenched t-shirt said, aw, c'mon, man.

Troy laughed. He asked about my family and went about his day.

I had a good relationship with Troy throughout his 12-year career with the Pittsburgh Steelers. Talking about our families and soccer and anything but football, as often as possible, helped that relationship.

It also helped that I didn't run with the clickbait crowd. I was still old school and worried more about my long-term relationships with players, and I felt I had one with Polamalu.

Troy liked the idea behind my last book, *Steeler Nation*. It was a road-trip book and his family appreciated that someone from Pittsburgh drove all the way to Oregon to talk to them.

I thought it was the best chapter of the book, and I got to know his family and friends there. It's what set this book in motion.

I brought the idea of a biography up to Troy a few years later, but he was apprehensive.

Well, perhaps repulsed is the better word.

"A book?" he said with a visible shudder. "I don't know. That doesn't interest me right now. Maybe I'll change my mind after I've actually accomplished something with my life."

This from the reigning NFL Defensive Player of the Year.

I figured I could conduct peripheral interviews while Troy waited for the right time. So I went back to Oregon in the spring of 2011. A few months later I boarded a plane for Los Angeles to interview the Southern California portion of the Polamalu family.

At the time, the NFL was involved in a lockout, so I thought I had the opportunity to slip out of my Westmoreland County home for some quick work on the West Coast before getting back to my day job of covering the team.

However, the league and the players came to an agreement, probably while I was in mid-flight.

I was determined to stay the week, and missed the first few days of the 2011 training camp. I did some interviews, checked out his Santa Ana hometown, walked around the USC campus, snooped through the sports information department's library, and called a guy I follow on Twitter, Alex Holmes.

He's Theodora Polamalu's brother, Troy's brother-in-law, and he agreed to an interview and invited me to an afternoon cookout. He told me there would be others there who could provide good information as well.

Alex gave me the address for my GPS, and I showed up – at Troy Polamalu's house.

Yeah, the guy from Westmoreland County showed up, and the guy who should've been there – the guy for whom this massive feast was to honor – Troy – was in Westmoreland County.

The money guys at Troy's house didn't like this.

At all.

But, I interviewed Alex, and he was great. Later I interviewed the hostess – his sister Theodora – after she had finished cleaning up from the massive feast she had prepared.

She was so polite. Theodora sat down for a 30 to 40-minute interview. It was on the digital recorder that also held interviews with, among others, her brother Alex, Keneti Polamalu and Dan Rooney, all for this book.

The next day I began my trek back to St. Vincent College. Of course, the first player I saw was Troy. I told him I had been at his house.

"So I heard," he said as we started walking up the hill following practice.

I made my case for the book again. He wasn't upset, but remained opposed to sitting down for a long interview about his life. He stressed again that at 30 he had only lived a portion of his life and really hadn't done anything worthy of a biography.

"Ask me again in five years," he said.

He never did do it. But he would help, for example, with asides following mob interviews. I remember him at Super Bowl 45 turning to me during media day and saying, "You'll appreciate this," before dropping a gem of a small story that no one else really could use on that news day.

He wasn't against the book. He just couldn't bear to <shudder> look at 400 pages of stuff about himself.

Of course, Troy had helped with every other request I made during his 12 years in Pittsburgh. Much of it was his reflections of historical events some years later. Those are the interviews that are offset in this book. It's been styled that way after reading Alan Paul's exceptional books on the Allman Brothers Band (*One Way Out)* and Stevie Ray Vaughn (*Texas Flood*).

I, in fact, asked Alan if I could not only steal his style but if he would edit this book. Who better to edit a stolen style than the guy from whom you're stealing?

As a lifelong Steelers fan from Squirrel Hill, Paul, the accomplished rock-and-roll author, said yes to both requests.

Those interviews that are reflections are broken out with the speaker's name bold-faced. The other quotes were either given to me in locker rooms throughout my 26 years on the beat or found via research in the Library of Congress or in local news files in Roseburg, Oregon.

I do regret that Troy performed some kind of a mind meld on the digital recorder I brought into his house. The interviews with Alex, Theodora and Rooney were pronounced lost after even the experts could not revive my recorder. Keneti and Malaefou MacKenzie both agreed to be re-interviewed about nine years later.

Troy never did interview for this book. I have a thousand guesses as to why not, but it really wasn't necessary. He would only pour his humility all over these cool stories anyway.

I once asked Troy at his third Super Bowl why he continued to play the game. He had the money and the rings, and we know he's not driven by ego. Why wouldn't he just tuck his health safely inside his home and spend his time with his family? What was he getting out of football?

His eyes sparkled as he spoke of the joy he saw in his teammates when they won. He played for them, he said, and he wanted to see that joy one more time by passing around another Lombardi. The joy in Troy's face as he spoke told me this was the plain truth.

This book is an example of those teammates and coaches turning around and giving that love right back to him. Their callbacks came fast and with enthusiasm.

Guys were giving me hours on their back porches, on their cellphones, and, in the case of Heath Miller, on the side of the road in a car after driving to the top of a hill for better reception. These guys couldn't wait to tell their favorite Troy Polamalu stories.

And that's what this is, a collaboration of their joy.

I'm just the collator here. I typed some words between theirs, but for the most part this is the universe's gift to our future athletes and leaders and philanthropists.

There IS an athlete worthy of this type of intensive life study. And that story needs to be passed on to future generations. It's a story of beauty, power and grace. It's a story that needs to be told.

CAST OF CHARACTERS

TROY POLAMALU *Perhaps the greatest strong safety ever to play football. Born April 19, 1981, Garden Grove, California.*

AOATOA POLAMALU *Troy's uncle; Penn State nose tackle (1984-87).*

BRANDON POLAMALU *Troy's first cousin in Tenmile, Oregon.*

JOE POLAMALU *Troy's first cousin in Tenmile, Oregon.*

KENETI POLAMALU *Troy's uncle; USC fullback (1982-85); USC assistant coach (2000-03, 2010-12); NFL assistant coach (2004-09, 2017-current).*

SALU POLAMALU *Troy's uncle in Tenmile, Oregon.*

SHELLEY POLAMALU *Troy's aunt in Tenmile, Oregon.*

RANDY BAUMANN *host of The DVE Morning Show on WDVE-FM.*

JOHN BOVE *Penn State DB coach (1979-84); administrator, recruiting coordinator (1985-09).*

PETE CARROLL *USC head coach (2001-09); Seattle Seahawks head coach (2010-current).*

RYAN CLARK *Steelers free safety (2006-13).*

KEVIN COLBERT *Steelers general manager (2000-current).*

JERRICHO COTCHERY *Jets wide receiver (2004-10); Steelers wide receiver (2011-13).*

BILL COWHER *Steelers head coach (1992-06).*

DAVID DECASTRO *Steelers guard (2012-current).*

JASON DICKOVER *Douglas High athletic director, asst. basketball coach.*

TOM EGGERS *The News-Review (Roseburg, Oregon) sports writer.*

ALAN FANECA *Steelers left guard (1998-07).*

JAMES FARRIOR *Steelers inside linebacker (2002-11).*

STEVE FISHER *Douglas High basketball coach (1985-98).*

JAMES HARRISON *Steelers outside linebacker (2002-12, 2014-17).*

CASEY HAMPTON *Steelers nose tackle (2001-12).*

CAMERON HEYWARD *Ohio State defensive end (2007-10); Steelers defensive end (2011-current).*

CHRIS HOKE *Steelers nose tackle (2001-11).*

CHRIS HOPE *Steelers safety (2002-05); Tennessee Titans safety (2006-11).*

RAY HORTON *Steelers secondary coach (2004-10).*

BRETT KEISEL *Steelers defensive end (2002-14).*

CARNELL LAKE *(Steelers DB 1989-98/DBs coach 2011-17).*

DICK LEBEAU *Steelers defensive coordinator (1995-96/2004-14).*

MIKE LOGAN *Steelers safety (2001-06).*

MALAEFOU MACKENZIE *USC running back (1997-02).*

HEATH MILLER *Steelers tight end (2005-15).*

MIKE MILLER *Steelers offensive assistant (1999-03); Arizona Cardinals WR coach/offensive coordinator (2007-12).*

JUSTIN MYERS *Troy's childhood friend in Tenmile, Oregon; sports talk show host in Portland, Oregon.*

SHAUN NUA *Steelers defensive lineman (2005-07); University of Michigan DL coach (2019-current).*

CARSON PALMER *USC QB (1998-02); Cincinnati Bengals QB (2003-10).*

MARCEL PASTOOR *Steelers assistant strength coach (2001-current).*

DARREN PERRY *Steelers defensive backs coach (2003-06); Steelers free safety (1992-98).*

JOEY PORTER *Steelers outside linebacker (1999-06); Steelers OLB coach (2015-18).*

ROB RUCK *author Tropic of Football; history professor University of Pittsburgh.*

RYAN SCARPINO *Steelers PR staffer (2010-16).*

AARON SMITH *Steelers defensive end (1999-11).*

JOHN SOWELL *The News-Review (Roseburg, Oregon) county government reporter, Oregon high school football official.*

CURT STOOKEY *father of Troy's childhood friend and high school teammate Erick Stookey.*

IKE TAYLOR *(Steelers cornerback, 2003-14).*

TIM TESSALONE *USC sports information director (1984-current).*

DENNIS THURMAN *USC secondary coach (1993-00); Baltimore Ravens assistant coach (2002-07); New York Jets assistant coach (2008-14).*

MIKE TOMLIN *Steelers head coach (2007-current).*

DESHEA TOWNSEND *Steelers cornerback (1998-09).*

ROD TRASK *Douglas High baseball coach (1992-00); Dr. Stewart's American Legion baseball manager (1994-98).*

LENNY VANDERMADE *USC offensive lineman (1999-03); Steelers offensive lineman (2004-05).*

HINES WARD *Steelers wide receiver (1998-11).*

KEN WHISENHUNT *Steelers offensive coordinator (2004-06); Arizona Cardinals head coach (2007-12).*

CRAIG WOLFLEY *Steelers Radio sideline reporter (2002-current).*

TABLE OF CONTENTS

CHAPTER I

MIKE MILLER'S WAR (*WE'LL SEE)

Like many of us, Bill Cowher was doing pretty well in the early part of 2020. He had just been inducted into the Pro Football Hall of Fame and was celebrating that milestone in Miami at Super Bowl 54 where he was being congratulated by the elite of the football world.

One former player who came to pat Cowher on the back could actually take some of the credit for that recent induction. Few would've recognized this person, and Cowher didn't at first.

"How about this," Cowher said after returning home. "I ran into Dexter Jackson at the Super Bowl. He came up to me, I was at the bar. He said, 'Coach, Dexter Jackson.'"

Jackson wasn't sure if Cowher would remember him, but how could Cowher forget him? Jackson was all that had stood between the Steelers and the drafting of Troy Polamalu in 2003.

Polamalu was also elected to the Hall of Fame Class of 2020 along with Cowher, as well as another former Steelers strong safety, Donnie Shell.

Cowher said he looked at Jackson and just said, "Wowwwww."

Dexter Jackson never made a Pro Bowl during his 10-year NFL career, but he was the primary target of the Steelers' 2003 free agency plan.

A month earlier he was voted Super Bowl MVP after intercepting two passes in Tampa Bay's win over the Oakland Raiders.

The Steelers, meanwhile, had been eliminated from the playoffs by the Tennessee Titans in the second round after rallying past the Cleveland Browns in the first.

Ranked 20th in pass defense in 2002, the Steelers allowed their worst and third-worst passing totals of the season in those playoff games, so they were looking to bolster a secondary that was letting strong safety Lethon Flowers leave in free agency.

Chris Hope, the backup free safety, had been drafted in the third round in 2002 and "had a chance" to fill Flowers' spot, according to defensive coordinator Tim Lewis.

But the Steelers preferred a veteran strong safety and weren't sure if 28-year-old Mike Logan would recover from the knee injury he suffered in the playoffs.

So, the Steelers honed in on Jackson.

The draft-world chatter as far back as early February had the Steelers looking at a strong safety from USC named Troy Polamalu.

He played a little linebacker early in his Pac-10 career. They called it dimebacker. But Polamalu became a strong safety much earlier in his career than the strong safety Cowher missed so much from his Blitzburgh defense of the 1990s, converted Pac-10 linebacker Carnell Lake.

The draft match on paper made sense to the media.

However, the Steelers continued to pursue Jackson. He visited Pittsburgh, talked to the media and passed a physical as negotiations heated up.

A week later, convinced they had Jackson locked up, the Steelers went off in search of a running back to draft with their 27th pick.

Cowher and General Manager Kevin Colbert headed to the University of Colorado to watch the pro day workout of running back Chris Brown. The Steelers' private jet stopped in Nebraska for fuel and Colbert checked his messages. One was from team vice-president Omar Khan.

Colbert called him back and heard what at the time was considered bad news: Jackson had changed his mind and signed with the Arizona Cardinals.

Cowher was enraged by the development. He came across Jackson's agent, Peter Schaffer, the next morning at the Colorado workout and gave him a piece of his mind.

"Big time," Schaffer told CBS Sports in 2014. "I had to explain to Bill, 'Who thought we were going to get 30 percent higher in a half hour?' Really, it was 15 minutes."

The Cardinals snuck in the back door and stole Jackson.

Back in Pittsburgh, fans were disappointed.

"It's a sad, sad day in Pittsburgh," one in a long line of callers told talk-show host Stan Savran.

Savran, the respected chieftain of Pittsburgh sports radio, didn't argue.

Of course, in retrospect, what seemed like a collapsing plan was one that actually was just taking shape.

While in Colorado, Colbert heard back from Lewis, the defensive coordinator who'd been dispatched to the USC pro day. Lewis reported that Polamalu's workout was phenomenal. The Steelers timed the 5-10 1/4, 213-pound Polamalu in 4.35 seconds over 40 yards. He benched 405 pounds, squatted 600, power-cleaned 353, jumped 38.5 inches vertically and broad-jumped 10-4.

Those are freakish numbers, but they were just the math of an historic football workout.

What the organization's braintrust would see later on the tape of that workout began the process of the team trading up in the first round for the first time in organization history.

So, yeah, Cowher knew who Jackson was.

"Boy," the coach told the safety nearly 17 years after it all went down. "How significant are you in terms of Troy Polamalu being inducted?"

Another question: How significant was the Jackson-Polamalu trade-off in terms of *Cowher* being inducted?

Troy Polamalu would mean that much to the Pittsburgh Steelers.

The Steelers don't like to veer far from their scouting reports in the months leading up to a draft, and college scouting coordinator Ron Hughes graded Polamalu as a Round 1-2 player in February.

These were some of the highlights from the veteran personnel man who had once mentored a young Kevin Colbert with the Detroit Lions:

* *Positives:* "Outstanding quickness, good straight speed, is both tough and aggressive, best in zones, reacts well once he sees it. Not a lot of knockaways, gets his PBUs hitting through receiver. Great timing on release of ball, can play off blocking or step around them. Flies around. Big time hitter."

* *Negatives*: "Playing injured in games viewed, still does not look real nifty, not the smoothest in his drops, may not always be in the right position, question man cover skills, unless can turn and run with receivers, goes so hard that he does not always break down well and he will miss some in his tackling attempts."

* *Summary*: "Can't help but like him, but he does appear to have some liabilities – looks athletic, has good size and good straight speed, was playing hurt in tapes viewed, did not see hands, question any type of extended man coverage – tight turning, very aggressive in support, big time hitter, tries to hurt people but not always consistent breaking down and will miss – will probably be good on teams, if he is smart enough

could contribute early – possible nickel linebacker because of size and temperament for game."

From there, the scouting department handed the ball to the coaching staff.

DARREN PERRY, *Steelers defensive backs coach (2003-06):* The first time I saw Troy's college tape, I said, "We've got to have this guy," because we needed a strong safety who could do the things that Carnell did during our time together (1992-98). When you have success and you're putting together a defense, you want to find guys who match the personnel that you had. So you look for a guy like myself, who's smart and can play the free safety position and can communicate all the calls. We thought we had that in Chris Hope. Chris had more athletic ability than I had when I played, but you look for guys who can match the qualities of the guys that you had. We didn't have a Rod Woodson but we were looking to find a Joel Steed when you look at the nose tackles. You're looking for Levon Kirkland. You're trying to find a Greg Lloyd because you know if you can get these kinds of players, you can have the same success. We wanted a safety who could cover, yet be a linebacker type in the run game, and that's where Troy fit. And I remember watching two or three games on Troy at SC and calling Bill and saying, "We need to get this guy."

BILL COWHER, *Steelers head coach (1992-06):* I knew of him and I watched him. I knew USC had a history of great defensive players. I remember going down to watch Junior Seau when I was in Kansas City. Man, he had those old socks on. He was almost like Pete Maravich with those old socks he used to wear all the time. But they had a history of just great defensive players. I wasn't even at Troy's workout, but he was one of those guys you knew was a really good player, so we all started taking a closer look at him.

PERRY: That was the one thing I respected about Bill – as a position coach he really allowed you to have a lot of input in terms of players we drafted, because it's so important to have high-character guys, guys that you think can play the Steeler way, that you know are going to come in and do things the right way. And he trusted you in that, whereas some organizations don't allow the coaches to have that much input. That was the thing I appreciated about Bill. You're going to be coaching them, so he would come back to the position coach and ask them, "Do you like him? Do you want to coach him? Can he be a Pittsburgh Steeler?" That goes back to the Rooney belief and that's one of the reasons why they've been so consistent. If there are guys out there who they don't think can be a Steeler in the ways and examples that you look for, they won't be on their draft board. That's why Kevin has done such a great job in drafting.

KEVIN COLBERT, *Steelers general manager (2000-current):* When you're watching film or you're watching games, he's just a kid in a helmet. You don't know who he is until you talk to him. The first impression of Troy was he was 100 percent different than his on-the-field personality. That's why we brought him back in for another visit because we wanted to dig deeper, because his on-the-field personality didn't match his off-the-field personality and you've got to make sure you feel good about having that type of person, that type of player, that type of mental make-up. It's not a negative. It's just not usual.

PERRY: A lot of times on the video, people's actions speak to what they are. You can watch tape of a guy and their communication; they're talking to you with their body language. Character will show up in a lot of different forms in terms of how they get to the ball, how they finish plays. You can tell if a guy's an effort guy, if he's smart, just in terms of his footwork, and what his assignments are relative to the defense. We have guys that go out and talk with these guys, and they'll bring them in pre-draft and you get a feel for where they are mentally and character-wise. They do a lot of homework and the scouts are heavily involved in that. There's more than just looking at height, weight, speed.

COLBERT: Usually the great players are probably a little more extroverted, you know, high-tempo kind of guys. Troy wasn't off the field. Again, what they do on the field is the majority of what we're concerned about. As long as they're good people off the field, their personalities and mannerisms don't matter. We just want to make sure those personalities and mannerisms aren't going to change too quickly. Obviously he was able to turn it on and off.

COWHER: The more you talked with him you could just tell this was a guy. He was one way when his hair was up, but on game day he let his hair down and went from Clark Kent to Superman. When his hair was up, he had the glasses on, he was very cerebral. But all of the sudden he goes in between the lines on game day, the hair comes down. You don't see ANY of that during the week. It was like, wow, this guy just turns it on and he's flying all over the place.

PERRY: Really, the only negative I had personally on Troy coming out was we questioned his ability to cover in the deep zones because he played so much closer to the line of scrimmage in college, like a linebacker, that we were wondering about his discipline in the deep zone and being able to stay back and not let things get behind him.

MIKE MILLER, *Steelers offensive assistant (1999-03)*: I was going into my fifth year as the quality control guy on offense, and I love the draft. Ever since I was a kid and they started putting it on ESPN, I always followed it. They would show it on a weekday, such an innocent time. My parents would say "Well, as long as your grades are OK you can stay home with your buddies." We did it every year.

Now, I'm with the Steelers, my hometown team, and every day's just a blessing working with Coach Cowher, Tom Donahoe, Kevin Colbert, all those guys. That whole scouting staff with Bill Nunn, Phil Kreidler, Doug Whaley, Dan Rooney, Jr., Mark Gorscak, all those guys are great people and certainly some of the best who've ever done the job, so in no way do I want you to think I'm taking credit for something that happened. I'm simply going to tell you the story. I don't know if it had anything to do with anything, but it did happen.

We're getting ready for the draft, and Tim Lewis, our defensive coordinator, and Willy Robinson, our secondary coach, both great coaches, I was hanging out in their office and they said, "Hey, you've got to take a look at this kid." So they put on Troy's pro day from USC, and let me tell you it was amazing. Just. Amazing. They worked him out at I believe both corner and safety. That's how talented he was. Troy was head and shoulders better than anybody on the field, and they had a ton of players. So explosive. So instinctive. And I'm an offensive guy, but I can respect this because I study defenses. It's very rare in the NFL draft that you can fill your biggest need with who could quite possibly be the greatest to ever play that position, right? I'm watching this, saying we have to get this guy.

As an offensive guy, traditionally you're pushing for offensive players, right? But I really, really liked this guy. So we were picking 27th, and now it's Mock Draft Day, the day before the actual draft. Mock Draft Day is like Christmas for me, so we're there and I'm sitting in the back. Now, anybody who's anybody as far as football goes with the Steelers is in the scouting room at the South Side facility, every scout, every coach, with Mr. Rooney coming in and out. The board is magnetized on the wall and they do a great job putting up different scenarios from all the information they've gathered. It's just great fun. And I would do a mock draft, one every hour in the offseason. I mean, I'm crazy with this stuff. And we're going through all these situations and we get all the way down to the end of the first round.

They would always group it with five players, so we were picking 27th, and they would go to 22 and say, "At the 22nd pick, in this scenario, here are the five players we think we would consider. Do we feel comfortable with this group of five? That one of these guys would make it to us?" And then a discussion would ensue about maybe we would make a move up, maybe we would move back, maybe we would take this guy, or the other guy, and why we would take him. You know, for preparation. So, we were there for a few hours, and it was getting towards the end. There was a scenario that came up with the 22nd pick. It was the Jets. And they said, "OK, on the board here's Troy Polamalu. Would we trade up to get Troy?" It was determined, no, we would not do that. That was from the main table with all the big wheels sitting there – Kevin, Coach, Phil Kreidler, Ron Hughes. They made their determination that, in that scenario, they gave the Jets Troy. I think we picked in that one example Doss, the safety from Ohio State.

So, we get done. At that time, Dick Hoak would always do the last mock draft, and so Kevin gets up and said, "OK, Dick, you're up." He goes, "Nah, I didn't do one this year, Kevin." And Kevin said, "Dick, c'mon, you're killing me. You do this every year." He goes, "Nah, nah, I'm good. You guys have it covered." Well, Kevin looks around the room and he sees me and he says, "Miller, I know you've got one." And I said, "Yeah, I've got several." And he goes, "Well, c'mon, put one up." So this is one of those moments that I thought, well, you either believe in something or you don't. I'd been there five years and felt a little more comfortable. But everybody who's anybody is in that room and we just had said what we would do in that scenario about trading up. So, I get up there and Doug and Phil are pulling names off as I'm calling them out. Carolina takes this guy, Bengals take this guy, and so forth. So we get down to the New York Jets at 22, and I said, "OK, with the 22nd pick, the New York Jets select – " and I'll never forget this, I said – "wait a minute, they don't select. They just got a phone call from Kevin Colbert with the Pittsburgh Steelers, and the Pittsburgh Steelers WILL trade up to the 22nd pick and we WILL select safety Troy Polamalu from USC." Coach Cowher looks up at me and goes, "You are aware that just a little bit ago we said we wouldn't do that." And I said, "Yeah, Coach, I'm aware of that." So, I started walking away. Kevin goes, "Well, wait a minute, aren't you going to finish up the draft." And I said, "Nah, we don't have to. We've got the best player on the board. Congratulations. We just drafted a Hall of Famer."

The guys kind of laughed, but I wouldn't back down. I'm not going to name names, but I took an incredible amount of grief from a few members of our staff who were really, really angry. They were like, "You just showed you don't know anything about football. You just embarrassed yourself in there. You just showed you don't have any idea what you're talking about." And I was shocked by it. I said, "What are you talking about?" And they said, "You never draft a safety that high. You only draft corners. You would never take a safety with that kind of pick. That's just ridiculous. What do you think you were doing?" And I said, "Excuse me. Excuse me. Have you guys seen this guy's film?" They said no, and I said, "Well I think you need to watch this film before you say anything else. This kid is unbelievable." And they said, "Listen, there's only one safety that you would ever draft in the first round, and that's Ronnie Lott. So I guess you're telling us this kid's going to be as good as Ronnie Lott." And I said, "No, I'm not saying that. I'm saying he's better than Ronnie Lott." They mocked me over that. "Oh, now he's better than Ronnie Lott. You never game plan for safeties. Name us one." And I said, "When we played Houston, don't we game plan for Robertson and Bishop?" And they were like, "Yeah, but that's a defense." I said, "Those are safeties." They said it doesn't matter, and I told them, "Listen, this kid will revolutionize the game. He'll be in the Pro Bowl by his second year." And then they mocked me again, "Oh, now he's a Pro Bowler!" And I told them he will be a perennial Pro Bowler and he'll be in there his second year. I was pretty angry myself at this point. So I leave.

COWHER: All of the sudden we heard about this workout, and then I went back and I started watching him. It was kind of like with Ben. The same thing happened with Ben the next year. You hear about Ben and you go back. I watched every game Troy played, and I was like "Wow this is a pretty special player," like, "This is the guy." He was that special. So I think the more you watched him, and then you saw the workout, you were like, OK. Troy just killed it. He had that suddenness. He was so quick. And he had this amazing burst in short range, and he had this unbelievable change of direction. He had a suddenness to everything he did, and I just remember like, "Wow, this is a pretty special player." That's when we figured we had to trade up to get him.

MILLER: I come in the next morning. It's the first day of the draft and I'm excited, as always. I come upstairs and I see these same members of our staff and I'm still kind of bent out of shape about it. But I was the low guy on the totem pole, so I kept my mouth shut, but they said, "Welp, I hope you're happy." And I said, "What do you mean?" And they were like, "Yeah, like you don't know." But I had just got there and had no idea what they're talking about. They said, "Talk about impact. I hope you're happy. You're getting your guy. We're trading up with Kansas City to take Troy Polamalu at 16." I went, "Wowwwww!"

COWHER: I was talking to Carl Peterson, the Kansas City GM, and Carl was convinced we were taking a running back. He wanted Larry Johnson. I said "We're not taking a running back." So we were talking to him and they finally agreed to it and the deal was done the day of the draft. I think they were seeing what else was available, and we gave him a third and a sixth. And we had not been known as people who traded that much. It wasn't something we did very often. But he was a special guy and fit what we needed. Our division was becoming more of a division in which you HAD to be able to cover tight ends. He was so skilled. He could cover in the slot; he could cover tight ends; he could blitz; he could play the run. He was so multi-talented. He could blitz like a linebacker; he could play like a strong safety; he could cover like a nickel back; he could also play half the field like a safety. I mean, this guy was like a corner, safety, linebacker all molded into one. And then you couple that with talking to him. He was so quiet. We talked to him at the Combine and it was like, "Wow, this guy's a really quiet guy." But he was cerebral. You could just tell how smart he was.

COLBERT: He was unique. He had linebacker physicality with corner athleticism and that's a hard thing to find. But it was unanimous. I say this all the time: We're not going to make a pick unless it is unanimous. It may take a lot of discussion, a lot of meeting, to get to a unanimous point, but once we make it unanimous it stays that way.

MILLER: Some of the scouts were good-natured. They were actually very supportive. They were having fun with me saying, "Hey, wow, look at you. That took a lot of guts to get up there in front of everybody." And I told them I just did it because I believed in it. They gave me a chance to give my opinion. But the real gratifying thing was when he came in. We got to meet him and we got to see the type of person that he is. He's 10 times the human being than he is as a player, which is saying a lot. I never really got to know him that well, though, because I left. But I was always a fan, was always proud of him. And I would keep in touch through all my friends who were still there, and they would tell me just how great a human being he is and they'd pass along a story every now and then. You can't help but be such a fan. You want that kind of guy to be the face of your organization, and really the face of your community.

◆◆◆

PART I:
DOUGLAS HIGH SCHOOL

◆◆◆

CHAPTER 2

DESCENDED FROM ROYALTY

"The chronicle of your tragedy is simply the prelude to the memoir of your triumph."

- Ryan Clark, March 2020

Pretty heady stuff, even for a quick-thinking, championship-winning free safety.

Of course, Ryan Clark was and is close to Troy Polamalu, so perhaps Clark has known about Polamalu's self-defined juvenile delinquency.

Here's the roll call of what Troy has told newspapers about his childhood as it took shape in Santa Ana, California:

* "I was just a little hood rat walking around parks by myself, hanging out with homeless guys. I witnessed that side of things."

* "The break-ins were an everyday thing because the influence was all around me. When you don't know right from wrong, it's different than it is for a kid who's just living the high life, doing it because he's spoiled and out of resentment. For me, breaking into homes was an everyday, survival thing."

* "One day, a friend and I stole a woman's dog. Then we saw there was a reward on the collar, so we gave it back to her and collected."

TROY POLAMALU: Growing up in Southern California, we had people coming in and out of my house and I had free rein. The world was my playground. If I found a quarter on the ground, I would walk a mile, mile and a half, two miles from my house in the middle of the night, like two, three o'clock in the morning, just to go buy candy.

And then I would walk home. I was so scared. What scared me were kidnappers, so what I would do was walk in the middle of a four-lane street because I knew I could outrun anybody if they jumped out of the bushes. If I was on the sidewalk, I wouldn't have time to react. So I walked in the middle of this four-lane boulevard. Then I knew I had time to run away from him, or her, the kidnappers. So that was the biggest thing I was scared of when I was growing up in Southern California. I would get home from school and be out till 9-10 o'clock at night and I'd come home. I had zero parental supervision. So, I could leave in the middle of the night. I could leave all day long.

On or around the day Troy Benjamin Aumua was born, on April 19, 1981, in the Los Angeles suburb of Garden Grove, California, "Tommy" Sitala Aumua left his newborn son to be with his other family.

Father left mother, Siuila Polamalu, to raise her eldest son Sakaio, three girls – Patricia, Sheila and Talalupe – and baby Troy by herself in Santa Ana.

"My sisters had babies in high school, my brother was in and out of jail," was how Troy described his siblings to *Gentlemen's Quarterly* in 2006. "I'm in first grade. My brother's in the backseat of a police car, waving for me to open the door. What am I supposed to do?"

What was he supposed to do?

Troy's brother Kaio, seven years Troy's elder, deserves credit for stoking Troy's interest in football. The day after Troy was drafted by the Steelers, Kaio told Joe Starkey of the *Pittsburgh Tribune-Review* about the rolled-up socks they used for a football in running past each other in the front yard.

"I used to punch Troy in the legs and flip him," said Kaio. "He had a lot of moments when he landed on his head, but I remember one time I went to flip him and he looked like he would land on his head and kind of did a hand-stand and never went down. He just ran right by me. I was like, 'Wait a minute.'"

It might've been Troy's first flash of football greatness. Kaio also talked about Troy's first big hit, when, as an 8-year-old, he belted a high school sophomore running for a pass.

"Troy hits him," Kaio said, "and the next thing you know the other kid is crying, holding his shoulder. It was separated."

Kaio could play a bit himself. Uncles describe him as "a taller Troy," and at 6 feet 1, 205, Kaio played defensive end at Rancho Santiago Junior College in Los Angeles, where "he just walked in the door one day and wanted to play," RSJC Coach Dave Ogas told the *El Paso Times* in 1993.

"He was undersized as a lineman, but he was so quick. We couldn't block him."

Nobody knew much, if anything, about Kaio because he had been kicked out of Mater Dei High School and matriculated through a reform school.

But Kaio, with 7 sacks and 2 interceptions, was Rancho Santiago's second-leading tackler in 1991.

He bulked up to 220 pounds in 1992 and led the team with 10 sacks and was named team MVP and All-Mission Conference.

Kaio transferred to UTEP in 1993 and played fullback – or "ace back" – in the team's run-and-shoot offense, and was playing so well that by Thanksgiving he was featured by *Times* reporter Don Henry.

The Q&A with Aumua opens with him at Southern California scholastic football power Mater Dei.

KA: Well, I haven't played football since I was a freshman in high school. I played linebacker and running back then.
And then as a sophomore?
Only went half a year ... because of grades.
What did you do as a junior?
Didn't play.
Why?
Had some problems, got locked up.
What for?
Drugs, lots of things.
And as a senior?
Played volleyball.
What was behind all of this?
Gangs. Even when I got to junior college I was always getting in fights with players on the other teams who were members of the other gang (Bloods) from ours (Crips). But after my freshman year, I met this girl, Joy, at school, and she started taking me to church. The thing that first got to me, we went to this church service where they had eight ex-gang members give their testimony. That was the start. I got out of gangs.

UTEP recruiting coordinator Bill Patterson had told the *Times* prior to the season that Aumua was "the best speed we've gotten."

Of course, Kaio's checkered past had left the door open for 1-10 UTEP to recruit that kind of elite speed.

"We looked at Rancho Santiago game films," Patterson said at the time, "and I thought it was an Aumua highlights film. He was making just about every tackle."

It's not difficult to imagine a taller Troy Polamalu doing exactly that at the junior college level.

UTEP coach David Lee moved the JC transfer into his backfield in the run-and-shoot in 1993 and Kaio led the team in rushing. His 642 yards (5.0 ypc.) were the most at UTEP in five years.

But the Miners again went 1-10 and Lee was fired in the middle of the season, replaced by defensive coordinator Charlie Bailey, who later changed the offensive alignment to the I-formation.

Quarterback, fullback and tailback were considered UTEP's strengths entering 1994, according to *Sports Illustrated*, which ranked the Miners 106th out of 107 Division One teams prior to the season.

Kaio bulked up to 238 pounds to become the blocking back in the I, but sprained an ankle in the opener. It was the start of an injury-plagued season that ended with Aumua finishing with only 123 rushing yards (4.2 ypc.) in 8 games as UTEP finished 3-7-1.

Former Steelers offensive line coach Sean Kugler was UTEP's tight ends and assistant strength coach at the time.

SEAN KUGLER, *Steelers offensive line coach (2010-12):* Obviously I didn't know I was coaching Troy Polamalu's older brother at the time. I found out recently. But, yeah, I remember him. He was a real physical kid. He carried the ball, was a good blocker, tough kid. He really was an excellent football player. Good ball skills as a runner, good fullback as a blocker, tough kid, good kid. Well-respected on the team. The coaches all liked him. He was a hard worker, a great teammate.

BRANDON POLAMALU, *Troy's cousin:* Kaio was a phenomenal athlete. Troy would tell you that Kaio hands down was a better athlete than him. Growing up in this family, you had all of these role models to look at.

Brandon Polamalu is the youngest of three sons to Salu and Shelley Polamalu, the uncle and aunt in Tenmile, Oregon, who took in young Troy Aumua when he was nine years old.

Salu and Shelley called it "Greyhounding," because the young and oftentimes troubled members of the wide-ranging Polamalu – or Pola, as many had it shortened – family were bused to Oregon for a taste of Salu's discipline.

Salu often joked about his "iron fist," but when he wasn't in that fatherly mode he was clearly a gentle giant.

"Most Samoans are very good-natured, easygoing," Shelley said. "But, man, don't make them mad."

That description fit Salu Polamalu, Jr.

Fa'asasalu "Salu" Polamalu, Jr. was born in American Samoa on June 15, 1945, the first of 11 children to Fa'asasalu and Ta'eleese Pomeli Polamalu.

He was raised in the tiny village of Siufaga.

American Samoa is not to be confused with Samoa, which was ruled by New Zealand until 1962, when the country became known as Western Samoa, and then just Samoa in 1997.

The International Date Line separates Samoa from American Samoa and its main island of Tutuila, located some 5,000 miles southwest of Los Angeles and 2,500 miles south of Hawaii in the Pacific Ocean.

Further east of Tutuila is the Manu'a Islands chain of American Samoa. Among that cluster of islands is Ta'u, and on the island of Ta'u is the village of Siufaga.

That's the village in which Salu Sr. and Ta'eleese Polamalu began their family with Salu Jr., the future uncle and father figure of Troy Polamalu.

In the 2018 book *Tropic of Football*, author Rob Ruck wrote that "Samoans have long considered Manu'a – the small but majestic volcanic isles of Ta'u, Olosega, and Ofu – the fount of their culture. According to legend, Samoa was created there when the paramount god Tagaloa fashioned the Manu'a Islands so that he had a place to stand amid the seas."

Salu Sr., according to Ruck, was a "high talking chief married to a woman whose (Pomeli) lineage descended from the tui Manu'a," which, according to Ruck, held "the most prestigious matai title in the Manu'a Islands. The tui Manu'a traces its lineage to Tagaloa, the supreme deity who created the Samoan islands."

Simply put, Troy Polamalu is a direct descendant of the most supreme king of Samoa and therefore a descendant of the supreme god that created the islands.

Maybe Ron Hughes should've put *that* in his scouting report.

SHAUN NUA, *Steelers defensive lineman (2005-07)*: Yes, Troy is literally from the village where the tui Manua'a is from. I'll try to explain it to you in a very, very simple way. There are chiefs, and then there are the island leaders, high chiefs, talking chief, orators, but there is a king. There was a king back in the day, and Troy is literally from the part of the village where that king's from. So having blood lineage directly to him, yes, it's 100 percent true. To explain to you the direct lineage, I would need to come to Pittsburgh and spend a whole night at your house. But it shouldn't surprise anybody that Troy is from kings, should it? Don't bring that up to him, though. Troy won't promote that kind of thing. He would rather be from the servant's mindset.

Nua, a teammate of Troy's with the Steelers, comes from the same village – Siufaga – as the Polamalu family. Nua's father was still village chief at the time of this 2020 interview.

NUA: I knew a little bit more about his family than about Troy when I first met him. He comes from a very big, a very athletic family. Obviously there's Keneti Polamalu. And he has another uncle (Aoatoa Polamalu) who played at Penn State. It's a family with great athleticism and size. But the family back home was just like another family farming, fishing and living the simple life in the village. You have to understand, the island we're from is separate from the main island. You have to fly to the main island, then you have two options to get there: a couple-hour flight or an eight-hour boat ride. We're from a very small island of three villages, and I can't believe I'm from the same village as Troy's family.

Following a typhoon on Ta'u in 1957, Salu Sr. moved his family to American Samoa's main island, Tutuila, and the small village of Matu'u. That's where Salu Jr. became an undefeated local boxing champ and where he learned the siva afi, a traditional Samoan dance that involves a flaming war club.

He became so skilled as a "fireknife" dancer he was recruited to perform at the World's Fair in New York City in 1964. That led to a job dancing in Honolulu at the Royal Hawaiian Hotel.

Salu Jr. toured clubs throughout Waikiki, where he caught the eye of Rochelle "Shelley" Redenius. They married in 1970 at 'Akaka Falls State Park on Hawai'i Island.

Shelley is the Texas-born daughter of Skip and Billie Fae Redenius. Skip was born in South Dakota and joined the Navy in World War II. He was aboard a destroyer that was ashore briefly in Seattle. During leave, he stayed in a cabin on a nearby lake and met Billie Fae, who, after graduating high school in Texas, was spending the summer with a cousin in Seattle.

They eventually married and lived briefly in Salem, Oregon, before moving back to the north Texas town of Perryton – just south of the Oklahoma panhandle – where Shelley and her brother Jerry were born.

Skip convinced Billie Fae to move back to southwest Oregon and they bought a seven-acre tract of land in Tenmile, a tiny town of 539 that rests about 20 miles southwest of the Douglas County seat of Roseburg.

Skip and Billie Fae bought the land next to Olalla Creek and raised their two kids.

SHELLEY POLAMALU, *Troy's aunt:* This was a *fun* place to grow up, full of history. I went to Oregon State for a couple of years, and then I decided I wanted to go live in Hawaii a while. I wanted to see some of the world. I wasn't thinking about where I wanted to live but I ended up marrying my husband. I met Salu and I brought him here to meet my family and he fell in love with it. He said, "I want to live in Tenmile." It really wasn't what I had in mind, but we did live in Samoa the first year. He wanted to come back and go to UCC (Umpqua Community College), and he did, so we've been here ever since.

SALU POLAMALU, *Troy's uncle:* I brought her back. She was trying to find some place. She went all the way to Hawaii to find me. She said, "I come all the way here to find it. I want to live here. Now you want to go to Oregon and live? I can't believe it!"

SHELLEY POLAMALU: He said, "I want to go back and live in Olalla." I said, "What?" He said, "Olalla." I said, "Are you out of your mind?" Olalla is a little side road right over here. But he loved it.

SALU POLAMALU: That's my spot. I just love the quiet. I lived in New York, L.A., Hawaii, San Francisco. I come over here, this was it. I just kick back. Got everything I want. Build a fire –

SHELLEY POLAMALU: I didn't realize it was a different way of life until I was a teenager and would spend the night with some of my friends occasionally in Winston (Oregon). Wow. You could walk to your friend's house. It's a whole different life. Jerry and I never had anybody, but we would climb trees, play in the creek. We built rafts. We were Tom Sawyer and Huckleberry Finn. We had sports everywhere, and so did my kids. There are sports still everywhere you look.

With World War 2 over, the U.S. Navy pulled out of its base in American Samoa in 1951 and arranged for the passage of Samoans to Honolulu or California if they wished to continue working in the military. Thus began the great Samoan diaspora to the United States, and ultimately the NFL.

Following the typhoon in 1957, Salu Sr. moved some of his family to Tutuila. Salu Jr. was 12 when he moved to Tutuila. His younger brother Tone was born before the infant Sefulusene had died. They had another younger brother, Talati ("Lucky"), before Siuila – Troy's mother – was born in 1953.

Following Siuila were brother Sokimi, sisters Talalupe, Moana and Tofa, and then the football stars of the family, youngest members Keneti (or Kennedy) – born the day John F. Kennedy was assassinated – and Aoatoa, who was born in 1965.

The latter two boys were eventually coached on the U.S. mainland by Tone, a Viet Nam veteran who established a family homestead in California before moving back to the islands to become a high talking chief.

Tone was a linebacker at Cal Irvine before becoming, as Ruck quoted Aoatoa in *Tropic of Football*, "a mean son of a bitch" as a trainer.

AOATOA POLAMALU, *Troy's uncle:* Tone went to Viet Nam when he was like 14, lied about his age. Came back, went on to junior college in Santa Ana. He was the first one to play football in our family, played middle linebacker at Santa Ana Junior College. Got his associate degree there. Went to a small local college for his degree in economics, and then he got his master's in economics at the University of Cal Irvine. But, yeah, when he was training he would come after work in the summer and we would have to do a mile run and then go in the weight room. I want to say me and Keneti were in fourth grade and sixth grade, around that time, and we would do a mile run, go lift, and then we'd play either racquetball, basketball, handball, a sport, and then we'd run again. He ran us so much.

Tone's tough coaching paid off for the young Pola boys. They became star players at Mater Dei, a Catholic school in Santa Ana, California, that's turned out Heisman Trophy winners and several NFL quarterbacks among a long list of professional athletes.

Keneti eventually committed to Penn State, but backed out when Salu Sr. developed health problems following his move to California. Keneti opted to stay close and became a fullback at the University of Southern California. He did recommend his younger brother Aoatoa to Joe Paterno, and Aoatoa eventually became a nose tackle on Penn State's 1986 national championship team.

Salu Jr. didn't play football. He played rugby, cricket, soccer and boxed on Tutuila before becoming a world-class fireknife dancer, which led him to New York City, Honolulu and eventually to Shelley, Tenmile and Troy.

SALU POLAMALU: Life in Samoa is not easy. My dad worked for the government and didn't make that much money, but enough for the necessities. We raised our food on the plantation: taro, banana, papaya, pig and chicken. Our family called it communal land. It's shared by the whole family. If you're related to me, you can put up a house. We have a lot of land outside of Pago Pago, the capital city. My dad was still working when I left in '66. I made a pretty good living, but it can't last long. Once you get heavy and old it's gone. I met Shelley in 1969. We moved here to Tenmile in 1970. But growing up, the sport we played a lot was rugby and volleyball and cricket.

SHELLEY POLAMALU: I sat through many, many a cricket game, and the losers always beat up the winners.

SALU POLAMALU: That's the way. They don't like to lose. No sportsmanship. If my village got beat, and the team that beat us lived on the opposite side and had to cross our village, they just stoned that bus. Real bad sports. No rules. They say the Samoans stopped fighting wars between the islands and they concentrated on sports. That's how they participated in war.

SHELLEY POLAMALU: So they killed each other.

SALU POLAMALU: I'd grow up and hear talks about how people on my island would travel on the outrigger, 10 of them or so, and they'd go to different islands like Tonga and they'd just whip up on the Tongans and take all their important goods and claim as their own. If you'd spend the weekend with your grandpa he'd tell stories about how they traveled using the moon and all that. I know my dad, when he used the longboat to go to different islands, you'd see the stars and the moon and go five days, come back, and bring a lot of birds. We'd use the birds for family meals.

SHELLEY POLAMALU: This is his original knife from the '60s when he danced professionally. He'll tell you about the hook.

SALU POLAMALU: According to the legend, this was the plate made out of ironwood in Samoa. The hook on the end was for after the war, when your enemy was killed, you chop off the head and hook him up here and then carry him to the village. Now we use them for entertainment to make money. I got hooked on the leg one time doing my routine. It was pretty bloody. One time I got burned because we light both ends of that knife. It gets pretty warm on that plate and sometimes your hand slides on it. You soak them with gasoline or kerosene and then you light them. You see it on TV, all you see is the face when you spin a circle. I think it was Disney that came to Samoa and asked if we'd like to represent the Polynesian islands. They picked people who could understand a little bit of English and perform all different kind of dances from the different islands. First time I ever been on an airplane, I went from Samoa to Hawaii to L.A. to Chicago and then to New York. The highest thing I'd seen in Samoa was a coconut tree. Oh my God, I just looked up at all these buildings. It was fascinating. I stayed there for a year until the World's Fair was closed.

We stayed in Flushing. They rented a big, old house. There were 40 of us, a high school group. I didn't really have no reason to go out. A few kids from in town knew a little bit about going out. There were a few who liked to drink beer. Most of us were always worried about embarrassing our family.

In a lot of ways my dad was strict. I lived in a hut when I was little. We had sugarcane all over and that's how they thatch the roof. Pick the dry leaves, and the women will weave them and the men will put them on top of their huts. It protected us, and when there's a hurricane it's very easy. They just cut them in half and dropped the whole frame down.

SHELLEY POLAMALU: That's pretty much the way everybody lived. You didn't need anything else. You didn't need windows. You didn't need walls. The wind went right through and cooled everything.

SALU POLAMALU: Shelley and I got married in 1970 and we moved to Samoa. Troy's mom, Siuila, was the last one born in Manu'a. She used to follow Shelley around all the time and carry her purse. She loved that thing.

SHELLEY POLAMALU: Siuila is three years younger than me. One Sunday we were swimming and I was diving off the rock, and she did it and broke her head open. She never told anybody. We took her to the hospital for stitches but we never told Salu's parents.

SALU POLAMALU: My entire family moved to California by '78. My dad wanted to improve my younger brothers' and sisters' opportunities through education. I came to Oregon because of Shelley. The weather is excellent. It's a little warm and a little winter. The fall and spring are just gorgeous. I like the change of seasons. I worked in a lumber mill but it was the same old thing every day, so I applied with the state and they hired me as truck driver maintenance. I didn't like that, either. I was going to school at Umpqua, so I applied for the engineering department and they hired me there. I worked as an engineer and became a project inspector before I retired.

Salu and Shelley bought a double-wide mobile home and parked it on the seven acres of property belonging to Shelley's parents, overlooking Olalla Creek. Their family grew to include sons Joe, Darren and Brandon, who's now called by his Samoan name, Tafea, after his great grandfather, Salu Sr.'s father. The remainder of the migrating Pola(malu) family settled in Santa Ana, Ca.

SALU POLAMALU: They went to Hawaii first. There were a lot of Samoans in Hawaii and they don't have a good reputation. They became troublemakers, so my dad thought they were better off going to Santa Ana. My dad was ahead of his generation. He was able to communicate, even with Shelley. My mom didn't speak English at all. My brother Tone was responsible for my mom and dad moving to Southern California. Tone, Siuila, Talati, Keneti and Aoatoa all came to Southern California and everyone came later. They all grew up there. They bought a house with four or five bedrooms and a converted garage, so there was a lot of room and about 30 people living in it. Siuila was probably 17 or 18 when she met Troy's dad in Santa Ana. His name is Tommy Aumua. Really, a nice guy.

SHELLEY POLAMALU: His real name is Sitala Aumua. "Tommy" Sitala Aumua. He was a very talented person. He was pretty much raised in Southern California. I met him after they were married at a holiday gathering. We went down for three or four days.

SALU POLAMALU: Siuila was still attending a small community college in Santa Ana. Tommy was working as a salesman but he would always walk away from a job. That was his nature. He don't like something, he just walked away. He always figured he could get another job. Yeah, I remember Tommy. I liked him a lot. He was in a real bad wreck in New Zealand with a church group. He came back and had some memory loss. One time a car pulled in here, Tommy and my brother Tone and another friend. I asked them what they were doing here. "We escaped the law in California." I said, "Oh my God." They said they beat up one of the guys who took my sister out without my mom and dad's permission. The Samoans are very protective of their sister. Sometimes there'd be big wars between families because of it. You gotta make sure you ask permission from the old man. It was my sister Tofa. Tommy and my brother and another guy beat that guy up to pieces. He was in the hospital when the cops came for them and they were here. I told Shelley we were accessories. So they were here for a week. I had so much fun with them. We built fires out there, drank beer. That's how I really got to know Tommy.

Tommy and Siuila married and lived in a house on Richland Street in Santa Ana.

Sakaio Richland Aumua was born in 1973, followed by Patricia in 1975, Sheila in 1977, Talalupe in 1979, and Troy Benjamin in 1981.

SALU POLAMALU: That was the family Mr. Tommy Aumua left behind.

SHELLEY POLAMALU: The bad thing is where they lived, drugs were really prevalent.

SALU POLAMALU: Kaio got with the bad crowd but he had a chance to go to Oregon if he had his transcript sent. He would've played for the Ducks. That's how good he was. Good basketball player. He could really go up in volleyball. His skill was what got him out of drugs. He met a great girl that helped him, but now they're divorced.

SHELLEY POLAMALU: He left Texas and was coaching for what, 10 years?

SALU POLAMALU: A private school in California. But Tommy left them just about the time Troy was born. He met somebody else, some other gal. Matter of fact they have a daughter about the same age as Troy. He was with two women at the same time.

SHELLEY POLAMALU: It was a rough area for kids to grow up. We would go down every year to visit when Troy was a baby. He wasn't any more than four when he was crossing that freeway by himself to go play in Miles Square Park. I would've been afraid to cross that freeway myself.

BRANDON POLAMALU: My first memory of Troy was at my grandma's funeral in the late 1980s. We were down there for a week and it was a really big Samoan funeral, which means hundreds of people, a week-long event of food exchanges, people bringing mats from Samoa, extended family coming in and paying respects, chiefs there. But he was just this little kid who was very familiar, I think, with that scene down there and he was attracted to the idea of getting to know Darren and I. Everywhere we turned, me and my brother, Troy was there. I was four years older than Troy, who couldn't have been more than five or six years old. I don't think Troy had many toys but he had some stashed away, like a couple Matchbox cars. He was really proud of them, and through the week he was showing me and Darren these cars. Here in Oregon, my dad worked very hard but we had plenty of toys. That was not an issue here. And when we went to leave at the end of the week, after we had been playing with Troy and got to know him all week, he tried to give me and Darren those cars. He was really intent on giving us those cars. So, yeah, he was an amazing kid from when I first got to know him. When he got to Oregon, for the first time ever he could have possessions to himself. But he was a very, very giving person at a very young age.

SHELLEY POLAMALU: Troy saw his older brother and friends have problems, gang related, drug related. Troy was headed nowhere. He couldn't even play sports because he didn't have anybody to get him there. His mom and dad were split. He saw how uncomplicated our lives were compared to what he knew.

BRANDON POLAMALU: You have potential of getting into trouble anywhere, even here, but the stakes are higher when you start talking about gang activity. I didn't really see where Troy lived as a bad neighborhood, but I did think some of our family was connected to some bad things. They were our first cousins and they were connected into some gangs. But our family's got really strong, smart men in it, guys that you as a kid looked up to and were blown away by: Keneti, Kaio, Joe, my dad, Talati, my uncle Famasile, the chief. I had cousins named Lua and Wayne. As a kid, we looked up to all of these symbols of masculinity. They were really strong dudes. They were cultural symbols of what it meant to be Samoan. They were heroes. We had people who were in the military. We had people who were football players. Uncle Keneti, fullback for USC. Uncle Ao, nose guard at Penn State. Kaio, Wayne and Lua were tied up in gangs, but they were all very strong, intelligent men. Those guys were just as intelligent, just as athletic, just as good-looking, all that stuff for a young kid looking up to them. As an adult, maybe it's easier to look back at the lifestyles they were leading, the decisions they were making, and say "This is wrong and this is right." Even as a kid we knew what was wrong and what was right. But they were very cool still. They weren't monsters by any means. They'd do good things for you – take you out to the park, play football with you. But they had chosen this other path, and I think that's important because Troy was surrounded by this. Kaio was his brother, his first hero, and he, Wayne and Lua were like a pack. To me they're still my heroes and they're all very good, kind people.

Nicky Sualua's another one of those men. He's our first cousin, the oldest of the Sualua children. He's Moana's son. Very quiet, soft-spoken. Another very kind person. He came up here and visited us his sophomore year in high school. He was probably 5-10, 230 pounds. He played basketball, dribbled between his legs, would spin, nimble-footed, an amazing athlete, very humble, very smart, very kind. He might be the quietest dude in our family.

[Sualua was Eddie George's fullback at Ohio State and successor to Daryl Johnston with the Dallas Cowboys.]

Kaio ended up spending a large amount of his pre-adult years in multiple juvenile facilities. Wayne and Lua both have been to prison; Wayne for probably the majority of his adulthood. Lua spent pretty long bids in prison, too. But they're all out and doing well. I want to note that. But, yeah, Kaio was very easy to look up to. He could 360 dunk a basketball with no problem. He's like Troy. Troy can pick up stuff so quick. If you give Troy a guitar, he can learn to play it. If you give him a piano, he can learn to play it. Kaio's the exact same way.

In Santa Ana, 9-year-old Troy Aumua had smoked a cigarette, stolen lunches from grocery stores, broken into buildings, and pretty much forced his mother, Siuila, to make a decision.

She called her oldest brother Salu for help, and he and Shelley agreed to take Troy in for a respite, and, more importantly, some discipline.

"I needed it in a military boot camp way," Troy said in 2006. "That's the way he applied it to me."

It was clear to those around Troy that he was a good boy who just needed some supervision. Uncle Aoatoa, the youngest of Salu and Taeleese's 11 children, saw that when he returned from college.

AOATOA POLAMALU: I had just finished up at Penn State and I go back to California with my hotel/restaurant degree, so I'm in restaurants out there. I'm staying at my sister's house saving up some money to get an apartment. I noticed every day when I come back from work all the kids are doing is playing outside. They're not doing homework. They're not doing anything. So I started leaving math problems for Troy to do after school. In the morning I leave math problems, come back, it's done, check. He's out there playing and it was OK. Well one day I come back and he didn't do the math problems. I say, "You didn't do your math problems. What's up?" He said, "Uncle, I didn't want to do them." I said, "What?" He turns and takes off. I take off after him. I mean, I just finished college, OK? I take off after him and he's getting distance on me. I said, "You know, you're going to have to come back and eat tonight." And I left him go. I just couldn't catch him, and I think he was in first grade.

Tenmile, of course, was a stark departure from Santa Ana for Troy. He's told reporters about the first pine tree and first cow he had ever seen there, the lush green, the seven acres of land, and more beyond what his new family had owned. There was the basketball court - replete with light standards and homemade press box up in the trees – that had been paved in front of the mobile home.

And the cousins! Troy was 9, Brandon was 13, Darren was 15 and Joe, away at Oregon State on a football scholarship, was 22.

While Troy grew into an NFL Hall of Famer by 2020, Brandon became an English professor at nearby Umpqua Community College, Darren became a government and history teacher, and Joe a counselor. Darren and Joe both served successful stints as high school head football coaches. Salu passed away in 2018.

SALU POLAMALU: Siuila and Troy came on vacation and then asked us if we could help, so we made a deal. We could keep him, but he don't follow the house rules, we'll send him back. I wanted to make sure his grades were good.

SHELLEY POLAMALU: He loved it. He wouldn't go back. Siuila came up to visit later and he didn't want to leave. He cried and cried and cried, and it was the end of July and I told his mom to come back and get him on Labor Day weekend. That came and he didn't want to go. He never wanted to go back. But she didn't come, so we went down on spring vacation to see them all. He was so afraid we were going to leave there without him that he wouldn't unpack his little suitcase.

SALU POLAMALU: He had good grades. He was good until he got cocky with Shelley when she gave him his chores. We used to have a wood stove. The guys would bring some wood in for the night. Sometimes he didn't want to do that kind of stuff. He'd get a little lazy, plus I was not here. I was working away from home. I walked in through the door one day and Shelley was scolding him. I heard him say, "Why me? Can't the other boys do that?" That's when I backhanded him and he flew over that couch and I said, "Don't you ever. Not in this house." So he went over to see Grandma and said I want to turn Uncle into the authority for child abuse.

SHELLEY POLAMALU: My mom was worried he would end up in a foster home, or back in L.A.

SALU POLAMALU: I said I'm going to put you on the bus. That was my rule.

SHELLEY POLAMALU: He told him a couple times, "You know it's real easy for us to put you on a bus with a one-way ticket back to Santa Ana." He understood that.

SALU POLAMALU: Troy was very bright. He knew he'd better listen to Uncle, because I said I don't care.

SHELLEY POLAMALU: There was a bit of an adjustment period.

SALU POLAMALU: His older brother was here one time with another cousin – Kaio and Wayne. Troy was still little then. They got bandana tied around their head, another one tied around their leg. That was the beginning of their gang thing. We went to my son Joe's baseball game and they had their box and played that stupid thing and were singing their rap. I had to go down and say, "Get out of here. Go to the parking lot and play your thing, and don't ever let me see you dress like that again." That was it. They never dressed like that again.

SHELLEY POLAMALU: I have to say, Kaio spent a couple summers with us. He was the sweetest kid. I loved him.

SALU POLAMALU: I'd come home on weekends and I'd talk to the boys. I didn't raise my voice, but I always had a truckload of logs piled back there. So when there was punishment, we'd all cut firewood all day long until they were exhausted. I ran the chainsaw and they split them and stacked them. They had their big music going. Oh, it was fun.

SHELLEY POLAMALU: And then we sold it and they had to unload it and stack it wherever we sold it. That was their spending money. Troy wanted the best of everything. He wanted Air Jordans, all the stuff we hadn't even heard of around here.

SALU POLAMALU: He loved shoes.

SHELLEY POLAMALU: The first year we had him here for Christmas, he wanted a Los Angeles Raiders coat. It was a gang thing. We didn't even know that. Mom and I were shopping at Penney's and the sales clerk asked us, "Do you really want to buy this for your little boy?" I said, "Well, that's what he wants." And she said, "This is the sign of a gang." But we didn't know.

SALU POLAMALU: We're so far up here in the country we don't know nothing about it.

SHELLEY POLAMALU: We didn't want to know. And we didn't want him telling us. So we had to get all of that out of his head.

SALU POLAMALU: It took about three to five years to get the L.A. out of him.

SHELLEY POLAMALU: No, I'd say it was one year. Otherwise I wouldn't have kept him. I was living day by day with him and he was driving me crazy. I had him in grade school, Brandon in junior high, Darren in high school, and Joe in college. I was back in PTA and Little League again.

SALU POLAMALU: And you'd get called by the principal.

SHELLEY POLAMALU: Oh, every month I was down there for something he did. When he got in junior high it was accelerating because of some of his friends. And I told him – and of course by then I knew we had him; after the first year he wasn't going anywhere – and I told him before he got in high school, I said, "You know I work there in the main office and the vice-principal is a best friend of mine I grew up with. I do NOT want to see you ever in his office. Only kids that are in trouble go to his office. I don't EVER want to see you in there."

SALU POLAMALU: She put his locker right where she could see him from her office. He fought about that, too. He wanted to move his locker to the end of the lockers so she couldn't see him.

SHELLEY POLAMALU: Oh, all my kids; I knew all their teachers and all their friends. I knew their grades before they did. They never got into any trouble, but Troy – oooooh. I got so in his face about that, that he thought it over really well. But from the time he entered high school his freshman year he was never in trouble and he started getting straight A's.

SALU POLAMALU: And he was always a religion person.

SHELLEY POLAMALU: He wasn't a talker about it, though.

SALU POLAMALU: No. It's the same thing now. He doesn't talk about it now unless he's asked.

SHELLEY POLAMALU: Just visiting with him he never brings it up. But when we're with him he shows his mischievous side to me. Oh, yeah. He gets that look in his eye when I'm around like to see if he can still push my buttons. But, you know, the principal who lived through those years in Tenmile, even to this day he says Troy was a wonderful kid. He did have a mischievous streak, but the principal loved him. So it wasn't like he went through school offending those in authority. They loved him. But I had to deal with it. You know, I didn't love it (chuckles).

SALU POLAMALU: It was so good for Troy to have us. We had a ski boat and we did a lot of outdoor stuff and he was feeling so perfect. The weekend I'd load up the boat, we'd go to the reservoir. And he LOVES to boogie board behind. He just loved the openness of the outdoors. We'd go up to the mountain and snow ski, and to see that little devil go around just covered with snow and just roll all over the place.

SHELLEY POLAMALU: He was good at anything he put his mind to.

SALU POLAMALU: We noticed he was athletic as soon as he came over here. He never played soccer before, but when he touched the ball you couldn't get him. He'd dribble right between all the players, nine years old. He was so good. And then he played baseball. He was the cleanup hitter and he was blind.

SHELLEY POLAMALU: The coach told me, "You know Troy's a helluva batter. If he could see the ball it would be incredible." I said, "What do you mean?" He said, "He can't see anything. He senses it. The only reason he can hit it or catch it is his sense. He can't see it."

SALU POLAMALU: He said, "The ball's four feet before he can see it."

SHELLEY POLAMALU: I took him to the eye doctor and he said, "Yeah, he can't see anything." He got contacts and has worn them ever since.

SALU POLAMALU: But he played Babe Ruth (League) and, God, he was a great hitter. Joe was a great baseball player, too.

SHELLEY POLAMALU: Brandon was a fantastic basketball player.

SALU POLAMALU: If Joe didn't blow out both knees, he'd have played somehow. He was very good, disciplined athlete. Darren has turned into a very good coach. Brandon and Troy have lots in common. They were close. They always played together and they'd laugh, go to the show, have friends. Troy gave us so much and made us very proud. Not only did he make our name popular, but his actions: good person. He cares a lot about people. Some reason that both my son Joe and Troy had the same idea to work with unfortunate kids, handicapped. They spent a lot of time working with those kids. And they loved them for it. I think that's the spirit that really made them stand out. He helps the unfortunate ones feel like they're on the same level.

BRANDON POLAMALU: I saw seeds of his spiritual side immediately when he came to Oregon. He prayed every night. He had a Bible with him pretty quickly. I think he grabbed one. There were several lying around here. By the time Troy got here we were pretty inactive, as far as church goes, which is pretty rare in Samoan families. But I definitely saw a lot of curiosity, and he was very devoted to saying his prayers, but Troy kept that to himself. That was part of his own journey, so it was never anything that he was pushing outward onto other people. As Troy continued to do good things, I think he attributed that to his faith, and a lot of good things happened. When things wouldn't go well, I think maybe he checked himself also in that way. By the time he was in high school he had memorized verses. It was definitely something he was seeking answers for.

JOE POLAMALU, *Troy's cousin:* I was at college. My younger brothers spent a lot of time with him. He was a young kid that just really kind of fit right into our family. With the old man it's pretty simple to understand: We all walked that tightrope making sure we did what we were supposed to do, and Troy followed suit. He took care of school. He was respectful at other people's homes. Darren and Brandon pretty much took him in and made him a country boy for a while.

BRANDON POLAMALU: We played a lot of basketball out there on that court. We'd had these imaginary leagues in which we would create scenarios and Troy would think about how he was going to approach this game or that game. Just a lot of sports.

SHELLEY POLAMALU: There were a lot of kids down through the years who can say they grew up at the Polamalu house. That's all they wanted to do was come out here. They had the pool, the basketball court, the creek.

BRANDON POLAMALU: Erick Stookey especially. He lived about a mile up the road. It was me and Troy against Darren and Erick every day: whiffle ball, touch football. The teams never really changed. Erick on a local scale was a really good athlete, the all-time leading scorer for Douglas in basketball, and he and Troy had a great chemistry. But in touch football of course we never lost, me and Troy. I thought I was that good of a quarterback. I'd drop back and just loft it. No matter where I threw it Troy would catch it. And then of course you couldn't touch him. It was touch football and you couldn't even touch the kid. And then one day we switched teams and I had Erick and I realized I'm not that good of a quarterback. I couldn't complete a pass. I was frustrated. My whole ideal broke down.

SHELLEY POLAMALU: By the time Troy came, Joe was in college, so that opened a room. Darren and Brandon always shared a room.

SALU POLAMALU: And then Troy take over Joe's room.

SHELLEY POLAMALU: It's funny because Joe was a huge Steelers fan growing up.

JOE POLAMALU: I was going to be Lynn Swann.

SHELLEY POLAMALU: When he was about four all he wanted for Christmas was a Steelers outfit – shoulder pads, the whole bit – with No. 88 on it, and he got it.

JOE POLAMALU: I was young and that's all we had on was Franco Harris, Donnie Shell, Mel Blount, like a lot of people around here. It's amazing, when Troy signed, everybody in his group and probably a little bit older, are Pittsburgh fanatics. They think Jack Lambert's president. They want him with his missing teeth and everything. So it was weird when he signed.

BRANDON POLAMALU: Every family has a dynamic. In our family, before Troy ever got here, Joe was the hero. He blazed the trail, played all the sports.

SALU POLAMALU: We thought Joe was going to go a long way. I still wish he played baseball. He was a helluva hitter. Joe was good in all three (sports), just like Troy. Too bad he hurt his knees.

JOE POLAMALU: I don't think I would've advanced the way Troy did. He's one where you know it as soon as you see it. I didn't have that speed. I don't know if we ever knew how fast he really was. I don't know if you can measure that game speed.

SHELLEY POLAMALU: Brandon graduated high school and the next year Troy came in as a freshman. Troy, for the last four years, was an only child. It should've been a no-child time for us, but we didn't mind. Not by then.

SALU POLAMALU: Nah.

SHELLEY POLAMALU: He was being such a good, almost perfect kid. He had a lot of friends. He was just overall a very easy and fun child to raise – after the first year.

CHAPTER 3

ONCE A TROJAN, ALWAYS A TROJAN

Throughout an illustrious career at Douglas High School, Troy Aumua did it all. He was a straight-A student, worked with kids who had special needs, made furniture for his friends and family, was the Homecoming king, gained 350 yards in a football game, blocked the shot of a future NBA forward to turn around a state basketball playoff game, and stole home to propel a big baseball win.

But nothing made his uncle, Salu Polamalu, more proud than the day Troy enrolled at Tenmile Elementary School in fourth grade.

"He asked me if he could use our name," said Salu's wife, Shelley Polamalu. "I said sure. He's gone by it ever since."

Troy Aumua didn't officially become Troy Polamalu until January, 2007, when he legally changed his name in a courtroom in Pennsylvania's Allegheny County. But the mere act of asking meant everything to Salu, the eldest of 11 Polamalu children, the big brother of Troy's mother Siuila.

"My proudest moment," Salu said. "He said, 'I live here and I want to be like Darren, Brandon and Joe.' For such a young kid, he already saw to be part of my family here. He asked for that. That, to me, will always stand out."

Not that it softened Salu's proverbial "Iron Fist" of discipline.

Troy was in fifth grade playing Pop Warner football in Roseburg. It was tackle football. It was probably the first touchdown Troy ever scored and he jumped up and down. He looked up at his Uncle Salu, who wasn't happy.

"Don't you ever do that again," Salu told him after the game.

Lesson No. 1: don't celebrate.

"Well, like Troy always say, I'm a disciplinarian," Salu said 16 years later. "I don't tolerate that rah rah rah type of thing. Play the game like it is and be humble. Give the ball back to the official."

It's part of the Samoan heritage known as Fa'a Samoa – act like a gentleman off the field and a warrior on it.

Troy understood the concept, but accepting the discipline wasn't so easy. He recalled Salu's tough love years later.

In Troy's final NFL season, during a November game against the Baltimore Ravens, Polamalu belted a runner, but the runner spun away and banged into another Steelers defender before pinballing into the back of Troy's legs. It was a freak occurrence that looked scarier than the result, but the sprained left knee caused Troy to miss the second half, and then the next two games. After the game, in a one-on-one interview, Troy talked about one day as a Douglas Trojan.

"My junior year in high school, I got picked off first base," he said. "I played center field, so I go out to center field and my uncle was out there saying 'You beep beep beep. You stink, blah, blah, blah.' So I went to rob a home run. There was a chain link fence with the little spikes on the top, and my face and ear got torn up and I was bleeding all over the place, and I heard this voice, 'That's what you get. You deserved that, blah, blah, blah.'

"So the funny thing is when I missed that tackle, I kind of looked back and saw the guy spinning and he was still up and then all of the sudden he lands on me.

The first voice that came to my mind was, 'That's what you get!'"

Wounds remained. But Troy grew to be grateful for the discipline impressed upon him by Uncle Salu.

"He would do that in basketball, too, just start yelling at me if I played bad," Troy told the *Orange County Register* in 2001. "I was mad at him for a long time. But now I'm thankful."

And in 2005: "I knew that I had it tough compared to children around me," Polamalu said. "But I felt like I needed it. I think I had the wisdom as a child to know that it would help me later on."

JUSTIN MYERS, *Troy's childhood friend:* Troy showed up in the summer. My parents were teachers so my dad knew his aunt because they worked at the same school. It was such a small town, we all knew each other anyways. You had to wait to play football, so soccer was the only thing we played in the fall, and all of the sudden here comes this Samoan kid that nobody's ever heard of, who's faster and stronger and more competitive than anybody else. I was like, "Wait, who's this guy?" So, yeah, I hated him.

CURT STOOKEY, *father of Troy's childhood friend Erick:* The first year we went in to play football on the worst team they had in the league. A good friend of ours called and asked – since they didn't have enough kids to field a team – if we could bring kids in. I said, "Well, I've got a few I can bring in." Man, by about the end of the first quarter, those kids, who'd never won a game, after they saw Troy make a couple of runs, they thought "Maybe we can win a few games." It was a big turnaround and the same thing happened in basketball.

KERRI STOOKEY, *Curt's wife:* The first experience I had with him in basketball, Troy and Erick's team beat Jennifer's team 40-something to 1. I thought, "Who are those jerks on Tenmile?" People used to not believe that they all came from out here. They thought they were dragging them in from everywhere.

SALU POLAMALU: There was one guy saying, "I hope you're not bringing more Polamalu from California."

MYERS: There are four communities around. It was Winston and Tenmile and Looking Glass and a little town called Green, all in the same Rec League. It was funny because Winston, we were the city kids, even though it's the furthest thing from an actual city. But we had a City Hall and a sewage system, and we all played every sport, so we played against each other all the time. It was football, and then it was basketball, and then it was baseball. It was pretty intense – at least what my brain remembers of being 11 years old.

CURT STOOKEY: We were playing in the Babe Ruth Regionals, 13-year-olds, and we were playing for the championship to go back to the World Series. We had to beat this team twice. Troy came up to me before the game, real serious, and said, "I forgot we have a luau this weekend. My whole family's going to be there." I told him there's no way I can get him back in time. The best advice I had was to get out there and win these games and get back before everybody leaves. He got back pretty late but everybody was still there.

SHELLEY POLAMALU: What was the luau event?

SALU POLAMALU: We buried pig. Any reason needed?

SHELLEY POLAMALU: Weddings, engagements, graduations, junior high through college, or just people coming to visit. There's always a reason for a luau, so we have one almost every year. Rod, you remember, right?

ROD TRASK, *Douglas High baseball coach:* I can't remember the end of a lot of them, but I remember the beginning of all of them.

At family luaus, Troy would often showed off his skill as a Samoan fireknife dancer. Of course, he had the perfect teacher in Salu.

SALU POLAMALU: He watched me practice. He wore out a place in the lawn outside the fireplace.

SHELLEY POLAMALU: The rhododendrons back behind the fireplace, that was his place. I was his audience and he would do it for hours. He works at everything until perfection. He totally wore out the lawn here. It was years before it ever grew back. He was pretty darn good. He made money at USC dancing for luaus. And he danced for one of the sports channels.

SALU POLAMALU: He was interviewed by Rod Woodson and Lincoln Kennedy. He wanted me to do it. I said, "No, Troy can spin a knife."

SHELLEY POLAMALU: Yeah, the NFL went out and bought a knife. They had to go all over the islands. That was the Pro Bowl. But he is such a dancer. He doesn't want to be in the limelight, but that's his thing: dancing and music. That's his love.

Troy, by Shelley's estimation, practiced dancing two hours per day. That perfectionism was a precursor to his athletic training.

BRANDON POLAMALU: Here in Oregon is where we got to see Troy experimenting with being a really hardcore workout fiend. I started seeing it about halfway through high school. He built a trail that went up the mountain. He saw the famous video of Walter Payton running hills, and started understanding that he wanted to push his mind and spirit to levels that other people wouldn't push, because that was even more important than just being able to run faster, bench more, whatever. So you would see him out on summer days in the middle of the heat running hills.

MYERS: I don't think people understood how hard Troy worked on his own. Playing 3A high school football in Oregon, all he had to do was show up and he was going to be the best player, but the day after a game he would get up, work out on his own, run hills, and just crazy, crazy workout stuff that he would try to figure out how to do. It's still the most impressive thing about him. He could've showed up, been the best player in the history of our high school, probably would've still gone to college and been drafted, but the reason he's going to the Hall of Fame is he worked harder than anybody ever did or anybody even asked him to. It was all internal. His wiring was so different than the rest of us.

BRANDON POLAMALU: When I went to Pittsburgh, Troy showed me a video of Rickson Gracie called *Choke*, and it shows his workout. He's a Brazilian jiu-jitsu master. There's one documentary that follows him to a tournament in Japan and shows his family life, shows his workout, shows his spirituality. It kind of shows his humanity. When Troy showed it to me, he was just stoked. He's fascinated with people who pour their entire self into whatever it is they do. It could be a mechanic, a pilot, whatever, but this particular video showed a workout, again, like the Walter Payton one, only it went into a lot more depth. That might be the closest video that's aligned to his approach to working out; it was very much about a sort of spiritual fitness.

SHAUN NUA: Troy's against lifting heavy weights, and I wish all of us would listen to him. Every time he went in the weight room in Pittsburgh to bench we made fun of him. We were like "Whoa! That's against what you do!" But that's Troy. He thinks outside the box, but with a great heart. He's huge on high reps, huge on flexibility, on mastering your body weight. He told me one time "Why are you trying to lift more weights if you can't control your own body weight?" Huge on those types of workouts, a lot of hydro water workouts. I used to go visit him when he would lift in San Diego, and I don't think I've yet to complete one of his workouts. I'm like dang I didn't even lift any weights but I'm dead. He's huge on recovery, and his diet. He used to make his own almond milk. I've seen him cook almond and strain almond on his own. It's pretty impressive, the dedication and commitment he gave to his mind and body to prepare himself to be a Hall of Famer.

BRANDON POLAMALU: I know it changed dramatically when he started working out for the (NFL) Combine with (Marv) Marinovich. I think up until then Troy's workouts were pretty conventional. He was extremely strong, naturally. He's since told me he never lifts more than 20 pounds, year around. I don't know if that's still accurate, but that's a dramatic difference from benching 400 and power cleaning 350, things he did in high school that he completely let go of. Now he's very much focused on balance and explosion.

NUA: He would say, "Can you believe our people years back didn't have shoes and walked around with strong feet?" He believes everything starts from the bottom up. Everybody says from the top down, but he would always say your feet are your most important thing. It carries all your weight. So it was all for the purpose of strengthening your feet, your base. I remember when I first met him, when I first went to a store with him in Pittsburgh. We went for the five-finger shoes he used to wear.

MYERS: Who thinks like that? Who says I need to strengthen the soles of my feet so my ankles are sturdy? It's just a thought process on a whole different level.

NUA: I can't teach it his way. Michigan has a strength and conditioning staff, an equipment staff. Every department has its own staff. If I do what Troy says, as the D-line coach, I'm overstepping my bounds. But when I do move up to head coach, you're going to see my whole team wearing no shoes and we might not have a single bench in our weight room (laughs). I'll wait until I have the authority to do that. But you grow up as a kid and you're like, "Gotta lift weights, gotta squat, gotta do this and that," and then this guy comes around saying, "Yeah, I don't do that." It's almost like a change of culture.

BRANDON POLAMALU: This is another thing about Troy being a great observer: He observed things from Darren, who's a daredevil. He could climb up to a 50-foot cliff. Where it takes me a half hour to build up the courage to jump, Darren will turn back and do a backflip. Troy was the same way. He always wanted to test the limits of what he could do. "What can I do with this body? I want to take it to the extremes. I want to do creative stuff that nobody else would try," like flip over somebody into the end zone – not in celebration, but actually try stuff within the flow of the game. At the end of the day, whatever Troy does, he wants to look back and say, "I did everything that I could do with that body. I held nothing back." Troy's an extreme dude. He really is. He's an extreme person and he's a perfectionist in a lot of ways, and he has a fascination, I think, with those qualities of other people in life.

Troy Polamalu was still a few years from those 400-pound bench and 350-pound power clean days in 1995. He was a 5-8, 135-pound freshman at Douglas High and, other than leading the middle school team to the county title, he was relatively unknown.

Until the "jamboree" at nearby Roseburg.

On one of the first plays of that preseason tournament, Polamalu, the freshman free safety for the Douglas Trojans, announced his presence by walloping a receiver over the middle – and gave himself a concussion.

"*Probably* a concussion," corrected Douglas coach Neil Fuller.

Reports on the number of concussions suffered by Polamalu throughout his football career are varied. During his time in Pittsburgh Troy wouldn't admit concern over the number, nor admit that some were in fact concussions. And it sometimes became a point of contention with reporters. Troy felt that once he let his hair grow in college – from his days with a tight, Marine-style cut in high school – it served as a secondary buffer and the concussive impacts lessened.

Polamalu doubled as a slotback for the 1-8 Trojans as a freshman, and made the biggest play of their only win.

With a 7-0 lead against 5-0 Brookings, Douglas lined up to punt from its own 26-yard line. Polamalu was a gunner, but the upback saw that he was uncovered and called for a fake. Polamalu took the pass from Caleb Robbins and sped 74 yards for a touchdown, a 14-0 lead and ultimately the win that broke Douglas' 13-game losing streak.

"I about died of heart failure," Fuller told local reporters about the call made by one of his players.

Troy was the only freshman to start on a team that was packed with sophomores, so the future was bright for Douglas despite its record. And in Troy's sophomore season, having been moved to tailback, the Trojans jumped out to a 3-0 start when, as *The News-Review* sports writer Phil Lueck wrote in his lede on Oct. 10, 1996, "The legend of Troy Polamalu grew."

Polamalu rushed for 206 yards, added another 124 yards receiving and threw 20 yards on what Lueck called "an improvised pass to Casey Dawley after a broken play." It added up to 350 yards of total offense, and Polamalu scored six touchdowns – three on his first five touches (a fourth called back) – in a 47-8 win over Gold Beach that made Douglas 4-0.

"He's one of the best backs I've seen in this league," opposing coach Robert Van DeZande told the Roseburg paper.

"He's an O.J. Simpson type of back," said Fuller. "He's the best high school tailback I've seen."

Lueck did note that Simpson, of USC fame, had also been a Trojan.

Troy was interviewed for the first time after the game, and he told Lueck exactly what those who've interviewed him through 12 professional seasons would have expected:

"I can only do as good a job as my line does," Polamalu said. "I have confidence in the guys up front. They're the ones who are responsible."

Then Troy gave a nod to his Samoan ancestry.

"And the long runs," he said, "that was family blood right there."

SALU POLAMALU: Keneti ran the 100-yard dash for Mater Dei. Ao was fast. They both had good speed. I was fast. Matter of fact, when Joe was in high school I raced him. But I ran out of gas because he was so young. I was shoulder to shoulder with him for a while. When I was young and played rugby, I was pretty good, pretty athletic. I was a tough runner. And you get tough when you use a coconut as a football. We didn't have a football. We'd take a coconut on the soft end and pound them to the ground until they're soft, and when it hit you in the head at least you got some coconut (laughs). That was our football.

JOE POLAMALU: Our Uncle Keneti is pretty fast. He clocked out at a 4.3 or 4.4, which amazed me for his size. The old man had pretty good speed, too – when he was chasing us.

Above *The News-Review* headline that read "Douglas runs G.B. out of town" was a picture of Troy carrying the ball in his right hand ahead of the pack. His No. 41 made many close to him proud. It was Joe's number, Darren's number, Curt Stookey's number and Shelley's brother Jerry's number.

SHELLEY POLAMALU: His freshman year he couldn't get 41 in high school, so he asked for the closest number to it. So his freshman year he was 43. The senior graduated and then the next year Troy got 41. But he had 43 his freshman year and he doesn't even remember that. I discovered it by accident.

Douglas improved to 5-0 for the first time in 30 years with a 31-0 win over Coquelle. Troy scored two touchdowns as the young Trojans crept into the Oregon state Top 10 rankings at No. 7 in Class 3A.

Up next was Brookings, the team Douglas had upset the previous year, and Brookings returned the upset.

Troy scored three touchdowns and piled up 165 yards of total offense as Douglas held a 30-22 third-quarter lead, but eight turnovers eventually did Douglas in.

Troy's 1-yard run in overtime the following week gave Douglas an 18-12 win over Myrtle Point. His 154 yards of offense resulted in Douglas clinching at least a tie for first place in the Far West League and a playoff berth for the first time in four seasons.

MYERS: Troy scored the winning touchdown against Myrtle Point. He jumped over the pile but he didn't have to. It was his Walter Payton moment. The play was there. He could've run around the side, but he just decided to jump over the pile. It was one of those things that stuck with me, like, "Dude, you've always wanted to do that and you finally saw your spot." He became a safety but he wanted to be a running back. He was a frustrated running back always at heart, even when he was an All-Pro defensive back.

"Frustrated running back is the perfect way to put it," Troy told Justin Myers during a February 2020 interview on Portland talk radio.

"It's funny," Polamalu continued, "but whenever I was helping out other safeties, I always said, 'Listen, we're better running backs than the running back because as a safety we have our run gaps and our run keys but we have to find the gaps before the running back finds it.' So it actually helped me so much as a safety. But jumping over the line definitely stems from my brother, who at a young age was a huge Walter Payton fan, so whenever him and I would play one-on-one football when I was six or seven years old, he'd toss me the ball and make me jump over him and he'd just launch me higher, he'd take out my legs. To me, that's how football is experienced. You jump up like jumping on the bed before coming to a crash landing. So there's definitely some correlation between my love for Walter Payton jumping over the line and the way I did that playing defense as well."

Douglas lost its regular-season finale to Reedsport 30-13 and the Trojans ended in a three-way tie for first place at 7-2 (5-2 Far West League).

Douglas went up against the Skyline Conference runner-up Henley in the first round of the playoffs at Klamath Falls. Douglas fell behind 14-0, but Troy – who entered the game with 1,300 yards rushing at 8.0 per carry – scored on a 41-yard run, and then returned an interception 35 yards for the tying touchdown in the second quarter. However, Henley shut Troy down the rest of the way and romped to a 56-22 win to end the Douglas season.

Steve Fisher coached a Douglas basketball team that he said utilized a four-guard offense.

Troy Polamalu, a sophomore, was one of the four guards, as was his buddy Erick Stookey.

The tallest player was 6 feet 2, and the Trojans went 19-7 as Troy averaged 11 points per game and was named to the All-Far West League's first team.

In previewing the Class 3A state tournament in Portland, Fisher told *The News-Review*, "Without Troy we're a JV team. Everything we do relies on Troy's ability to put pressure on the ball defensively."

In the first round of the playoffs, second-seeded Douglas beat Ontario 50-47, but was crushed by Sutherlin 60-38 in the second round, which, of course, opened the door to baseball season.

Troy was coach Rod Trask's center fielder and leadoff hitter, and Douglas finished second in the Far West League with a 20-5 overall record (12-2 in league). Douglas had been to the state tournament every year since 1988, so the 1997 team was following a solid tradition and aiming for its second state championship in five years.

Douglas beat Philomath 12-5 in the first round of the 1997 state playoffs, as Troy went 3-for-5, but the Trojans lost in the quarterfinals 5-4.

The News-Review photographed Polamalu looking skyward after striking out for the final out with the tying run on second base. In the background, players from The Dalles celebrated their win.

MYERS: In our community, baseball was huge. The majority of college athletes from my high school, we all played baseball somewhere. It's funny because you have Troy and then Josh Bidwell from Douglas. They both played in the NFL and in the Pro Bowl, so you would think we were a big football school, but everybody at Douglas loved baseball. And in Oregon, summer baseball is almost bigger than high school baseball because it rains in the spring time, so in the summer it's perfect. The American Legion team in Roseburg was made up of the best players from like five local high schools, so we would all play on one team and travel throughout the state.

The big Fourth of July tournament we were in every year kind of showed another side of Troy. We stayed at a hotel for the tournament and Troy and Caleb Robbins thought it would be funny – actually we all thought it was funny; they just got caught – to throw water balloons out the seventh story window of the hotel. Coach Trask found out, lost his mind, drove them to the Oregon State campus, found a track and said, "You guys have a hundred laps. I'll be back at the end of the day." I don't think they got their 100 laps done, but they ran all day. That's the thing I think people should know about Troy. The whole "Troy's so soft-spoken and humble and nice and gracious" thing, all of that is true. But he was also the biggest prankster growing up. He loved messing with people. When he stayed the night at our house, he couldn't sleep in. He was always up early and he thought it was very funny to turn on the Lion King, the very opening part of the Lion King, as loud as it could possibly go and scream along with it until everybody else woke up.

Troy was the leadoff hitter and center fielder for Doc Stewart's, the American Legion team in Roseburg. On a day in July of 1997, when the Pittsburgh Steelers were playing an NFL preseason game at legendary Croke Park in Dublin, Ireland, Troy was helping Doc's clinch a playoff berth. However, in the state sub-tournament, Troy's throw to the plate with two outs in the bottom of the ninth inning of a tie game was a bang-bang call that didn't go Roseburg's way. Once the ump signaled safe, it was time for Troy to turn his attention to the most anticipated football season in Douglas High history.

The Trojans entered the 1997 football season ranked 16th in the state's 3A classification. They assembled at their University of Montana camp with nine starters returning on offense and 10 on defense.

Neil Fuller, in his third season, counted junior Troy Polamalu on each side of the ball, but it was the senior-dominated offensive line receiving most of the attention.

"The key was the Trojans' massive offensive line," *The News-Review* reported following Douglas' 48-6 opening-night win over rival South Umpqua.

"Anybody can run behind a line like that," Polamalu said after carrying 10 times for 135 yards and 3 touchdowns.

He ran all but one play of the opening drive, which he ended with a 32-yard counter for a touchdown.

His 20-yard touchdown run gave Douglas a 14-0 lead, and his 42-yard touchdown run put the game away.

"We flat couldn't take him down," said South Umpqua Coach John Srholec. "I think the rest of the state is going to have that problem, too."

Douglas beat its old (and future) coach, Rick Taylor, and Glide 48-0 the following week. Troy rushed for 170 yards and scored five touchdowns – two on carries (9 and 52 yards), another on a 40-yard fumble return, another on a 70-yard punt return, and the fifth on a 93-yard reception off a fake punt.

Douglas opened its FWL schedule by thumping Reedsport 31-6, and improved to 4-0 the following week with a 35-20 win over Bandon in which Troy rushed for 200 yards on 15 carries and also caught a 66-yard touchdown pass.

Polamalu scored from 5 and 40 yards in a 20-6 win over Siuslaw that made Douglas 5-0 for the second consecutive season and vaulted the Trojans to the top of the Oregon state 3A rankings.

The previous year's Douglas team lost three of its final four games to finish 6-3, but this 1997 team learned from the experience. Douglas blew out Coquille 54-8, behind Troy's six touchdowns, and then Gold Beach 37-8 to improve to 7-0.

However, on the first play against Gold Beach, Polamalu sprained his ankle. He sat out the rest of the game and returned the following Friday with the ankle heavily wrapped.

A 56-20 rout of Brookings-Harbor made Douglas 8-0 and clinched the FWL championship.

"This is the biggest win in my career, in any sport," Polamalu told *The News-Review* after rushing for 112 yards on 11 carries. "It didn't matter what shape I was in, what percentage I was at, the fact is the line did such a great job all I had to do was follow them."

Douglas finished its regular season undefeated for the first time in school history by beating Myrtle Point the following week 55-20.

Troy was able to rest his ankle during a bye week in the playoffs, but Douglas lost offensive lineman Eric Koegler with a broken ankle. Fellow linemen Willie James and Peter James were also struggling with knee injuries, which didn't bode well for their opening playoff game.

At home, top-seeded Douglas was upset by unseeded Scappoose, 21-7.

Douglas trailed 14-0 in the fourth quarter but Troy caught a 28-yard pass on fourth-and-14 to set up a touchdown.

However, Scappoose and its spread offense – with future Cleveland Browns quarterback Derek Anderson a freshman wide receiver – beat the elements and the Douglas defense for the game-clinching touchdown with 4:32 remaining.

Polamalu caught five passes for 124 yards in the loss, but was held to 44 rushing yards on nine carries.

MYERS: It was beyond crushing. We were undefeated. No one was ever really close. We all figured, "Hey, we've got Troy. We've got the best player in the state, if not the best player anybody was ever going to see. There was no possible way we were going to lose this game." But we got smacked in the mouth by a team that was ready to play and we did not handle it well. It was devastating. That loss came from out of nowhere.

BRANDON POLAMALU: Troy would never say this but I'll say it for him: His ankle was badly rolled. Watch the video. He couldn't plant. Troy was an amazing running back. He still had a good game, but, yeah, that Douglas team was a great team – in terms of Oregon football. I think that was the most talented team to come through Douglas. Troy had a lot of help, but by his senior year the help was gone. That group of seniors when he was a junior was a good group.

JOE POLAMALU: That junior year I came back and helped coach. Some of that stuff I can remember like it was yesterday. His moves, his sidesteps, it was almost effortless. Up at college, I'd seen some athletes, and I came back and saw him and said he's the real deal. I may be biased. I know he's family. But you don't see that kind of stuff.

MYERS: I played middle linebacker. He played safety behind me. And he beat me to the ball a lot. *A lot.* The thing that translated, because obviously he got physically better and smarter and got better coaching and everything else, but the thing that has always been a constant, going back to high school, to USC, to when he was in Pittsburgh, he was 100 percent confident in the play he was making and he never stopped his feet. He never second-guessed himself, especially on defense.

BRANDON POLAMALU: His defensive skills were absolutely there at the time. He was a phenomenal defensive player. But as a running back, he was awesome. It was also the Far West League. People don't throw a lot. They run a lot. The weather's bad in Oregon. We played on the coast a lot with high winds, so you had a lot of just running football. He was really small his freshman year. His sophomore year he started putting on muscle and he started making these hits that you'd think didn't have any business being on this field. Some of those hits were like car wrecks. I thought, "He's really going to hurt people with these hits." I think if Troy was playing down in Southern California with some other athletes that were maybe at that level, they could elude some of those hits better. But by the time he was a junior, oh, he made some crushing hits. There were some hits that hurt to watch. They really did.

JOE POLAMALU: As a senior one time he had a penalty for too hard of a hit or something, and I'd never heard of that.

JASON DICKOVER, *Douglas High athletic director:* It wasn't a blow to the head or anything, it was a personal foul, "You hit the kid too hard."

JOE POLAMALU: I used to cringe when I saw a quarterback throw that lazy pass over the middle. You do not want to do that because you'll see a blur coming through there. He was a safety. That was clear to me at the time.

MYERS: Joe's 100 percent right. You didn't throw lazy passes. You really didn't put people over the middle. Troy has, I would say, a mean streak. The nicest person ever. He's my best friend. He's like a brother to me. But there are times when he needed to turn it on in high school and get a little bit ornery, and he could turn it on.

TOM EGGERS, *The News-Review sports writer:* My main memory of Troy was after Douglas lost to Scappoose in that first-round state playoff game in a rainstorm. Douglas was muddy. It was the home field. Douglas was favored. I remember standing in the rain trying to have dry paper and talking to him. They didn't do much offensively. It was a slick field. Scappoose focused on him because Douglas probably didn't have much else. Even though they lost to an unseeded team, he was still willing to stand there in the rain and talk to me. That's typical of him. He didn't hang his head. I don't remember him trying to get into the locker room and out of the line of fire. He didn't have any qualms about standing there in the rain answering questions about a bad loss.

JOHN SOWELL, *The News-Review county government reporter:* I've refereed football the last 25 years at the high school level. When he was at Douglas, he didn't always have a very good team behind him. I never saw an instance where he got up after being tackled and started yelling at his teammates, like, "If you'd have made that block – ." We see that quite a bit. It's interesting that there are some guys who, for whatever reason, don't feel the need to do that. They've had it ingrained upon them by other people not to take out frustrations on other people, especially teammates and such. But there are other people who have – maybe not the talent that he had – but are good players and for whatever reason have to do that. So it always impressed me that he just went and did his job. Of course, at that time none of us knew where he was going to go from there.

Troy Polamalu was one of three returning starters – along with Erick Stookey and Ty Worthen – on the basketball team his junior season.

Douglas finished third in the Far West League at 9-5, and beat Myrtle Point 73-60 in the first round of the district playoffs behind Troy's 19 points. Douglas lost in the second round to Reedsport 77-65 when Troy was held to five points. Douglas finished its season 13-12 overall.

In baseball, Troy hit .565 and Douglas went 18-3 overall and 14-0 in the FWL. Even though Troy homered to give the Trojans a 3-1 lead in the first round of the state playoffs, Douglas lost to Pleasant Hill 6-4.

Troy missed several American Legion games that summer due to football recruiting, but Doc's won the Area 4 title. In one doubleheader, Polamalu hit a two-out, bases-loaded single for a 9-8 win, and in the second game stole home in the first inning to spark a 14-4 win.

Troy finished the regular season with a .373 batting average and was second on the team with five home runs.

In the state playoffs, Doc's needed to beat 4A Oregon state high school champ Beaverton twice to win the championship. Troy went 5-for-8 in the doubleheader, and led Doc's to one win, but Beaverton won the second game 16-9 and walked away with the title.

The recruiting from colleges was only part of what Troy Polamalu endured the summer following his junior year at Douglas. The recruiting pitch from big-school football neighbor Roseburg was also picking up.

Coached by Oregon legend Thurman Bell, Roseburg, in the highest classification, 6A, was coming off a school-record 32 consecutive regular-season wins from 1995-97. Roseburg had won state championships in 1995 and 1996, and was loaded for the 1998 season. It hoped to add Troy, the younger cousin of former Douglas-to-Roseburg transfer Joe Polamalu, who went on to play linebacker at Oregon State from 1986-90.

Troy told *The News-Review* of Roseburg that he had received an anonymous letter "practically begging me to put on the orange and black."

Joe had previously made the complicated transfer, which included much sacrifice by his parents, Shelley and Salu. So, Troy, who would be entering his senior season at Douglas as a running back behind a young offensive line, was a logical target.

SHELLEY POLAMALU: (Salu) and Joe actually had to move to Roseburg and we had to get a legal separation so that he could have custody of Joe and he could live in Roseburg and he could go to Roseburg.

We did it. We paid for two houses, rent for the apartment. I had two houses to clean. I had two different places to cook. I thought "God this is awful."

SALU POLAMALU: Joe went for his last two years. That was after we looked into Douglas and saw there was no future. No baseball, no basketball. There were some good individual players at Douglas. Josh Bidwell played with Darren, but he was a kicker. He was a big kid, like 6 foot 2. He could kick the ball very well. When he played soccer for me, I was like "Geeeeez, the only thing he's good for is kick the ball. The mouth goes all the time." Dennis Boyd (Seattle Seahawks 1977-82) was just a big kid. He came here from somewhere else for one year and then went to Oregon State. But there were some other players I thought Douglas had over the years. Kevin Tommasini went to Notre Dame for baseball. Joe had two kids when he coached that I thought JC should've looked at. They were fast and had very good work ethic. To me, those are the things you've got to look at, compared to some bigger, lazy, picky kids, like at Roseburg. When Joe was there they had a front line that averaged 6-5, about 300 pounds. In Joe's first year he came home and said "What a luxury to run behind that line."

SHELLEY POLAMALU: Believe me, Joe's transfer was a BIG subject of conversation here. But the times were different with Joe. We had *nothing* at Douglas then, not football, basketball or baseball, and Joe was good in all of those. When Troy was here, every one of our programs was doing very well. Basically we were ruling the Far West League. There was no reason to move him. And besides that, how could a family do that *twice*? And I work for the district.

SOWELL: I always found it interesting, too, that Troy played summer baseball for the Roseburg Legion team. I know some of his baseball teammates were trying to get him to come to Roseburg for his senior year and play football for them. That was the year Roseburg football lost in the state championship game. He would've made the difference. I never had conversations with him about why he stayed with Douglas his senior season, but it seemed to me he had a loyalty to that program and to the kids around him and that he didn't feel he had to go to the bigger school down the road.

While Roseburg was gearing up to attempt a third consecutive 6A state title run during Troy Polamalu's four years at Douglas, the Trojans entered the 1998 season ranked sixth in the state in 3A.

Of course, the media was basing that on the fact Douglas had Polamalu among nine returning starters. But the rebuilt Douglas offensive line consisted of two freshmen, a sophomore and two juniors.

Douglas blasted Phoenix in the opener 48-0 as Troy rushed for 211 yards on only 15 carries. He scored touchdowns on runs of 10, 23, 11 and 77 yards.

But Douglas was drilled the second week by Henley 30-7. The third game was a repeat as Myrtle Point hammered Douglas in the Far West League opener 51-16. Troy didn't play in that game due to what later was diagnosed as a bruised kidney. He did return for Week 4 against Reedsport and had his second 200-yard game – 226 yards on 29 carries. But Douglas fell to 1-3 with the 20-12 loss on Oct. 4.

On Oct. 7, Troy was voted Douglas' Homecoming king, with his high school sweetheart Shawna, but on Oct. 8 doctors told him about his bruised kidney, from Week 2, which had been hit again in Week 4. They told Troy his season was over.

On Oct. 9, Douglas lost to Bandon 90-6 as the Trojans were forced to become accustomed to life without Troy Polamalu.

Or so they thought.

SHELLEY POLAMALU: He doesn't even know what particular hit he took or when it happened. Troy was so targeted. It's just the game plan every team had: get him out of the game. We had seen the same thing with Joe, who played a whole game, the first game of his senior year, with a seriously broken arm. Ugh. But Troy, he told me about three days after the game that he thought something was wrong with him. He said his urine was bloody. I'd never had any experience with that with any of my kids, so I packed him up and took him to the emergency room to Dr. Norris, our family doctor. He said Troy had a pretty seriously bruised kidney, and he told me that he absolutely cannot practice or play. This is very serious. Of course, you don't tell someone like Troy or Joe you're not going to play anymore. In Joe's case it was his senior year and yes he did come back. It was Troy's senior year also, and it was probably midway through the season. This was South Umpqua and they were told without a doubt Troy would not be playing that game that Friday. So they geared their whole game plan all week long on the knowledge that Troy would not be there. Well, he didn't practice that week, but I think he was undergoing some mental rebellion about this. I mean, everything about his being told him he has to play. So Friday, game day, South Umpqua's coming to Douglas and he concocted this story – which I believed; maybe because I wanted to believe it – but he called Brandon and asked him to take him to the doctor. Troy actually checked himself out of school basically right underneath my nose. Everybody in the offices knew him. I think he just walked out and no one felt like they needed to question what he was doing. Brandon picked him up and they went somewhere. And when they came back it was just prior to the game.

BRANDON POLAMALU: I don't remember that actually. It might've been Darren that took him. I just remember that they told him they didn't want him to do any type of physical activity that would put any strain on his body, so he had to essentially quit working out. My mom and dad always cooked every meal at home. We ate lots of red meat, lots of rice, typical Samoan diet. We ate differently than say the Samoans of Southern California because we didn't eat as much Spam. We also drank lots of soda. Troy's an extreme person so when he decides to let go he might drink like 12 Mountain Dews a day. As soon as they told him he couldn't do anything, he just started eating candy and drinking soda and just really let go. And this time was really hard for him, but I think his way of coping was to just relax and have as much fun as he possibly could have, so it was really a fun time because we shot a lot of movies during this time and we stayed up really late all the time. And then when he actually got back, they cleared him to play and he was in horrible shape. He'd run a couple of plays and have his hands on his knees. But it was still awesome to watch because you could see this is what Troy would be if he was an undisciplined, unmotivated person. And it was still a really impressive game, his first game back. It was a fun time.

SHELLEY POLAMALU: I was working the ticket booth that night until game time. Both teams were out on the field warming up, pre-game stuff. Everybody was up there. The locker room was empty. Troy was dropped off and he went in the locker room, got all his gear, put his jersey on, and proceeded up the hill and joined the team in the pre-game warm-ups. I saw him coming out of the locker room and I hollered at him and he came over. I said, "What are you doing?" He said, "I went to the doctor. I got cleared." And he said, "I gotta go." He didn't give me any chance to even think about what he'd just said. So he charges up on the field and kind of blended in. South Umpqua did not have a clue. And then the kickoff and the South Umpqua coach went berserk. He charged out and went to the referees, "He's not supposed to be in the game!" It wasn't his business and nothing happened, but he saw red. Neil, Troy's own coach, didn't know what to do, either, but Troy said "I got cleared." But did anybody ask him for a note? I mean, isn't that law for God's sake? He went right past the AD up there, a friend of our family, right past the assistant coaches. Joe was one of them. And he just joined in. Nobody was going to challenge or question him. Troy said he was cleared, so he was cleared. And Troy was dynamite that game.

Troy rushed for 149 yards on 21 carries in a 28-6 Douglas win over South Umpqua. He scored two touchdowns and ran for two conversions. He also made a play that might be remembered more than any other at Douglas.

"It was our Homecoming game," Neil Fuller told the *Daily Inter Lake* of Montana more than seven years later. "He hurdled a kid and ran 70 yards. And our quarterback was running down the field with him. Right before he would've scored, Troy pitched it to the quarterback and he scored the touchdown. It was probably his first touchdown."

SHELLEY POLAMALU: He was told not to play anymore that season, and he was told not to play basketball. He even told me he wasn't going to play basketball. He knew the recruiting time was going to hit hard and basketball's a very time-consuming game and he plays it like he plays everything else.

Of course, Troy did play basketball. He felt good, and he felt as if the recruiting from colleges – which had begun with a letter right before his 350-yard game early in his sophomore season – was under control. He in fact settled on USC in January of 1999.

"Once a Trojan, always a Trojan," said Troy, who was so named, according to his Uncle Keneti, because of the USC Trojans.

"Yes," Keneti recalled. "He was born a few months after I committed to USC. We're all close and my sister (Siuila) was taking care of my mom in Fountain Valley."

Troy, of course, was the city comprised of Trojans in Greek mythology.

The University of Southern California would now become the campus comprised of Troy, and he would become one of the greatest of Trojans ever.

CHAPTER 4

LEGACY STORIES

SHELLEY POLAMALU: Troy did change his mind, on his own, about basketball. And I really wanted him to play because he can't function without a sport. He's too focused on everything to take something like sports out of his life. I really felt for his sake he needed to play basketball. The team needed him, too.

JASON DICKOVER: Troy called basketball his fun sport. That's what he termed it because he was being recruited so heavily in football and baseball and so he got to have fun with basketball. My favorite memory of Troy on the basketball floor was actually our first home game his senior year against Brookings. It was a pretty close game up to the end. Erick Stookey stole the ball and threw it ahead to Troy, and Troy and his 5-10-ness dunked the ball and it really kind of broke open the game for us. We had a capacity crowd and it just went nuts. I looked at my assistants in disbelief. Then I looked up in the balcony at Salu and the big guy was doing a little Samoan tap dance up there. I couldn't hold it in. I had to start laughing.

SHELLEY POLAMALU: His senior year he and Erick Stookey, one or the other, was the leading scorer way above everyone else. They played together from the time they were little on this court right here, so Erick and Troy could just communicate without talking. They made a good pair.

BRANDON POLAMALU: I love basketball, and I played so much basketball with that kid. That was my baby with Troy, basketball. I wanted to push him to see what he could do. We were hard on Troy, too. When he got up here he was a little thing and we were rough with him. There were times on the basketball court that I saw Troy do things that blew me away by the time he was a senior, but mostly I'm talking street games, pick-up ball. I saw Troy throw down some dunks, make some blocks, just do things that I was in awe of. It's different when you saw it all manifest, unfold, from a 7-year-old to this 19-year-old who's doing a 360 windmill, cocked dunk.

TOM EGGERS: I covered him more in basketball than football. God, the quickest kid on the floor. I remember in the state tournament he just disrupted the whole other team with his defense and quickness. Steve Fisher could tell you more.

STEVE FISHER, *Douglas High basketball coach:* In basketball, he brought athleticism to the game. He would put pressure on the ball, get the rebound, lead the break, finish it, that sort of thing. He was unselfish. I begged him to shoot the ball. I couldn't get him to score more. But he made everyone around him better.

DICKOVER: I was driving a van back from a tournament. We were taking the boys out to the buffet after the game and something was going on in the back, and one of the boys said, "Jesus Christ," or something like that. And I said, "Hey, you guys knock that off. I don't want to hear that." Pretty soon the quiet voice from way back was Troy, and he said, "Coach Dickover, do you believe in God?" I looked in the mirror and said, "Yeah, Troy, I do." And he started up a discussion that lasted the rest of the drive to the restaurant. We talked about God and where He belongs in our life. It wasn't the typical post-game discussion you have in a van full of teenage boys. But I did hear him raise his voice one time, and it was actually one of the saddest days in Troy's high school career, the day Salu had the heart attack.

SHELLEY POLAMALU: He didn't want to play in that game.

DICKOVER: We had a game the next day and Troy stayed the whole night in the hospital. He was awake all night.

SHELLEY POLAMALU: Salu made him go.

DICKOVER: I fully didn't expect Troy to show up, but he showed up for the bus ride. We talked a little bit. He was so heavy-hearted, so sad, just not Troy, and we got over to Bandon and there was an incident in the game. Again, he stole the ball late in the game and he went in, dunked the ball, and this little freshman from Bandon, who didn't know any better, undercut him and Troy ended up landing so hard on his head and his shoulder that the mesh from his jersey was imprinted in his skin. I know it scared him, and he got up and the whites of his eyes were all I saw. He was going for it. I got out there on the floor and it was hard for me to hold on to him. He was close to out of control at that time. He wanted to do something. That was the only time I'd actually come close to seeing him lose it.

SHELLEY POLAMALU: Troy did go, and it was probably a mistake. He was just so full of emotion. He had (football) scouts there, too. I didn't go to the game, either, but I heard there was a cheap shot. Normally he would handle that just fine, but he wasn't in a mood to be messed with. So, he got sent to the locker room. After the game, Troy came home and I asked him how did it go, did we win? "No. We lost." I said, "How did you do?" He said, "I got kicked out of the game." That was unheard of. He'd never shown any kind of anger or bad behavior. I couldn't imagine it. I thought he was kidding me. I said, "Oh, yeah, right. I'm not in the mood for jokes." He said, "I'm not joking." I asked him what he got kicked out for, and he said, "I was just about ready to get into a fight." I thought, this is getting worse and worse. It wasn't until the next day I found out that what he was saying was true. I also found out later that all of Bandon sympathized with Troy. Even today, people in Bandon talk about that game. They remember it with pride. The whole Far West League considers Troy theirs. The majority of his career he was such a good sportsman that everybody loved him. But that basketball season definitely came with some highs and lows for us all. The distractions were just incredible.

DICKOVER: In the playoffs in basketball, the one we lost his senior year, we were playing against the team that ended up winning the state championship. They had size and we didn't have any size. They had a 6-7 post player.

CURT STOOKEY: It was against Cresswell and Luke Jackson was the star. He was 6-7, 6-8, drafted by Cleveland out of Oregon. Put Troy on him. Put Erick on him. Those two took turns guarding Luke, and Luke was a great, great ballplayer. We held him down for two quarters. Troy did a heck of a job on him bringing the ball up. Luke brought the ball up for Oregon.

FISHER: They were loaded, nobody less than 6-foot. We were outmanned at every position. I think they scored the first 13 points. We called timeout. We were quick but we weren't as talented as that group. I remember during the timeout, "Stick with the program. Stick with what we're doing. Maybe we'll get back in the game." That sort of thing. Well, the next time the ball comes down the floor, we're fronting post and they lob over the top to Jackson and he's on the block and he turns and he's going to lay it up. Troy covers down from the point and he lifts – and I kid you not – he's like *this* far above the rim, Troy. And this kid turns like it's an everyday lay-up. Troy slaps it up into the seats. And then all of the sudden everybody on our team, me included, said, "He's on our team and guess what fellas? You're in for a ball game right now!" And that's what happened. They became a little deflated, "Whoa, did you see that?" And then our kids got all puffy. It's probably the best example I can tell you about his influence on the kids that played with him and everybody elevated at that moment, and guess what? We had a halftime lead. We were within a point with a minute to go. We lose the game, but we would've been blown out. That one moment right there changed the entire face, color of that game. It just elevated everyone here. That's the one I remember the most.

SHELLEY POLAMALU: Troy thought he would have problems with recruiting that season, but he only missed two games. What was bad, we would have like seven football recruiters at a basketball game from different colleges and they'd seek Salu and I out like magnets and sit with us. Troy would see this from the floor and it had to have been distracting. One game, Keneti went with us – he was with Colorado but he could do that, family – and we had two other football coaches that traveled all the way to Florence for a basketball game. We had a whole group that followed us to Reedsport. It was just – whew. In a way, that basketball season was almost a nightmare. They were all vying for our attention, too. And all of them were really pissed off that Keneti was there because he was coming home with us and had all the access to Troy. He's sleeping here! Keneti knew most of these recruiters really well and he would joke about having a beer with Salu.

The baseball season his senior year was another nightmare that way. We went all the way to Glide to a baseball game with 26 baseball scouts. There were more scouts than parents watching. You could pick them out. They were all dressed too nice for a baseball game and they all had briefcases. That fired Troy up. He hit a grand slam batting left-handed, which he'd never done before. It was the first time I ever saw him bat left-handed. He did amazing things in the field. It wasn't that he was showing off; it was almost the opposite. "You guys came to see me do something? OK, watch this." Of course, they were impressed.

EGGERS: That was the sport I thought he had a chance to go. He was a center fielder with power, speed, good arm.

DICKOVER: He could cover any ground that needed to be covered in the outfield. And any ball he hit to the left side of the infield was a single. They weren't going to throw him out. I always thought he was a good football player in high school but that he was probably too small to play major college football. But I thought he really had a chance to play pro baseball.

SHELLEY POLAMALU: That was my thought and prayer, please, baseball, because I already lost one son's knee to college football. It's a brutal sport. Joe tore up his knee at Oregon State, his senior year, major knee surgery, and he never did get to play baseball. Troy got that same offer. He could've played baseball at USC, and they would've let him, but after his second year they changed coaches and Troy didn't want to miss spring football with a brand new coach. But he came home that Christmas with his bat, his bag, his uniform, everything for USC baseball.

ROD TRASK: We went down to Dodgers Stadium for a tryout and stayed with Keneti and got to see everything. He did well. He really did well. He was already signed to USC but I thought they'd draft him anyway. I was really surprised they did not. They were coming in for cross checks and all that kind of stuff.

Troy didn't play American Legion baseball the summer of '99 because he parted for USC soon after graduating from Douglas. But he did have a few pro baseball tryouts.

The first was with the Atlanta Braves in Oregon in April of 1999. Braves scout Kurt Kemp was in his first year scouting the Pacific Northwest. He had watched Polamalu the previous fall and, according to *Yahoo Sports*, had noted in his reports that "Polamalu ran hard after every ball and closed the gaps unusually well. Polamalu's musculature was forming." A note was made of Troy's "broad shoulders, thick neck and loose but powerful arms that produced a potent swing." Kemp liked the way Polamalu's bat sounded when he made solid contact, even though the sound was "the awkward clank of aluminum."

Kemp had been an assistant baseball coach at Oregon State when Joe played, so the scout was naturally drawn to Troy, and visited the family in Tenmile.

"Troy and his family were very honest about football, which was very nice," Kemp told *Yahoo Sports*. "They spoke candidly about what football meant to Troy and their family. It was no secret. It's not like they had you there to see if they could get the right offer."

Troy thanked Kemp for scouting him, which Kemp noted with delight. Kemp then concluded that, "You sure had a good feeling about that young man. You had to do the due diligence, as if football wasn't a factor. The honesty was uncommon."

Troy had another tryout with the Los Angeles Dodgers a week before the June 2, 1999, Major League draft.

He had already committed to USC after then-coach Paul Hackett agreed to let him play baseball. But Troy never got to play a game at USC, so his tryout with the Dodgers was pretty much his last hurrah.

JUSTIN MYERS: People were debating whether he should go to college and play baseball or football. My dad was adamant that he could make it to the bigs as a catcher. I think my dad was still the only coach that put him at catcher, and Troy kind of hated it. He wanted to be a center fielder, but my dad was like "He's so athletic. He's so quick. He's a born catcher." His arm was fair. I'll joke with Troy about this because everybody called him a five-tool player, but he was four and a half. His arm left a little bit to be desired.

KENETI POLAMALU, *Troy's uncle:* I went to the Dodgers workout when they brought him out. He had the fastest time from home plate to second base. You could see him in center field, he could just cover everywhere. He was so good. But at that time, outfielders were hitting 30 home runs and you needed to do that to play there or first or third base. The Dodgers, along with the Cubs, and I think the Atlanta Braves, they were looking at him to play second and shortstop because of his speed. At the Dodger workout, one of my former teammates' father was there with Lasorda, Tim Shannon, Sr. Tim Shannon was a safety with me at USC. Both Lasorda and Shannon just loved Troy's bat speed and how he could get on base. They thought he could be like Steve Sax, just that athlete who could get on base and steal. But they wanted him to give up football. Then they would take him in the high rounds. That's how talented the kid was as a baseball player. One of the Cubs' scouts thought Troy could be as good as Ryne Sandberg, and he's the scout who had signed Sandberg. He thought Troy had the ability to be better. Obviously, when you look back and see all the athleticism and explosiveness, you can see that.

Troy Polamalu wasn't the only big-time athlete at that Dodgers tryout. Ricky Manning was there. He was eventually drafted by the Carolina Panthers in the same 2003 NFL draft in which Troy was drafted by the Steelers. But at the time, Manning was about to begin a dual minor-league baseball/UCLA football career after being drafted by the Twins.

There was another speedy Polynesian switch-hitter at the Dodges tryout by the name of Shane Victorino, who was drafted in the sixth round by the Dodgers the following week. He later told the author of his book, *Shane Victorino: The Flyin' Hawaiian*, that he hit 3 home runs at the camp and "outran everyone else at the camp … including Troy Polamalu."

Victorino became a Major League star. Troy wasn't drafted.

"I wasn't good enough, first of all," Polamalu explained years later. "But I was all football and I was committed to go to USC to play baseball and football there."

Troy Polamalu and Pete Carroll would come to celebrate the way Troy's baseball career played out – or didn't play out – sometime around the middle of the 2001 football season.

As a Samoan growing up in a county that was 94 percent white, Troy learned how to deal with racism. It wasn't something he liked to discuss; it wasn't something he tried to avoid.

He would drop the topic to reporters close to him in Pittsburgh, but then back away when he sensed resulting fuss. He also knew many good people in Douglas County weren't racist at all.

SHELLEY POLAMALU: Talk to our sons and they'll agree with Troy. They try to keep it from us and they don't really talk about it but they've all experienced it.

BRANDON POLAMALU: This starts with the history of the area. Obviously this area has been ethnically cleansed of Native Americans. There was a strong Chinese community here that was brought in to mine and build railroads. There were taxes imposed upon them. And there were whatever African-Americans here in the earlier part of the 20th century. There were taxes imposed on them to where it was basically impossible for them to live here. This is stuff that's researchable, but it's certainly not what we learned in history books going to school here. It's also well-documented that there were sundown laws all the way into the late '50s and '60s here in a lot of these towns along I-5 where you had to be out of town by sundown if you weren't white. When I was in college, I saw pictures of the KKK marching right down Main Street in Grant's Pass in the '60s, and right there with the football team and fire department, a very normal part of life. So I put that into context with the fact my dad came here in the late '60s. He was called nigger a lot. My dad's way of dealing with that was he beat a lot of people up.

FISHER: This is what I hear, too. Aside from coaching the basketball team, I'm a bar owner, so everybody tells me these legacy stories, "I knew Salu when he first came to town." The story pretty much is, "You can piss us all off, but don't piss off that big Samoan, man. You'll get in trouble." Those stories still linger around from when he first came to this community.

SALU POLAMALU: Yep. I still hear them.

BRANDON POLAMALU: By the time I was born he had a reputation for having been in many fights and never lost. Ever. Not even close. My dad put people in the hospital. I want to be clear on this: It wasn't for no reason. He got in trouble at work for people calling him that name and him addressing it with his fists. That was his way of handling it. I think by the time we came through he had paved a path for us. But all of us got called that name at least once, some of us a lot more – me and Darren a lot more.

SHELLEY POLAMALU: I heard a horrible story about Salu coming home from work one night on a dark, lonely road. They cut him off and he pulled over. Four guys got out of the car and four guys ended up lying on the road as Salu drove home.

SALU POLAMALU: I was tough enough to take care of myself.

FISHER: Salu and Shelley came into this community about 30 years ago, and it's rural America. It's no different than Michigan, or flat land, or anywhere else, but for someone of Salu's stature to come in this community and to add parental guidance, moral guidance, he coached all the sports, and he and Shelley have been pillars of the community. It was fortunate he happened to land in this area.

BRANDON POLAMALU: I have to also say that this is a beautiful community full of love and great people. Even a lot of the people we are great friends with, we had to come to terms with this idea that they would say very controversial things, but at the same time they treated us very well. I think it was an ingrained part, maybe because this area doesn't have a lot of diversity when it comes to skin color.

SHELLEY POLAMALU: Joe kind of paved the way for all the boys. He kind of broke the water, made the great Samoan race something to be proud of as good people, and it made it a little easier for each one down the line.

BRANDON POLAMALU: My dad has one of those bigger than life personalities who people are really attracted to. We'd have these luaus and there'd be 300 people out here. The community loved him so much, too, that I think it gave them permission to let down whatever guard and ignorance they had. A lot more than his fighting, there was just a lot of love coming from that guy. I think it was amazing how my dad started doing these umus, where he'd bury a pig and have all these people and they'd participate. They would eat it afterwards and they would drink. He was inviting them in to participate. It was very hands on. "This is my culture. This is how I grew up." And they loved it. It was a very educating process and I think he did a pretty amazing job of breaking down a lot of walls. I'm very impressed with the way my dad did that. I can't say he was just a fighter by any means.

KEVIN McDANIEL, *Douglas High principal:* I wasn't here when Troy was here. I was the AD at a rival school. My joke was I was glad to see the guy graduate because he was killing us. I've been in southern Oregon my entire career and I've seen two remarkable athletes – Troy and Danny O'Brien, the decathlete. I wasn't here when he was here, but Troy was very much involved in the center for educational partnerships, disabled students, kids with Down syndrome, mental retardation, autism. He was very closely connected to that. The truth be known, he sneaks into town and that's one of the first places he goes, down to visit that program. There's a picture that kind of captures his last visit. A retired teacher set this up. They had Troy on some kind of a video clip and the kids are around watching it – and Troy walks in the back door.

JOHN SOWELL: The year after Pittsburgh won the first title with him there, I was refereeing a junior high basketball game in Winston where one of his nephews was playing. There's an open area on one end of the court that leads back into the rest of the school building, and usually there are two or three people hanging out, just standing there watching the game. We had been down at the other end of the court for a while and then came back and suddenly there are 25 or 30 people. I was wondering, "What are these people doing there?" And then out of the corner of my eye I saw Troy there. At halftime I went to the bathroom and there were mothers in the hallway and I could hear one of them on her phone going, "It's Troy Polamalu! He's here! He's here!" And before the end of the game there must've been double the number of people in the stands that obviously other people had called. Afterwards they went up and asked him for autographs and photos and he seemed to accommodate everybody.

SALU POLAMALU: Troy was a gain for us. We were very fortunate. We worked on it to get it to where he is. When he interviews he says, "Yes, the real discipline for me was my uncle in Oregon." He's always credited me with that. And I was. I really was. I don't think Troy would be where he's at if he didn't come here. I really believe that. Kaio was just as good an athlete and a little taller than Troy. Solid. Good athlete. But he never had any home life or somebody to back him up until he got married.

BRANDON POLAMALU: It's a very, very good question, but I hesitate because I think me and Troy disagree on this. I think Kaio absolutely could've made it as an athlete. But it could be either way because I really do believe very strongly that if you give a lot of those kids down there access to the opportunities, they will flourish. A lot of them, their opportunities were more narrow. You do see kids come out of the hood and make it. You see that. But it's very important for me to put it in terms: That's an anomaly. That's a freak accident when anybody makes the NFL – not an accident, but it's very unlikely. Again, the more opportunities you have maybe the greater chances you have. But it's important to understand that I think that the struggle also makes people who they are. But, yeah, I think it was critical that Troy came here when he did. I think it's critical that he came here after he had had those experiences, because that's what defined him, or part of what defined his childhood, because this is the other thing about Troy: He's a great observer of people. He was in the garage when he saw the decisions that Kaio made, that Lua made, that Wayne made. Yeah he looked up to those decisions a lot, too, but he also had examples like Keneti, like my dad, Darren, Joe, me. All of us had a lot of flaws. None of us were like these glowing examples of perfect people, and he knows that. But he was such a great observer of people. Troy would see people do things one way, and it wouldn't work out for them, and you would watch him and he'd do it the other way. I think he had a very advanced wisdom when it came to observing people and making his decisions based on that, at a young age.

EGGERS: Him coming up here from Southern California was the best thing that ever happened to him. He stayed out of the gang environment and was raised in a small community. It worked out beautifully.

TROY POLAMALU: My mom made a very brave decision. It must have hurt her a great deal. But she let me stay. She knew it was best. I loved it up there. Of course, the sun was out then.

CHAPTER 5

HERE COMES THE SUN

Before he took on his full last name, Keneti Pola was a star running back/linebacker at Mater Dei High School and was recruited by Penn State and USC, among others.

And make no mistake, there were others.

"My mom said, 'Do you know anybody named Paul Bear Bryant?'" recalled Salu Polamalu. "I said 'Paul Bear Bryant? Is that the guy from Alabama?' She said, 'Yeah. He's here recruiting Keneti.'"

Keneti was born in Pago Pago, American Samoa, on the day John F. Kennedy was assassinated.

"A nurse came in and told my parents that the President was assassinated. They didn't have a name for me at the time, so they named me after the President," Keneti explained to the *Los Angeles Times* in 1982.

Like Troy, Keneti made a big move at the age of 9. He came over from American Samoa to Santa Ana with his parents without knowing the English language. He learned it, explained to his parents that, no, football was not rugby, and showed them he could play this new game a bit.

Living in a crowded house and struggling to make it to practices, Keneti convinced his parents to allow him – and his younger brother Aoatoa – to stay with his junior high basketball coach, Ray Alvarado.

After a year at Santa Ana Valley, Keneti enrolled at Mater Dei, the Catholic school with the legendary athletic tradition.

At Mater Dei, Keneti became the student body president and an All-America football player. He set a school rushing record as a senior, but – at 6-1, 215 and with what the *Los Angeles Times* reported was a 320-pound bench press and 4.5-second 40 – he was recruited as a linebacker.

In his mind, that meant there was only one school for him: "Linebacker U."

He intended to continue his epic journey from Pago Pago all the way to Penn State.

KENETI POLAMALU: I really wanted to play linebacker, and at the time everyone around me was telling me that if you want to play linebacker, this place had a pretty good history of linebackers. Like anything else, you wanted to compete and see how good you are.

JOHN BOVE, *Penn State recruiting coordinator:* We went after Keneti. Really great family, but Keneti's father was suffering at the time. When Keneti came for his official visit, his host was Leo Wisniewski, Stefen's father. Leo was a really good player for us, obviously. He was a middle guard and another super young guy. At Penn State, you didn't really have any kids who were going to cause you a lot of trouble. Joe (Paterno) told us, "Make sure you know who and what you're getting." He'd say, "Go to the candy store he buys candy in. Go to the Boys Club if he goes there. Go to the barber shop and find out what they have to say about the prospect. Go everywhere the kid goes." And he always made sure they came in with their eyes open, that's for sure.

KENETI POLAMALU: Man, if you're looking for glamour and glitz, the visit back to JoePa was not it. I think I was on the cot in the dorm rooms, not my own hotel room. I flew into Pittsburgh and met Franco Harris and Jack Ham. They were tough guys. I really felt at home there.

BOVE: We never went far away for a kid unless there was a reason to go outside our 300-mile radius. That was what was generally established. One time the running back Leroy Thompson called my office wanting to know why we weren't recruiting him. I told him we really don't recruit around the country unless there's a need at a position we can't find within our recruiting radius. I told him to send me some film and we'll get back to you. And he was great. He was the MVP in the state basketball championship, he was the sprint champion, and he was Mr. Football in the state of Tennessee. I told Jimmy Caldwell to go recruit him, and Jimmy brought him in, and at the same time Sam Gash out of North Carolina met up with them on the recruiting trail and he and Leroy really hit it off. So we found out Gash was a great one and we got them both. They became great buddies and both of them turned into NFL players. But Keneti was interested in Penn State, and of course Mater Dei had the great program. You look at him and say, "Oh, yeah, this guy's good."

KENETI POLAMALU: I really don't know how they heard about me or who contacted them. I just know that coach John Bove came out to recruit me.

BOVE: Keneti comes and he loves Leo and he liked Penn State for some reason. But we're recruiting him and Southern Cal's in his backyard every day, as you could imagine. Here we are, five hours away by plane and we don't run around that neighborhood much. What happens is Leo's going to play in the Hula Bowl all-star game after the season in Hawaii. So the Penn State Alumni Club in L.A., they booked Leo on the way back to stop in L.A., talk to the alumni, and lo and behold Leo was able to hook up with Keneti. There was a coach coming in to visit on the day Leo took Keneti to go play basketball somewhere off the school grounds and that guy never found Keneti. The rest of the story goes back to Keneti's father being sick and Southern Cal really tugging on his heart strings. Keneti probably preferred Penn State, but because of his father's condition he stayed and went to USC. And I understood it. John Robinson did a good job of making him understand we were a five-hour plane ride.

AOATOA POLOMALU: Keneti was two years ahead of me. At Mater Dei, my sophomore year, I was the starting fullback and he was the tailback, and we both started as inside linebackers. Keneti was one of the top recruits in the country, and he actually committed to go to Penn State as a linebacker, but two days before the signing day my dad had a stroke, so Keneti decided to go to USC. Two years later, I'm a senior getting recruited, and my brother looks at me and said, "You're going to Penn State." I said, "Where's Penn State?" He said, "In Pennsylvania." I said, "Where the hell is Pennsylvania?" He said, "On the other side of the country." I said, "OK." And that's how it ended up.

BOVE: Ao was a defensive lineman, built a lot differently than Keneti. You know how wide and thick Samoans can be? Keneti was that way, but taller than Ao.

TOM BRADLEY, *Penn State assistant coach (1979-11):* Coach Paterno told Keneti, "Hey, I'll be back for your brother Ao regardless of what you do." Keneti went to USC and we went out and recruited Ao. They're good people.

AOATOA POLOMALU: I didn't even know they were even talking about me. USC looked at me and said I was too short and too slow. I'm 5-10 and USC wanted 6-1, 6-3. Now, if they would put me at fullback, yeah, but I would have to run a 4.6, 4.7 and I was at 4.8, 4.9, too slow for that. At linebacker I was 5-10. Back then they were looking at Jack Del

Rio and all those guys at 6-3 and taller, so I was too short for that. My arms are too short for the defensive line. But Joe looked at it and said, "What does an inch really matter?" And he offered me the scholarship.

BOVE: Ao was a middle guard and you couldn't get under him. If you were an offensive lineman, you would have to be a worm to get under him. If an offensive lineman and defensive lineman take off, the guy that gets pads under pads will have leverage and probably win that battle. You couldn't do that to Ao Pola because he was so close to the ground when he got in his stance, and he was explosive. He was really *POWerful*. And he was tough.

AOATOA POLAMALU: That was just what I was taught to do. My arms weren't really long enough to shed blocks. Those guys are pretty big, too. I played against Stepnoski. I was a freshman when Fralic played at Pitt. I watched him play and said, "Holy crap. I have to play against people like this?" Luckily I redshirted that year.

BRADLEY: Ao played nose tackle on our '86 national championship team. He was very tough. Very athletic. Strong at the point of attack. Team guy. He was one of those guys who fit into our team and we could do a lot of different things with him because of his athletic ability. He played some really good games in '85 and '86.

AOATOA POLAMALU: We had some great leaders on that championship team. We had Shane (Conlan) and John Shaffer and D.J. (Dozier) and Tim Johnson. Ray Isom. They didn't talk much. They just showed it. They didn't have to yell. They didn't have to motivate. It was just playing for your brother, and you didn't want to let them down. Any good team has that. Luckily, we found it the year before, going into the Orange Bowl No. 1 on New Year's Day of '86 and we lost to Oklahoma and ended up No. 3. In that locker room you could just tell we were going to do something special the next year. That's when it all started.

BOVE: We had the linebackers, Shane Conlan, Donnie Graham. But figure, if you're playing a guy like Flutie or Turner Gill at Nebraska, those guys drove you crazy chasing them around, and your defensive line wears out. So we made sure that we rotated people all the time, especially those defensive linemen, to keep them fresh. That's how Ao helped us. You say he was listed third on the depth chart, but that makes no sense to me. Ao played a lot of football and started his share of games. The way we operated, it didn't matter where you were on the depth chart.

AOATOA POLAMALU: I tell you what: That Miami team we beat for the national championship was the most talented team I've ever seen. Those guys were fast. Remember that movie *Remember the Titans?* That guy comes off the sideline, "What'd you see? What'd you see?" "They're fast." "Yeah." "They're fast." "I know. You said that." "Yes. They're fast." Well, that was Miami. The defense that we ran was a defense we had never run before. We had Shane out there doing whatever he wanted to do. He did like Troy. He was literally freelancing. He played rover pretty much. Other than that, every position pretty much just concentrated on their part. I just listened for my numbers and that was it. I played nose guard. We held before it was illegal. How do you think we had so many All-American linebackers? We weren't going to let those big offensive linemen try to get to him. That's all we did. Just create a pile and let the linebackers flow, which was perfect for me. I really enjoyed being on that team and being a good teammate. I played the whole national championship year and the following year on about 70 percent strength in my left knee. It was never damaged, I just couldn't strengthen it from an old injury.

In '87 I started the whole year. In '88 I walked into Joe's office and said, "I've had enough." And we both agreed. I couldn't walk anymore. Like right now, I dance one day and I suffer for two. But I loved my time at Penn State. Loved it. You know how crazy Penn State people are. Now, I'm not as crazy as them but I bleed blue and white. I'll give my honest opinion because Penn State's not for everybody – but, yeah, that was probably one of the best times of my life. I still live in Pennsylvania.

BOVE: Ao had a nice career and was a gentleman and has a nice family. His one son [Maika Polamalu] played ball at the Naval Academy, and they played at Penn State when he was on the team, so I went on the sideline with Ao. Those guys are solid citizens. Keneti was a real gentleman, too.

SALU POLAMALU: We followed both of them in college. Grandpa bought that big satellite over there to watch Keneti play for SC. We had terrible reception here – one channel. So when Keneti was on, we know and grandpa put him over there.

SHELLEY POLAMALU: Whenever he changed channels, ours did too.

SALU POLAMALU: We didn't mind that.

SHELLEY POLAMALU: We kind of learned don't ever watch movies because it's going to flip before it's over. Fortunately games never got flipped because they shared the same love of the same teams. But if it was a movie or something, forget it.

Keneti, of course, wanted to play linebacker, but instead of getting stuck behind Jack Del Rio until his senior year, Polamalu accepted John Robinson's request to move to fullback late in his freshman season.

Robinson told the *Los Angeles Times* that Keneti reminded him of former Trojan Mosi Tatupu, because "when Pola blocks, you can hear the collision, and he's quick as a runner."

Keneti started eight games at fullback as a sophomore in 1983, but before his junior season underwent a fifth knee operation. During the surgery, his heart failed and his lungs filled with water. He was revived with the help of a lung specialist who "was walking down the hall and knew exactly what to do," Keneti told the *Times*. "I never did find out what went wrong. I tried to read the doctors' reports but they didn't want me to see them."

Keneti remained at fullback as a junior in 1984 and helped USC to the Rose Bowl, where coach Ted Tollner's Trojans beat the Ohio State team that included Keith Byars, Chris Spielman and Mike Tomczak 20-17.

Keneti had a strong game. He rushed for 51 yards on nine carries.

Del Rio was named USC's Defensive MVP for the game.

SALU POLAMALU: We went down to see that Rose Bowl.

SHELLEY POLAMALU: We won the Rose Bowl that year.

SALU POLAMALU: Yeah, it was really a surprise because SC lost their quarterback, Rodney Peete. Keneti never lost a yard when he was at SC. Never. They were punishing, punishing and then they gave the ball to the tailback to score. That's life as a fullback at SC. He had a chance for the NFL. When Tampa went after Bo Jackson, they had Keneti to be his blocking back. Keneti got married and his knee was so bad, and Bo Jackson went to play baseball for the Royals, so Tampa lost everybody.

SHELLEY POLAMALU: We wanted to be in Arizona the year Aoatoa played for the championship, but we didn't go.

SALU POLAMALU: It wasn't the popular thing, like with Troy and Keneti. Those are familiar names on the West Coast.

SHELLEY POLAMALU: Troy grew up watching Keneti play. That USC jersey he wore all the time was Keneti's.

Keneti's senior season ended with a 24-3 loss to Alabama in the Aloha Bowl and he began coaching the following season at Crespi High in Los Angeles. After three seasons there he moved on to Westlake High in Thousand Oaks, and in 1992 Keneti became a graduate assistant at UCLA.

His coaching odyssey then took him to San Diego State to work for Tollner as a running backs and special teams coach.

Keneti left SDSU in 1997 for Colorado to work under a coach he had met at UCLA, Rick Neuheisel. It was during this period that Keneti began paying close attention to what his sister Siuila's son, Troy, was doing in Tenmile, Oregon.

KENETI POLAMALU: During that time, Troy was tearing it up in baseball, and everything. But, again, people around there said transfer to Roseburg because it would get him looks and give him an opportunity because it's a bigger school compared to Douglas. I told him just keep his head down, do the right things, just like he's been doing his whole life, and we will get you a scholarship. Troy was a 4.0 student at Douglas. He did everything right. Obviously my older brother and his family, Troy's cousins, and the whole community did such a good job with him. We brought him out – at the time I was at the University of Colorado going into his senior year – and nobody knew who he was. Before that, Troy was getting recruited more for baseball. But I brought him out and he stayed with us and we put him in our camp, and he just lit it up. Rick Neuheisel was the head coach and I'm selling him, like, "Hey, look, this is my nephew. He's at a small school. He's very talented." But in those times, everybody recruited off all the recruiting analysts with their grades and then the *Parade* All-Americans. Troy came in there and just ran, in tennis shoes, like a 4.48, verticaled over 40 inches, played receiver, caught balls from one of the Clausens, who went on to start at Tennessee, and just lit it up. By the end of the three-day camp, he would stay with us instead of staying in the dorm with the other players. He would just stay with my wife Diane and I and the kids, and he really liked that environment. And so they offered him a scholarship, and he committed.

DENNIS THURMAN, *USC secondary coach:* We had just gotten an assistant coach from the University of Oregon, Steve Greatwood, and Greatwood was coming to SC with Paul Hackett to coach the offensive line. He was recruiting Troy at first. At some point, he went to Hackett and said, "Look, we need to get somebody else involved." Hackett came to me and asked me if I would get involved, and then he asked me if I knew Keneti Pola.

KENETI POLAMALU: Even though Troy had committed, my brother Salu said, "Hey, look, I really want him to play baseball." Well, the University of Colorado doesn't have baseball, and I was also trying to work the Rockies into drafting him, because there were guys like

John Elway doing things like that. And I wanted him to go see other schools just to keep his options open. So, during that time I'm still thinking that he can go to USC, but the competition was hard. Then he goes through his senior year in high school football and gets hurt. He has internal bleeding, ends up not playing a lot. I'm still with Neuheisel at the time, but it turned out that God had a better plan. Rick ended up leaving Colorado to go to Washington. When the head coach leaves, all the assistants are up in the air, so I'm up in the air and I'm trying to tell Troy I really like Colorado and would want to stay but I didn't know if the new head coach, whoever he may be, would want me.

SALU POLAMALU: It always was Troy's dream to go back down south (to USC). Keneti was coaching with Neuheisel, but Troy didn't want to go to Washington. Every Pac-10 team came by, so did Illinois – they were the first one. Troy might have gone to Oregon if he could have played baseball. The one he didn't like for some reason was Stanford. Something about his application. From then, all Troy wanted to do was beat Stanford.

SHELLEY POLAMALU: Our buddy Steve Greatwood was at USC at the time, so he came after Troy. He had been in our house many times, was a good friend. Troy visited Illinois, too. One of the Illinois coaches had coached Joe at Oregon State and he loved Joe, so immediately he picked up on the name and started watching Troy. He came out. Troy also went to Washington State, and then he went to USC. He was going to go to Stanford, but he cancelled. Troy had his back up about Stanford for some reason. Troy actually seemed to feel good about contacting Stanford and saying he wasn't going to visit. You can make five visits and Troy only made four: Illinois, Washington State, Colorado, USC.

THURMAN: I had watched tape of Troy before I went up to visit. He was a high school running back but I liked what I saw. We wanted to convert him to defensive back and I had to determine if he had the foot quickness and hip movement, things of that nature. As a running back I saw him make some cuts and he had really good balance. But what you noticed about him was that he was tough and he was competitive, and so they asked me if he could make the conversion. I said I'm pretty sure he can, even though I never got to see him play defense. We had converted Daylon McCutcheon, Kenny Haslip and Antuan Simmons from offensive skill positions to DBs. We were in the business of converting good athletes to defensive backs. We felt like Troy fell in that category.

KENETI POLAMALU: Rick got me to come out to Washington, and was like, "Hey, you've got to get Troy to come." And I said, "Yeah, Troy doesn't have any family in Colorado now. There's nobody there." So I flew down to see Troy.

THURMAN: Keneti wasn't with USC at the time, but he let me know he thinks Troy's No. 1 choice would be SC.

KENETI POLAMALU: Paul Hackett called and said, "We've lost some guys and we have some scholarships available. Why don't we meet?" So I got on the flight with Troy to L.A. He was supposed to come later to the University of Washington, knowing that he had a scholarship there and felt safe. But the whole time he was just like, "Uncle, I just want to get away from the rain if I could." And I was just hoping that if he didn't get the offer from USC, that, hey, we'll go to Washington, which had baseball, too. But, man, he just wanted to get out of the rain.

THURMAN: (Laughs) Yeah, the rain might've had something to do with it then. I wasn't sure. But he committed and came to us. From there, it was pretty much history.

KENETI POLAMALU: [Baseball] Coach Gillespie was another advocate, a person who was pushing for Troy to come to USC because he thought he would be a really good asset for the baseball team. And, if he's on a football scholarship, that's a free scholarship for baseball. So, he was pushing for Troy to be there. I had gotten a call that they were going to offer him. They met him and realized how humble he is. What they hadn't come to realize yet was that when they get him between the lines they're going to uncage a pretty good athlete, a pretty good player. So it all worked out. I called Troy and he told me what happened on his visit. And then I walked into Rick's office and took another job. I left for San Diego State to get back closer, and eventually ended up at USC with Troy for his sophomore year.

TROY POLAMALU, *to Justin Myers:* I grew up here in Southern California, in Santa Ana. My uncle played at USC in '82-85. So I just, from birth, was a big USC fan. I had a USC jersey that I wore literally every Halloween. I definitely grew up just having a passion for USC football, as well as the fact I lived here for the first nine years of my life. My family's in Southern California as well, so to me it wasn't like I was moving away from Oregon. I was just kind of re-engaging with my family down here in Southern California and my youth. Oh, the rain had a lot to do with it, for sure. That's the reason why I didn't go to Washington or Washington State. I wasn't really too highly recruited coming out in the first place, and USC was definitely one of the top places that recruited me, so I also wanted an opportunity to compete against the best football players in the country as well. And USC had one of the top recruiting classes in the country that year, and again I came from 3A high school, so I'm looking at the No. 1 100-meter runner in the country, the No. 1 200-meter runner in the country, the No. 1 shot-putter, the No. 1 defensive lineman. Everybody's the No. 1 something in the class that I joined at USC. I definitely saw that I really had to raise my level and was really intimidated by that situation.

The 1999 USC recruiting class was ranked 10th in the nation by *Student Sports Magazine*. That's how it was reported on Feb. 4 in The *Orange County Register*. The story didn't even mention Troy Polamalu, beyond his name being buried in the agate list of 21 new players.

He wasn't hyped like Darrell Rideaux or Kareem Kelly or Bernard Riley – 1999 recruits whom Hackett called "instant impact guys."

Also mentioned in the story was a player who would become one of Troy's close friends, Lenny Vandermade, an offensive lineman from the same Santa Ana hometown as Troy and the same Mater Dei High as Troy's uncles.

The biggest recruit at the time was Markus Steele from Long Beach City College. He was hyped in the story as "the premier junior college linebacker in the nation" and drew comparisons to Trojans LB Chris Claiborne, who would in 10 weeks be drafted ninth overall by the Detroit Lions.

Hackett lamented at the time that his second class as USC's head coach didn't include enough linemen or defensive backs. Hackett was also down about his inability to recruit any more than three out-of-state players.

Even though Paul Hackett had just added the greatest out-of-state DB ever recruited by USC, the coach merely shrugged his shoulders over the letter of intent signed by Troy Polamalu.

♦♦♦

PART 2:
UNIVERSITY OF SOUTHERN CALIFORNIA

♦♦♦

CHAPTER 6

NEXT THING YOU KNOW, TROY'S TAKING THE BALL

Paul Hackett was known in Western Pennslyvania as the Bill Walsh-trained offensive coordinator who moved up to replace Mike Gottfried as the University of Pittsburgh head coach late in 1989.

Hackett promptly turned Gottfried's 8-3-1 Panthers into 3-7-1 Panthers.

Hackett and Pitt recovered to go 6-5 in 1991, but his 3-9 record in 1992 led to his firing and return to the NFL as offensive coordinator of the Kansas City Chiefs.

In 1998, USC hired Hackett to replace John Robinson, and, as many NFL coaches prefer, Hackett moved the Trojans' training camp away from home to provide, in theory, more solitude and better focus.

Robinson's second tenure at USC ended with a 6-5 record. Hackett's Trojans went 8-5 in 1998, so there was hope as the team, with freshman recruit Troy Polamalu, reported to the University of California at Irvine, some 45 miles south of the USC campus, 10 miles east of Newport Beach, in the summer of 1999.

KENETI POLAMALU: The kid came down without a license, without anything. Nobody knew who he was around there. He just built a pretty good camaraderie with his teammates. Never been so proud of him. Again, they didn't know where to play him. His freshman year he was an outside linebacker at 5-10. But he just played. He made plays as a special teams player, just doing anything he could to get on the field and help. He eventually found a spot at safety and then kind of just took off when Coach Carroll came in.

MALAEFOU MACKENZIE, *USC running Back (1997-02):* They gave me the chance to host Troy when he visited. They said, "Hey, we have this Samoan kid from Oregon and he's going to come on a recruiting trip, so we'd like you to take him out." I'm like, "Awesome. I'm in." He was so soft-spoken, such a nice guy. You almost wanted him to come out of his shell. Every other guy you host and take out, they wanted to go out and party, they want to see the girls, they want to go and just live it up, right? He was the complete opposite. I'm like, "Hey, after dinner we can go out." I gave him all the different options. He's like "No, I'm OK. I'll just go back to the hotel." I'm like, "Are you sure? I can take you anywhere you want. There are different places that we can go and see. This is L.A. and I know you're from Oregon, so we can go anywhere. We can go to the movies, whatever you want." He's like, "No, it's OK. I just want to go and hang out at the hotel and kind of soak it all in." I'm like, "Well, OK." He was a good, sweet kid from a small town who just wanted to hang out, and this was his idea of living it up in L.A.

CARSON PALMER, *USC quarterback (1998-02):* I was a year older than him and I met him on a recruiting trip. We went to a USC-UCLA basketball game. I remember hearing a bunch about him, and when I first saw him he was maybe 5-10, 180 pounds, and I remember thinking, "This is the big guy they want?" He was no different than he is today: very quiet, very soft-spoken, not trying to be the center of attention, not standing in front, just very laid back and kind of calm, cool and collected. He looked more like a baseball player to me and I couldn't believe he was the guy we wanted so badly. He turned out to be who he is today, but I never saw it coming.

MACKENZIE: Troy loves the Samoan culture. He absolutely loves it. So when you say he calls me one of his mentors, I am extremely humbled and honored. I think part of that was because I was born and raised in Western Samoa and I've been there. I came here when I was nine, so he would always ask me about Samoan culture, even during that recruiting trip. Even to this day we still talk about the values and the spirituality of our people. We always use the term "Muamua Le Atua," meaning "put God first" in anything that we do. If you start off with God first, family second, then everything else will fall into place. I've always seen Troy as a little brother. He's always asked advice and I've always tried to play that older brother role and try to be a good example for him.

LENNY VANDERMADE, *USC offensive lineman (1999-03):* I met Troy the first day we moved into the dorm for camp. We moved into Fluor

Tower, which is where the freshmen stayed for a week before the rest of the team joined us at Cal Irvine. Troy had just gotten off some crazy bus ride, like 50 hours or something from Oregon. He obviously brought everything with him because he wasn't going back. I didn't bring as much because I was local and I could go back and get the rest of it. I just remember seeing the look on his face. I felt bad for my guy. He was quiet, reserved, real respectful. I introduced myself. My parents were there. He was real respectful with them. And after we moved in we had lunch and the rest was history. We just kind of took to one another. Obviously it's easy, a lot of similarities. He's Samoan, I'm Samoan. He had a lot of family out in Santa Ana, where I grew up. I knew all of his siblings and cousins, so it was an easy connection.

MACKENZIE: One of the tight ends from Oregon came with him, Chad Cook, and they came out and started hitting. They were practicing a couple days before we came out, and I could just tell his initial pop. You can hear the distinctive difference between somebody that's a good hitter, somebody that has that pop. Chris Claiborne had "it." When he hit people you could feel it. When Troy hit Chad, I was impressed. His hips turned, he was running, and they said he had a 40-inch vertical.

VANDERMADE: Shoot, it was maybe the first or second practice, when we first got the pads on. That's when the colors come out and you can tell who's ready to go and who's not. My freshman year, I was not. I got baptized. But Troy was flying around, smacking people, making plays on balls. Kind of what he's done his whole career.

KENETI POLAMALU: Troy's leaping ability and explosiveness is really unbelievable. And his ball skills. Now he wasn't going to wow you when he walked into the room at that age. But as he matured and got that big butt, the thickness in his legs, you knew he was going to get the Samoan side naturally pretty soon.

TROY POLAMALU: My freshman year I had to establish that everyone on the practice field was equal. They threw a bad pass, and R. Jay Soward – he was the big star at the time – was kind of trotting through this route, and I went over and blindsided him. He got up cussing me, but later he told me I was OK. I think that got me noticed a little bit.

AOATOA POLAMALU: I heard the story about how he knocked out a receiver. Keneti said that kind of described Troy's freshman year at USC, wanting to make a statement. It was during practice and Troy just nailed him. Of course, everybody was just going crazy. That's when Keneti said, "Yeah, he's got it." And he was only like 170 at that time.

THURMAN: We felt like it may take him a year or two to find his footing, but the characteristics and traits that he showed on tape – just being a naturally good football player – were beginning to show up once we got to training camp. There was one particular play that he made. We had recruited this junior college All-America running back, Jabari Jackson, from San Francisco City. The offense had run an iso, hitting right up the middle between the guard-tackle, and Troy met Jabari in the hole. I mean, they collided. But what happened after that made us all just look at each other. They collided, and the next thing you know Troy's just taking the ball from him. And we all were like, "What just happened?"

MACKENZIE: They were coming out from about the 15, 20-yard line. Troy hit him and literally just ripped the ball away. That little burst from the 15-yard line, 20-yard line, to the end zone, was the fastest I had ever seen at that time. It was crazy.

VANDERMADE: That was our first major scrimmage. Troy's personality off the field is that of a reserved guy, not at all a show-off, or a guy who needs attention. You hear the old adage let your play do the talking. Well, that was him. Here's this grown man, this JC transfer who's probably three or four years older than Troy, and Troy just put a hat on him and took the ball away and scored.

THURMAN: It was one of those eye-opening plays that you had to see to believe because trying to describe it really does not do it justice. You don't see defensive backs hit running backs in the hole as fast as he hit this guy in the hole, and not only did he stop him, he had taken the ball. You can't describe what really happened because it was a once-in-a-lifetime play. I didn't see it before nor have I seen it since. O.J. came from San Francisco City, and some people thought he was the next O.J., so we had to think either he's not as good as we thought or this other guy is just that much better. Right away, we defensive coaches knew we had to get this guy on the field, that we've got to find ways to play him without overloading him with too much information. We were looking for different packages and ways to get him on the field, because he just had this natural ability to find the football – or the football found him.

After camp, coach Paul Hackett announced that Carson Palmer would open the 1999 season at quarterback over junior Mike Van Raaphorst.

As a true freshman in 1998, Palmer had replaced Van Raaphorst on Halloween and guided USC to a 3-1 record before its Sun Bowl loss to TCU.

Hackett didn't make any such pronouncement about freshman Troy Polamalu, who was merely being groomed to play dime linebacker in sub-packages for second-year defensive coordinator Bob Young and seventh-year secondary coach Dennis Thurman.

Polamalu had come to camp as a no-name recruit at the strong safety position, and once again couldn't get the number – 41 – that so many of his friends and family had worn during their football careers.

A senior, cornerback Antoinne Harris, was wearing No. 41. He wasn't expected to play much, so the staff was going to keep its promise to Polamalu and give him the number. But the freshman refused to take the number from a senior. As he had as a freshman at Douglas High, Troy asked for the closest available number. And once again, Polamalu was given 43.

This time, he kept it.

THURMAN: We tried to get him on the field his freshman year in packages. We played him at some dime. We played him at some safety. We felt the closer he was to the line of scrimmage, the better he played as a young player. Didn't want to get him overly involved in trying to read keys and all that kind of stuff, just put him in position where he could go play football and make plays. We had figured that much; if he's on the field, he's going to make some plays. One or two might be for them, but hopefully eight, nine or ten would be for us. Because you know we would rather him be what he was – a naturally aggressive ball-seeking type guy – then trying to pull him back and make him do things the way that would take his natural, God-given talent from him. We gave him one assignment and that was it. He was either covering a back or a tight end, or just playing football – you see the football, go get it. That's how we played him. He was getting better and better and better.

PALMER: I thought it happened kind of slowly. He wasn't a star right away. It was kind of like how it happened in Pittsburgh. His freshman year he was on the field in situational things, wasn't a full-time starter, and you just kind of slowly started to see him grow and develop, and get bigger, get faster, start to recognize things, start to be a ballhawk, start to blow people up when he had open-field tackles. It was something he worked very hard at. It wasn't like God gave him the ability and he just showed up. He worked extremely hard – first to put on weight, then to get faster, then to work on his tackling. It just kind of slowly progressed as the years went on, and by his junior year he was a superstar. He was unbelievable.

MACKENZIE: I could see he had a future in this game on the first play of his freshman year in our opener against Hawaii. At SC, every great player always played special teams. And I remember the opening kickoff in Hawaii, going down, Troy almost took somebody out. He ran and jumped through somebody. I don't think he got the tackle but that first initial hit set the tone for the rest of the game. He was very impressive, even as a freshman playing special teams.

VANDERMADE: He actually leapt over the wedge. He jumped over it on the opening kickoff. He's going down covering the kickoff, and back then you were able to wedge. He just jumped over it. He didn't make the play but he scared the crap out of the return man. The guy stopped his feet and everyone else gang-tackled him. Yeah, Troy totally left his feet. He didn't get upended, which is crazy. It was almost like that play you see over and over where he jumps over the linemen to make the play on the quarterback in short-yardage. It was similar to that. Chest and arms first. He scared the crap out of the returner for sure.

Troy Polamalu may have set the tone for the 62-7 win at Hawaii on the opening kickoff, but it was sophomore Carson Palmer who led the Trojans to six scores in their first six possessions for a 41-0 halftime lead.

Palmer completed 14 of 16 passes for 167 yards and 1 touchdown pass. He also scored on a 9-yard run.

MacKenzie, the tailback once described by Polamalu as being his "spiritual advisor," scored touchdowns on runs of 3, 1 and 1 yards, while starting tailback Chad Morton rushed 13 times for 95 yards.

Polamalu got in to notch a sack for a 20-yard loss. He also forced a fumble and made four tackles in his debut.

Up next for USC was San Diego State led by coach Ted Tollner and featuring linebackers coach Keneti Polamalu. Those former Trojans nearly made their return to Memorial Coliseum a triumphant one, catching the 17th-ranked USC looking ahead to an upcoming trip to Oregon. Favored by 23 points, USC jumped out to a 17-0 lead and held on for a 24-21 win.

Moving up to No. 16 in the Associated Press poll, 2-0 USC traveled to Oregon, and got beat in triple overtime, 33-30. It was the longest game in USC history, and the Trojans – the most penalized team in the Pac-10 in 1998 – set a team record and tied the Pac-10 record with 21 penalties at Oregon.

The USC kicking game cost the Trojans. USC missed two field goals in overtime, and was also penalized 15 yards before missing an extra point with 3:08 left, which would've given USC a four-point lead.

Polamalu nearly rendered all of those misses moot by forcing a fumble on the ensuing kickoff. USC recovered at the Oregon 22, but missed a 30-yard field goal with 2:20 left. It allowed Oregon to tie the game with 30 seconds left. The Oregon kicker tore his ACL after a teammate crashed into him during the celebration, but the Ducks won in OT with backup kicker Josh Frankel's 27-yarder in the third overtime.

To compound the loss for USC, Palmer was ruled out for the rest of the season with a broken collarbone sustained during a scramble just before halftime.

Palmer finished his two-and-a-half-game season with a sizzling 74 percent completed and 490 yards passing. He was eventually granted a redshirt.

Aside from his near-heroic special teams play late in regulation, Polamalu was involved in meaningful defensive snaps at Oregon, and had another sack among his four tackles. He also broke up a pass by Oregon QB A.J. Feeley.

USC rebounded with a 37-29 win over Oregon State in its 1,000th football game. The following week, Polamalu made a "highlight-reel"/"teeth-rattling" hit on Arizona punt returner Dennis Northcutt.

The future Cleveland Browns WR who would finish second in the nation in punt-return average in 1999, Northcutt attempted to field a punt at his own 1-yard line, but he was drilled by Polamalu, fumbled, and nearly allowed a USC touchdown before recovering it himself.

Northcutt did finish with 121 yards receiving to lead Arizona to a 31-24 win that knocked USC to 3-2, 1-2.

The Trojans suffered a gut-wrenching 25-24 loss at rival Notre Dame the following Saturday. Ironically, the game marked the 25th anniversary of USC's comeback win from a 24-0 deficit to Notre Dame.

In a reversal, the Irish rallied from a 24-3 deficit on this day, mostly in a driving rainstorm, and mostly on the back of critical USC mistakes.

The loss dropped USC to 3-3 overall.

"It's a thrill to be part of," Hackett said after the rivalry game. "But, God, it's painful."

The pain continued into the week, particularly for Polamalu, who suffered a concussion during practice and was forced to miss the next four games – Stanford, Cal, Arizona State and Washington State.

USC went 1-3 in those games and fell to 4-6.

Troy Polamalu returned to the field for a home game against intra-city rival UCLA (4-6), which had won the last eight games against USC (4-6). It was the first time in 58 years that both teams entered this game with losing records.

Polamalu made one tackle, as a punt gunner, on UCLA return man Ricky Manning, as the Trojans salvaged some dignity with a win.

The Trojans concluded their season not in a bowl game but with a 45-19 Friday night home win over 25th-ranked Louisiana Tech.

Tech QB Tim Rattay threw 68 passes to set a USC opponent record. He also became the NCAA's No. 2 all-time passing yardage QB during the game. But USC pulverized the La. Tech defense with 309 yards rushing.

The only 2000 NFL first-round pick from USC would be WR R. Jay Soward. He was the third-leading receiver with 51 catches for 655 yards and four touchdowns.

Strong safety David Gibson was also drafted in 2000, in the sixth round.

Jabari Jackson, the infamous "next O.J." from the City College of San Francisco, scored his one and only USC touchdown against Louisiana Tech, the Trojans' final touchdown of the season, courtesy of a blocked punt in the fourth quarter by Polamalu.

Troy finished his freshman season with 12 tackles in eight games, two sacks, two forced fumbles, a PBU, a blocked punt and a clear resolution to come back as a starter the following season.

However, he almost retired.

CHAPTER 7

LET THEM SAY I LIVED
IN THE TIME OF POLAMALU

One of the more prominent USC recruits in 2000 impacted Troy Polamalu more than anyone could've realized at the time.

Not the five-star recruit, Matt Grootegoed, who was said to be rugged enough to play in the box and fast enough to cover deep. He was a much-ballyhooed strong safety, the position Polamalu was hoping to handle upon the departure of David Gibson to the NFL.

No, it was the other top recruit, a tight end who figured to attend Michigan, where his father had played. But Alex Holmes chose to stay home at USC, and the Trojans considered his commitment a major coup. Polamalu would, too.

Holmes' high school coach at nearby Harvard-Westlake called him the best player he had coached in 35 years, and USC Coach Paul Hackett said of Holmes, "He has the ability to redefine the tight end position."

Holmes' pedigree was that of more than a football player. He had been a three-time winner of a national Latin exam, spoke fluent Greek, played the violin and had "a keen interest in computers and their gadgetry."

Holmes' father Michael played at Michigan before working for the Saudi royal family, and his mother Katina, "a classicist," according to the *Los Angeles Times*, stressed classical literature to her three children.

"Renaissance Man" read the headline at *usctrojans.com* above a feature on Holmes more than a year later – about the time Holmes' little sister Theodora entered college.

Theodora Holmes changed her last name to Polamalu in January, 2005.

MALAEFOU MACKENZIE: Troy was focused on his studies and on football but he was very popular with the girls, too. In Troy's senior year he asked Alex, who was very protective of Theodora, for permission to date his sister. That's how that started. Troy also played a big role in me meeting my wife. Not that he planned it that way. One weekend Troy said, "Hey, my cousin's graduating. They're having a huge celebration." All we were thinking was there's going to be food, drinks and a lot of music. I didn't even know he had a girl cousin. When he said cousin I just assumed it was a guy. So Lenny, Troy and I went over and we were eating, drinking, and next thing you know the emcee says "And the graduate ..." and here comes my current wife. She comes out in a hula outfit and does a full-on Tahitian dance and I'm like, "Wow!" Lenny and I were looking at each other and Troy caught that and said, "Hey, c'mon. You guys are family." I was dating somebody else, but, man, this girl's gorgeous. I'm like, "Wow!" We talked and I asked her out. We got married in 2013, and four kids later that was our story, all thanks to Troy. Troy's mom and my wife's mom (Moana) are sisters. What a small world. Lenny wound up marrying my sister, so he's my brother-in-law on the other side.

LENNY VANDERMADE: Norm Katnik and I lived together that second year, but Troy and I were always at each other's apartment. Troy kind of has more of an O-lineman's mentality. O-linemen are like mules. You can whip 'em, you can drive 'em, you can give 'em a hard time and they'll keep showing up. That's Troy's mentality, so we hung out.

MACKENZIE: I met Theodora before I met Troy. Carson and I were trying to recruit the No. 1 tight end in the nation, Alex, her brother. So we drove out to where they lived and they had a get-together and I met Theodora. I met and fell in love with their whole family and I knew right then that Alex was going to come to SC.

In other family news, Troy's Uncle Keneti made the expected jump to USC from San Diego State. Hackett, who at this point had decided against allowing Troy to play baseball, named his uncle the running backs coach.

"Thank God he's not the secondary coach!" Troy joked about his demanding uncle. "But I'm happy to have him here and around. It's made it so much easier on me to have somebody to talk to and someone to help me out."

Troy also made his first trip to American Samoa that year to visit his mother. When he returned, there was the business of fending off the other hotshot recruit, Grootegoed.

DENNIS THURMAN: Matt was a good football player. He was more of a thinker, whereas Troy would just play instinctively. Both were good football players but you know how some guys the ball just ends up in their hands? Well, that was Troy. Troy had that natural gift. I really don't think you can coach that. I think you either have that or you don't, and Troy had that. That's why he was able to play sooner. He made plays.

MACKENZIE: Matt came out of Mater Dei and was a big-time recruit, but Troy was ready. I remember it was raining outside right before conditioning practice in spring ball. We had to run indoors. We were on the basketball court and Troy was coming in first in every sprint. But I looked over and saw his hamstring was black and blue and I wondered, "What is he doing?" I asked him and he said nothing. He had this look of concentration that it didn't matter what was going on physically. He was so focused on running and getting first place that nothing could've stopped him. So I talked to him afterwards, I was, "Hey, what's wrong with your leg?" He said, "What do you mean?" I lifted up his pant leg and it was black and blue, up and down, from the back of his knee all the way up to his glutes. I said, "What are you doing?" He said, "I have to keep running." I said, "Why? You're injured." He said, "No, I can't give up. I want to win my spot." "Dude, this is spring ball. This is not the season." But his mentality was that every single rep, including the sprints, was more important than anything else. What also was amazing to me was we had some really fast guys, guys who won the 100 meters in California, like Darrell Rideaux. Troy, with an injured leg, was still beating them. I'm like, "This guy is something else." I was amazed. He did that and wasn't pushed. To me, that was more telling than anything, any play, scrimmage game. Nothing on the field surprised me after I saw that. I've had injuries. I've had ACL, PCL, meniscus, multiple hamstring injuries. There comes a point where no matter how mentally tough you are, that injury will always win. Yeah, you can do one or two reps, but this guy was running for 45 minutes. He didn't even skip a beat. Afterwards he was icing down like there was nothing wrong with him. I'm like, "Wow, this guy is a freak."

Troy began getting attention from teammates, even the media, for staying after practice – *well* after practice. It actually turned into a movement at USC, one that may not have been directly responsible for a decade of excellence, but it certainly helped set the tone.

TIM TESSALONE, *USC sports information director:* He was always the LAST player – by about 45 minutes – off the field after every practice. He would conduct his own private workout after practice and the beat guys would all have to wait around if they wanted to talk to him.

VANDERMADE: He started it. You see your best player out there getting extra work, I wanted to do the same. I saw what it did for him as a player. I want to do the same and try to better myself that much more each time. But he would always do that, and he would never try to make you feel bad, like, "Hey, man, you need to stay out because I'm staying out." He would just go do it. We got to see him work and were like, "Man, you know what? I'm going to get some extra work, too." Just by example. The guys got behind it.

TROY POLAMALU: I used the time to think about what I did during the last game. I think about what I need to work on. ... There are so many things you can do to get better. A lot of people take things for granted. They just want to get through practice. I just want to do whatever I can to become the best. ... I believe that God has blessed me with a gift, an ability, and that it's something I need to keep working on. I never walk away when I can still push myself and try to improve. ... Sometimes I burn myself out during practice and I know that's not good, but I believe that you get everything you work for, so I always want to work hard.

VANDERMADE: People always point to the process, and that's what it was. He focused on being the best he could be, and by doing that he motivated people around him. I started doing extra work, whether it was core or stretching, after seeing him doing it. That's kind of what drove him. He was a guy who had a chip on his shoulder. He never expressed it too much. He just focused on bettering himself day in and day out. The most impressive part was the discipline. He would always do it. He never cut a corner. He would never try to find a way out or make an excuse.

Dennis Thurman was an eighth-year assistant and appeared to be a USC lifer. He was a freshman flanker under John McKay when the

Trojans won the 1974 national championship, and was moved to free safety by new coach John Robinson in 1976 and led the Pac-10 with 8 interceptions. Thurman intercepted three passes in 1977 and was named team MVP. It was also the year he took a freshman defensive back named Ronnie Lott under his wing.

Lott, in turn, cited Thurman in his induction speech into the Pro Football Hall of Fame in 2000.

Lott's was one of the names thrown around by the media as a quick comparison when the Pittsburgh Steelers drafted Troy Polamalu in 2003.

THURMAN: No. No. It's really not a good comparison. We played Ronnie at corner his freshman year. He came in as a safety, but was athletic enough to go play some corner. After I left he and Dennis Smith became the SC safeties. Ronnie converted back to corner his rookie year in the NFL. His first couple years in the NFL he played corner because he was a good athlete. Ronnie had good ball skills and instincts. I never saw Troy as being that type of a guy who could go out and play corner, and Ronnie was taller and leaner, just different type of bodies. But as safeties they both obviously knew how to find the football and were around the football and had their share of big hits, even to the point where in Troy's sophomore year he was concerned about concussions.

Troy suffered his second diagnosed concussion at USC during training camp prior to the 2000 season. It became a point of such concern that Polamalu considered retirement.

THURMAN: He came and sat down and we talked in my office, and I told him Ronnie had similar issues but he learned how to tackle using his chest and shoulders. So I gave Troy Ronnie's number and they talked about tackling. Ronnie loved using his head and his helmet, so he and Troy talked about that and Troy felt more comfortable after that and he tried to keep his head out of his way and use more of his body and his chest and his shoulders. I think that really eased some of the anxiety Troy was beginning to develop. He played in that kamikaze style. When you do that, you don't really have a lot of regard for your body. You only do that once a week, though, 12 or 13 times in college. And then you go to the pros and start to do it more. But it's not good for you and Troy was concerned about it. He told me that he contemplated walking away from football if he continued to get concussions. I think talking to Ronnie really helped him.

Troy Polamalu opened the 2000 season in the Kickoff Classic at Giants Stadium in East Rutherford, N.J. as USC's starting strong safety. His first-half interception and 43-yard return through the middle of the field ended with him diving into the end zone for his first college touchdown. The play gave USC a 20-3 halftime lead and the 15th-ranked Trojans cruised to a 29-5 win over No. 22 Penn State.

AOATOA POLAMALU: Both sides were having a great time because, one, it's opening day, and, two, it's a great matchup between two historic programs. I had a lot of friends in town. My family was there, I got to see my nephew and Keneti, so it was pretty exciting. Of course, I wanted Penn State to win, but as long as those guys did well we were good. When Troy took that one back, everybody was like, "Well, he deserves it." The Penn State people around me cheered for him. I cheered for him. It was great. They turned around and pointed, congratulated us, and went back to cheering for Penn State. We lost the game, but, hey, Troy had made a big play, a memorable play. That was basically the beginning of where we're at now.

VANDERMADE: The first game of the season he has a pick-6, dives in the end zone and stands up and does the baseball safe sign. Everyone interpreted it as his it's over sign, that he sealed the deal. I thought so, too. I said to him, "Man, that was tight." He said, "No, I did a safe sign because I dove and slid into the end zone like a baseball play."

USC kept the Nittany Lions out of the end zone and held them to six yards rushing, a record low for Penn State.

Carson Palmer, with 87 yards passing, didn't exactly pick up from where he had left off the previous season, but the redshirt sophomore QB did direct the Trojans to the win.

New USC starting tailback Sultan McCullough rushed for 128 yards on 29 carries, while Penn State RB Larry Johnson was held to 21 yards on five carries.

"What struck you was how fast that USC defense was," broadcaster Marty Schottenheimer told the *Orange County Register*. "They can really run."

Troy was no doubt one whose speed stood out.

VANDERMADE: By this time, everybody kind of knows Troy is special – everyone on the inside anyway. He was powerful in the weight room and set all kinds of records, can jump out the building, can run. We were just waiting to see, and then the first game of the season he takes that pick to the house and we're like, "All right. There he is."

Palmer got his groove back the following week when the No. 11 Trojans defeated Colorado 17-14.

The QB completed 25 of 30 passes for 275 yards and drove USC 72 yards for the game-winning field goal with 13 seconds left.

Polamalu set up USC's second touchdown with a 19-yard return of a fumble recovery to the Colorado 21 in the third quarter.

The Trojans moved up to No. 9 with the win, and followed up by winning their 500th game played in the L.A. Coliseum 34-24 over San Jose State in a game USC trailed in the fourth quarter 24-12.

The win pushed USC up to No. 8 in the nation, but that was as high as the Trojans would get that season. In fact, the bottom fell out once again with another five-game losing streak that gave USC its first 0-4 conference record in school history.

The Trojans lost to Oregon State (ending a 26-game win streak over OSU), Arizona, Oregon, Stanford and Cal with future Ravens QB Kyle Boller.

Polamalu had his moments during the losing streak.

Well, he had one moment anyway.

JUSTIN MYERS: One funny moment. I was going to college at a little school north of Eugene. Where I grew up we were all Oregon fans. I was watching Oregon and USC in Troy's sophomore year at a sports bar in Eugene with a bunch of Oregon fans, and Troy made a diving interception of Joey Harrington. That was a really good Oregon team that really should've been in the national title game. But Troy makes an interception and of course just on instinct I jump out of my chair, and I get the weirdest looks from Oregon fans throughout the bar, like "Whaaaaat?" I'm like, "Hey, the guy's from Douglas! I know that guy!"

Otherwise, Harrington picked USC apart. He passed for 382 yards and four touchdowns in the breakout game of a college career that would end with him being drafted No. 3 overall in 2002.

Injuries weren't helping the USC secondary. Senior free safety Ifeanyiu Ohalete broke his foot against Oregon State. The backup free safety, Antuan Simmons, nearly died – twice, according to reports – from complications arising from two surgeries to remove a benign abdominal tumor.

USC also lost Matt Grootegoed, the promising freshman, to mononucleosis early in the season, sprint champ Darrell Rideaux to a sprained ankle, and junior Kris Richard to a knee injury.

It left Polamalu and fellow sophomore DeShaun Hill at safety, with sophomore Kevin Arbet and JC transfer Chris Cash at cornerback.

All of it added up to one red hot seat for Paul Hackett, who was on the way to USC's second consecutive non-winning season for the first time since 1960-61.

"The month of October's been a nightmare," Hackett said after USC lost its eighth October game of its last nine.

Overall, in two college head coaching jobs, at USC and Pitt, Hackett was 7-19 in college football's defining month.

The calendar changed and so – it seemed – did USC's fortunes with a 44-38 overtime win at Arizona State. Polamalu led the defense with his new college-high 14 tackles.

THURMAN: It was a night game and Arizona State had this really, really good tight end, Todd Heap. We put Troy on him and Troy had a great game against Todd. We won and Troy played well. I mean, Todd could run, and run routes, obviously had great hands. He was a No. 1 draft pick by the Baltimore Ravens. Troy did a very, very, very good job that night. I can't remember how many catches Todd had but it wasn't a lot. His defense on Heap was a big factor in why we were able to win the game.

While Heap became the most prolific tight end in ASU history that night by catching seven passes for 51 yards, none were longer than 11 yards. In ASU's 26-16 win over USC the previous year, Heap had caught seven for 100 and a touchdown and set up another touchdown with a 37-yard catch-and-run to the USC 3.

The 6-5, 252-pounder went on to play 12 NFL seasons with two Pro Bowls, and, in the final regular-season game of the 2002 season, before the Steelers made Polamalu their first-round pick the next April, Heap caught seven passes for 146 yards and a touchdown.

In Heap's next 16 games against the Steelers, since Draft Day 2003, he never gained more than 58 yards in a game and caught only four total touchdown passes – two in a game Polamalu did not play.

THURMAN: We used Troy differently than how the next staff at USC used him, so he may not have been in coverage much his junior and senior seasons. But I think over time you could ask Troy to do most anything and it wouldn't have mattered. He still was going to show up on game days and make plays.

That next staff was coming soon. Even though USC did beat crosstown rival UCLA for a second consecutive year, the Trojans lost to Washington, then lost the 2000 finale to Notre Dame.

In the *Orange County Register*, the day before the loss to Notre Dame, USC running backs coach Keneti Polamalu wondered what the expected firing of Paul Hackett would mean to the assistant coaches.

"You can put it aside when you're on the field," Keneti said, "but you can't help thinking about it sometimes when you're off the field. Your family wants to know if you're still going to be at the school."

"He definitely should stay," senior RB Petros Papadakis said of Keneti. "All he cares about is his group of players. He didn't come here to use this job as a steppingstone to something else or to become the coordinator here. He wants to coach the running backs at USC and he does a great job."

Major strides had been made by tailbacks Sultan McCullough (1,163 yards rushing/5.9 avg. in first season as the starter) and Malaefou Mackenzie (284/6.1).

"Many Trojans players from all positions are lobbying for Pola and defensive backs coach Dennis Thurman to be retained no matter what happens," wrote Todd Harmonson of the *Orange County Register*.

Hackett was fired three days later. The Trojans finished 5-7, 2-6 and tied for last place in the Pac-10.

USC bought out the remaining two years of Hackett's contract for $800,000. He finished 19-18 in his three seasons at USC.

The *Orange County Register* reported that athletic director Mike Garrett's top choices to replace Hackett were Oregon State's Dennis Erickson and Oregon's Mike Bellotti. The paper also reported that Mike

Riley, Barry Alvarez, Ron Turner, Norv Turner and Randy Walker were under consideration.

"If the other recruiters are any good, we've got no time," Keneti warned.

Carson Palmer later called the moment his lowest at USC. "I think that's when I got to see how nasty everybody could be," he said in 2002. "It was just a low, nasty time."

And Hackett's final words?

"There's a hell of a team in there."

CHAPTER 8

ROCK YOURSELF A LITTLE HARDER

P aul Hackett wasn't there to say no.

Peter Carroll wasn't yet there to say no.

So, Troy played baseball in 2001 for Mike Gillespie and USC, the national champions as recently as 1998.

Well, Troy played briefly.

TROY POLAMALU: After my sophomore year there was that lame-duck period between Coach Hackett and Coach Carroll and I actually played baseball. As soon as Coach Carroll came in, he had watched the game tapes from the previous couple seasons. He sat me down and said "Hey, you're going to go all-round on football. We're going to do a lot of really cool, special things with you," and that really excited me because he kind of had a history of coaching safeties and really making them the focal point of the defense.

JUSTIN MYERS: I think Troy was a little surprised by the level of play by the SC baseball team. He came back during spring break and was like, "Dude, you don't even know about this place." Now, I had played junior college baseball, so I knew who Mark Prior was, and Troy was just like, "Man, you don't even know what these guys are doing."

TROY POLAMALU: I was scrimmaging against Mark Prior. They literally were one of the best teams in the country and I was facing Major League pitching. As soon as I saw that first off-speed pitch, I was like, "Oh my gosh this is a whole different level." It was a big slap in the face in the realization that this truly is a skill sport that needed to be practiced over these last few years. I kind of lost those qualities and I definitely realized that I wasn't going to be a very good baseball player if I was going to try to play both.

Thus ended the great baseball experiment for Troy Polamalu, who put his glove and spikes away until Defense played Offense in softball at the end of his first Steelers training camp.

Vanderbilt transfer Mark Prior went on to win the Dick Howser Trophy that season, along with the Golden Spikes Award and the Rotary Smith Award before becoming the second overall player taken in the 2001 draft. Two years later, he was 18-6 for the Chicago Cubs and finished third in the National League's Cy Young voting.

Prior led the Trojans into the College World Series, but as the third seed they lost to eventual champion Miami in the second round and then to Tennessee in the loser's bracket. It's been the last appearance in the CWS for 12-time NCAA champion USC.

Troy could justifiably blame Prior for ending his baseball career, but, of course, the decision was ultimately made by Pete Carroll, whom USC hired on Dec. 15, 2000.

A 49-year-old from San Francisco who graduated from the University of the Pacific, Carroll once was cut by the Honolulu Hawaiians of the World Football League, so he began coaching wide receivers and defensive backs at Pacific at the age of 22.

He coached secondaries at Iowa State (1978) and Ohio State (1979), and moved to the NFL to coach defensive backs for the Buffalo Bills (1984) and Minnesota Vikings (1985-89).

Carroll became defensive coordinator (1990-93) and ultimately head coach (1994) of the New York Jets, but was fired after a five-game losing streak – begun by Dan Marino's famed fake spike/game-winning touchdown pass – had ended the Jets' season at 6-10.

Carroll went home to coordinate the defense of the San Francisco 49ers in 1995-96 and was hired as head coach by the New England Patriots in 1997. Even though the Patriots made the playoffs twice, Carroll was fired after the 1999 season, replaced by Bill Belichick.

Carroll sat out coaching in 2000. And even though he left the NFL with a winning record (33-31), his hiring at USC wasn't met with much enthusiasm.

"I'm sure Carroll, like Hackett, knows his X's and O's," wrote Tom Dienhart of *The Sporting News*. "The problem is the college game Carroll doesn't know. It was the same one Hackett had trouble grasping. I'm talking about things like academic issues, recruiting and dealing with alumni."

Dienhart lamented USC's facilities, the 85-scholarship limit, and Los Angeles housing costs and traffic in deciding that USC "is not that good of a job because it's not 1975 anymore."

But the columnist sprinkled wisdom in writing that "Carroll needs a positive start and would help himself by retaining defensive line coach

Ed Orgeron and running backs coach Kennedy Pola, a pair of Hackett assistants who red-line their intensity meters."

Orgeron, future head coach of 2019 national champ LSU, was retained by Carroll as the recruiting coordinator. He was eventually named National Recruiter of the Year in 2004.

Keneti Polamalu was kept as the special teams coordinator.

PETE CARROLL, *Seahawks head coach (2010-current):* (Keneti) was a great SC guy. He had it deep in his heart about representing the university. He is a very unique character guy in terms of the energy and creativity he brings and the way he commands respect from the players. He was just a really fun guy to work with and he was a great part of our early days of putting together the mentality and kind of the history and tying it all together for the future.

KENETI POLAMALU: Coach Carroll and I went back and forth, and he said, "Everyone tells me that I should keep you. But I don't know what position because I already hired the running backs coach from Washington." He had gotten my job when I left (Washington) and they just went to the Rose Bowl. So, Coach Carroll was debating back and forth, and Troy's on the baseball team. I remember Coach Carroll talking about him, like, "Well, (Troy)'s a little stiff." Knowing Pete well now, I think he was trying to get my competitive juice going, saying, "I don't know if that guy can play." I'm starting to get really pissed off. I'm like, "Well, you don't know him." And he said, "I don't know if he has the hips to play safety." I said, "Well, you're going to have to see that." That's when Troy gave up baseball and came out and proved himself to Coach Carroll in the spring. They were throwing the basketball around, and Pete loves basketball, but he didn't realize how good Troy is. They said, "OK, let's have a little dunking contest." Well, it was over then. As soon as Troy got into dunking it was over. After that, Coach Carroll said, "Wow." And I said, "Yeah." But knowing Coach Carroll now, I think he egged that on trying to get the competitiveness out of us. And he got it.

MALAEFOU MACKENZIE: Little did he know Troy's 40-inch vertical was like a Vince Carter 40-inch vertical. Any of the guys would tell you Troy was doing almost the same dunks as Michael Jordan and Vince Carter. I remember Vince Carter at that time was the dunking champion, and Troy did every single one of his dunks. Coach Carroll was an awesome basketball player. We would play 3-on-3 tournaments, we'd team guys up 3-on-3, and at the end we'd have a dunk contest, and Troy was the star of stars. Oh, it was ridiculous. Ask any of the guys about his windmills, 360s. You name it. And he's not very tall. He's a half-inch shorter than me, and I remind him of that every time we see each other. It was amazing how high he would jump. You could tell his athleticism just by watching him play basketball. You could tell he was special.

Carroll had a reputation for encouraging, and participating in, 3-on-3 basketball with the Jets. He even had a court painted into the parking lot of the team's practice facility.

He also had a reputation for molding defenses, particularly secondaries, and his first hire was Dewayne Walker, a 40-year-old secondary coach who had been the New England secondary coach the previous three seasons and understood Carroll's defensive system. Walker replaced Dennis Thurman at USC.

Carroll also hired an offensive coordinator, Norm Chow, who was known as something of a quarterback whisperer. As an assistant at BYU, Chow was instrumental in the development of QBs Jim McMahon, Steve Young, Robbie Bosco and Ty Detmer, and had just coached Philip Rivers through his freshman season as the starting QB at North Carolina State.

Chow was about to turn "Student Body Right" into a vicious passing attack by simplifying the offense and cutting Hackett's playbook in half.

MACKENZIE: I really didn't think Coach Hackett's offense was complicated. I think it was just his delivery. He's an amazing offensive coordinator, but as a coach, the guy wasn't the best in terms of motivating, especially in college. There's a big difference between college and pros. In college, they're still just developing kids, so you have to be able to motivate young men to play, and he didn't have any of that. In a professional setting, yeah. If he would tell a guy to run H2Foxtrot, or whatever, they'll run it because they're professionals. Now, Coach Carroll's amazing. As a piano player, he's amazing. As a basketball player, he's so competitive. He was one of us. It felt like he was one of the guys, whereas Coach Hackett was almost like your grandfather out there trying to preach to you.

TROY POLAMALU: One of the funny things was, with Coach Hackett, we kind of had a military approach. Everybody woke up at 5 in the morning and trained. One of Coach Carroll's first sayings was, "We don't play at 5 in the morning. Why should we get up at 5 in the morning?" So we got rid of those mandatory workouts early in the morning and it just set a different tone for us. We definitely had more of a team-building environment, because we never lacked in talent.

What he had seen was that had we all just been pulling in the same direction, we could do some special things.

LENNY VANDERMADE: One of the first things he did, he had us meet at the Coliseum at 10 p.m. He had this big, old rope out there, one of those ropes that ties down a big boat or something. He told Carson, who was the quarterback and kind of the captain of the offense, to grab 10 guys and take one side, and he told Troy, who was being looked at as the defensive captain, to grab 10 guys. Coach had us do a tug-of-war. People pulled back and forth, and people started cheating, guys started jumping on the offense's side. We all ended up in a pile. And then he told us all to get on one side to pull the rope. We pulled the rope, and obviously it's easy, right? But he said, "Hey, if we all pull together, that's how it will be around here. It'll be easy and no one can get between us."

MACKENZIE: That's why we gravitated to Coach Carroll. He was almost like one of our guys at 1013 coaching us.

"1013" was the name given to Troy Polamalu's new residence in the second semester of his sophomore year at USC. Of course, Pete Carroll wasn't "one of our guys at 1013." He only seemed that way.

MACKENZIE: 1013 West 24th Street. It's a two-story, old Victorian/Craftsman type of house. I moved in with Carson and we all lived separately my freshman year, and then sophomore year it was Carson, Charlie Landrigan, Zeke Moreno, Grant Mattos and myself. And then the next semester Troy and Lenny moved in. There were 10 guys who came in and out of the house before we left.

CARSON PALMER: Troy and I stayed there the longest, and as guys graduated and left we would take on new roommates: Matt Cassel, Keary Colbert, Lenny Vandermade, Norm Katnik.

MACKENZIE: Carson and Matt Cassel were roommates. I was downstairs with Lenny. Keary Colbert was upstairs with Troy. It was great. It was a lot like a fraternity when we were at home. We all woke up in the morning, worked out at 6 a.m. and went to classes.

PALMER: Very relaxed. Very mellow. I wasn't a big partier in college but I went to my fair share of parties. I can't think of a time when Troy was there. If he was, he wasn't there for long. He was in his room a lot listening to music. When we would play dominoes or cards or video games, he was right there in the middle of it. He was always part of the group but not the leader of the pack or making all this noise or starving for attention. He was there to hang out, laugh. He was always smiling. But he wasn't in college to party. He was in college to play football and get an education. Little else was important to him. He'd go out for a little bit and head home, but he was probably very much the way he is today.

MACKENZIE: I wish it was more of a party house but the landlord lived right next to us (laughs). Poor planning, but it still didn't prevent us from having get-togethers. I mean, c'mon, we tried to be serious students (laughs). We tried. I think we did the best that we could, especially with the tutors. Thank goodness they had tutors. We tried to focus, tried to make sure that each other was accountable. Sometimes we didn't want to go to class and it rubbed off on the others. But it was a ton of fun. My fondest memories of college were over there at 1013.

ZACH BANNER, *former USC, current Steelers offensive tackle:* To me, the talk of a bad neighborhood around campus is overrated, but you have to look at it with perspective. To a kid from Orange County, a nice area, it might be a little scary and alarming because it's new. But if you look at it from a historical perspective, a USC professor once told me that when the riots happened in the '90s, and people were going through the streets of L.A. destroying stuff, there was only one reported broken window on that big campus in the middle of South Central Los Angeles. That, he said, was a reflection of how much SC has done for the community. When SC was founded, Compton was a nice area, but it was still the inner city. Now it's a private school that's very expensive, very nice and very prestigious, and they take the time to help the surrounding community. If you were on that campus, and you were just enjoying your time, and you're not going around starting things and acting stupid, you're more than welcome to walk around the campus. I'm telling you they have it very secure. I never felt unsafe on that campus. Ever.

MACKENZIE: What a small world, right? Growing up I lived two houses away from, in my opinion, the greatest strength and conditioning coach, or mind, ever, Marv Marinovich. My dad was very strict with me. He made me run up and down the hills, and then there's a little high school, Capistrano Valley Christian, right down the street from the house. And I was running with my tire up and down the field, run up and down the hills, and then Marv would come over and say, "Hey, I train athletes for a living and I live two houses away. I would love for you to come over." I was such a shy kid that it took me about three months to go over there and start training.

I was probably 12 years old. I went over there and Marv Marinovich had The Barn. They converted it to a weight room, training facility, and athletes from all over the world would come. One of my first days over there, Marv got me on the rowing machine and I looked over and saw this tall guy. I looked over and saw another girl doing some jumping jacks. I saw somebody else doing plyometrics out there on the grass. I started noticing these people and I thought, "Hey, this is cool." A couple days later, my dad was reading the front page and I'm like, "Dad! That guy right there on the front page, he was doing the rowing machine right next to me." Turned out it was Kevin Brown, the first $100 million pitcher for the Dodgers. I was like, "Whoa." And I love training in general and how athletes use their body, mind and everything, so I started paying attention and started going there pretty much every day. Marv was like a second dad to me.

Fast forward to college – I still trained with Marv in the offseason – and Troy asked, "Hey, how do you get the balancing disconnect?" I'm like, "Dude, I'm going to take you to a guy named Marv Marinovich and I'm telling you right now you're going to love him." Troy was just as infatuated and just as insanely addicted to training as I was, so I took him down and he met Marvin. From that day forward he adopted all of Marv's philosophies about training. He bought all of his stuff, the iso-kinetic machines, the ball, all of that stuff.

In a 2006 interview with *GQ*, Polamalu explained his "spirit training" regimen: "When you're really intense in your training, you transcend your body. If you go till your mind says you can't go anymore, but you keep going, where you start making crazy sounds, where you really lose yourself, where you have to pull all the love and hate out of yourself, that's spirit training."

MACKENZIE: Troy had that special it. Dude, this guy's legs – I think he could've squatted 1,000 if he wanted to. He used to put six plates on and it would look like it was just the bar on there, up and down. They did rep maxes at SC until they stopped them, but I think he still has the squat record there, and then his bench was close to 400 pounds. When I introduced Troy to Marv, I think the instinct clicked right away because Troy was still so advanced physically, but he was humble enough that he still took the input from Marv.

VANDERMADE: Marv loves Malaefou and loves Troy. If you're a strength coach, you love guys who train as hard as they do. They both go hard and they take pride in doing things right, doing things at a high level. I would go down there and train. I wasn't at their level but I would train with them. And Marv would light up, man. He would see Troy and Fou [pronounced Foe] walk in and he'd be like, "Here are my guys. Here are my Trojans." He would get so excited about them.

MACKENZIE: Marv's the guy who said you don't need that weight. In the end, when you start learning about your body and the different systems in your body, you start learning you don't need that much weight. It's how you apply that weight, how you apply that force.

Troy Polamalu had started all 12 games his sophomore season and finished second on the team with 83 tackles and tied for the team lead in interceptions (2) and pass deflections (7). He was named honorable mention All-Pac-10.

Any comment, Troy?

"Last year was such a disappointment," he told the *Orange County Register.* "There is so much that we could've done better, and I take that as a personal responsibility."

Pete Carroll appreciated the accountability. He named Polamalu one of three captains for the 2001 season, along with seniors Charlie Landrigan and Antuan Simmons.

"That just says a lot about the kind of person and leader Troy is," Carroll said of naming a junior captain.

Carroll did even more with Troy. Much more. After reviewing tape, he designed his defense around the darting, sudden playmaker of a strong safety.

CARROLL: Heck yeah we did. We put him all over the place. We thought of him everywhere we could and gave him special freedoms that we didn't give other players, because we could trust him and he could take advantage of it, and he is still doing it. I'm sure (the Steelers) are still allowing him to do those things now. Early on when you first looked at the guy you probably thought he was guessing. But he has great savvy instinct and takes advantage of it. You can see him go and make plays that some guys just don't even think of making.

TROY POLAMALU: So as we were going through that whole spring training, I started to see how he really allowed me to move around, have some freedom within the defense that I wasn't accustomed to in the previous two years. That was really exciting. You could definitely feel a different energy from Coach Carroll.

CARROLL: First off, he has extraordinary speed. People don't realize how fast he is. Running in the 4.3s at the Combine is a ridiculously fast time. That explosion he has and his willingness to use it, because he is so instinctive and so tough, you have to feature the guy.

TROY POLAMALU: A huge influence. He gave me a lot of freedom. He taught me a lot about defenses, to find freedom within certain responsibilities, taught me a lot about the strong safety, or safety, position in general. I had a great coach before him in Dennis Thurman, and Coach Carroll continued to add to that. I'm very thankful to him for that.

For the second consecutive season, Troy Polamalu opened as USC's starting strong safety. He was joined in the secondary by Comeback Player of the Year candidate Antuan Simmons, and also by two cornerbacks who would become the team's only 2002 NFL draft picks, Kris Richard and Chris Cash.

Young lions Shaun Cody and Keneche Udeze had joined veteran Bernard Riley up front. Matt Grootegoed moved into the lineup as a linebacker.

On offense, Carson Palmer led a QB room that included two other future NFL players in Matt Cassel and Matt Leinart. The previous year's 1,100-yard rusher, Sultan McCullough, returned and was joined in the backfield by fullback Charlie Landigan and top reserve Malaefou MacKenzie. Kareem Kelly and freshman Keary Colbert were Palmer's primary targets. Each would sit atop the all-time USC receptions list by the time they left. Alex Holmes was the tight end. Left tackle Jacob Rogers and center Lenny Vandermade anchored the offensive line.

The Trojans were unranked in the Associated Press Top 25 poll for the first time in three years, but it would be the last time they would be unranked throughout the next 18 years.

MACKENZIE: A lot of the scouts every year would come through SC and say the same thing: "You guys are in the top 5 most talented guys athletically, but for some reason nothing's jelling." That meant, to them, that it's the guy leading, that if you get the right guy in there, it'll change everything. And Coach Carroll really did change our culture. It was fighting with and for each other, whereas before things were more individualized, like "Hey, I'm trying to get to The League" versus "We're going to move forward as a family."

The young family moved forward into the 2001 opener against San Jose State focused on stopping 5-6 tailback Deonce Whitaker. And they did – after a 40-yard first quarter. Pete Carroll moved Polamalu into the box and Whitaker gained only 25 yards the rest of the game, a 21-10 USC win.

Carroll was doused with Gatorade after the game as the players left the field chanting "Pete! Pete! Pete!"

Up next was another home game, this one a step up in class, and USC lost to No. 12 Kansas State 10-6.

It was Carroll's first loss, Bill Snyder's 100th win, and Troy Polamalu's first controversy.

PALMER: Something happened in that game against Aaron Lockett, who was the top returner in the country. The special teams coach had told them, "I don't care what happens, whoever gets down there first lay this guy out and make him think about returning punts the rest of the game." And Troy's the type who'll do what he's told to do. He lined up wide, eluded a couple blockers, and the instant the ball touched Lockett's chest, Troy just hammered him. People called it a dirty shot but it wasn't. Troy was doing what was asked. Whether it was worth the penalty or not, his coach asked him to do it and he did it. That's just the kind of player he is.

MACKENZIE: You ask what Troy's greatest game at SC was and there were a lot of them. But the one that really impressed me, and I don't know if it's the right game to say, but he changed the game when we played Kansas State. I don't know, the Kansas State folks probably hate hearing that. Do you know what play I'm talking about with the kick? At that time they didn't have the halo rule, and so it was fair game. They still penalized him, but that one play gave us a chance to win.

Polamalu did actually drill Lockett – the nation's top return man in 2000 – before the ball touched him, and USC was penalized 15 yards for interfering with his right to catch the ball.

Kansas State had a 10-0 lead at the time and USC punted following its opening possession of the second half.

MacKenzie was correct that the play sparked the Trojans. A third-down sack by Lonnie Ford caused a fumble that was recovered by Riley at the K-State 27. Four plays later, McCullough was in the end zone and the Trojans had cut the lead to 10-6.

The extra point was blocked and the momentum stalled. A late fumble by Palmer at the K-State 27 was the final blow.

But the controversy over Polamalu's "dirty" hit was just beginning.

"I didn't like it," Snyder said after the game. "My understanding of the rule is that you're supposed to be ejected from the ball game. I don't know what was on the young man's mind, but that's a helmet in the face, No. 1."

"I wasn't going to give him any room," Polamalu said after the game. "But it wasn't intended for me to hit him with a cheap shot. I'd like to make a public apology to the Kansas State fans, (Lockett) and their coaching staff. We needed some momentum and apparently that helped us, but that was by accident."

Two days later, on his Big 12 conference call of Sept. 10, 2001, Snyder called for Polamalu's suspension. "Ejection also carries over into the next ball game as well," Snyder said.

"It's a mistake of a split second," said Carroll. "It's a split second. I think that's really out of line to be going that far."

On a positive note, Snyder did say that Lockett was OK.

On a negative note, the controversy would be forgotten the next, awful day.

September 11, 2001 was of course a day that shall live in infamy for all Americans. For Malaefou MacKenzie – Troy Polamalu's "spiritual advisor," the running back who would marry the daughter of Troy's Aunt Moana and become Moana's son Nicky Sualua's brother-in-law, and who would become a fireman, in fact a record-setter in the well known Biddle Physical Ability Test for Long Beach firefighters, who would help supply masks and protective gear to those working the front lines of the COVID19 crisis – it was the day he lost his father, Vernon, to prostate cancer back in (Western) Samoa.

MacKenzie eventually reached a state of depression that alarmed Polamalu and all of those close to him. MacKenzie left for Samoa a month later and didn't expect to return. He spent hours at his father's grave, "looking for answers," as he told Bill Plaschke of the *Los Angeles Times*. "I was looking for my father to tell me what to do next."

MacKenzie stayed away the rest of the season. And Pete Carroll called and told him that his scholarship was still available.

"I realized I had more than one family," MacKenzie said.

He returned to school in January of 2002 and the NCAA granted him a sixth year of eligibility.

"This is the best man I've ever met in my life," Palmer told Plaschke. "I just wish everyone would have a chance to meet him."

"He's the best," Polamalu told the *Orange County Register*. "Every one of us would do anything we could for Malaefou."

If the football gods saw the brutal – albeit incidental – hit Troy Polamalu put on Aaron Lockett, the karma to both Troy, the special teams captain, and his Uncle Keneti, the USC special teams coach, struck almost instantly.

Following a week off, USC traveled to Eugene to face Oregon. Troy entered the game 0-2 in his adopted home state, and his third game back in Oregon started with a brawl 45 minutes before the Saturday night kickoff.

Troy was one of the 30 players involved. He rushed to help teammate Antuan Simmons, who later said he had been bumped by the Oregon player who allegedly ignited the brawl. Oregon Coach Mike Bellotti helped break it up, while Pete Carroll didn't emerge from the locker room until the brawl was over.

Carson Palmer threw for 411 yards and touchdowns of 75 yards to Sultan McCullough and 93 yards to Kareem Kelly, but Palmer also threw three interceptions – all by Steve Smith – which allowed Joey Harrington to rally the seventh-ranked Ducks to a field goal in the final minute of a 24-22 win.

Polamalu was suckered on a halfback option pass to tight end Justin Peele for the first Oregon touchdown, and was beaten by Peele for a second touchdown in the loss. Troy was also flagged for two personal fouls for the second consecutive game.

While his uncle's special teams blocked an Oregon field goal with 1:30 left, the kickoff coverage unit allowed 228 yards on six returns.

The USC losing streak then reached three with a 21-16 home loss to Stanford. USC fell behind in the first half 21-0 with the help of Sultan McCullough's lateral to Stanford instead of to Palmer during a flea-flicker. And when USC missed a 26-yard field goal just before the half, the Trojans were booed on their way to the locker room.

USC rallied in the second half, but couldn't stop Stanford from grounding the clock late in the game.

Troy returned an interception 22 yards for a touchdown the following week at Washington, but the Trojans lost their fourth consecutive game 27-24 to the No. 11 Huskies. A 32-yard field goal by Washington with three seconds remaining was the game-winner.

At 1-4 overall and 0-3 in the Pac-10, USC was off to its worst start since 1958. Another loss would match the worst start since the 1957 team went 1-9.

In danger of enduring a five-game losing streak for the third consecutive season, the Trojans prepared for Arizona State, the second-highest scoring team in the nation.

And USC responded. The Trojans won in a 42-17 blowout. Troy led USC with 8 tackles, all solo, and his future brother-in-law, Alex Holmes, wrapped up the win with a 4-yard touchdown catch in the third quarter.

But the euphoria faded the next week as USC reached the depths of the Pete Carroll era with a 27-16 loss at rival Notre Dame to fall to 2-5.

The Trojans had taken a 13-3 first-half lead on a pair of Palmer touchdown passes, but a disastrous fake punt on their own side of the field in the second quarter went nowhere.

Notre Dame scored four plays later, and then held USC to a field goal after a first-and-goal at the Notre Dame 1. Notre Dame controlled the game from that point forward.

After the game, Carroll said he hadn't called the fake punt. The punter, Mike MacGillivray, said, "I was trying to get something going."

Yes, on his half of the field with a 10-point lead.

The next day, special teams coach Keneti Polamalu told the *Orange County Register*, "It's my fault."

And Carroll told the paper, "It was my fault."

There were no fingers being pointed in Trojan land – by anyone besides Troy Polamalu. The junior co-captain took matters into his own hands in the locker room after the loss.

VANDERMADE: He got up and had it out. He exploded, let it all out, as far as everyone having to step their game up. "We're better than what we're showing out there!" He didn't always explode like that, so when he did it had more meaning. At this point, he's fired up. He's tearing up and he's just had enough. Here was our best player telling us what time it was. "Let's stop BS-ing and get to work!" It helped change the culture.

Prior years, when things were like that, the leaders would talk about "Oh, it's time for me to get ready for the NFL." That wasn't Troy. He wanted to leave it better than how he found it. You could just tell that it mattered to him that much. Shoot, he could've said the same thing, "Hah, it's time for me to get ready for the league." But he didn't. That's a testament to his character and integrity. Instead, he started with himself, like he always does, held himself accountable and then said, "The rest of us need to step our game up, too." When the hardest worker says that, it's time to listen.

Carroll, the coach who was judged to have already failed in the NFL, was 2-5 with a team that had Carson Palmer and Troy Polamalu as its primary playmakers.

Not much was looking up for a coach who was clearly at a career crossroads.

TROY POLAMALU: No matter if we were losing or winning, we always had a winning attitude. And Coach Carroll was so enthusiastic, you couldn't help but feel good no matter what the situation was, personally as well as what your team was going through. That's one great thing that I've taken from him.

CARROLL: There really was a moment. There was a game. We were playing against Arizona and we were 2-5 and we had just lost to Notre Dame. Late in the game we were ahead but Arizona was coming back. We made an interception and ran it back for a touchdown and separated the score and that play signified that we can make things happen at the end of the game and win it. In the locker room after that game I told the guys that we don't have to lose anymore. We don't have to lose football games because we don't believe or don't have the ability to make those plays. So, there was a moment really that I thought it turned around. From that time on we won a lot of football games and really got rolling. It was a significant changeover. I think that does happen. You don't know when it's coming.

VANDERMADE: We were 2-5 but we were losing close games. The cool thing was Coach would show us what was costing us. One of them, we lost to Stanford and, to be honest with you, it was my fault. I had a couple personal fouls that stalled drives and we ended up losing by three. We get a field goal out of those two drives and we win. Things like that, he pointed it out, made it tangible, explained why we were losing and how we could fix it. By that time, the leaders on the team – Troy and Carson and later Malaefou and Justin Fargas; Kris Richard was another guy like that – they would be like, "OK, stop pointing fingers. Stop talking about The League." Those are the kind of guys I hung around. It was constantly get better, constantly improve. I'm just so grateful to guys like Troy. Guys respected him. Guys saw how hard he freakin' works, so shut up and get behind it. Myself, as a person, also as a team, everyone bought in and we were able to get back to 6-6.

At Tucson, USC blew a 31-13 halftime lead and Arizona had the ball with less than two minutes remaining in a tie game. Richard returned an interception 58 yards for the game-winning touchdown.

The win marked the beginning of a 95-14 finish at USC for Carroll after the 2-5 start to his nine-year run.

Carroll, of course, would move on to coach the Seattle Seahawks and became one of only three coaches to win both a college national championship and a Super Bowl. Barry Switzer and Jimmy Johnson were the others.

After giving up over 115 yards in kickoff returns for the third time A.L. (After Lockett), Keneti Polamalu infused his kickoff unit with speed. He put Troy, Kris Richard and Chris Cash – three-fourths of the starting secondary – on it and they held Arizona to 44 return yards in the 41-34 win.

The Polamalu-centric special teams could take another bow the following week. Troy blocked an Oregon State punt for a USC touchdown in the first quarter of a 16-13 home win for USC.

"Boy, that guy's a heckuva football player," Carroll said after the game. "I've coached a lot of great safeties, and he's right there with anybody."

The special teams, along with the defense, remained hot the following week in Berkley. Keneti Polamalu called a fake field goal for a touchdown and the defense knocked Cal QB Kyle Boller out with a bruised jaw in the third quarter of a 55-14 USC win, the Trojans' fourth straight in the Pac-10.

In concluding the regular season at home against rival UCLA, Troy blocked a punt that led to a USC field goal and intercepted a pass to set up a touchdown in USC's 27-0 win. For his efforts, Polamalu was named the Pac-10 Defensive Player of the Week.

For a team that appeared headed for its first back-to-back losing seasons since 1960-61 under another of athletic director Mike Garrett's so-called poor hires, USC was bowl eligible at 6-5 and 5-3 in the Pac-10. Four of USC's losses were by five points or less, with two occurring in the final 12 seconds.

USC sports information director Tim Tessalone had first recounted for us Polamalu's post-practice regiment, which set the tone for a program that was in the midst of changing its culture.

Tessalone's second memory?

"I'll never forget," Tessalone wrote in an e-mail, "the day I informed him that he was named a first-team All-American in his 2001 junior season, he started crying."

And, of course, Polamalu's modesty followed.

"I felt really undeserving of this," he told the *Orange County Register* following a late-November practice as the Trojans prepared for their Christmas Day bowl game. "There are a lot of great safeties in the country."

With one game to play as the Pac-10's fifth-place team in the Las Vegas Bowl, Polamalu had 98 tackles, three blocked punts, three interceptions, two returned for touchdowns and two forced fumbles. He was asked if he was preparing to leave early for the NFL draft.

"You have to be good to leave early," Polamalu said, meaning that he was not.

Two weeks later, Polamalu was named USC's Most Valuable Player of 2001.

That was preceded by his record-setting performance in the Las Vegas Bowl.

USC slept-walked and lost to Utah 10-6, but Polamalu had eyes wide open. His 20-tackle performance remains a Las Vegas Bowl record.

"Troy was the defense," said Maflaeou MacKenzie, who was warming up for a return in 2002. "Like I said after that day I saw him running with the bruised hamstring, and after what I saw him do on the basketball court, nothing would ever surprise me about Troy. He was just everywhere in that bowl game. The announcers, every time they mentioned a play they would say his name right after."

"People count on me to make big plays," Polamalu said after the game. "I just didn't come through today."

VANDERMADE: He had a monster game. It felt like he was making every play. But as a team, shoot, we lost 10-6. We didn't show up to play because I think we had a little too much fun out there. With Troy, we would hang out with family and hang out at the hospitality suite and then go to our rooms. We didn't really get out on the town like that. We walked around and checked out casinos, but we didn't indulge. That's the thing I admire about Troy. We could just have fun cruising in and checking it out and coming back to the hotel and calling it a night. He never felt like he had to be out all night to chase whatever. He experienced it the way he wanted to experience it and that was enough for him. I was probably a square, which was perfect for Troy. That's probably why we hit it off so well. But it was guys like him, guys like Malaefou, Carson Palmer, the leaders on the team took ownership by the end of that first year with Carroll. Whoever wasn't on board, there was – for lack of a better term – locker room justice, right? Guys weren't going to do that stuff anymore.

CHAPTER 9

CONQUEST

Theodora Holmes often stood on the sideline with family members and watched her brother Alex Holmes practice with the team, and his USC teammates often commented about his sister's beauty.

Troy Polamalu did more than comment. He approached Alex and asked if he could date Theodora.

"I distinctly remember I wouldn't let anyone date her, except Troy," Alex recalls. And so he gave his USC teammate permission to ask her out, and she accepted. Years later, Theodora became Troy's wife, and in a 2006 story *GQ* magazine described her this way:

"... [W]ho precisely resembled, physically and personally, the dream woman that Troy had prayed God would one day deliver to him. Given that Theodora is Greek on her mother's side and black, white, and Cherokee on her father's side – a heritage that gave her a lovely face that's pale in color but African in its contours, with a spray of freckles across her nose – this was a pretty tall order for God to fill."

MALAEFOU MACKENZIE: They are still like Bonny and Clyde. They are awesome. They're great together. I've known them for 20-plus years and she's the perfect wife, mother and companion for him, and vice versa. He's confided in me for advice about her, and they're so compatible it's crazy. It's almost sickening (laughs).

LENNY VANDERMADE: They started dating in the fall of Troy's senior year but honestly I can't remember much about them from college. I just know that she's been so selfless and so supportive of Troy, always putting Troy first. She's always been kind to me and Fou and anyone who's come over. She always goes out of her way to make us feel at home anytime we entered her house or anything like that. You could see when Troy played that she's hanging on every play. She really loves him and cares about him and doesn't want to see him get hurt. They're both very selfless people who try to put the other first.

Troy and Theodora became a dream match and later a dream marriage. Of course, there was football, too.

The loss to Utah in the Las Vegas Bowl put into question whether USC actually did play well down the stretch of the 2001 season, or whether the teams they beat were just bad teams, teams having bad days, or both.

The numbers on defense did improve for USC in 2001:

* In its first 7 games, USC went 2-5, allowed 19.4 points per game and 4.3 yards per carry. The pass defense allowed 56 percent completed at 11.7 yards per.

* In its final 5 games, USC went 4-1, allowed 14.2 points per game and 3.1 yards per carry. The pass defense allowed 54 percent completed at 11.0 yards per.

Polamalu averaged the same 10 tackles per game throughout both halves of the season. His 118 tackles were the most by a safety at the school in 15 years. He also blocked three punts, intercepted three passes (returned two for touchdowns), forced two fumbles and recovered another. He was the first USC All-America at his position since Mark Carrier in 1989.

None of it satisfied him.

"I don't feel like I've been that good," Polamalu said on the cusp of his senior season in 2002. "Coach Carroll puts together a defense that highlights the safety position. That's why I was excited when we hired him. But I could have a lot more sacks and interceptions. A lot of guys – Marques Anderson (UCLA), Tank Williams (Stanford), the guys at Washington State (Lamont Thompson, Billy Newman) – they could have done what I did."

Polamalu was named first-team All-America by the Football Writers and *College & Pro Football Newsweekly*, second-team by the Associated Press and third-team by *The Sporting News* and *Football News*.

It only seemed to embarrass him.

"I hate to get an award that separates me from the team," Polamalu said, echoing comments he had made at Douglas High and foreshadowing comments he would make with the Pittsburgh Steelers.

As he prepared for his senior season, Troy swore off haircuts, made progress on his degree in history, and met the woman of his dreams.

Life doesn't get much better than the summer before a student's senior season in college. The guys at 1013 West 24th Street didn't need to party like animals to make it the summer of their lives.

VANDERMADE: That summer, going into Troy's senior year, was my favorite summer as a football player. All the guys were on campus, working out together and doing stuff together. We had barbecues and team activities at our house. We weren't partying, drinking. We were all hanging out, playing cards, playing dominoes, those types of things. We got real tight and it showed during the season.

TROY POLAMALU: The barbecues. The barbecues, the summer workouts. I think those were the most fun times that we had: going to class, doing our workouts, going to breakfast every weekend. I think it was Pamela's we used to go to every weekend … just kind of that daily playing dominoes on the porch of our house that we rented out. Those are the best memories that I have.

VANDERMADE: We would put some money together from our stipend for summer school. We'd all pitch in, kind of like a pot luck. Fou would work the grill; I'd work another grill. We'd make some potato salad. College kids stuff: have guys over, have the team over and play dominoes, play cards, got on the sticks, just got to know one another as a team. I think it brought our team together. That was all Troy, Carson, Fou and Justin Fargas, those types of guys.

Fargas, who had been highly recruited out of L.A.'s Sherman Oaks neighborhood, had transferred to USC from Michigan prior to the 2001 season. At Michigan, he rushed for 277 yards (3.6 avg.) before breaking his right leg as a freshman. He redshirted in 1999, and the rehabilitation required plenty of hardware and several surgeries before he returned in 2000 and carried 18 times.

Midway through the 2000 season, Fargas moved to safety and made 10 tackles.

Fargas transferred to USC, sat out the 2001 season as he underwent a fourth surgery related to the broken leg, and came back to enjoy an outstanding 2002 spring.

The coaching staff was excited to put him in the backfield, along with the returning MacKenzie, to compete with incumbent starter Sultan McCullough at training camp.

Fargas would go on to run the exact 4.35 40 at the NFL Combine that Polamalu did, and, at 220, Fargas was almost 15 pounds heavier.

KENETI POLAMALU: Troy and Justin Fargas, they were competitive as hell.
VANDERMADE: Ultra competitive. A lot of times, if things were blocked up right, it would be the safety and the running back, so a lot of times they would have big collisions. Justin Fargas was the kind of guy who wouldn't turn anything down, and neither would Troy. They had some battles in the hole. There was so much respect for one another; there was never animosity. They appreciated each other because they made each other better. It was really cool to watch.

That camp – held for the second consecutive summer on the USC campus – was hot with competition all the way around. And Troy was a driving force.

CARSON PALMER: One play that I'll never forget. We were in practice and Kevin Arbet, another corner, was a younger player. Troy was an older vet. A receiver came down on a crackback block and cracked Troy, hit him right on the side of the helmet, absolutely lit him up, and the ball bounced outside and went for a long run. There was no yelling or screaming but Troy grabbed Kevin Arbet by his throat and by his shoulder pads and picked him up. It wasn't real loud, so the entire field didn't see it, but a handful of people saw it. If he wanted to pick this guy up and throw him over the fence he would have, but he picked him up and looked him straight in the eye and yelled, "If you ever don't yell out 'crack' on a block ... " I don't know how he finished the sentence but it was a defining moment of his career. Troy's main thought wasn't "Well, I just got blown up because you didn't yell crack." Troy's main thought was "They just had a 50-yard run because you didn't yell crack." It wasn't about him getting hit hard. It was about the defense giving up a big play because a corner didn't do his responsibility within the defense. I remember that like it was yesterday. That was Troy. He didn't need to verbally assault the guy, but when need be he can be the voice and the guy behind the defense who kind of runs the show. I know all the guys on the defense saw it and remember that. They'll probably never forget it, either.

Pete Carroll didn't forget it. That day in August of 2002, Carroll told reporters that Polamalu "needs to find a better way to react," but he also added that, "You can't be a great player like he is without the kind of unbelievable spirit he has about being great. He has it. Somebody put a little fire under it today.

"Do I wish that everybody would respond that way? Yes. I wish they all understood how important it is to be great. Not everybody understands that."

That was the second Troy Polamalu news event to come out of the two practices that day. The lede in the *Orange County Register* said that Troy was also "staggered by a collision with tailback Justin Fargas and likely suffered a concussion."

Polamalu, while hospitalized, turned out to be fine. So, the schooling of Kevin Arbet remained in the news, and would for years.

MATT LEINART, *USC/Arizona Cardinals quarterback (2002-09):* Oh my goodness, I've never seen him flip out like that. He was so mad that the guy missed his assignment. He picked the guy up, threw him on the ground and started cussing – and he never cusses. He's barbaric on the field.

CARROLL: And then he just ran around the field the rest of practice, controlling the whole football field. You couldn't take your eyes off him. He just wanted to prove that you couldn't knock him down without him responding. He was so determined; he was not going to be beaten. He's got extraordinary will. He's got the will of a champion who just will not allow himself to be outdone. There are a very few guys who I've coached over the years – in different levels – who have stood out so much. He's truly one of those guys who has that champion will about him. He just cannot live with the thought of someone beating him. And out of that comes that warrior mentality when he's playing, and he's fearless and ferocious and relentless.

VANDERMADE: You know, Troy's not perfect. None of us are. But he strived to do the best all the time. He practiced hard, he trained hard, and he lived his life as best he could, as hard as he could. His passion made him want to be good, want to be the best person he could possibly be. He does have a temper. He's lost it a couple times on the practice field. Kevin Arbet was one of those times. But right after practice he would go up to the guy and humbly ask him for forgiveness and apologize. He was accountable. I'm sure he did that with Kevin and explained to him why he was so pissed, just because I know how Troy is. I know he did it for one of the linemen, Norm

Katnick. This had to be '99. He threw Norm to the ground with kind of a jiu-jitsu toss, then he kind of shoved him in the face. After he did it, I could see in his face that he was so disappointed in himself. Norm was next to me in the locker room and Troy came up to him and apologized. He said, "Man, that's not me. It was bad and it was totally my fault. There's no excuse for doing that."

Troy and Carson Palmer were the 2002 captains, but the media guide told an interesting story: With Troy on the front and Palmer on the back, the safety was deemed the bigger star than the quarterback.

Todd Harmonson of the *Orange Country Register* listed Troy at the bottom of his Top 10 list of Heisman candidates, below Mike Doss of Ohio State under the heading NO CHANCE.

That was still better than Palmer, who didn't appear at all, though the following quarterbacks did: Rex Grossman (1st), Ken Dorsey (2nd), Byron Leftwich (5th), Dave Ragone (6th), Jason Gesser (7th) and Eli Manning (8th). USC didn't even launch a Heisman campaign for its QB, which actually was a relief to Palmer.

"I haven't done anything since I've been there," he said at the time, sounding like his friend and fellow captain.

Both Polamalu and Carroll disagreed with the assessment. In fact, Polamalu was certain a second season in Norm Chow's offense would help Palmer immensely.

"If the people around him can be consistent this year," Carroll said, "you're going to see what we know Carson can be: one of the top quarterbacks in the country and someone in high demand in the NFL."

Palmer, like Polamalu, had also met the girl of his dreams at USC.

Carson met soccer goalkeeper Shaelyn Fernandes at their freshman orientation, and through the next five years neither athlete would allow each other to slack from watching film or working out. They would be married July 5, 2003.

Another Palmer-Polamalu commonality: Palmer's brother Jordan had just committed to UTEP, where Troy's brother Kaio had played a decade earlier.

KENETI POLAMALU: There are so many moments that made me proud. The one I think of is probably Troy going into his senior year. He and Carson are the face of our program and they're roommates and good friends. I think his last spring practice we had at that time we had pretty good season-ticket holders. We weren't getting SEC numbers but we were getting up there with the spring attendance. And now we're planning to have a little family dinner after the spring game, but they decided they wanted guys to give autographs because it was an open spring. Well, that kid sat there and he signed everybody that came. It was hours. I'm like, "Troy, let's go." And he said, "Well, there are still people."

PALMER: I don't have a bunch of stories from college of what we did together. Troy's a man of few words and a man of few stories. His story is being told on the football field and on NFL Films. The other stories you won't hear about, the things that happen with his kids, how he's now teaching his two boys how to be a man, them watching him be a father and be a husband. Those are the stories that nobody will know about, and that's probably the way Troy wants it. He's a football player. But aside from that he's a man of faith and a man who takes care of his family. And that's all that matters to him.

The *Orange County Register* ranked USC third in the Pac-10 behind Washington and Washington State, but noted that "With the toughest defense in the Pac-10, the Trojans could shake off a difficult schedule and contend for the title," and that "safety Troy Polamalu could be the best defensive player in college football."

That may have been prophetic, because of the players who would be picked ahead of Polamalu (16th) in the next NFL Draft – Dewayne Robertson, NT, Kentucky (4th); Terence Newman, CB, Kansas State (5th); Johnathan Sullivan, DT, Georgia (6th); Kevin Williams, DE, Oklahoma State (9th); Terrell Suggs, DE, Arizona State (10th); Marcus Trufant, CB, Washington State (11th); Jimmy Kennedy, DT, Penn State (12th); Ty Warren, DT, Texas A&M (13th); Michael Haynes, DE, Penn State (14th); and Jerome McDougle, DE, Miami (15th) – only Suggs has a chance to enter the Pro Football Hall of Fame, as Polamalu did 18 years later.

As for the national media and their previews of the Pac-10 season, USC was ranked No. 2 by *Athlon Magazine*, No. 3 by *The Sporting News*, and No. 5 by *Street & Smith*.

Playboy named Troy to its preseason All-America team, which created an ethical dilemma for him.

After he considered not attending, Polamalu went, but said, "I never would go out and buy it. Actually, I wouldn't go out and buy any magazine that I was in."

Fame, of course, never appealed to Polamalu, even when he was a high school star.

TROY POLAMALU: It wasn't different. I had almost felt different in kind of being the odd man out in a lot of respects when I did first move to Oregon, because my family was literally one of maybe two or three minority families, not only in our town but possibly the whole county. So, it felt different in that respect. But I also remember growing up playing and people would pronounce my name wrong, "Polamal-uh", "PoLAMaloo." They would say our last name wrong. I had always been, "Man, if they could just understand me enough and respect me enough that when they start pronouncing my name correctly then I'll know that I've done something special and significant." These were literally my thoughts as a child growing up there. So I always felt that small-town fame a little bit. Aside from that, I was never really aware of how much people talked about me because I kind of shied away from that sort of spotlight. So when I came to Southern California, I'm going to college and receiving some of the recognition, it really wasn't much different for me. It was just another obstacle for me in the sense that, man, you dealt with it as a child, you don't like this, it's no different. It wasn't like I was out slamming the clubs, either. I was more of a Netflix kind of chill person anyway. So it didn't affect me too much.

USC, the team that was outrushed in the Las Vegas Bowl by 222-1, opened its 2002 season with a 24-17 win over Auburn and its exceptional running backs, future top-5 overall draft picks Cadillac Williams and Ronnie Brown.

Carson Palmer's 1-yard sneak with 1:26 left won the game for 18th-ranked USC.

Williams rushed for 97 yards on 14 first-half carries before USC dropped Troy Polamalu into the box in the second half and held Williams to -3 yards on seven carries.

Not that Polamalu was proud of the accomplishment.

"How tough was he to tackle?" Polamalu repeated. "I don't know. I never tackled him."

Polamalu led USC with 7 tackles, but was hardly impressed with himself saying afterwards, "I shouldn't have even been out on the field tonight. When you're a defensive captain, you have to play better than that."

USC entered the season with designs of recapturing its old glory running the ball. Pete Carroll moved Keneti Polamalu to RB coach and welcomed the return of the previous year's hurting, suffering and transitioning backs Sultan McCullough, Malaefou MacKenzie and Justin Fargas, respectively.

Two weeks later in Boulder, the USC rushing attack piled up 177 yards as the No. 17 Trojans romped to a 40-3 win over the No. 18 Buffaloes. It was Colorado's worst loss in 10 years and worst home loss in 19.

Polamalu led a stifling USC defense with 11 tackles as Colorado accumulated only 61 yards of total offense. He was named Pac-10 Defensive Player of the Week for the performance, and tempered the 2-0 start by saying, "We've done this before. It doesn't mean a thing yet."

Norm Chow's offense was also humming with 811 yards through two games. In addition to the great running, Palmer completed a red-hot 73 percent of his passes at a robust 12.1 yards per completion.

The key, though – and the running game would heartily agree – was the improved offensive line. Palmer, who had been sacked 36 times the previous season, was sacked only once in the first two games of the 2002 season.

Ranked 11th heading into its third game, USC knew the rematch with Kansas State would be difficult. And, sure enough, Wildcats linebacker Josh Buhl told the *Topeka Capital-Journal* that the team had a bounty out for Troy Polamalu, who had blasted return man Aaron Lockett a split second before he could field a punt the previous season.

"I'm not sure what it's up to. The offensive players have all that," Buhl said of the reward monies. "But if I see him on special teams, I'll be out to get him, too."

Nobody ever did "get" Polamalu, except on the scoreboard, where Kansas State posted a 27-20 win over USC in the Trojans' first-ever trip into the state of Kansas.

Polamalu did sting Kansas State pretty hard. Late in the second quarter, with Kansas State holding a 10-0 lead, Polamalu blitzed off the edge on third-and-9 and blindsided QB Eli Roberson at the K-State 15. Polamalu flung the QB around by the hips and the ball flew out of Roberson's hand toward his own goal line. USC DT Mike Patterson scooped it up at the 3 and cruised into the end zone for a USC touchdown with 30 seconds left in the half.

Unfortunately for USC, its extra point was blocked and K-State's Terence Newman scooped it up and returned it for 2 points, the first-ever such play allowed by USC.

So, instead of taking the momentum into the locker room, the crowd surged behind No. 25 K-State and its 12-6 lead.

The lead reached 27-6 early in the fourth quarter, but Carson Palmer threw a 5-yard TD pass to Keary Colbert with 10 minutes left and Sultan McCullough ran 25 yards for another TD with six minutes left, cutting the K-State lead to 27-20.

Palmer drove the Trojans to the K-State 33, but was sacked, and then threw incomplete on fourth-and-15 for the first USC loss of the season.

USC bounced back the following week against Oregon State, winning 22-0.

Sophomore QB Derek Anderson's first Pac-10 start was a difficult one. "The Moose from Scappoose" – who was on the other side of Polamalu's most difficult loss in high school – completed only 8 of 30 passes for 80 yards and was sacked five times.

USC allowed only 131 total offensive yards, eight first downs and 1.8 yards per rush to the Steven Jackson-led OSU ground game.

The second consecutive Pac-10 shutout kept USC at the top of the national defensive rankings, both overall and in pass defense. And Pete Carroll was doing it without his top three corners from the previous season, his secondary coach, who had also left for the NFL, and then without two injured replacements.

The nickel back in 2001, Kevin Arbet, was out for the year with a broken foot, and his replacement – opposite 5-8 veteran CB Darrell Rideaux – was Ron Nunn, who then tore an ACL against Kansas State.

Corners are important in a Carroll defense that asks them to play bump-and-run coverage and allow Polamalu the freedom to make plays.

Greg Burns, 29, was the new secondary coach, but Carroll was in command of the USC defense, particularly the secondary, which was his specialty.

"I love having a coach who's involved with everything we do on defense," said Polamalu. "You know what he's thinking and what he wants. The level of expectations is so much higher because of the way he coaches."

"If you don't do that directly – get your hands on them and coach them – it takes a lot longer for them to understand what you're all about," said Carroll. "It's something I didn't do in the NFL and, looking back at it, I really think I made a mistake."

Through four games, USC allowed only 13 percent of third- and fourth-down attempts to be converted, and only one touchdown drive had begun in opposing territory.

But all of USC's lovely defensive numbers were about to be shredded.

Troy Polamalu was "the best player on our team and one of the best in the country," said his friend, housemate and co-captain Carson Palmer.

And that's why Polamalu's injury in Pullman, Washington, was so devastating.

Polamalu sprained his right ankle on the artificial turf during the seventh play at Washington State, and the No. 1-ranked defense in the nation gave up 516 yards in losing to the home team in overtime 30-27.

Polamalu tried to pull up instead of letting loose on a Washington State WR, and he knew right away he was hurt and hobbled to the sideline. There, he begged Pete Carroll to put him back in the game.

After taking a cortisone shot at halftime, Polamalu was allowed back in, and Carroll even had him blitz.

"And he got great pressure on the quarterback," Carroll told the *Pittsburgh Tribune-Review* two years later. "He would go beyond what normal people would do to show his valor and courage."

Valor and courage weren't enough for USC, which could've used a better hold on a missed extra point that would've given the Trojans a four-point lead with 4:10 left to play. The miss allowed Washington State to tie the game on a 35-yard field goal with 1:50 remaining, and then win in overtime.

The loss snapped a six-game Pac-10 winning streak for USC as the defense fell from first in the nation to fourth.

"I had a shot, ice, pills, everything," Polamalu said after returning for "a handful of plays."

He also had an X-ray, which came out negative, but the injury kept him out the following week against Cal.

With Polamalu sidelined, USC fell behind Cal and QB Kyle Boller 21-3 in the second quarter, but scored 27 consecutive points for a 30-28 win.

Polamalu returned the following week against Washington, and his interception in the third quarter helped seal a 41-21 win at the Coliseum.

At 0-3 in return trips to Oregon, Troy Polamalu was looking at his last chance for a W there when the 15th-ranked Trojans traveled to Eugene to play the 14th-ranked Ducks. Troy even ignored ticket requests from family and friends in order to remain focused.

"I'm not even going to spend five minutes on it," he said. "We've got a game to win."

Polamalu played and made seven tackles, but it was Carson Palmer who shook off his own Oregon blues with a record-setting performance that thrust him into the Heisman frontrunner position.

Trailing 19-14 in the second half, Palmer led the Trojans to 30 consecutive points for a 44-33 win. He threw for a school-record 448 yards and tied Rodney Peete's school record of 5 touchdown passes.

Mike Williams, a red-hot freshman, had his best game yet with 13 catches for 226 yards and two touchdowns. It gave Williams 34 catches for 600 yards and seven touchdowns in the last four games.

The win improved USC's overall record to 6-2 and kept its Rose Bowl hopes alive at 4-1 in the Pac-10.

For Polamalu, the struggle with his high ankle sprain continued. He had another X-ray taken during the bye week, but it once again showed nothing broken.

By Saturday he was feeling better and led 10th-ranked USC with 13 tackles and a sack in a 49-17 blowout at Stanford.

"It's about time, isn't it?" Polamalu said after the game. "I finally felt like I could fly around out there again."

Palmer continued his assault on the USC record book with four touchdown passes to give him a school record 61 in his career.

The win moved USC up to No. 8 in the AP poll, and Arizona State was no match in USC's homecoming. Palmer threw for 214 yards and two touchdowns, Justin Fargas rushed for 125 yards, and Polamalu made 5 tackles in a 34-13 romp over the Sun Devils.

It was the Trojans' fifth consecutive win and their fifth consecutive 30-plus point game.

The streaks both reached six games the following week at UCLA, where USC pounded its crosstown rival 52-21. The romp stood as the most points scored by USC in the rivalry in 71 years, as Palmer became the Pac-10's all-time passing-yardage leader with 254 yards and also 4 touchdowns.

The win made USC 9-2 overall and 7-1 in the Pac-10 with one more regular-season game left, this one at home against Notre Dame, which was riding a three-game series win streak against USC.

"They'll beat Notre Dame," said UCLA Coach Bob Toledo.

Troy Polamalu walked past a group of four reporters after the last practice of the last week of his last college season and said, "Now there are the Four Horsemen."

Yep, it was Notre Dame Week and the USC history major was looking at his last chance to beat the Irish in his college career.

Now a Thorpe Award finalist, along with Terence Newman and Mike Doss, Polamalu was *finally* beginning to feel like his old self. He had the reprieve against Stanford, but the sprained ankle otherwise hurt his performances and was a big reason why the Trojans lost by three at Washington State and were now dependent on many other occurrences to optimize their postseason chances.

Ranked sixth, 9-2 USC was hosting seventh-ranked, 10-1 Notre Dame in what would be Polamalu's last game at Los Angeles Memorial Coliseum. The tributes to Polamalu started the Tuesday before the game.

"Carson Palmer might be having a better year," columnist Steve Bisheff wrote in the *Orange County Register,* "but no one of recent vintage has had a better career than the team's extraordinary strong safety. No one will deserve the kind of tribute he is likely to receive Saturday from teammates, coaches and fans, either."

Bisheff relayed the story of an elderly USC football alumnus who had approached Polamalu in the locker room a few weeks earlier.

"You don't know me," the unidentified man told Polamalu, "but I just wanted to tell you how impressed I've been not only by the way you play but by the way you conduct yourself on and off the field. You are the perfect role model for this program. It's been a pleasure to observe you over these past few years."

"I can't even begin to explain what he's meant to all of us around here," said linebacker Matt Grootegoed. "He's like a mentor to everyone on this team. He teaches other players how to conduct themselves, but it's more than that. It's his spiritual presence."

In the same column, Polamalu again explained Fa'a Samoa, The Samoan Way, which he had been taught by his elders.

"You have to be a gentleman everywhere but on the field," Polamalu said.

MACKENZIE: He's always been spiritual, but he's almost like a whole different person once he gets on the field. When you talk to him, there's no way this guy can be that much of a badass on the football field. But he surely is. He just had that switch when he gets on that football field. It's almost like he puts a cape on when he gets on the field.

PALMER: Look at Mike Tyson. He's one of the fiercest guys out there and he has a soft, sweet voice. Troy's just soft-spoken. If he wanted to yell he could scream and yell at the top of his lungs and scare anybody, but that's not the way he handles things. That's just his demeanor. That's how he approaches life. That's his way of life. When he gets on the football field he never talks trash or yells or screams. He makes noise with his helmet and his shoulder pads.

Polamalu and the Trojans had it all their way on this Saturday night, thrashing the Irish 44-13.

The other numbers were even more lopsided. USC had 31 first downs to Notre Dame's 4, and outgained Notre Dame 610-109.

Palmer settled into the driver's seat for the Heisman Trophy with 425 passing yards and 4 touchdown passes. He was lifted from the game with 1:57 left.

Two plays earlier, on a second down, Polamalu sacked Carlyle Holiday for a 9-yard loss and Polamalu left the game to the cheers of the home crowd for the final time.

When it ended, Palmer was swarmed with interview requests, so Polamalu took the stand to conduct the band – fittingly named The Spirit of Troy – through a rousing rendition of "Conquest."

Palmer joined Polamalu on the platform as the school's traditional post-game victory song was ending.

ANNA POLAMALU, *wife of Troy's cousin Darren:* Darren and myself and Brandon and his wife and their baby, who was about three months old, went to the USC-Notre Dame game. After the game we were standing there waiting for Troy. Tons of fans were outside the stadium waiting, too, and we see Carson Palmer come out and jump in his car and take off. Troy comes out and we were standing there for four hours. He signed every single person's autograph after the game. People waiting for Carson Palmer and other players said, "Oh, we'll take Troy." And he didn't mind. He just stood there and signed and talked till midnight. When we got in the car and drove off, the first thing he said was, "Wasn't that great?"

College football is infamous for ending its seasons before they're finished.

Bowl season is a time for mathematics and politics, and the team that was being called by many the best in the country, USC, was kept out of the BCS title game in favor of undefeated Miami and Ohio State, which met in the Fiesta Bowl.

Fifth-ranked USC, co-champ of the Pac-10 with Washington State, couldn't go to the Rose Bowl, either, because of that 3-point loss at Washington State.

So, the 10-2 Trojans were selected to play in the Orange Bowl against 11-1 Iowa in a game matching just-named Heisman Trophy winner Carson Palmer and his vast array of playmakers against an Iowa team that started future first and second-round NFL draft picks Bob Sanders, Dallas Clark, Eric Steinbach, Robert Gallery, Bruce Nelson and Jonathan Babineaux.

The Trojans overwhelmed the Hawkeyes, even without Troy Polamalu, who was in only two plays, because, well, as he put it, "It's a long story."

Polamalu went into the game with a bothersome right hamstring. The plan was for him to test the hamstring in the first half and, if needed, take a shot at halftime.

Well, Polamalu took the shot before the game and – as a similar shot did to Jerome Bettis in a Pittsburgh Steelers playoff game a year earlier – it caused "an adverse, numbing reaction," according to USC sports information director Tim Tessalone.

Even without Polamalu, USC crushed Iowa. The Trojans overcame a 100-yard opening kickoff return and a 10-7 Hawkeyes lead after the first quarter by going on one of their patented rampages with 31 consecutive points.

Palmer again led the way (31-21-303), followed by phenomenal freshman WR Mike Williams (6-99-1), RB Justin Fargas (20-122-2) and a defense that ended the season without having allowed a 100-yard rusher.

It was USC's first 11-win season since 1979, and the first of what would be seven such consecutive seasons under Pete Carroll, who seemed to know at the time that his program was on the precipice of greatness.

"We're just getting started," Carroll said after the game.

Polamalu was in for an extra point, and returned for another play in the fourth quarter, but he otherwise found no relief for his hamstring. He ended his season with 68 tackles, nine tackles-for-loss, three sacks, three forced fumbles and an interception. None of that led USC, or even came close, but he was still noticed, even in his two-play finale.

BRETT KEISEL, *Steelers defensive end (2002-14):* I watched him for USC in the bowl game and he was hurt. That was the first time I had seen him, but the announcers kept talking about him, what a great player he was, how he was going to be a super-high draft pick. And I could see how upset he was not being able to play and be a factor in the bowl game, because he had hurt his hamstring. So there was a lot of footage of him on the sideline riding the bike, walking up and down the sideline. You could just see by him doing the things he was doing that he was having a hard time being out there. As a player, I like seeing that type of stuff. I want guys next to me who it means something to them. When you step out there and put your body on the line, you want to know the guy next to you is doing the same thing and cares about it as much you do.

♦♦♦

PART 3:

PITTSBURGH STEELERS

♦♦♦

CHAPTER 10

MASTER OF NONE

The 2002 Pittsburgh Steelers made the playoffs in spite of a pass defense that ranked 20th in the NFL, the franchise's worst ranking since the 1991 team – Chuck Noll's last – finished 26th.

That sad ranking didn't include the playoffs, when the Steelers allowed 740 yards in their two games, a 71 percent increase over the regular-season average.

Clearly things needed to change. Everyone knew it, certainly including coach Bill Cowher.

That offseason the Steelers allowed starting strong safety Lethon Flowers to leave in free agency, and intended to replace him with reigning Super Bowl MVP Dexter Jackson, who had intercepted two passes against the Oakland Raiders to lead Tampa Bay to the championship.

Jackson was leaving Tampa Bay and his secondary coach, Mike Tomlin, who would ultimately benefit from Jackson's late, surprising decision to turn down the free-agent offer from the Steelers and sign instead with the Arizona Cardinals.

The Steelers turned to the draft for their needed safety and traded up for future Hall of Famer Troy Polamalu. Tomlin would become his head coach four years later.

MIKE TOMLIN, *Steelers head coach (2007-current):* Interesting, isn't it? (Laughs) It was evident that Dexter was leaving. I didn't know where he was going. It was just the nature of free agency. We had won the Super Bowl. He was Super Bowl MVP. That's what comes with that. We had high-priced players in our secondary like John Lynch and Ronde

Barber. I had come to grips with the fact that he was leaving. I really didn't think about the relevance of the sub-plot of all of that until much later once I got here. I remember talking to Dexter Jackson when he was in a bathroom on his visit in Pittsburgh. He was just letting me know how the day was going.

Jackson signed with Arizona for a few bucks more, and to rally at the draft the Steelers made their best trade since sending second and fourth-round picks to the St. Louis Rams in 1996 for a young Jerome Bettis and a third-round pick.

To move up 11 spots in an exchange of first-round picks with the Kansas City Chiefs in 2003, all it cost the Steelers were picks in the third (Julian Battle) and sixth (Brooks Bollinger) rounds. The Chiefs drafted running back Larry Johnson with the Steelers' pick at No. 27.

TOMLIN: I think Dexter was really more interested in wearing the responsibility of being a leader, and he thought there was more opportunity for him to do that in Arizona. He had been a significant young guy, a support guy, in Tampa. We had strong leaders like Derrick Brooks, and Pittsburgh had strong leaders, too. And I think the most significant thing for him was he wanted to be in an environment where he was challenged to be a leader, and Arizona gave him that.

DENNIS THURMAN: I went to Baltimore in 2002 and I remember when Troy was coming out for the draft. We had discussions about him, Mike Doss (Ohio State) and Ken Hamlin (Arkansas). The Ravens' personnel guys – Phil Savage, George Kokinis, Ozzie Newsome and Eric DeCosta – were there. I was new to the coaching staff, so I was sitting there listening to their reports. They were questioning whether or not Troy had good cover skills or ball skills, because they hadn't seen them. Pete used him differently than how we had with Paul Hackett, so people didn't know he could cover. I was asked by the people involved how well he can cover, and I said, "Well, we put him on Todd Heap and he did a really good job. You guys drafted Heap in the first round (in 2001)." I told them that was Troy's sophomore year and maybe you guys didn't see the tape.

TOMLIN: I didn't scout Troy heavily for Tampa Bay. With where we were positioned in the draft, he wasn't a realistic discussion. Sometimes I try to save my energy. Obviously I was aware of him and what he was capable of. I had a close relationship with Pete Carroll. He and

I used to get together in the spring and have defensive back coach clinics. That's probably the first time I met Troy, the spring before his junior year. I was out in L.A. at one of those defensive back coach things, and a couple others used to get together and bounce ideas. So, very aware of him. Seriously scouting? No.

THURMAN: My guys had more questions than answers. I listened to them talk about all these other safeties, and at one point I just raised my hand like I was in elementary school and said, "Wait. With all due respect, you guys have this kid all wrong. This guy can play football. He's a better football player than Mike Doss. He's a better natural football player than a lot of these guys you are talking about." They had sent me to Ohio State's pro day. Bill Cowher was there. We both watched Mike Doss. They sent me to SC's pro day. Tim Lewis was there. We both watched Troy. After I had my say in the pre-draft meeting, I left it alone. I told them, "The guy's a better football player than you guys are giving him credit for." And they were like, "DT, we hear you, we hear you."

CARSON PALMER, *first overall pick 2003 draft:* I was in New York for the draft and I couldn't believe Troy was not a top-10 pick. I just couldn't believe it. As I was going through my little media rounds, I was trying to listen to the background to hear his name called. I remember thinking, "He's gotta be a top 10 pick." I wanted to know where he and our other roommates and other guys on the team were going, but I knew Troy would be the next to go. So I remember trying to listen, trying to hear in the background his name get called. They kept calling other names and I was thinking, "Man, this is crazy. This guy is the best football player I've ever seen, played against, played with, whatever." He finally went to the Steelers, and then it took me a little while to realize, "Wait a minute. I'm going to have to play against him twice a year in our division!"

RAY HORTON, *Steelers secondary coach (2004-10):* I was coaching for Detroit, and viewed him as the best safety in the draft, and at Detroit I kind of got laughed at for my grade. They didn't think he was worthy. I got ostracized. The next year, I end up in Pittsburgh and, for me, the rest is history because he validated what I thought of him.

THURMAN: I was sitting in my office and Pittsburgh traded up to the 16th spot to draft him. Our scouting department sent some people down to my office and said, "Oh, by the way, on our final board we had Troy rated ahead of Mike Doss." And I just looked at them and thought, well, OK, I don't know if you did or if you didn't. I just couldn't sit and listen to them talk about Troy and not understand how good of a football player he was. I just couldn't listen anymore to what they were saying. It wasn't bad. They. Just. Didn't. Know.

HORTON: What didn't the Lions like about him? Well, it would be easier to tell you what they liked about him: nothing. They didn't like him. We're there in Detroit watching the draft. Everybody's in the draft room. The commissioner says, "There's a trade. Kansas City has traded with Pittsburgh." In the room, they're wondering who did Pittsburgh trade up for? Obviously nobody knew. So when the commissioner said it's Troy Polamalu, everybody turned and looked at me. I put my hands up like "I told you. I told you." They were stunned that that happened. Really, the look in that room towards me was the look on Aaron Rodgers' face a couple years later as he sat there and sat there and sat there and sat there. It was just reversed. They thought it was unbelievable that someone would trade up to get him. We already drafted Charles Rogers, and I think Troy ended up with more catches of the football than Charles Rogers did. [No. 2 overall pick Rogers had 36 career catches; counting playoff games, Polamalu had 35 career interceptions.]

KEVIN COLBERT: It was no different than any other evaluation. USC had a bunch of good players, like they tend to have. Three of us went in at three different times during the fall. Ron Hughes, myself and one of the scouts. He didn't work out here. He worked out at his own pro day. He had a great pro day.

MIKE MILLER: Troy's pro day tape was unbelievable. They had him doing ball drills, turning and flipping his hips, and running and changing direction, high-pointing a ball, time him, three-cone drill, all those kinds of things. Did he cover guys running routes? I don't remember, but I do remember him flipping his hips and running to the sidelines catching the ball, redirecting, change of direction. It was just effortless. It was just one of those things that amazes you with how fast and quick and explosive; and his ball skills. The guy's just amazing. And then, then you put the film on and you just see how fearless and physical and unselfish. I started watching more on him, just on my own. He just jumps off the screen. Blowing guys up with menacing hits. So physical. Just awesome.

THURMAN: When I got to Baltimore, the safety positions were interchangeable. The safeties had to learn both jobs. We started two rookie safeties my first year there [2002], Ed (Reed) and Will Demps. Demps was a free agent from San Diego State. They used to be on the field, rock-paper-scissors to determine who was going to play which safety position on a particular play. They not only did it in practice, they did it in games. You could've put Troy in Demps' position and it would've been obviously phenomenal because of how we used our safeties. They both would've played the middle of the field, they both would've blitzed, they both would've played half the field, they both would've covered, because the defense would've afforded them the type of flexibility to do things they were comfortable doing. With Troy and Ed together, the way we were playing defense at the time, the flexibility would've allowed the both of them to play together and be successful.

MILLER: I love the theory, I always have, that if there's a guy that you really want, you go get him – just like they did last year with (Devin) Bush. Draft picks are nice to have, but if you have a chance to cash those in for a guy you really want, you do it. What they did with (Minkah) Fitzpatrick was outstanding.

COLBERT: Everybody here liked Troy. It didn't seem like there was a hole in his play. After we picked him, I told the media, "This kid plays safety like a linebacker." He was unique. The linebacker physicality with corner athleticism? That's hard to find.

BILL COWHER: We had Carnell Lake, and when we lost him we kind of lost a lot of the flexibility we wanted in our defense, having a strong safety who could cover guys. We wanted to get back to that with Troy.

MIKE PRISUTA, *WDVE sports director:* All of Steelers Nation recalls it as the Polamalu draft, but some of us in the media recall it as the Pearl Jam draft. When they traded that third-rounder, that opened up the night for us and Pearl Jam was in town. As I remember, somebody – *somebody* – reminded me that I work for the radio station. Somebody said something like, "Gee, if only we knew somebody who could call and get Pearl Jam tickets at the last minute." So I called the front office, and, bingo, I must be in the front row. We only missed a couple of songs. Kevin Colbert, God bless his soul, assured us he would not trade back into the first round, so we had that scoop going for us. We didn't even need two sources.

The drafting of Troy Polamalu – the first safety shorter than 5-11 drafted in the first round in 10 years – crossed off one of the four needs General Manager Kevin Colbert had provided to the media at the NFL Combine.

In order they were: defensive back, offensive lineman, tight end and quarterback.

Colbert would get his quarterback the next year, and the year after that he would get his tight end.

The Bengals added QB Carson Palmer with the first pick of the draft. The Ravens drafted Pac-10 Defensive Player of the Year Terrell Suggs of Arizona State with pick No. 10, then traded up to No. 19 to draft QB Kyle Boller of Cal. The Browns, at No. 21, chose Notre Dame center Jeff Faine.

All of those players knew Polamalu from one rivalry or the other, and they obviously knew him better than their personnel departments had, because the team starting the day at No. 27 ended up with the first Hall of Famer in the draft.

JOEY PORTER, *Steelers outside linebacker (1999-06):* I had never heard of Troy when he was at SC, but Cowher was fired up. I remember certain people in the building being super excited and I didn't know what the buzz was about. I called a buddy who played at San Diego State against Troy, and he said, "Man, you guys just picked up a real good safety. This dude's crazy good. He's just a normal-looking guy and you don't know he's that fast." It was kind of funny to me because you would think a guy running that fast would look like Ike – tall, chiseled up, something like that, but Troy doesn't look anything like that. Still, he's moving faster than all the strong, buff-looking guys. He's flying by everybody. It was awesome to watch him as a young player.

The Steelers added more to their defensive secondary that weekend by drafting CB Ivan Taylor in the fourth round.

"Call me Ike, please," Taylor told reporters on his first conference call.

Taylor, raised in New Orleans, had been a running back at Louisiana-Lafayette but moved to cornerback his senior season. At 6-0 1/2, 191, he was timed at 4.33 and 4.35 at his campus pro day.

The two rookie defensive backs were roommates from the beginning, and have remained close friends into retirement.

TROY POLAMALU: I came in early with Darren Perry after I was drafted. We went over a lot of different things. It was kind of one-on-one time.

DARREN PERRY: The first thing I noticed about Troy was his study habits. From Day 1 he was right beside me in the meetings and he took about as good of notes as anybody I've ever been around.

IKE TAYLOR, *Steelers cornerback (2003-14):* They had us come in after the draft for rookie minicamp. We were roommates at the Hilton downtown. You know Omar Khan? Omar put us together. That's the best thing he ever did for me – other than get me three contracts (laughs). But, yeah, I had heard about Troy. I saw him a few times at USC. He was known for the hit he put on that kid on that punt return. When he came in the room, I was butt-naked on the floor fresh out of the shower doing sit-ups. So he thought he had the wrong room. I was like, "Troy?" and he said, "Yeah." And I said, "It's me. Let me finish these sit-ups and I'll put on some clothes." And that was how we met.

TROY POLAMALU: We were roommates and we hit it off. What's funny about it is we're completely opposite in almost everything, but we match together perfectly. I love him as much as I do any one of my family members. Obviously the expectations for first-rounders are much different, and he definitely helped me along the way. I remember one time he was on speaker phone with somebody, and that person was talking about how much of a bust I was. This was my rookie year. And I was just, "Aw, man, that sucks. That's hurtful." It was definitely hurtful. It was one of his friends. Ike told him, "You know you're on speaker phone right now."

TAYLOR: I don't even talk to this person anymore because of that. You really have to be on the field to understand what we go through. Yeah, you see all the glitz and glamour off the field, but we work. Can't nobody tell me nothing about Troy. I just flipped out.

CHRIS HOPE, *Steelers safety (2002-05):* Going into my second year, I had a real good offseason coming off a great first year on special teams, and to my knowledge I was the only strong safety on the roster. Lee Flowers, the veteran safety who played the year before me and taught me a lot, was moving on to the Denver Broncos. The entire offseason I was supposed to be the strong safety, and, again, I was really focused on getting stronger, faster, learning the defense and trying to keep up with the high-paced, fast-paced style of NFL football. I had no intentions of focusing on moving to free safety. I had no intentions of even thinking about the draft because that was behind me. I was supposed to have been a first-round draft choice when I came out, but I didn't get picked until the third round. That was a torturous thing to go through, so I wasn't thinking about the draft again. I didn't even watch it. And here we draft Troy Polamalu. I got a call from someone and they told me they drafted a strong safety and they wondered what that meant to me. All I knew was that I was going to be one of the safeties on the team. I wasn't going to get cut or released just because they drafted another safety. So, before I even met Troy, he sparked a fire in me.

MIKE LOGAN, *Steelers safety (2001-06):* To me, it wasn't a slap at Chris. I think it was more towards me. I was an aging safety at the time who went from strong to free back to strong safety, played some nickel and dime, and I really thought he was drafted to come in and take my position. Being in the league that long, I knew that time would come. But watching that draft, when they moved up to actually pick him, I knew there was some writing on the wall. And then after I saw this kid play, I knew why they did what they did.

TAYLOR: As soon as he stepped on the field, it was like "Oh shit. This dude here, he not just good, he different." I was good, played great about four or five years. That extended my career for another four or five years. But Troy was different. Still, we had to earn it. That's one thing I like about Coach Cowher, boy. He made you earn that shit. Boy, he made you. Coach Cowher pushed you mentally, like to the point where you've got to decide if you want this to be your occupation or not.

Troy Polamalu was given No. 43 and – with Mike Logan still injured – the No. 1 spot at strong safety next to veteran free safety Brent Alexander through the early portion of his first set of spring practices.

It was clear that Chris Hope was the free safety of the future, so he worked behind Alexander.

But Troy had to miss the final two weeks of spring practice in 2003. He aggravated the hamstring that had given him problems throughout his senior season at USC. He believed it was a result of overcompensating for the ankle injury earlier that season.

TROY POLAMALU: We had a complex defense under Coach Carroll. The difference is that I'm going from a 4-3 front to a 3-4 front. The 3-4's a lot more flexible so you really don't know where you're supposed to fit in as the eighth man in the front.

BRETT KEISEL: Troy got thrown into a whirlwind of things at the safety position by Tim Lewis and Cowher. So many things that you've got to put together: red, blue, yellow; seam, curl, flat; corner, back, safety, hook, nickel. And as a rookie coming in, with the pressure of being a first-round draft pick that you had traded up for, there was a lot to mentally gather. And that's really the separator in the NFL, the mental part of the game. Too many great athletes come through who can't piece it together. As young players in certain situations it can be overwhelming, and I think it was a little bit for him at first. Cowher has admitted that he probably put too much on his plate right off the bat.

LOGAN: Troy held out of training camp for a couple of days, but he wanted to just get in and play football. I remember when he did show up, he didn't have his luggage, so he came to me and asked to get a shirt to throw on until his stuff came. I looked through my haberdashery to find something Polynesian or Hawaiian. I ended up giving him just a t-shirt and some new shorts. But I ended up immediately just really gravitating to the guy. You could feel his spirit, just from an introduction. I didn't really know him but I could tell he was a kind-hearted person. I mean, this was a first-round pick the Pittsburgh Steelers moved up in the draft to get, and his attitude was that of humility. That struck a chord with me right away.

CHRIS HOKE, *Steelers nose tackle (2001-11):* He was interesting to watch because off the field the guy was just respectful to everybody. He was kind. You hear about guys, the older guys who wouldn't even give you the time of day, that actually treated you poorly – and I saw it when I was a young Steeler. The day before a game you would have your tickets and your parking pass. They'd come up and say, "Hey, man, give me your parking pass." I would say, "I only got one." They would say, "You're a young guy. You're not even going to play tomorrow." I'd be like, "What!?" That happened on a routine basis.

LOGAN: I wanted to know more about him. From Day One, just observing him through the first training camp and how he handled himself, the times he would just go walk off around St. Vincent campus. I'm like, "What is this dude doing?" Now I understand that was his peace and his solace and this is who he was. His faith was so significant and important to him that it was above everything else that was going on, no matter what he was doing, what his stature was, how much money he had, what team he was playing for. His faith was first and foremost in his heart, and that's what he was going to do. He was just going to serve.

PORTER: Even with his mistakes, the flashes Troy would show in practice were something none of the other safeties could do. They couldn't run like he ran. That was back when we had those old-school two-a-days. He filled holes like they couldn't. He did a lot of things they couldn't do, and you could see it.

The preseason saw Troy Polamalu grab the third safety spot in the new nickel defense the Steelers were patterning after the world champion Buccaneers.

Their nickel defense was designed to A.) keep Kendrell Bell on the field as a second inside linebacker with James Farrior, and B.) use Polamalu as a slot corner to cover Todd Heap of the Ravens in the opener.

The Steelers had used the dime as their primary – and usually only – sub-package on passing downs throughout Bill Cowher's tenure. By the second preseason game, Polamalu had taken the dime spot away from Chris Hope. That position had Polamalu lining up deep next to Brent Alexander, while the other starting safety, Mike Logan, moved into the box as a dimebacker next to Joey Porter.

Cowher gave Polamalu as much playing time in the preseason as he could, and he led the Steelers with 17 total tackles.

In other team developments, Jerome Bettis was benched in favor of Amos Zeroue at running back, and Mark Bruener lost his starting tight end job to free-agent acquisition Jay Riemersma. And James Harrison – the runaway leader in special teams tackles – was cut for a second time, which, as Joey Porter would say 12 years later, didn't sit well with some of the veterans.

PORTER: We were actually pissed. Not to take anything away from Matt Cushing, but one year we kept four tight ends. We cut (Harrison) and kept Cushing twice. We were like, "How can you tell me Cushing's a better special teams player than Harrison?" We were always mad, especially because of The Cowher Rule: I won't get rid of good special teams players. And he did it twice. So that caught us off guard. The second time we released him and brought in Erik Flowers, and he was terrible. He was like trippin' over the bags. We were like, "We let Deebo go for him?"

Polamalu didn't create a turnover or tackle-for-loss in the four preseason games. And while he routinely beat the rest of his teammates down the field in kick coverage, he made only two special teams tackles.

Polamalu himself was unimpressed with his play.

"Everything's coming so slow," he said. "Hopefully, I can get better, but this probably isn't permanent anyway. It's probably just to give me a look at seeing what it's like to play with the first team."

HOPE: We had Mike Logan and Brent Alexander starting at safety and me and Troy as the backups. The only part that made it difficult for me was that I couldn't play until Troy played. If I played and Troy didn't play, it would look like "Why did we waste that draft pick when we already had Chris Hope on the roster from last year?" I understood, but I was 22 years old. I felt I was ready, but I was nowhere near ready yet. Later I appreciated that they had so much talent and could let a young guy grow up and learn the game before they put him out there.

LOGAN: People were talking about the mistakes Troy was making early on, but nobody walks into the Pittsburgh Steelers as a defensive back and just picks it up. There are a lot of things that go into our defensive schemes, especially for a guy who has the range he has. They're going to ask you to do a lot and expect you to know a lot and move you around in different positions. I was impressed with him on the field, but more so off the field. We would go out as defensive backs on our days off. Gather and things happen. But Troy wasn't a participant in that. He was going to stick to the integrity of who he was and what he believed in. I admired that. So here you had the old guy learning something from the new dog, and he didn't even know.

PORTER: Brent Alexander and Mike Logan were smart guys who knew the defense, but you knew how Troy and C Hope were, and that was going to be the tandem. It was just a matter of time.

LOGAN: I called one of my friends and said, "Man, this young man is going to be a helluva ballplayer because he's got it together." He had a level of maturity that I don't think I had until maybe four, five, six years into the league. That thoroughly impressed me. It got to the point where I was taking heed of some of his actions. I saw that his faith was a high priority on his list, and I said I have to structure myself a little bit. I have to change. And I really re-dedicated myself to my faith and started reading my Bible again and started getting involved in some of my church ministries. That was like a light for me. One of the scriptures that I kind of had taken from my times and observation of Troy was Psalm 1:1, "Blessed is the man who does not walk in the counsel of the wicked or stand in the way of sinners or sit in the seat of mockers." I thought, OK, maybe I need to change my environment.

The 2003 season quickly became a pain in the ass for Joey Porter. The Steelers' defensive captain went into a Denver bar after his alma mater, Colorado State, played rival Colorado, and he was shot in the rear end.

It occurred in the parking lot and was considered by police to be a random, gang-style shooting in which one person was killed. Porter was among five injured.

"I think my night life is over," the 26-year-old said at the time. Bill Cowher announced the injury would keep Porter out two to eight weeks, and it was clear Porter would miss the opener four days later against the Baltimore Ravens.

The Steelers beat the Ravens 34-15, so Porter wasn't missed. Neither was he forgotten as he and Ravens linebacker Ray Lewis engaged in both pre-game and post-game squabbles.

Troy Polamalu had no tackles as the nickel back in the Steelers' 5-DB alignment, which was used extensively against the Ravens' TE-driven offense.

Todd Heap caught six passes for 55 yards, and Ravens rookie QB Kyle Boller was fairly impressive, but it was the Steelers' day at Heinz Field.

Plaxico Burress caught six passes for 116 yards and Hines Ward caught nine passes for 91 yards and two touchdowns to help QB Tommy Maddox win AFC Offensive Player of the Week.

The line of the day belonged to Ravens CB Chris McAlister, who had criticized the Steelers' wide receivers during the week. McAlister turned to Ward during the game and said, "I respect the shit out of you." An official overheard the vulgarity but not the context and penalized the Ravens 15 yards.

As for Polamalu, he spoke the same way he did as a freshman at Douglas High, and as he would after his final game in 2014.

"We won," he said. "That's what's important. But I made a lot of mistakes."

The next Sunday the Kansas City Chiefs hammered the Steelers 41-20 at Arrowhead Stadium.

TAYLOR: Dante Hall lit fire on us in Kansas City. I think he ran two back (3-146-1 KRs/4-62 PRs). They called him "Human Joy Stick." I remember we had really good special teams, but that day the Human Joy Stick caught fire and Troy felt like he didn't have a good game. He and I were talking and he was like, "Man, there's pressure out there." And I said, "They got us here for a reason. Every time ain't gonna be like how you want it. They got us here for a reason, man. We're going to ride this season out and we'll come back next year."

MERRILL HOGE, *former Steelers running back:* Troy Polamalu's the first player I ever saw on tape literally stand there when the ball got snapped because he didn't know what was going on. It was his rookie year against the Chiefs. He went out on motion and a linebacker hit him on the side of the head, telling him to go back because he was doing the wrong thing. They snapped the ball and he was just lost. It spoke to two things: The complexity of this league, and how much harder the transition from safety to the NFL is than from corner. Safeties have to understand motions and shifts.

COWHER: That was James Harrison his first year. James used to just stop in the middle of a play in practice and it drove me crazy. I said, "Just make a decision and go with it." Seriously. Be decisive. Don't be hesitant. And if you're wrong, we'll correct you.

PORTER: There have been plenty times where we would have to help Troy out. This was before he was good enough to want to switch with you, like once we got to play with each other a few years. As he got into his second year, he would make a mistake but he would make up for it in the same game. He would have a bust, then come up and make a turnover or a big third-down stop or something, and you would be like, "Man, he paid it back." That first year, Cowher didn't really worry about it. Neither did Tim. We played it. Our defense has always been complex, but the coordinators wanted us to have access to our whole playbook. Some coaches say things like, "OK, this guy doesn't know this, we can only go in with this." But we played it and everybody had to be ready for it. That got Troy a little bit early in his career, but once he picked it up, man, it became what it did. He definitely went through his growing pains. He and Kendrell Bell were the only two guys in our defense that we were OK with them making mistakes. We still wanted them on the field. That just does not happen. I've been on that defense and you get bawled out when you mess up. But we weren't in a rush to push either one of them off the field.

The lament about an offensive change in philosophy was already underway in 2003, courtesy of Ward. But the Steelers got back to their basics against the Cincinnati Bengals. So much so that Alan Faneca was nominated by Cowher for AFC Offensive Player of the Week after the left guard's dominating performance in a 17-10 Steelers win.

"I have never seen a game by an offensive lineman any better than that," Cowher said.

ALAN FANECA, *Steelers left guard (1998-07):* Yeah, those couple of years were my sweet spot. That year I had to play some left tackle, too, and I always gave Marvel (Smith) shit after that. "Man, that was the easiest year in my career. You guys are stealing money." I was fresh on Mondays, not in there banging. Tackle's easy.

Cowher was asked a couple of days later at his weekly press conference to provide "a preliminary report" on Polamalu's progress. The rookie made two tackles on defense and a special teams tackle against the Bengals.

"I think Troy's doing fine," Cowher said. "It's just the expectation level. People say 'What's wrong with him?' and 'He's not starting' and 'Number one pick.' Mike is playing pretty well. Troy plays in all the dime and nickel packages. He's playing safety in those. Then last week when Mike doesn't practice, he moves up to the dime (linebacker). It can happen that quickly in a game. We've got him playing a bunch of different positions. But he's doing fine. I mean, he had a tough day the other day but that's to be expected."

Cowher also blamed the example set by the Steelers' new punt gunner, Chidi Iwouma, for Troy trying to do too much on special teams.

"He's trying for the Chidi kill," Cowher said in reference to a big tackle Iwuoma had made in the opener.

Tim Lewis, the defensive coordinator, castigated the media.

"They don't have a clue," Lewis said as he gestured toward the media room at the Steelers' practice facility. "Somebody read something to me today that said Troy looked lost. Look, he's way better than he's ever been. He's doing a great job. He's very instinctive and he'll be light years ahead down the road. I think the way we're doing it will be good for him. We're bringing him along slowly, the way (Cincinnati Coach) Marvin (Lewis) is doing with Carson Palmer. But we're getting him some time in the nickel and dime. He'll be fine."

Marvel Smith broke a 45-game streak of consecutive starts when he missed Game 4 against the Tennessee Titans because of a pinched nerve in his back. The 30-13 home loss was a precursor of what was to come. The Steelers would go on to lose eight of the 11 games Smith, their left tackle, missed.

Polamalu made a critical mistake against the Titans. He gave away his lone blitz attempt too early on a third-and-4 play. He was stopped by the left tackle and in frustration flipped the tackle by the facemask.

The penalty helped the Titans score a touchdown three plays later for a 23-13 lead early in the third quarter.

LOGAN: He might've been overwhelmed. He was playing safety in the sub-packages and linebacker in the dime. He could cover in the slots, plus rush from the dime position and get pressure on the quarterback so efficiently and effectively, they were like, "We're going to move this guy all the way around." And then even on the back end, from him being the support strong safety and moving up into the box, and then you're moving the free safety and he's got enough speed and range to cover from the middle of the field to the sideline, so you're like, "Where can we put this guy so he can have success?" When you're basically the jack of all trades – well, I won't say master of none because he eventually mastered **that** strong safety position quite well – but he came in as a jack of all trades and they were trying him at every position. That's a lot of different terminology.

COWHER: I probably did him more of a disservice because we put him in so many positions. It was a tough year, but I wanted him to understand conceptually what we were doing because he could do all these things for you. Each week it could be something different depending on how you want to match him up. We probably put him in a lot of situations where he made a lot of mistakes early because he only knew how to play a certain way. But because of that, he evolved and began understanding the defense so well that you then could utilize that skill set he had and it made him a special player. But he had to go through growing pains to understand exactly what his role was. We didn't clearly define it because it really changed week to week.

MILLER: Those same offensive coaches from the draft were killing me that year. And I said, "Guys, our defense is a little complex. It's going to take him at least a year to get it figured it out." I reminded them I said he'd be in the Pro Bowl his second year. And you could see him going through that process. I know he was really frustrated. But you could see glimpses of his potential that first year. I mean, it's the NFL. It's tough.

After four games, the Steelers had the No. 2 pass defense in the league, and assumed they were ready for Tim Couch and the Cleveland Browns.

They were not. Couch, the No. 1 pick of the 1999 draft, enjoyed his last NFL hurrah in a 33-13 Browns romp, dropping the Steelers to 2-3.

The poor play of the inexperienced offensive tackles, and the struggles of right guard Kendall Simmons, recently diagnosed with diabetes, led to a poor performance by the offense as Tommy Maddox surged to the AFC lead with eight interceptions – three were returned for touchdowns, a fourth to the Pittsburgh 1.

The Steelers next hosted Denver without injured QB Jake Plummer, but his replacement, 38-year-old Steve Beuerlein, threw a pair of touchdown passes in a 17-14 Broncos win.

The Steelers entered their bye week with a 2-4 record. So, they practiced. Polamalu was on the scout team, where he had a hard time doing the job right – because that sometimes meant allowing the offense to succeed.

TAYLOR: Me, Troy, Deshea Townsend and Chris Hope were all on the scout team together. That's where it started, on the scout team. We were going against Plax, Antwaan Randle El, Hines Ward. Ain't had no choice but to get better.

HOPE: Troy didn't believe in false advertising, so he didn't really like reading a card on the scout team, doing what's on the card and giving the offense a false sense of security. Those cards they drew up in practice were designed to make the offense succeed. As young guys, we had to give the offense a look, and ironically that's the starting secondary that won the Super Bowl a few years later. But we were the scout team then, and as a result we grew the biggest climbs ever up the board on those scout team practices every day, because we told ourselves that we were going to challenge Plaxico Burress and Hines Ward. We were going to check those guys. We were going to dominate those guys. And sometimes the cards were designed to let the offense win, and Troy never did that. His punishment was to wake up early in the morning and look how the play was supposed to have been run and how he messed it up.

PERRY: I remember meeting with Troy at 6:30 in the morning watching practice tape from when he was on the look team. He was out there just being Troy. I said "Troy you can't do this. You've got to read the card and do what it tells you because you're trying to show our offense what our opposition is going to be doing, and you're not giving us the look. You're hurting us right now." I remember

Thursday and Friday being up extra early watching practice tape of our scout team, not our opponent.

HOPE: That's Troy: "I'm not practicing those bad habits just to get them some self-esteem and make them feel they're doing it right." He didn't do that. He was going to play football and use his natural instincts. As a result, he got better.

PORTER: Even on the bad plays you still saw the flash from Troy. And even when Ike and C Hope were young, you saw the flash of their potential. So even when it wouldn't translate to game day, you would see those guys do things in practice that would make you say, "You know, that was pretty good right there."

HOPE: Me and Troy learned so much about each other being on the scout team. That's where I learned who Troy Polamalu was; that's where he learned who Chris Hope was. We bonded as real brothers.

They were critical weeks in the formation of an elite, dominating NFL defense that would lead the Steelers to two championships in the coming five years. But there was something else that occurred in those few weeks in the middle of the 2003 season that was equally significant.

KENETI POLAMALU: It was after the Denver game and I'm still at USC. It was a Sunday and we played and I'm now going in, and I was listening to the radio and they were just ripping him. I guess he made some penalties and they were just ripping him, "Wasted draft pick!" Jumping down on him on the Steelers radio. I don't know who it was, but they were just speaking their disappointment that he wasn't panning out. If you remember, they didn't really play him much. He was playing behind Logan. Then I realized, I looked at the film and he had his hair tucked up in his helmet. So I caught him when he was on the bus. You know, he's disappointed and I can feel it in his voice, "How you feeling? What's going on?" And I said, "I noticed something there, Troy. You're not yourself. What's going on?" And I said, "You've got to let your hair down, man. They knew you had long hair when they drafted you. Just let it out. Just be yourself." I didn't believe there was a rule, so I said, "Hey, be yourself. Let it go. Be a free spirit. Play with the energy and the spirit and the Samoan fire that you have."

It would become one of the great pep talks in Pittsburgh Steelers history.

CHAPTER II

SAMOAN FIRE

The struggles of Troy Polamalu's rookie year would become fodder for national media through three Super Bowls.

"There's a funny story," he said from the podium at Super Bowl 45 in 2011. "I came to Pittsburgh on a visit, and I came from Southern California. I remember calling my agent and I said, 'There's no way I can fit in here. There's no way I could come here. It's cold. It's dreary. It's rainy.'

"And then when I was drafted here my rookie year, it was very tough. The whole culture was tough for me, for one. But then the media was very tough on me mainly. I remember telling my wife, 'There's no way I'll ever live here. And if I ever want to live here, then you should slap me.'

"And then, like three years ago, I was telling my wife, 'So do you want to settle down somewhere in like Sewickley or something?'"

Polamalu laughed before finishing.

"And she said, 'Well, maybe.'"

They did settle down in the north Pittsburgh suburb of Pine Township. The weather? It didn't get any better. But the culture? The media?

"Yeah, you guys were tough on me," he said. "It was deserving, though. I didn't play very well at all."

Yet, as the weather got worse his rookie year, Polamalu got better.

He had been waiting for his first start to do as his Uncle Keneti suggested and "Let your hair down, man." But that first start wasn't coming anytime soon.

Even though changes were being made as Steelers losses piled up, Polamalu was still performing his slot duties in the nickel and splitting between deep safety and linebacker in the dime.

"He's progressing," Tim Lewis said after a game in which a potential big play slipped through Polamalu's hands for a Rams touchdown.

"He just needs to make a play," Lewis said. "He needs to make a play for his own confidence."

The entire team needed a shot of confidence. A five-game losing streak had the Steelers at 2-6 at the midway point of the season, their worst first half since 1988.

A win over Dexter Jackson and the Cardinals snapped the skid, and the Steelers prepared for a Monday night game in San Francisco against the 4-5 49ers.

Deshea Townsend had replaced Dewayne Washington at right cornerback, and Ike Taylor received praise for his work in sub-packages as he was moved into Townsend's old role.

Townsend actually made two of the game's biggest plays in the win over the Cardinals. Chris Hope played, too, and was spotted getting a chest bump from Bill Cowher after one play.

The greatest scout team secondary in Pittsburgh history was moving up in class, and the youngsters were gaining respect.

In an unofficial poll taken in the locker room the week after the Arizona win, players were asked about the hardest hits of the season.

Polamalu, Taylor and Hope were named, along with Clint Kriewaldt, Larry Foote, Clark Haggans and Lee Mays.

Only one player was named by everyone polled.

"Chidi," said Hope. "He's an assassin."

"Chidi just got back from Iraq," said Plaxico Burress.

"Chidi Iwuoma plays fast and with utter disregard," said special teams coach Kevin Spencer.

Polamalu showed some utter disregard on the opening kickoff Monday night in San Francisco. He was first down the field, hit return man Cedrick Wilson, lifted him off the ground and planted him on his back.

There was something else about Troy that night, something he would later call "my fifth appendage ... part of my identity, a part of my body."

It was his hair. It was flowing out from under his helmet like a Samoan war flag.

TROY POLAMALU: My goal was not to let it down until I actually started a game. But when I went there, being back in California really made me feel back home, and it was really where I felt I could finally let myself loose and start playing ball like I always wanted to. I never had any hesitation in anything, so it's a good memory.

DARREN PERRY: When we were in warm-ups in San Francisco, so much was going through his mind and he had his hair tucked up under his helmet. I said, "Troy, let's get out there and play, let's just have some fun." And he said, "Coach, I'm letting my hair down tonight." That was the first indication that he's going to finally try to be himself and not try to do too much and not play so uptight. We ended up losing but I think he was telling everybody, "Hey, I'm going to be Troy now."

At 3-7, Cowher simplified his approach in preparation for the game in Cleveland, and told his defense to simply "hit harder."

It worked. Kendrell Bell and Joey Porter both forced turnovers with big hits, as the Steelers forced five in a 13-6 win.

Hope also made a big hit that impressed Cowher so much he moved the second-year safety into the sub-packages full-time ahead of Mike Logan.

It didn't pay immediate dividends as the Steelers fell to 4-8 with a loss the following week to the Jon Kitna-led Bengals. One Steelers coach confided that the Steelers made eight defensive breakdowns in the loss, and that veteran cornerback Chad Scott made four of those. Scott was placed on injured reserve later in the week and was done for the season.

The Steelers rebounded at home with a 27-7 win over a Raiders team that was called "the dumbest team in America" the previous week by its own coach, Bill Callahan. That kept the Steelers' playoff chances mathematically alive at 5-8, but, realistically, thoughts among fans and media turned to the end of the college football season in anticipation of a potential top-10 draft pick.

Veteran Steelers scout Mark Gorscak sat down with this beat reporter in the middle of the week to watch some MAC-tion involving Miami (Ohio) quarterback Ben Roethlisberger.

MG: You can't pass on a franchise quarterback. You get a guy like Roethlisberger here, he keeps the sticks moving. All of the sudden your line looks better, your defense looks better.
Is he better than Eli Manning?
Manning's the top guy. You have to look at that team he's on. They don't have much, and they're not in the MAC, either. He's their team.
He looks immobile.
He can move. And that fifth year is big. That's what the other guy (Roethlisberger) lacks. Quarterbacks mature so much in that fifth year.
How high will they go?
Manning's a top-5 guy and Roethlisberger's in the top 10. Look at him up there.
He looks like Jim Kelly.
I see some Elway in his movements. Look at the way he bounces out of his drop.

What about the other guys, J.P. Losman and Philip Rivers?
I love Rivers.
And?
Isn't that enough?

To Gorscak, the secondary wasn't much of a draft need. Townsend was proving to be the team's best cover man and Taylor was showing enough potential to handle the other cornerback spot.

"Ike's coming along," Gorscak said. "So is Troy. Those guys are in the nickel and dime, which is just right for them right now. Troy's really coming on. You're going to be surprised when you see him next year."

The mathematics for a playoff berth dissipated the following week in a 6-0 loss to the New York Jets. But the mathematics for nabbing one of the three potential franchise quarterbacks improved, and the shutout at The Meadowlands screamed for such improvement.

Meanwhile, the first of many awards throughout Polamalu's NFL career began rolling in that week when he was voted the Steelers Rookie of the Year by local writers. It produced the first of many acceptance speeches that rang out with humility and bordered on embarrassment.

"Quite honestly," said Polamalu, "I was really the only rookie that played this year."

The only competitor – the only other rookie to play since the first game of the season – was Taylor, who finished a distant second.

"I would like to thank God," Polamalu said, "not particularly for the award but because the beginning of the season for me was pretty rough with learning everything and not actually playing very well. I really started to feel comfortable late in the season."

MIKE LOGAN: Late in that first year he was starting to get it. He started thinking a little out of the box, too. They moved me to free in one of the sub-packages and he was playing strong, and I remember we were supposed to be playing half coverage on the field, but he's up at the line of scrimmage and the quarterback is in his cadence. I'm like there's no way in hell he's getting back to his half of the field. They were getting ready to snap the ball, and literally a half second before the snap he makes a bee-line dart to get to the half side of this field, and he does it. I'm almost in bad position because I'm thinking I'll have to cover the middle of the field to even get a chance to get over there. But he was able to do it. We got back to the huddle and I said, "Troy, dude, I'm an older man. You almost gave me a heart attack. You

148

can NOT be at the line of scrimmage when you've got half field." He said, "I got it covered, man. I got it covered."

JOEY PORTER: It started happening for him right about then. We would watch film and everybody would be like, "Did he just beat me on a play underneath to a back?" He has the B gap or the C gap and he'll be blitzing through there, and out of nowhere, right before you would make the tackle, he'd beat you to the tackle. That type of play just lifted everybody on the team. Here's this young player who already knows where the ball's going. Look how fast he's playing. As a professional, you never want to be outdone by another player, so he made everybody step their game up even more. That's the first thing he brought to the defense. You could see it was going to be different. Like, man, they made a great pick with that one.

In the following week's game against San Diego, Polamalu made his first game-wrecking play, and it may have done more for the future of the Pittsburgh Steelers than anyone realized at the time.

The Chargers entered 3-11 and had changed quarterbacks the previous week from 41-year-old Doug Flutie back to youngster Drew Brees. The Chargers were 1-8 in games started by Brees, their second-round draft pick in 2001, and were losing faith in him as the QB of their future.

Polamalu didn't help their thinking.

The Chargers rallied from a 21-0 deficit to trail 21-17 early in the third quarter. They had the ball on their 25 on third-and-10 when Polamalu blitzed off the defense's left edge. He was pushed well behind Brees, who stepped up into the pocket for more comfort, but Polamalu came like a blur and hacked Brees' right arm to force a fumble. Townsend recovered and two plays later Hines Ward was in the end zone and a 40-24 Steelers rout ensued.

Chargers coach Marty Schottenheimer pulled Brees later in the game and the two engaged in a shouting match on the sideline. The Chargers, of course, came out of the next draft with Rivers as their QB of the future. That left the Steelers with the underclassman from the MAC.

CHRIS HOPE: We had an exit meeting after the season and I sat down with Coach Cowher before I went home. My last game was a Sunday night game against the Baltimore Ravens. Troy and I played a lot in the packages. I played pretty well, scored a long touchdown on a fake punt. Coach Cowher sat down and said he learned a lot about who I was as a football player and said "You're ready. This offseason you work hard like you've always done and we'll look at you again." He pretty much gave me the go-ahead, the green light, that it was my time, that he was going to give me my chance.

PERRY: I remember Bill asking me distinctly during the offseason, when we were putting together our depth chart, "Troy Polamalu and Chris Hope are going to be our starting safeties next year?" And I said "Coach, they're ready." That was the same year I'd gotten promoted to the secondary job. I remember telling them at our first meeting that this had to work out. I said, "Guys, we've got a lot to prove this year." I said, "Hey, my ass is on the line, too, because if you guys don't step up I may not be here."

KENETI POLAMALU: At the end of that first season I told Troy, "Hey, I want you to stay back there. I want you to work out. I want you to prove to the organization that you're a Steeler." Then he called me. First I had to roll my window up because I'm in nice 80-degree weather in Southern California, and he's like, "Uncle, it is so cold here." I had never coached in the NFL, so I didn't know that, boom, in the NFL they're all gone. And I'm making him stay there to prove himself. I told him to go talk to Coach Cowher and talk to the Rooneys. He went in there and Mr. Rooney said, "Troy, what are you doing here? Get out of here. Go do Hawaii." So, that tells you not all of my advice was on the money.

There are said to be three distinct teachers needed for the development of a successful person's craft. Troy found his third teacher, his polisher, the man who turned him into a Hall of Famer, soon after the 2003 season ended in Dick LeBeau.

It all happened so suddenly, and surprisingly, as if prayer was working behind the scenes.

Bill Cowher had no intention of firing defensive coordinator Tim Lewis, but after the loss to the Ravens in the Steelers' season finale in Baltimore, Lewis was overheard at the exit telling people goodbye, that he would soon be fired after the 6-10 season.

Dan Rooney was asked the next day about Lewis' replacement, and that was the first Rooney had heard of any departure involving Lewis, who still had a year left on his contract.

Rooney informed Cowher, who verified the behavior, called Lewis into his office and fulfilled his defensive coordinator's prophesy by firing him.

Lewis, who had pushed the hardest for James Farrior over Earl Holmes, had pushed the most for Deshea Townsend over DeWayne Washington, coordinator of the No. 9 overall defense in 2003, was suddenly gone.

LeBeau had left Cowher on bad terms in 1997, with LeBeau leaving a championship-level defense and team for the same job with the .500 Bengals.

But Cowher showed a championship-level maturity in reaching out to LeBeau eight years later.

LeBeau was pondering retirement in Buffalo while working as a consultant for the Tom Donahoe's Bills. Cowher called LeBeau, assured him the defense would be his, and asked him to return.

LeBeau drove to Pittsburgh from his home in London, Ohio, and attended a University of Pittsburgh basketball game the night before his interview with Cowher.

"About 25 people said, 'Good luck tomorrow, coach. Come on back,'" said LeBeau. "I was thinking that this is pretty neat. I haven't been in this city for seven years and there are not very many towns in the country that would recognize me and be so supportive. That did make the whole thing feel like going back to a place where I had been before."

LeBeau accepted the job on Jan. 16, 2004, 10 days after the firing of Lewis.

TROY POLAMALU: When Coach Lewis got fired, the first thing I did was call Coach Perry to see what the situation was and to wish good luck to Coach Lewis. Coach Perry told me about some of the other guys they were thinking about, but he was hoping Coach LeBeau would get the job. All he talked about was his character and how he was like a father to him and how I would love to play for him as well. And I think I'm very similar to the type of person Coach Perry is, so I could obviously take his words for it and so I was on his side all the way.

CHRIS HOKE: It was great for the franchise to get their quarterback that offseason, but, really, the key to our success in '04 was our defense. I think in '04 we were number one in the NFL in almost every category that was important. And Troy was a *huuuuuge* part of that. That was the year he came out. And I think a big reason behind that was Dick LeBeau. LeBeau is the best. There was a different mentality in our defense.

DONNIE SHELL: *Steelers strong safety (1974-87):* A lot of coordinators want you to fit into their schemes, but (LeBeau) fit the scheme around Polamalu. You see the results when a coach or a defensive coordinator thinks more about the team and the ability of the player rather than you coming up in a game plan and you fitting into the scheme of the defensive coordinator. He fit the scheme around him and he really excelled at it.

LOGAN: I wouldn't say he changed things, at least not when I was there. He created different defenses because of the ability of Troy. We had our zone blitz down and all of our blitzes in packages together. But he definitely created new defenses because he had that playmaking ability. I've seen Coach LeBeau come to the sideline and draw up a defense. We would put it in our mental rolodex and go out there and operate it positionally. That might've had something to do with the way Troy played in 2004.

DICK LEBEAU, *Steelers defensive coordinator (1995-96/2004-14):* I had some experience with big defensive backs, and I would call Troy big. He's 210 pounds. So, I knew there was a spot in our defense for someone like that. Carnell, Rod, they were big, fast guys. I thought Troy should be able to take that role, and he did from Day One. He was always attentive, approached his profession like he wanted to go to the top – which he eventually did – but I mean there was no great revelation or anything. He fit the mold of Steeler DBs. I didn't know everything about his first year. It's not unusual for players to come from college into the NFL and have a little transition stage in there.

TROY POLAMALU: Of course, everything worked out for us. He's such a great guy to play for and is definitely one of my top two favorite coaches I've ever played for.

LEBEAU: From a coaching standpoint, Troy presents a dilemma. He's so good at everything. He's gifted at the line. He can blitz. He can read runs and blow them up for negative plays. He's a great interceptor. He erases big plays because of his diagnostic ability and his speed. And as a coach you're a little perplexed. If you keep him in the back, he's going to cut down the big plays, but then he can't blitz and make those plays. If you blitz him, they run away from him. But it's hard to run away from him when you've got him back in the middle of the field; he can just get to everything. You try to figure out a balance there. Fortunately Troy is very unselfish. He'll go wherever we put him. I should say he'll start wherever you put him. He may end up somewhere totally different. It didn't take me long to realize he's a joy to coach.

CARNELL LAKE, *(Steelers DB 1989-98/DBs coach 2011-17)*: The bottom line is LeBeau's defense allows flexibility for Troy to do what he does. The biggest part of the defense for a playmaker was LeBeau's willingness to let Troy improvise, as long as it didn't hurt the overall scheme. I think that's why Troy was able to develop into an artist at what he does.

LEBEAU: The defense very much went through a transitional stage in '04. At one point we had seven new starters because Casey (Hampton) got hurt that year. Ike had not started; Deshea had only started two or three games; Troy had not started; Chris had not started; Larry Foote had not started; James Farrior was in his third year here; Chris Hoke started most of the year for Casey. I've never seen a defense with that many new faces on it. Every one of them turned out to be an outstanding player, which doesn't happen very often.

AARON SMITH, *Steelers defensive end (1999-11):* I really like the changes LeBeau brought, the attitude he brought. The man had been in the league 40-some years and still had that enthusiasm and youthfulness and attitude. Every day we went out there the man was hootin' and hollerin' during warm-up stretches. He just enjoyed the game. It wasn't a job. He loved the game. I think you can't help but get infected with that.

HOKE: We're working in OTAs that first spring and we have this play called "tight close zebra zone y." That calls for me as a nose tackle to play the A gap away from the tight end side, the closed side. The closed side/tight end side defensive end is supposed to scoop, long scoop, down into that A gap. I'm supposed to play the open side, the A gap away from the tight end. Play the run first, and when I recognize it's pass there's a call – Lou or Roy. If it's Lou, it's the left side of the strength; Roy is the right side of the strength. Whatever call it is, I drop to the opposite. So the ball's snapped, I step into the open-side A gap, I lock out my center, and I think it's a pass so I turned to run to drop to the weak hook, right? But as soon as I open up to turn, it's a draw. It's a run. I go to turn around and I get knocked off the ball three or four yards and they go for a gain. It wasn't a big deal in OTAs, in terms of how far he went, but I yell, "Freak!" Now in years past, I get cussed out after that kind of mistake. But Dick Lebeau comes out to me and said, "Hokie, listen, that's a tough one. Just be a little more patient. Just sit in there a little longer, and you'll be fine." And that was it. He walked away and I went "Bro!" In the past, when we watched film on that stuff, I would get chewed out by Tim, and then (line coach John) Mitch(ell) would come down on me. It was like a double whammy. So I'm sitting there in film, the first OTA with Dick LeBeau. The play comes up. I'm sweating bullets, and Mitch says, "Hokie!" and Dick says, "Hey, Johnny, I've already talked to him about it. Hokie, this is the one we were talking about." And then we went on to the next play, and I'm like "This is awesome." That's the kind of guy he was. He was a coach. He was a teacher. That's the way he treated everybody. He endeared himself to everybody. We loved him so much. That was, I believe, THE change from '03 to '04. People were able to relax and just play, rather than going out there being scared to make a mistake.

One of the Cleveland Browns beat reporters tells the story of sitting in then-Browns coach Butch Davis' office when an ESPN feature on Ben Roethlisberger appeared on the screen. The reporter asked Davis what he thought of Ben.

"Not a fan," muttered Davis.

Soon thereafter, Davis became not a coach. He was fired after 11 games of the 2004 season with Kellen Winslow II, the sixth pick of the draft, sitting on five catches and 34-year-old free agent QB Jeff Garcia sitting on three wins.

The Browns, of course, had passed on the Ohio born and bred Roethlisberger for Winslow because they already had Garcia.

Going into the 2004 draft, the Steelers rated Roethlisberger and Philip Rivers equally, and figured Eli Manning would be long gone by the 11th pick.

The Steelers also liked cornerback Dunta Robinson and offensive lineman Shawn Andrews. As draft day drew near, the Steelers' interest in Andrews increased, but wiser heads prevailed.

Steelers GM Kevin Colbert was bubbling with enthusiasm as he greeted the media after picking Roethlisberger.

"We think this kid's potential is unlimited," Colbert said. "I don't even think he's scratched the surface yet."

The Steelers traded up in the second round for cornerback Ricardo Colclough and drafted massive offensive tackle Max Starks in the third round. The rest of the choices proved rather insignificant – until after the draft.

DICK HOAK, *Steelers running backs coach (1972-06):* After the draft you start to call free agents. They give you a list of people to call and you work with one of the scouts, and I worked with Dan Rooney, Jr. So I came out of the draft meeting and after about 10 minutes he comes down the hall and said, "Hey, I got your two backs. We don't have to sign anybody else." One was Willie Parker and I forget the other name. But I said, "Who's Willie Parker?" He said, "This is a kid I watched in high school who went to North Carolina. He never played but I think he should've gotten a chance."

By the time the 2004 season started, the Steelers had four new starters: Troy Polamalu and Chris Hope replaced Mike Logan and Brent Alexander at the safety positions; Clark Haggans replaced Jason Gildon at left outside linebacker; and Chris Gardocki replaced Josh Miller at punter. The Steelers also signed Duce Staley to replace Amos Zeroue as the complement to Jerome Bettis in the backfield.

The Steelers promoted tight ends coach Ken Whisenhunt to replace the departed Mike Mularkey as offensive coordinator, opposite new defensive coordinator Dick LeBeau.

Cowher hired another defensive assistant. He promoted Darren Perry to replace Willie Robinson as DBs coach, and filled Perry's job with Ray Horton, and the groundwork was laid for the Steelers to forget their 6-10 2003 season.

PORTER: In 2003? Six and 10? Man, I have a short memory. I remember thinking we had a good defense. We had won with Tommy the year before, and when Troy started playing with abandon that meant everybody was coming along. Casey Hampton had turned into a monster. Me and Aaron had been there since 1998. Kimo (von Oelhoffen). Farrior. We felt like our defense was ready. We were missing a couple of pieces, and with Jerome and the offensive line, man, I totally forgot about 6 and 10. I was ready to argue with you. Wow.

It was a year Porter could forget some 17 years later because it might've been his worst year personally and professionally. His five sacks were the fewest in what became 11 NFL seasons as a starter, and personally, as teammate Brett Keisel dryly noted, "Speaking as a hunter who's seen butts get shot, I could understand his difficulties."

Porter would return with a vengeance in 2004. Good health was also returning to the offensive line. But one injury cropped up that would come to completely alter the Steelers' defense.

Haggans broke his hand lifting weights in the offseason. Said Cowher: "It's a golden opportunity for Alonzo Jackson and (fifth-round pick Nathaniel) Adibi."

Cowher made no mention of a player he had cut two seasons running, James Harrison.

The Steelers did sign Harrison to replace Haggans on the roster and gave him Gildon's No 92, but Harrison remained just a camp body as the Steelers added veteran OLB Adrian Ross following another injury.

The hordes that attended practice at St. Vincent College to watch rookie QB Ben Roethlisberger rarely saw the work put in by Troy Polamalu. The phrase "Champions are made when no one's watching" suited the second-year safety.

After morning practice, he stayed an extra half hour to catch balls off the JUGS machine, or sometimes, all alone on the field, pushed a blocking sled up the hill. There were also strolls around campus during which he would pray. Or, he would find a comfortable spot to watch film.

HOKE: Troy was a studier. He was one of the first guys who had an I-pad. He watched film on it. You would see all the studying, the extra time. It was important to him. People thought he was just guessing. The instincts that he had came from preparation, too. He had a whole offseason to really study the defense, and study film, and that's why you saw such a huge jump from '03 to '04.

LOGAN: One day after practice he was throwing the ball with my son Trey, who was six. There weren't a lot of fans out there but Troy was doing what he was doing after practice: going through his drops, getting extra conditioning. Meanwhile I'm up on the hill entertaining friends, and I remember my son being down on the field with Troy playing with him. The media cameras were coming down and he waved them away. I thought, "Wow, this dude went down there after practice, put in his conditioning, worked on his technique, and then he took the time out to play with my son."

ALAN FANECA: You could just tell he was more comfortable that camp. He just had a better feel for things going into the year. He was moving a lot faster and making decisions. Some of those early beginnings of Troy making those crazy reads, of being able to see things before they happen, were starting to peek out a little bit. When you look between Year 1 and Year 2, that's when he just exploded.

CHAPTER 12

CELLULOID HEROES

Willie Parker led the Steelers in preseason rushing by nearly twice as many yards as the next best rusher, and nearly three times the totals of Duce Staley and Jerome Bettis.

It earned Parker the label of "camp surprise" by Bill Cowher and the nickname of "Fast Willie Parker" by the team newspaper, *Steelers Digest*.

Cowher didn't take his infatuation with Parker too far, though. The coach named Staley the starter for the opener against the Oakland Raiders and decided that Bettis would be the team's short-yardage specialist and game closer.

The NFL's worst running game in 2003 opened 2004 sluggishly with 107 yards on 33 carries (3.2 ypc.) in a 24-21 win over the Oakland Raiders, and Bettis' unique game line pretty much defined his new role: 5 carries, 1 yard, 3 touchdowns.

As for the new safety tandem of Chris Hope and Troy Polamalu, well, the Raiders passed for 305 yards and struck deep for two touchdown passes, both of which Polamalu felt, in his first NFL start, were his fault.

He bit on a fake on the 58-yard pass to Doug Gabriel late in the first half, but Polamalu's self-blame on a 38-yard touchdown pass to Alvis Whitted was a bit dubious. It stemmed from him whiffing on a third-down sack attempt the play prior to the touchdown. The subsequent two-point conversion tied the game with 4:51 left.

Fortunately for Polamalu and the Steelers, Jeff Reed kicked a 42-yard game-winner with seven seconds left to win the game.

"I'm disappointed definitely with my own performance," Polamalu said afterwards. "But a win's a win."

Bill Cowher was asked at his Tuesday press conference if the mistakes in the secondary were correctable. Cowher replied, "They better be."

"I looked at Troy's and I talked to him this morning," he said. "I don't want him to quit jumping routes. I've been around too long to watch safeties sit back there and play half the field and be afraid to jump things. I can go back there and play half the field. I want players to be special. I want them to study film, as he's done, and learn from that. And he will." It wouldn't get any easier the following Sunday against the Ravens and tight end Todd Heap.

"No, but that's why Troy's here," Cowher said. "I told him he's here for Heap and Winslow."

At least Polamalu was playing. His roommate, Ike Taylor, had a poor preseason and was replaced as the fifth DB in the nickel by rookie Ricardo Colclough and as the sixth DB in the dime by retread veteran Willie Williams.

Against the Ravens, Polamalu played his best game to date, holding Heap to three catches for 27 yards while making 11 tackles, but the Steelers lost 30-13.

If Polamalu's play was a silver lining, so, too, was the injury to quarterback Tommy Maddox. Rookie Ben Roethlisberger replaced him.

Teammates didn't exactly begin calling Maddox "Wally Pipp" that week, but some 16 years later Roethlisberger was still in the lineup.

The loss to the Ravens would be the last loss by the Steelers for three months.

Ben Roethlisberger made his starting debut in a crossfire hurricane – Hurricane Jeanne – in Miami the following Monday night. The game was postponed a day because of the storm.

Roethlisberger was the first rookie quarterback to start for the Steelers since Bubby Brister in 1986, and it was no doubt the best debut by any Steelers rookie QB ever. Roethlisberger's numbers – 74.6 passer rating on 22-12-1 for 163 yards – were average, but the conditions were abominable, and his low-and-away fastball to Hines Ward in the howling wind and rain was the game-winner.

"That may have been one of the greatest catches of all time," Roethlisberger crowed in the locker room. "My sophomore year at Miami I threw a 73-yard Hail Mary to win a game, and I was still more excited about Hines' catch."

The Steelers also got their ground game rolling as Staley rushed for 101 yards on 22 carries in the Miami slop.

The defense was led by its young safeties. Hope forced a fumble on the game's first play, then knocked Dolphins RB Lamar Gordon out for the season with a separated shoulder.

Polamalu helped set the tone with his first career interception, a first-quarter pick of former University of Oregon rival A.J. Feeley.

"To be honest," Bill Cowher cautioned, "that was not a very good offense. I think we'll get a better test this weekend."

Up next for the 2-1 Steelers: the 1-2 Bengals and their young QB, Carson Palmer.

Polamalu and Hope were playing with more chemistry each week, and they were also coming together as friends. They hugged each other before games and shook hands in their own unique way, as Troy spoke the mantra, "Brother from a different mother."

Polamalu and his other BFADM, Carson Palmer, were about to face each other in the NFL for the first time.

While Troy entered the game as the Steelers' leading tackler and owner of his very first professional interception, Palmer entered as the NFL leader with five interceptions thrown. He opened strong in a high-scoring loss to the New York Jets, struggled in squeaking past the lowly Dolphins, then threw three interceptions against the Ravens.

"He's been making some dumb decisions," Steelers pro scout Doug Whaley said at the time. "Throwing off his back foot, just throwing it up, lobbing the ball into three-deep on a post. He's just not seeing the field."

"Ed Reed picked two of them, and he'll pick off more than just Carson," reasoned Cowher. "Ben's got his share too. Any young quarterback will.

Those windows don't stay open too long in this league."

The Steelers beat the Bengals that day 28-17, with Troy making one of the more memorable plays of his career.

That fourth-quarter, game-clinching play is the one Palmer remembers, but another play stood out for Troy: his drop of what would've been a "pick-6" on a third-and-2 pass to the fullback with the Bengals at the Pittsburgh 17. The Bengals instead kicked a field goal and pulled to within 14-10 in the second quarter.

"I had the ball in my hand and dropped it with 80 yards to go and no one in front of me," Polamalu would tell *Point of Light* magazine two years later.

"I thought, 'Dang, there went my chance to make everybody happy, to get all these doubters off of me.' I was so angry and frustrated that I started crying on the sideline. I sat there with my head in my hands, oh man, crying as I was praying! Then I heard a song on the PA: Los Lonely Boys singing 'Lord, take me from this prison. I want to get away.' Just like that, I felt everything was going to be great."

He was right.

The Steelers clung to a 21-17 lead and punted into the end zone to give the Bengals the ball at their 20 with 2:19 remaining. Palmer dropped back against the Steelers' cover-2 and threw to the right hash for T.J. Houshmandzadeh.

Polamalu recognized the formation and thought he knew the play. Lined up as the dimebacker, he had faked a blitz and dropped into coverage. He reached up to pluck the ball at the 26, headed to the sideline, cut back and up through the field, broke four tackles and scored. The last attempted tackle he broke was that of his buddy, Palmer, and Polamalu ran him over at the goal line.

CARSON PALMER: I tell him my shoulder still hurts to this day. I had my back to the goal line. I was trying to protect the goal line. He had a full head of steam and he just ran me right over. I still have a knot on my AC joint on my shoulder from where he put his helmet. I had no chance. I should've just run off the field and got out of his way.

DICK LEBEAU: He's hard to get on the ground. That's his competitiveness. He doesn't want to go down. He doesn't know that you can get tackled. That's his biggest strength I think. He's an aggressive competitor and you know he's real soft spoken and would just as soon be out of the limelight, but the way he plays he's always going to be thrust into the limelight. Troy does not want to lose, and Troy does not want to be beaten by anybody on any play and that makes him a fierce competitor. And he's very aggressive. He's one of the most aggressive Steelers that we've had. It makes him ideal for a defensive back.

MIKE LOGAN: We were talking about the run afterward. I said, "Bro, you might have to get some offensive snaps or return kickoffs. That was impressive, man."

CHRIS HOPE: Troy was becoming a star right in front of our eyes.

BRETT KEISEL: That play right there was the start of the demon Troy Polamalu, Steelers safety, first round, first ballot Hall of Fame.

PALMER: It was an incredible play, but it's not something he would ever bring up. He's a complete competitor and whether we're halfway decent friends or best friends in the world he would've made the same play. Maybe when we're old and gray we'll bring it up, but I'm not bringing it up. I don't like thinking about that.

BILL COWHER: I remember another play from that game. We called a cover-2 where he's supposed to be playing half the field. And Troy was down at the line of scrimmage, moved the linebacker over. And I'm thinking, "OK, get out of there Troy. Get out of there Troy." And then I said, "Dick, he's not moving. I don't think he got the call." And I go, "TROY!" And he's waving, like, shut up, shut up. I'm like, "NO! Cloud, cloud, cloud!" which was the corner rotation. And he's like "Shut up!" And all of the sudden the ball's snapped and I go, "Oh, my God, he didn't even get to his half of the field. What's he doing?!" Carson goes back, throws it in the flat, Troy comes up and makes the play. We come off the field and I go, "Thank God. He had everyone screwed up. What the hell happened out there?" As it turns out, he knew it was cover-2. He knew it was Carson Palmer. He told Deshea, "You take half the field. I'll take the flat. I'll be in the box. They'll think it's a single-high defense." He told Chris Hope, too. And Carson indeed thought it was single-high, didn't see anybody in the flat. And Troy came up at the last minute and made the play on the guy in the flat. So we actually were playing exactly what we needed to play. And he came off the field, I go, "Troy, what the heck?" He explained it all, told me what he knew about Carson, that he had communicated with the other DBs. "I knew where I needed to be, coach." Then he goes, "Quit yelling." I go, "Troy, just next time could you let us know? I'm having a heart attack over here."

DARREN PERRY: Cowher yelled at me "What was Troy doing? He can't do that!" I told him that sometimes I don't know what Troy was thinking. When he came to the sidelines, Cowher was glaring at me as I was talking to him. I asked him what he was thinking. I knew Cowher was watching me – and I'm only in my second year coaching so I'm nervous. Well, I told Bill what happened. He asked me if that was right. I told him it was right on the tip sheet. Cowher just said "Well, tell him to be careful!"

COWHER: So we started to do a lot of things that utilized his skill set, some unconventional stuff. His flexibility and his ability to understand the defense, you had his input. He literally would take a defense and put his own blueprint on it. Like I said about him against Cincinnati, "I know what the defense is, but I'm going to put in this little wrinkle within the game." He was built to be in a defense that we had, but also to have the coaches that we had. A lot of people may be bothered by some of the things that he did. I think for Dick and myself and Darren, we were OK with him doing that. I would get mad at times, but the more you're around him, you're like, "Wow. You're going to have to live with some of the stuff because this guy's really special." He knew certain formations. He saw little things. He studied the game. Preparation was everything to him. Why would you harness that? If you didn't make the right call at the right time and he knew what the play was going to be? He knew what the weakness was. He knew he had to get there before the ball went to a certain area. What he did was not freelancing, they were calculated risks.

The 3-1 Steelers were in first place in the AFC North, and the secondary could take pride in having the NFL's second-ranked defensive passer rating (58.2) after finishing 23rd a year ago (82.4). The pass defense ranked fifth in yardage allowed.

But there was that old danger sign of the safeties making too many tackles, which is often a sign the front seven isn't doing its job. Troy Polamalu was leading the team with 30 tackles, while Chris Hope made 10 in the win over the Bengals, giving him 24 for the season.

"Way too many tackles. That's not a good thing," Bill Cowher said that week.

It was also a small sample size.

"I will say this about those safeties," Cowher added. "They can run. Troy is everywhere. We ran a blitz and he was supposed to be in a hook. Carson Palmer scrambled the other way and Troy came from a hook position, 12 or 13 yards deep, and ran him down out of bounds. This guy, he can run."

Of course, the news in Pittsburgh was largely focused on Big Ben, who won his third consecutive start against the Browns – a team that had traded a second-round pick to move up one spot to draft tight end Kellen Winslow instead of the local QB.

In the 34-23 win, Roethlisberger completed 16 of 21 passes for 231 yards with a touchdown. He also ran six yards for another score.

Roethlisberger's impressive start continued the following week in a win at Dallas. He completed 21 of 25 for 193 yards and a pair of touchdown passes, the second of which cut into a 10-point Dallas lead early in the fourth quarter.

The Cowboys still had the lead and the ball and were driving well enough to burn through the Steelers' three timeouts – and their nose tackle. With 2:36 remaining, Casey Hampton tore the ACL in his right knee and was finished for the season.

On the next play, a third-and-13, a free blitzing Polamalu startled Cowboys QB Vinny Testaverde, who stepped up into a strip-sack by James Farrior. Kimo von Oelhoffen recovered at the Dallas 45 and the Steelers had the ball with 2:20 remaining. Jerome Bettis finished the drive with a 2-yard touchdown run for another Steelers win.

At 5-1, the Steelers were cruising, but their Pro Bowl nose tackle, Hampton, had to be replaced by Chris Hoke, an anonymous reserve who earned his way onto the team as an undrafted free agent the same year, 2001, that Hampton was drafted in the first round.

The Steelers also lost cornerback Chad Scott to a knee injury. No one knew at the time that Scott was done in Pittsburgh. He was replaced by 33-year-old veteran Willie Williams, who would become the only Steelers player in Super Bowls 30 and 40.

Polamalu made a key play in the second quarter that was remembered by few, but in breaking up what looked to be a sure TD pass to Jason Whitten, Polamalu forced the Cowboys to kick a field goal. The play saved four points for the Steelers, who won 24-20.

Following the bye week, the 5-1 Steelers hosted the reigning champion Patriots, who were riding a 21-game win streak. The Patriots' last game against the Steelers, a 30-14 win to open the 2002 season, was a bit unsettling.

Marc Edwards, their fullback at the time, admitted, over a decade later, to being in the huddle late in the first half of a 7-7 game when Tom Brady told the offense, "We have their signs."

The Patriots scored on five of their next seven possessions to turn a 7-7 game into a rout at Gillette Stadium.

The Steelers were now attempting to beat Brady and Bill Belichick – whose defenses allowed rookie QBs a passer rating of 40.6 since taking over the Pats – with a rookie QB.

On Halloween.

But they did. Patriots shutdown cornerback Ty Law limped off the field in the first quarter with the Patriots leading 3-0, and two plays later the Steelers led 7-3.

Six plays after that, courtesy of a Joey Porter strip-sack, it was 14-3.

And on the next snap, Deshea Townsend's pick-six made it 21-3.

The Steelers waltzed to a 34-20 win.

"They outcoached us," said Belichick.

"We haven't done anything yet," Bill Cowher said in the locker room.

As for the Hampton-less run defense, the Steelers held the Patriots to a franchise-low 5 rushing yards. Porter led the way with eight tackles, three sacks and two forced fumbles, both of which led directly to Steelers touchdowns. Porter was named the AFC's Defensive Player of the Week.

Duce Staley rushed for 125 yards to give him 707 after only seven games. But his season took a bad turn when he injured his hamstring the following Friday at practice. Staley wouldn't get the chance to play against his old team – nor the three ensuing games – as Jerome Bettis returned to the starting lineup.

The Philadelphia Eagles came to Heinz Field with the best record in football, and perhaps the best wide receiver in Terrell Owens. He was coming off his fifth-consecutive 100-yard game.

The Steelers hardly broke a sweat in a 27-3 win as Owens' was blanketed by Troy Polamalu on third downs.

Owens, as the slot receiver, drew Polamalu on pass downs, and the Eagles were 0-for-8 on third downs that day. Owens did catch one third-down pass – for three yards – on third-and-9.

Bettis plowed his way for 149 yards, as the Steelers rushed for 252 – 4 yards off the their 54-year-old team record – to become the NFL's No. 1 ground game.

As for the run defense, the Steelers allowed 28 yards on 15 carries in two games with Chris Hoke on the nose.

While Polamalu was primarily responsible for holding Owens to 53 yards, he deferred to Farrior – known as "Potsie" to teammates – as the game's defensive star.

"He was all over the field making plays," Polamalu said of the Steelers' emerging leader at the critical buck inside linebacker position.

DICK LEBEAU: In '04, James did something every week. Every week he'd either intercept a ball, recover a fumble, cause a fumble. Philadelphia had a great halfback (Brian Westbrook) who was almost impossible to get with one guy in the open field. They threw a swing pass to him and James went over there and made a great play. I'll never forget that play. It was as good a play as I've ever seen in the open field.

IKE TAYLOR: Man, you talk about rejuvenating his career when he switched teams. There was no linebacker more physical than Pot-Dawg – and that includes Ray Lewis in his prime. And no knock on the Hall of Famer. I swear to God, no knock to Ray. But give me James Farrior all day.

CHRIS HOKE: Sure, 2004 was a huge year for me, but what I remember about that year was that some of those older guys, the guys who just didn't treat the younger guys with respect, they were leaving and the culture was changing. You had Aaron Smith, Brett Keisel, Alan Faneca. Troy was just coming on. You had James Farrior. Good. Dude. These were good guys who just wanted to play football. The culture shifted. You got rid of the Dewayne Washingtons and the Chad Scotts, those guys, it was ridiculous the change in our team.

MIKE MILLER: Tim Gribble, who's now a crossover scout with the Redskins, was with the Steelers back in 2002 and he told me I had to go to Kent State's pro day. He wanted me to look at James Harrison in particular. He said, "Watch some film on him. This guy's really tough." The thing about James that was interesting, when you're at these things inevitably every one of these kids at some point during the workout they're going to come over and ask for their times or what they jumped, ask how they're looking. Even though they've been told a hundred times, "Don't ask. You'll find out at the end." But James acted like this was the biggest inconvenience of his life. He was so unimpressed with the entire process. He'd get up, run his 40, and go sit down. And he would have that stare. He's just staring at you. And we'd be like, "OK, now we're going to do this." Not until it was his turn would he get up. He'd come over, do it, then go sit down. Then he'd get on the bench and put up some ridiculous number, because he's so strong, and then he'd go sit down. I thought, "Wow, this guy doesn't seem very impressed with this whole thing." So I got back and said, "If his demeanor says anything about how tough he is, then we'd better get him." So, we brought him in as a free agent.

Teammates at that point in 2004 had given James Harrison the nickname of "Silverback."

"They're big, strong gorillas from the Congo, the silverback gorilla," explained Clark Haggans. "They spend their days swinging on trees and breaking stuff. All the other apes and everyone in the jungle are afraid of him."

But at the time, the only people who feared Harrison – aside from perhaps his own coaches – were kick returners, because he wasn't seeing any defensive snaps.

But special teams were the reason Harrison was active on game days over the guy ahead of him on the outside linebacker depth chart,

Alonzo Jackson. It's why Harrison, and not Jackson, was active the Sunday morning Joey Porter was ejected for a pre-game fight in Cleveland. It allowed Harrison to make his first NFL start.

The guy who had been cut three times by the Steelers was in the starting lineup against the team that caused him to cry as a kid following devastating losses to John Elway.

Harrison made tackles on two of the Browns' first three plays, one for a 3-yard loss and the other after a 1-yard gain on third down, and almost recorded a safety, but Browns quarterback Jeff Garcia eluded Harrison in the end zone and just got a pass away.

Harrison sacked Garcia on a third-and-5 play in the third quarter and played a key role in Russell Stuvaints' fumble recovery for the touchdown that clinched the win.

Harrison led the Steelers with six tackles, all solos.

James Farrior forced another fumble and Chris Hoke keyed a run defense that allowed only 68 yards on 22 carries. Hoke also had his first career sack, which he punctuated with a Rockettes' style dance routine that became known as "The Hokey Pokey."

Harrison, the youngest of 14 kids growing up in Akron, played in front of 18 family members. Troy Polamalu played in front of four uncles, including Keneti, who was coaching the Browns' running backs.

Troy intercepted two passes, one at the Pittsburgh 2 to stop a Browns drive late in the first half. His second pick put the Steelers into victory formation, and Polamalu responded to hecklers by blowing them a kiss.

"Some guys take things way too seriously," he said. "It's nice to overcome some of that selfishness, or evil, whatever you want to call it, with love."

"Troy will hit you and knock you into tomorrow," said Aaron Smith, "and then smile at you and help you back up."

"Troy has been very constant," said Bill Cowher. "This kid has had a heck of a year to this point."

Up next, a rematch with Carson Palmer and the improving Bengals.

The Bengals were 1-4 the week after losing in Pittsburgh, but they won three of their next four games and hosted the 7-1 Steelers with a 4-5 record.

Carson Palmer was getting better every week, with help from WR Chad Johnson and RB Rudi Johnson.

Johnson the receiver – later to be known as Ochocinco – put the Bengals up 7-3 with a spectacular TD catch over Deshea Townsend.

The Steelers rallied behind James Farrior, who continued his season-long rampage with the first pick-6 of his career.

But Troy got beat by Kelley Washington's 19-yard TD catch and the Bengals took a 14-10 lead into halftime.

Ben Roethlisberger's 8-yard TD pass to fullback Dan Kreider in the third quarter gave the Steelers a 17-14 lead, and Palmer took a safety after being forced to ground the ball in the end zone. One fan heaved a bottle at the referee signaling safety as the Steelers left town with a 19-14 win.

The red-hot Steelers throttled the Redskins 16-7 the following week, prompting Hall of Fame coach Joe Gibbs to call the Steelers defense "one of the best defenses I have been up against."

Antwaan Randle El set up all of the Steelers points in spite of the presence of a most impressive Redskins defensive back. Rookie safety Sean Taylor showed his great range by streaking from the opposite hash to break up a deep pass to Hines Ward on one play, then cutting Jerome Bettis down at the line of scrimmage on the next.

"You're going to hear his name quite a bit," said Ward.

The following Sunday night in Jacksonville, Roethlisberger posted an almost-perfect passer rating of 158.0 in rallying the Steelers to a 17-16 win over the Jaguars.

On the final drive, Roethlisberger completed all three passes for 39 yards to set up Jeff Reed's 37-yard field goal with 23 seconds remaining to make the Steelers 11-1.

Bettis' four-game streak of 100-yard games ended in Game 13 against the Jets, but the Steelers rolled to a 17-6 win.

Polamalu got the Steelers rolling with a first-quarter interception of Chad Pennington. "Crazy Legs" Polamalu returned it 22 yards to set up a Reed field goal, which stood as the only points of the first half.

The Jets tied the score midway through the third, but the Steelers went ahead early in the fourth on a series that had Bettis' name stamped all over it. He went over the 13,000-yard plateau during the drive, and three plays later took a handoff from Roethlisberger, ran right, and flipped a 10-yard touchdown pass to a wide-open Jerame Tuman.

Bettis later scored his career-high 12th touchdown of the season on a 12-yard run to clinch the win.

Bettis ended the season with 13 TDs and 941 yards – and 13,294 career yards, fifth in NFL history at the time.

The defense had become the league's best behind Polamalu and Farrior, each of whom intercepted a pass against the Jets. They finished the season as Steelers interception leaders with five and four, respectively.

Farrior went on to finish second in the NFL Defensive Player of the Year voting behind Ed Reed, so what did that say about how well Polamalu was playing in his breakout season?

"He's the best safety in the game today," Bill Cowher said after his team improved to 12-1.

LOGAN: Once he got it, he had it. He has one of the best football IQs that I've seen, so once he got the terminology down it was like he knew it all along. He really has a genius football mind, and to go along with that he's a guy who's going to stay in and break down film and see it from different angles. Troy would watch the sideline view and the box view of what the linemen were doing and how the gaps may be changing or where he should enter. That's just a different dynamic of film watching. I'm watching the wide thing and thinking I'm seeing everything, looking at the DBs. He's watching the side angles and what the linemen are doing and what signals they're giving and how they're aligned. That's genius, man.

You know, strong safety is a tough position. You have to know how to play the back end and how to play in the box. You have to know specialties in our defense when we're zone-blitzing. I'm watching what I'm doing and where my position needs to be, where my alignment is. I know my assignment and the technique I'm going to use to do it. But he was at a different level. I remember peeking in on him watching film. I went from looking at him going into the room, to the next week peeking through the shades to see what he's watching, to coming in and asking him a question just to see what he's watching, to saying "Dammit, let me sit down here and watch a little of what you're watching to see how you're doing this." I learned stuff in my eighth year in the league from a second-year guy who was breaking down film and understanding it. I can't say enough about the guy they brought in to take my position.

After the loss, Jets defensive end Shaun Ellis, a Pro Bowler, was less than impressed by the Steelers. He told the *New York Post* that he hoped to see the Steelers again that season.

"We'll beat them," Ellis said.

The Steelers went on to beat the Giants, Ravens and Bills to finish 15-1, the best record in the NFL, and the best record in franchise history.

Roethlisberger finished the season 13-0, but he was driven into the turf and eventually out of the Ravens game on a late hit by rookie Terrell Suggs. Roethlisberger suffered bruised cartilage in his ribs.

He rested his beat-up body in the regular-season finale, and then the team enjoyed a bye week as the wild-card Jets eked past the San Diego Chargers in the first round to give Ellis his wish: a Jets-Steelers rematch at Heinz Field in the second round of the playoffs.

The Steelers were 9-point favorites, which seemed about right after Polamalu's first-quarter interception set up the Steelers for a 10-0 lead.

Polamalu had lined up in the slot over the tight end, but left his man alone and open when the eyes of QB Chad Pennington led him to undercut Santana Moss for the pick.

The play no doubt confounded Jets offensive coordinator Paul Hackett as Polamalu's 14-yard return to the New York 25 was followed five plays later by Jerome Bettis' 3-yard touchdown run.

The Jets fought back to tie the game 10-10 late in the first half on Moss' 75-yard punt return, then took a 17-10 lead late in the third quarter when Roethlisberger threw directly to safety Reggie Tongue, who returned it 86 yards for a touchdown.

The Steelers were driving early in the fourth quarter when, at the New York 22, Bettis was stripped by Ellis and the Jets recovered.

It was Bettis' first fumble in 353 carries, but the Steelers defense held and the offense tied the game on a 4-yard shovel pass to Hines Ward with 6:00 left.

Heinz Field was a pit of frazzled nerves as Pennington drove the Jets to the Pittsburgh 28, but Doug Brien's 47-yard field goal attempt with 2:02 remaining hit the crossbar and the score remained tied.

Roethlisberger was intercepted by David Barrett on the next snap and the Jets had the ball at the Pittsburgh 37 with 1:46 left. Judging by Brien's near miss from 47, the Jets needed to gain at least 10 yards to win the game. They gained 13, and Pennington even took a knee on third down. But Brien missed a 43-yarder as time expired.

The Steelers forced a punt to begin overtime, and drove from their own 13 to set up Jeff Reed's game-winning 33-yard kick.

The Steelers survived and would face another rematch – against the New England Patriots – at Heinz Field in the AFC Championship Game.

There was no public yearning for a rematch from the Patriots heading into the game, but there was the tongue-lashing Bill Belichick gave his players at Wednesday's practice "like we were 0-17," QB Tom Brady said. "It put us in the right frame of mind."

The Patriots didn't get out of that frame of mind until they finished crushing the Steelers 41-27.

The game would later come under scrutiny over the Patriots' sign-stealing practices, but just about every key Steelers player and even the head coach made big mistakes.

Roethlisberger's first pass was intercepted, and he later looked safety Rodney Harrison into an 87-yard interception return for a touchdown. Bettis fumbled again. Cowher chose to kick a field goal from the New England 2 early in the fourth quarter while down 14.

As for Polamalu, he was burned for a 60-yard touchdown pass to Deion Branch that gave New England a 10-0 lead in the first quarter.

JOEY PORTER: Double moves. That happens, man. I never really got mad because you never want to take Troy's eyes away from him. Then he ain't Troy. You ain't doing that. You ain't taking Ed Reed's eyes away from him, so are you going to count every time he gets beat on a double move? Or are you going to count how many times he changed the damn game with a play? We weren't going to make our young safety feel like this whole game came down to that. That's bullshit.

COWHER: Tom Brady got him in the 2004 playoff game. They motioned a guy across that put Troy into the middle of the field. They ran a dig with a post over top, and they knew Troy would jump the dig. So they got him into a position, and he jumped the dig, and Brady threw the post over the top.

PORTER: I was a young player when I dropped into the curl flat the year they came and beat us the first 13-3 season (2001). Bledsoe hit me in my hands. I could've run that ball in for a touchdown and won the game, but I dropped it, so I've been in that same AFC Championship Game and had a chance to make a play and didn't. Going through what I went through and watching Troy go through that when he was a young guy, man, it's all part of football. This game will humble you.

Polamalu did make the Pro Bowl after his second season, just as young assistant Mike Miller had predicted prior to the 2003 draft. There, he was teammates with Brady, and Cowher used the opportunity to see if his star safety had learned a lesson.

"The first practice we had I put the same play in," recalls the coach. "I put Troy in the same situation and said, 'Hey, Tom, get in there. I want to see if Troy learned from his last mistake.' And he did! Troy took the post, left the dig. He stayed back in the middle of the field. I said, 'Tom, you taught him well.'"

The talk about that AFC Championship Game changed over the next several years as evidence mounted of New England filming opposing sidelines to steal signs. Brady, remember, had the Steelers' signs in 2002. The Steelers are convinced he had them on January 23, 2005, as well.

HOPE: The year before I was drafted, the Patriots beat the Steelers in the AFC Championship to go and win that first Super Bowl, so I heard guys talk about it. They recall a few plays that game where they knew exactly what defense we were in, they ran the motion, they got the linebacker isolated on the receiver, and the play worked as if they were practicing it, like we were running the cards for them. I can't say if they cheated or not, but some of the plays they ran the time I played them, they caught us in the perfect defense for what they were running.

LEBEAU: Everybody maintains that. I don't know how true it is. If you're playing well, the other guy can know your defense and it still ain't going to do nothing. Make sure we know what the hell we're doing. I wouldn't attribute that loss to that. Others may. I think it can't hurt you to know what the other team's in, but Brady has done that over the years to a lot of people in a lot of situations. But I remember playing them out here that year and we beat them pretty bad, so they had our defenses then, too, supposedly. It comes down to how you play usually.

COWHER: Our guys will never accept it, but listen. They may have known the signs, but we also had a system in place to not have to use signs, to use wrist bands. Unfortunately, Coach LeBeau, after the first couple series, he hated the wrist bands, and in the middle of a series he'd go back to the signs. It wasn't too hard to know our signs. Circling your finger, you know it's man free, OK, so, like, "OK, Dick, we've got to come up with at least a different sign." (chuckles)

RAY HORTON: Someone asked me when I realized the Steelers organization was different. For me, it was right after we lost the AFC Championship Game to New England. We came back in on Monday, the day after the game, and Bill said a few words. He asked if anyone had anything to say. Hines Ward gets up in front of the team and starts talking about Jerome Bettis and he starts crying. I mean bawling. Not just a glimmer in his eye. I'm talking about big, big tears. "We didn't do it. We didn't get to the Super Bowl for Jerome." I was really taken aback, like "Wow, these guys are crying because of another player. This is really different." And from then on, I understood the culture and what they were talking about and what makes that team different. That's why it had made such a difference. I had been in a Super Bowl as a player and we lost. It was devastating but we didn't cry for one player. This was the best coaching experience of my life because of the family organization.

CHAPTER 13

SERENITY, NOW

Mike Logan may have lost his job as Pittsburgh Steelers strong safety to Troy Polamalu in 2004, but it didn't make him any sort of hater. In fact, the veteran marveled at how the youngster navigated himself through life; from the way Polamalu trained to the way he watched film to the way he chose his friends.

That circle of friends was led by Troy's future wife, Theodora Holmes, who had come to Pittsburgh in 2004 from LaJolla, Ca., and begun studying pre-law at the University of Pittsburgh.

"This dude was acting like a husband even though he wasn't yet a husband, and acting like a father even though he didn't have children yet," says Logan. "And the way he would treat Theodora every time he saw her, it was almost like the first time he met her. You could see the love between them and the anticipation of him just getting to her. That was amazing to me."

Troy called his uncle just before the AFC Championship Game in early 2005 to seek counsel on whether to propose to Theodora.

KENETI POLAMALU: I was privileged enough that he called and asked me if I would give the OK. I was just getting off a plane in Mobile at the Senior Bowl and walking to the baggage claim, but I had to sit there a little bit because he was taking his time trying to ask me, "Uncle, what would you think?" Like everything else, we sat there and planned, like picking Marvin (Demoff) to be his agent, and having to live on a budget, things like that. I wanted him to learn how to live as an NFL professional athlete before he settled down. I thought he'd be ready in two, three years. "You don't understand how to live on your own. You're coming from college. You were on scholarship with a training table. You didn't have the money. You didn't have all this." I wanted him to understand that.

He said, "Uncle, I want her. I want her here. I want to be with her." We talked and came to a point where, "Hey, if you respect Theodora, you've got to make sure of that." That to me, in my experience with athletes, is so important, because the hardest thing for most of them is that everybody's been doing things for them their whole lives, from Pop Warner through college, and those guys, in my opinion, just don't turn around and show respect to some of these people.

I went to the Jets playoff game, and before I left for Mobile we went to an Italian restaurant. Troy drove my kids and, man, those Pittsburgh fans were just jumping on his car. When we walked into the restaurant, everyone kept buying because they thought I was his father. "Hey, have a drink," boom, boom, boom. Before we left, he got up to everyone and bought their dinners. Instead of just going around himself, he took Theodora with him to say thank you. He took her to every table and introduced her. That left a pretty good imprint that he respects her. There are tough times in marriage, but when you have respect for each other you're going to stick together. So when he asked for my blessing, my inclination was to say, "Troy, you need another year." But when he answered my question about respect, and I remembered that dinner, I said, "Yes, young man. I will."

Troy proposed to Theodora in front of her mother Katina during dinner at Mineo's Pizza in the Pittsburgh neighborhood of Squirrel Hill. They were married soon thereafter in the magistrate's office in Squirrel Hill by one of Theodora's professors at Pitt.

"Troy picked me up right after class," Theodora told *WHIRL* magazine, "and we followed the judge to his office. It was Judge Firestone, his wife, myself and Troy."

No Steelers.

No family.

Only Theodora.

Theodora and Troy.

IKE TAYLOR: It was nothing big at all. That man's not looking for any light. He walks in the shadows. Troy's like a ninja, always looking for a shadow, whether it's there or not.

KENETI POLAMALU: Troy wanted to learn about wine, so for his honeymoon, Diane and I sent them to Sonoma and Napa and put them up at a bed and breakfast. I had a friend named Charlie Cline who ran a vineyard that helped him learn that kind of stuff. I told him it takes $10 million to make $1 million in that business.

Soon thereafter, Troy began preparations for the next season. He lost so much weight in the spring – down to 198 (from 213 at his pro day) – that his trainer, Marv Marinovich, ordered Troy to come home to get some of his new bride's cooking.

"He always pushed himself mentally, whether it's hanging with the monks in the cave in Arizona or fasting for 20 days," said Taylor. "Like, for-real fasting. No food, just water. Like I said, he different. Like, picture this: The Bible's originally written in Greek; Troy taught himself how to read and speak Greek fluently. Thea is Greek, but she can't speak it as fluently as Troy. Y'all should understand that Troy also is a pastor. He did a couple ceremonies in Pittsburgh while he was there. Hey, the dude different."

The Polamalus converted to Eastern Orthodoxy, eventually had two children – Paisios and Ephraim – and purchased a home in the north Pittsburgh suburb of Pine Township.

Troy relayed one neighborhood experience to *WHIRL* magazine in which a group of kids ignored the "No autographs" sign and rang his doorbell at 11 p.m. Troy signed and bid them a good night, but was soon back at the door to respond to a parent – who did not come to apologize for his child, as Troy had expected, but had instead brought friends for their own autographs.

Miscellaneous quotes about the famous couple were attainable merely by attending a sporting event at nearby Pine-Richland High School. A quick sampling from one evening of soccer:

* "He comes up to the track frequently to run."

* "His wife is so nice. She'll give us a $100 check and say, 'Oh, no hoagie.'"

* "Every time I drive by, there are more toys in the yard."

ALAN FANECA: Troy put his family in front of him. He leads his life by putting other people in front of him. He put Thea and his kids up in front, always took care of them and made sure whatever little thing, or big thing, it was, they were the center of his world.

LENNY VANDERMADE: They're both very selfless people who try to put the other first. When I was signed to the Steelers' practice squad late in 2004, he was very excited. In Troy fashion he was telling me, "Yeah, man, you gotta move in with me." I said, "Hold on, man. You're married now. This isn't college. As much as I appreciate you opening your home to me, I can't just be posting up." I stayed there a week or two to get my feet underneath me and find a place. I said, "Once I find a place, I'm gone." He was like, "No, you're not doing that. You're going to stay with me and Thea." Just so typical of Troy, open arms and trying to do everything he can to help me out.

The 2005 draft brought more new friends to Pittsburgh, namely Heath Miller and Shaun Nua, neither of whom Troy knew at the time.

Nua, of course, was more familiar with Polamalu's ancestry since Nua was born in – and his father was the village chief of – Siufaga on the tiny island of Ta'u in the Manu'a Islands chain of American Samoa. It's where Troy's grandparents were born, raised and started their large family.

SHAUN NUA: I walked into the locker room and he came up and said, "Hey what's up, us?" Us [pronounced oos] means uso; uso means brother. But I don't think I said hello. I think I was just starstruck. He told me he would see me after practice and then said, "Hey, Kimo's giving you his wife's car and I'll take you guys shopping." That was the introduction. He took us to a grocery store and me and Chris (Kemoeatu) lived well as rookies. Right away we were comforted. He didn't say we should do this, we should do that. All he did was help us out. When we went to lift, I saw him do all his flexibility stuff and he didn't force anything upon us. He's someone who led by example, and if you had questions he would answer.

HEATH MILLER, *Steelers tight end (2005-15):* What struck me right away was how he treated, first of all, Theodora. How much respect and love and admiration he had for her. Despite all the adulation that you may have from everyone on the outside he always held Theodora in high esteem and treated her, respected her, revered her as his wife. And on top of that, at training camp whenever anyone brings anyone's family, Troy always introduces himself to their significant other, their whole family. It doesn't matter how many people are there, he gives them a hug and treats them like family. From the first interaction with my wife Katie, that just made her feel totally comfortable. He and Theodora are great friends of ours.

NUA: Troy was very, very curious about Samoa. The main points of our conversations were songs, stories, legends. We would go out at night, but he didn't do that much. He's so focused. I never saw anybody study as much film as he does. And he loved, loved, loved his family, his wife Theodora and his kids. He's a great father and husband, first and foremost, and he's someone who's proud of his heritage and wants to represent it well, and he's still learning about it.

Polamalu, of course, was the first-team strong safety. But that didn't mean the third-year pro was off the scout team, which came as a surprise to the new first-round rookie.

MILLER: He would always be out there on scout team, and it'd be like, "Oh, great, Troy's out there." Being a young player in-season, I'm trying to remember my assignment. We just put in the game plan and I'm trying to figure out what route I had, what the cadence is on. Now I had to figure out what to do with this guy in my chest jamming me. I'm just trying to move and get open, but he's already on top of me. I think it was an awesome challenge as a young player. It definitely made me realize parts of my game I needed to improve. I thought it was awesome that he was out there giving us a look, and it definitely made Sundays much easier.

TROY POLAMALU, to friend and talk-show host Justin Myers: For a football player, especially a defender, it's hard to sit there and practice by yourself. If I'm a basketball player, I could go shoot a thousand shots by myself. If I'm a soccer player, I can go dribble. But as a defender, it's hard for me to actually get in-time game action, like, feel. I thought I could do that more during practice, so rather than just take the first-string reps, I took the first, second, third-string reps. I took all the scout-team reps. My philosophy was if I could practice twice as much as everybody else, as a five-year vet I would actually be a 10-year vet, given the fact I would have that many repetitions. So the more and more feel that I started to receive – like offensive linemen get their urgency to come to the line for a quick count, and kind of building upon these sorts of tells – I started to get a feel for those sorts of things. (Jumping over offensive lines) wasn't until the middle of my career, and it was never really a conscious decision for me. It was kind of a spidey-sense sort of thing, like "Uh, oh, they're going to sneak it," or "They're going to quick-count it here." I would just lay it on the line and gamble and really give in to my instinctual need to make a play at that moment.

MILLER: That was Troy. He put himself out there because the more looks he could get in a practice setting, the better prepared he felt for a game. I think that's just the type of detail, coupled with his mental acumen, that made him an incredible safety.

One time in practice, I'm on the sideline watching the defense. Troy's covering the flat, but he's kind of sitting still. He's in his spot so he doesn't need to be moving anywhere. I'm watching his feet, and just small details like the way his feet are staggered. Most people, naturally, when they move laterally to the spot, their feet would be parallel. But I'm watching Troy get to the spot and his feet are staggered because he sees the threat in front of him, he sees the route in the flat, and he's giving the quarterback the impression that it's open, but his feet were staggered. It's the tiny details like that that he would think of and put into his game on his own, which allowed him to make the plays that he made in the game. That was the difference between getting a fingertip on a ball and pulling it in and running it back for a touchdown.

His quickness and athletic ability are obvious. And he was so strong for his size. His punch felt like a punch from a linebacker jamming you at the line of scrimmage. He was in your chest so fast with all of that power. And when you throw his mental acumen of the game on top of that, the way he saw plays, he was playing chess while everyone else was playing checkers. He saw beyond your route. He saw the play developing. You may not be tipping the route or giving anything away, but based on everything else he saw as the play developed he kind of knew where you were going to go – which was frustrating. But his play strength and how physical he played, how heavy his hands were, I could tell right away that he wasn't a normal safety.

FANECA: My position and Troy's didn't do too much in practice, but you always had to keep an eye on Troy and never really believe where he was. If one of us was responsible for him, we always kept an eye on him a little bit longer, honored him a little bit longer, because you never knew if he might jump in there at the last second.

MILLER: The rookies went to a hotel and had a lunch send-off before the last preseason game, and we watched the highlight video of the previous season. That was his breakout year. He was all over the place – fumble recoveries, big returns, interceptions for touchdowns. That's when it hit me that this guy's really good.

The Steelers drafted three players they had graded as first-rounders: Miller, cornerback Bryant McFadden and offensive lineman Trai Essex. They had received scouting help on McFadden from his former college teammate Chris Hope. The Steelers liked that Essex could play left tackle as well as guard and center.

The Steelers still needed a receiver to replace departed free agent Plaxico Burress, and when WRs coach Bruce Arians stepped into the media room to talk about fourth-round pick Fred Gibson, Arians talked instead about their first-round pick.

"I'm a big Heath Miller fan," Arians started. "I like tight ends that can go deep also because now we have all areas of the field covered, as far stretching the field, and Heath is a very versatile guy. Having been a former coordinator, I would've taken that pick myself."

The Steelers signed Cedrick Wilson in free agency to replace Burress. Departed inside linebacker Kendrell Bell was replaced by Larry Foote, a Dick LeBeau favorite.

Also, Bill Cowher announced in April that Jerome Bettis would be coming back for the 2005 season.

Troy Polamalu, May 31, 2005

How's your conditioning going?
TP: I actually was overdoing it a little bit. I was really excited for this year to come up, maybe a little too excited, and I started training a little too hard too early. You know, once you get in great shape it's hard to really maintain it. What you want to do is build up slowly until the season comes and you're at your peak, really, before the first game of the season. The full season will slowly get you down.
Why are you so excited this year?
TP: Team-wise we have all the chemistry needed to be a championship team. The only thing we don't have is the experience of playing in those big games like New England or Philadelphia has. To end the season that we had last year was a big disappointment and I think that's the part of the building process.
Did you learn from some of those deep passes against New England?
TP: Yeah, definitely. As a team, we weren't all on the same level as we were throughout the whole year. I don't think that we played good team ball. Our team defense, team offense, were not pulling together with special teams. I know personally I made a lot of selfish mistakes.

Last summer you studied some of the better safeties. Will you do that again?
TP: Yes, I did. I watched every single play in the whole season of all the other big-time safeties in the NFL. I made a highlight tape of them; made a low-light tape of them. It's really nice.

The Steelers intend to start the scout-team secondary of your rookie season. Are you one of the veteran playcallers back there?
TP: Oh, no. Chris (Hope) is pretty much the playcaller. He makes all the calls and we just kind of react off him. But it's exciting, very exciting.

A note, a quote and some interesting numbers as the Steelers ended minicamp:

NOTE: Lenny Vandermade, after a strong season in NFL Europe, tore up his knee and was ruled out for the year.
QUOTE: "Maybe some of you could deliver a message for me to Ben and Tommy Maddox, namely that if they still got a brain in their head, the brain God gave them, they'll take their motorcycles to the nearest bridge and push them off, if for no other reason than they've got 50-something teammates depending on them. I don't know if that's ever crossed their minds. So, if you can, deliver that." – Steelers broadcaster Myron Cope during the press conference to announce his retirement after 35 years.
NUMBERS: The previous six teams to go from a losing record to the NFL semifinals all failed to return to the semifinals. ... Of the six 14-win teams in the previous 10 years, only one returned with a winning record. ... Only two quarterbacks had been named Associated Press Offensive Rookie of the Year since 1967, Ben Roethlisberger and Dennis Shaw. The latter, in his second year, had a passer rating of 46.1 while quarterbacking a 1-13 Bills team.

The future was certainly bright for the 2005 secondary, but it was puzzling that the Steelers didn't negotiate a contract extension with young, hard-hitting free safety Chris Hope.

The Steelers felt both he and WR Antwaan Randle El were making "unreasonable demands" as both players entered the final years of their contracts.

Bill Cowher became a bit testy with repeated questions about Hope. This brief exchange followed the third preseason game:

"What's the deal with Chris Hope?"

"The deal?" Cowher said as he turned slowly with an arched eyebrow. "The deal is I held him out with a shoulder."

Another reporter tried to ask a question, but Cowher continued his fixed glare on the first reporter.

"Is that OK with you?" Cowher asked.

The reporter nodded that it was.

"You're right, we probably can't afford to lose him," pro personnel coordinator Doug Whaley said about Hope. "Now, the other guy, 43, you better know where he is every snap. Dick LeBeau told me the defense will flow through him this year. I believe it. I can't say enough about how good of a camp he's had. Do you see how long he stays after practice and all the work he does? He's a special kid."

At cornerback, Ike Taylor enjoyed a strong camp and moved past Willie Williams for the job opposite Deshea Townsend.

"Ike Taylor is a more focused, more mature player," said Cowher.

The contracts of Hines Ward and Casey Hampton were renegotiated – Ward's ending a holdout – and the knees of Duce Staley and Joey Porter underwent cleanups that would keep them out until the first or second weeks of the season, but the Steelers were bubbling over with talented young backups such as Willie Parker and James Harrison.

Parker, asked to name the five fastest players on the team, said, "Willie, Willie, Willie, Willie, and then Ike."

And rookie tight end Heath Miller was proving to be everything the Steelers hoped when they made him their first-round draft pick.

"I like the way he's picked up the offense," said Cowher.

Undrafted rookie Nate Washington out of tiny Tiffin University made the practice squad along with Shaun Nua, Polamalu's "uso" from Ta'u.

The Steelers got off to a fast start in 2005, beating the rebuilding Tennessee Titans 34-7. Fast Willie Parker rushed for 161 yards on 22 carries and Ben Roethlisberger, after an ugly 32.8 passer rating in preseason, posted the first perfect passer rating (158.3) of his career.

In Week 2, the Steelers were led by Polamalu's pass-rushing rampage. He tied an NFL record for sacks by a safety with three, of the team's eight, in defeating the Houston Texans 27-7.

One of the sacks had Polamalu faking a blitz, turning his back to the line in an apparent bail, and then a re-turn back into the line to blitz and sack QB David Carr.

"I just wanted to mess with the linemen a little bit," explained Polamalu.

JOEY PORTER: He came up to me in practice that week and wanted to switch up a blitz. This is when I knew his ass was special because he started thinking out of the box. He was like, "Joey, I'm going to come down and I'm going to take your blitz and you drop." Now, normally, I ain't giving up my blitz for nobody, so I'm going, "You get your ass out there and cover." He was like, "Let's just try it in practice. Let's mess with the quarterback and see if he goes for it. I'm going to come in the hole, act like I'm coming, I'm going to turn around and act like I'm leaving, and then I'm going to come again." I just wanted to see if it works, so I said, "All right. Let's do it." And it came wide ass open.

CHRIS HOPE: Somebody looking at tape would say, "What is this guy doing? He's freelancing!" But this is stuff that he practiced. We practiced our disguise. He practiced staying on the line of scrimmage and seeing how far he could wait until the quarterback took the snap. He came up with a blitz where he would show, as if he was blitzing, the feet over the tight end/tackle. The quarterback began his cadence and he'd call out the blitz, and obviously he'd indicate to watch 43. By that time Troy would turn his back as if he was about to drop. They think he's dropping in coverage, he loops around, walks into a sack. Very, very clever. Very witty.

PORTER: For me to say, "All right, I'll give up my blitz. I'll take your curl flat," that's how much I believed in him getting there. That shit worked. It wasn't him being selfish. He was just thinking of different ways to win. We had a defense that if you told me something, and you believed in your heart it would work, and Coach LeBeau was OK with it, and he gave us that freedom, let's do it. Troy was always tweaking and thinking of how we can get there. He did the same thing with different people, and switched around stunts and angles. When it works, it always was a big ass play, a game-changing ass play. That was Troy.

MILLER: Years later, we would see other guys trying to do that on film, and I don't know if it ever worked because they didn't possess the timing or the athletic ability to do it. That was the first time I had ever seen it done, and maybe the only time I ever saw it done successfully. Every time I saw it I would say "Oh, there's Troy's move." But no one can do it but Troy.

HOPE: Sometimes it would bite Troy, but again it's not something he'd bring to the game on Sunday and just try for the first time. When we did walk-throughs and worked on our disguises, our blitzes, and put new blitzes in, Coach LeBeau would tell us where we need to be when the ball is snapped. Troy would be all over the place. We would always be selling, selling. Coach LeBeau always said, "Be careful. Don't show the quarterback what you're doing. But be careful what you're showing him. It has to be believable."

PORTER: We were growing as a family. We cared about the person next to us. Like Aaron Smith, I know his whole family. Kimo, his whole family. Hamp – I mean *everybody*, all the way down to J Reed, all the way down to Gardocki, our punter. We were close close. We did everything together. And when you have that type of closeness of a family, there's not nothing you won't do for somebody. That's why when Troy's saying, "I'm gonna blitz and you take my drop," shit, I believed him. That's what we had. We had our backups, the young Harrisons, Keisels, those guys were SO thirsty to play. They would run through whatever just to play. There was no selfishness. We were truly an unselfish, badass team. We actually loved each other, and that's what made us great.

HOPE: We are all so close. Troy even started coming out with us. He was like a groundhog – we'd see him out every 60 or 70 days!

LOGAN: If we went to a DB dinner at Morton's, we would get the private room in the back and be ordering champagne and wine. Troy didn't participate in that, but he would come in and truly have a fellowship with the guys. We got to see a little bit more of his personality in those closed settings. The first time I heard him crack a joke I was like, "Wow." Then he got so comfortable around us you got to see a little more of his outgoing personality, and that was a shock.

TAYLOR: Troy was like Michael Jackson. You know how women and guys react when they see Mike live in person. The people of Pittsburgh, when they saw Troy out, man, I done seen grown men cry – because he's a unicorn. It's like how people been in the woods and they say they've seen Sasquatch. That's how Troy was becoming to the city of Pittsburgh. When you see him out in person, and he's got long hair like Jesus, you're like damn.

PORTER: He's not judgmental. He done smelled the liquor coming in the days when we went hard. Sitting in the steam room, he's sitting over there laughing us. But we showed up for work every day. What

I'm saying it was the respect you had for him. You wanted to give him respect because you know he would give it to you.

JAMES HARRISON, *Steelers outside linebacker (2002-12, 2014-17):* Troy's kicking and screaming and yelling and all that, but once in a blue moon you was able to get him out.

PORTER: I would mention after games sometimes, "Troy, for the team, just come out. You ain't gotta drink. We're going to drink and party enough for you, but just your presence means everything. We know this ain't your environment, and you don't really too much care to be there. You're only here because you're hanging with us." We didn't ask him to come out every night, but after a couple big road wins, we were like, "Man, when we get back to the city, you gotta come out." And he did. And every time he came out those nights were special.

The legend of Polamalu, of course, grew along with his game and his humility. It wasn't that way with most football players, whose ego grew with their game.

PORTER: You thought you were a rock star – until you hung out with Troy. Even when we made the Pro Bowl. It was funny to watch Pro Bowlers trying to pull a seat next to him, trying to get close to him. That's how big of a star he was. That was the highest respect level. Everybody that we hated, that we played against in the AFC North, there was nothing negative they could ever say about Troy. You hated him because you had to go against him, but man did they love how he played. You wished he was your teammate. There aren't a lot of those kinds of guys walking around on this planet who can play and be humble and love the game to the max, and play the game to the max, and go home like it never happened. You don't get that. But that was Troy. So it made him unique because he never came over cocky, brash. He had 10 other guys doing that for him. We'll celebrate over Troy's plays like we made 'em. He was a star of stars. There's a reason he's going to headline the Hall of Fame class. There's always one guy out of each class. All you guys are big, but that guy's just a little bit bigger.

BILL COWHER: Troy is a very religious guy, right? He'd go to mass on Saturday night; he'd go to chapel on Sunday morning. One time I asked him, "What denomination are you? Are you Catholic? Are you Presbyterian? Are you Baptist?" And he goes, "No, I just like all religion. I like it all." OK. So in 2005 we were playing against the San Diego Chargers and we got a blitz zone called, and LaDainian Tomlinson circles out on a flare, and Troy takes the tight end. There's a miscommunication between him and James Farrior; both are on the tight end and no one's on the swing pass. He goes like 50 yards on a Monday night and they kick a field goal in the fourth quarter for the lead. We come off the field and I'm talking to the kick-return team. And then I wanted to talk to Troy because this thing was all screwed up. I go, "Troy." And all of the sudden Chris goes, "Oh, Coach, you can't talk to Troy." I said, "What do you mean?" He goes, "He's praying." I said, "What do you mean he's praying?" He said, "He's praying. You can't talk to him right now." I said, "Well how long is he going to be praying?" He goes, "It's gonna be a while. I'll come and get you." I go, "Well, I've got to talk to you guys about what took place out there! Chris!" He goes, "I will come and get you, coach, but you can't mess with Troy while he's praying." OK, "God dang, I've got to talk to you!" But I had to go back up there because we're getting ready to go on offense. Years later, I told Troy, "I will always remember coming over to talk to you, and Chris Hope would always stop me and say I couldn't talk to you when you were praying." Troy said, "You know, coach, I used to always tell Chris that I think coach is mad at me. If he comes over, I'll put my head down and tell him I'm praying."

TAYLOR: Boy, that's a cold hustle.

HARRISON: San Diego was the game he got pissed off about Keenan McCardell. You gotta ask them boys back there about that.

LOGAN: That was the only time I saw Troy get out of character. I don't know if something transpired between them under the pile, or something was said, but that was the first time that I saw him evoke emotion toward an opponent on the field.

MARCEL PASTOOR, *Steelers assistant strength coach (2001-current):* I've been with the team about 20 years, and in my entire career I only heard one bad word ever out of Troy's mouth. I should say I only heard OF one bad word – in the San Diego game.

HARRISON: Listen, Troy was so hot and fired up that game, he was acting un-U-sual. Yeah. You have to ask the other boys. I can't let that one out. If they want to let you in on that one, that's on them.

TAYLOR: I don't know what McCardell did to Troy. I think he blocked him in the back and tried to cut him, and you know Troy doesn't curse, but everybody on defense started hearing this high-ass voice, with the long hair, someone with the jersey number 43 for the Pittsburgh Steelers, curse. We all said, "What the hell? Man, I know this ain't TP." Oh yes it is. It was like the little brother coming home saying who did it, and then you got the whole clan coming for that one person.

HARRISON: Let's just say Troy wasn't being all light-toned talkin' Troy for a while there.

TAYLOR: He was talking that talk to McCardell. He was talking like a few of us at the bar with a few drinks talk. After that our intensity level went up. That's when Deebo got that interception, jumped over your boy, and if you go watch that tape you see Troy digging an offensive lineman out. I'm talking about smacking him right in the face and laying him flat on the ground. And then when the dude's on the ground, Troy's still digging him out. After we heard Troy say those couple of good words to Keenan McCardell, the intensity level went way up. Anyone with powder blue and yellow on wasn't safe.

HARRISON: That whole game I think we were just fired up, to be honest. After we heard Troy, it lit up anybody that heard him. We're not used to hearing that out of that voice. We were like, "Oh, yeah, it's game on."

James Harrison's first career interception was punctuated by his hurdle of LaDainian Tomlinson while Polamalu was laying waste to Antonio Gates with a block. The play set the Steelers up to take a 14-0 first-half lead in a thrilling game they eventually won 24-22.

Coming off a last-possession loss to the New England Patriots, the Steelers went to San Diego emotionally charged, and Polamalu lit the powderkeg after McArdell had pushed him late in the facemask.

BRYANT MCFADDEN, *Steelers cornerback (2005-08, 2010-11):* I remember Troy just yelling loud, "Fourteen and done! You're gonna be 14 and done?" Keenan was in Year 14 so Troy was basically saying this was going to be it for him. It was like hearing an angry Michael Jackson yelling at someone. I never saw Troy move as fast as he did in the next three or four plays looking for Keenan McCardell, shouting "You're 14 and done!"

LOGAN: Just imagine if that guy was out all the time. How would it play out? I always wondered that. Would he be more dominant? Or would it take away from who he was?

BRETT KEISEL: You turn it on, you flip that switch. That's what I try and say to my kids when the lights come on. It's OK to be a good person walking down the street. And it's OK to be nice and friendly and kind. But in sports, the great thing about it is when the lights are on, you can be angry and you can play angry with a nasty disposition. You can play physical and hit someone and they're not going to cuff you. They're going to celebrate you and buy your jersey and talk about you and emulate you on playgrounds. That's the amazing thing about sports. That's how Troy was. When the lights would come on, that animal switch got flipped up.

PORTER: Troy wanted him sooooo bad, I could see it in his eyes. So now I want him that bad! He's messing with my little brother and got my little brother so damn pissed, I'm that pissed too. And now, instead of them trying to stop Troy, now they've got to stop me because I feel like I have to make this right and was looking for Keenan. Keenan's one of my good friends now, but I was like "Somebody just tackle him and get him to the bottom of the pile, I'm gonna break his fingers." Hamp was like, "Peez, you can't do that." I said, "Man, get his ass on the ground and I'll come and break his fingers." I was that mad. I was so pissed because I had never seen Troy get that mad. I seen the anger in his eyes and, shit, I was that mad. Luckily it didn't happen.

CHRIS HOKE: When Troy got mad, when Troy got fired up, that got you fired up. I don't want this to be a comment that's going to devalue anybody else, but he was the heart and soul of that defense, man. He really was. There were a lot of *great* players on that defense, and I mean great players, some of the best in Steelers history, some of the best in the league at the time, of that generation at their positions. But I don't know if there's another player on that defense who's going to make the Hall of Fame. Troy might be the only Hall of Famer.

Ben Roethlisberger was knocked out of an overtime loss to the Jaguars, but returned the following week as the 3-2 Steelers embarked on the following four-game win streak:

* Ike Taylor, in a new role of "traveling" with the opposing team's No. 1 receiver, held Chad Johnson to four catches in a 27-13 win at Cincinnati.

* As reported in *Steelers Digest*, "Heath Miller broke Eric Green's team record for most consecutive games with a touchdown catch by a tight end in the 20-19 win over Baltimore. Miller also broke the NFL record for most consecutive touchdowns without acting like a jackass in the end zone." Miller was named NFL Offensive Rookie of the Month for October. Jeff Reed's 37-yard field goal with 1:40 remaining clinched the win, but Roethlisberger would miss the next three games with a knee injury.

* At Green Bay, Polamalu keyed the Steelers' 10th-consecutive road win by recovering a fumble – courtesy of Bryant McFadden's first career sack, a strip-sack of Brett Favre – and returning it 77 yards for a second-quarter touchdown. It turned away Green Bay's chance to at least tie the 6-3 game, and gave the Steelers a 13-3 halftime lead on their way to a 20-10 win. Polamalu's "disguise" of a Lambeau Leap further frustrated Packers fans.

Charlie Batch started again in a 34-21 win over the Browns, but left with a broken pinky and Tommy Maddox completed the easy win. Hines Ward passed John Stallworth as the franchise's all-time receptions leader and was named AFC Offensive Player of the Week with eight catches for 124 yards and a touchdown.

At 7-2, Bill Cowher made one of the best decisions of the season by convincing Roethlisberger to undergo surgery on a meniscus tear in his right knee. Roethlisberger injured it in the opener, and then Baltimore LB Jarret Johnson aggravated it with a low hit on Oct. 31.

The Steelers won two games without him, but lost the third, in Baltimore, on an overtime field goal that knocked the Steelers to 7-3.

Roethlisberger returned to the lineup Nov. 28 in Indianapolis for a Monday night game against the 10-0 Colts, who remained undefeated with a resounding 26-7 win, kickstarted by Peyton Manning with an 80-yard TD pass to Marvin Harrison on the Colts' first snap.

TAYLOR: Coach LeBeau called a deep cover-3 coverage, meaning corners got deep between the sideline and the hashes, safety got deep middle. He said, "Keep your eyes out the backfield." And I hit Dickie with the "Yeah, yeah, yeah, yeah. I got you. Chill, coach, I got ya." And Peyton Manning lied to me. He acted like he was about to give Edgerrin James that ball. And all I did was stop my feet for not even a second. And you know Marvin Harrison. Whewwww. Lawd, he was gone.

COWHER: We went in there and did not have a silent count. I thought we could get by without it. We were so bad on offense. And then, we told, Ike, don't look in the backfield. The very first play, play-action, and Marvin Harrison runs right past him.

TAYLOR: When you give up a play like that, there's nothing that needs to be said. All you've got to do is look at your teammates' body language and say, "Damn, I fucked up." I let my teammates down. I let the city down. After that play I told myself from that point on, it's going to be hard for somebody else to make me feel that way and make my teammates look at me that way. That play turned my career around. For real.

HOPE: Coach Cowher came in after that loss and told us that "If we suited up again, right now, we would beat that team." He said, "We'll be back and it'll be a different story."

COWHER: It was kind of a wake-up call for us, so it was like "OK, we'll be back here. They embarrassed us. We'll get a chance to come back here again.'" I just loved that team. That was one of the three games in a row that we lost. We lost to them, then Cincinnati, where T.J. Houshmandzadah was wiping his shoes with the Terrible Towel, and I'm thinking "Wow. OK. There's no more margin of error now." The playoffs start tomorrow.

HOKE: Dude, we were down. We had just lost three games in a row. We were beat up and demoralized. That was a tough moment. Coach Cowher made us go back and grade the film, like three points on each play, and we had to give it back to him. You know what he said? He brought us back in the room and said, "Some of you *think* you're playing pretty good. But you're not. You're a good football player, but you can play better!" That was his big thing, you think you're playing good but you're not. That's high school stuff, man, but it works. We didn't lose after that.

FANECA: We had to win out, all four games, so Cowher came in with the block-the-noise-out talk. He kept giving it every time we had a team meeting. He said, "We are all on a ship at sea and anybody not on this ship doesn't matter. Only the guys in this room. Block out the noise."

HOKE: The message was don't let history dictate your journey, but let your journey dictate history. He referred to the people telling Columbus the world was flat and he was going to fall off the edge, but that Columbus knew something was out there and he didn't let history dictate his journey.

FANECA: He gave different versions of that every meeting. Then one game, he started talking about a periscope. "Don't put the periscope up and look around. Just worry about what's going on around here, not what's happening around us." I caught up to him real quick after the meeting and I said, "Hey, coach, I'm with you. Block out everything. But I just want to know, are we on a ship or are we on a submarine? Because you said we have a periscope now." He started losing it, man.

TAYLOR: You know what started that Super Bowl run? When Bussy ran over Brian Urlacher in the snow in Pittsburgh. It was our defense vs. their defense; our running game vs. their running game. When Bussy ran Hall of Famer Brian Urlacher over, we won the Super Bowl.

CHAPTER 14

REDEMPTION SONG

The locker room bulletin board could've been loaded with material for the Steelers' first-round playoff game against the Cincinnati Bengals.

Instead, there was only a picture of Ben Roethlisberger and his junior-high prom date with a caption that read:

"Ben, Thanks for the dance, but I'm still a Browns fan. P.S. Call me."

Nothing on T.J. Houshmandzadeh wiping his cleats with a Terrible Towel? Reporters sought out Joey Porter.

"My wife told me about it," Porter said. "I guess he wants to make us mad. Well, we're mad. He wants to talk trash on us, he wants to wash his cleats with a Terrible Towel, fine. You want to make us mad, it worked. We're mad. Now what?"

CHRIS HOPE: Houshmandzadeh was not a liked guy on our team. He was trying to be Hines Ward, but he was a dirty version of Hines Ward. Hines hit people during the play; Houshmandzadeh did stuff after the play. He was a young guy trying to make a name. The night before the playoff game, Coach Cowher showed us that video and we had to go to sleep. If he would've showed that before we went out, no telling what we would've done to Houshmandzadeh.

IKE TAYLOR: I want everybody to get a clear picture of what the great Myron Cope and that Terrible Towel means. That Terrible Towel represents 4-1-2. That Terrible Towel represents Steel City. That Terrible Towel represents six Lombardis. That Terrible Towel represents blue-collar, hard-working, no-nonsense Yinzer City. That Terrible Towel has a lot of history. So, when T.J. Houshmandzadeh wiped his cleats with that Terrible Towel, it was like he was pissing on the great Myron Cope's grave. We ain't having that.

ALAN FANECA: T.J. came in through the tunnel and somebody gave him a Terrible Towel for some reason, and then he started wiping his shoes with it. It was disrespect that definitely added fuel to the fire. Coach Cowher was always good at finding motivation and waiting for the right time to use it. Coach Cowher, a lot of times, would come in on a Monday and he would start talking, give a full presentation, offense, defense and special teams. It was always a longer meeting every Monday. Coach would usually end it with his personal thoughts of the game, or what's going on with the opponent. And if something was pissing him off, he would say he was pissed off, but he would also say, "I'm not telling you why today." Then he would tell us what it was on Thursday or Friday. Half the time he never said anything again. Half the time he got you riled up about something that didn't even exist. He just had the cue for when to pull it, when not to pull it. But this one he pulled out and stuck that jaw out and got the room fired up: "You don't do that in OUR house to US!"

BILL COWHER: We had gotten comfortable in a weird way, but all of the sudden we got our edge back, and that team got very edgy at the right time of the season. Then it was a redemption tour.

Redemption started slowly in Cincinnati as the Steelers punted, James Harrison was injured covering the punt, and Carson Palmer hit Chad Henry for 66 yards.

But Palmer – who led the NFL that season in TD passes and completion percentage – was hurt on the play, done for the day after an accidental low hit by Kimo von Oelhoffen.

The Bengals settled for a field goal, but got the ball back. Rudi Johnson ran through Chris Hope and beat the charging Troy Polamalu to the pylon for a 20-yard touchdown and a 10-0 lead.

The Steelers came back with a 19-yard Roethlisberger screen pass to Willie Parker for a touchdown, but the Bengals drove for another touchdown, in large part due to a Polamalu mistake. He uncharacteristically lost his cool after diving and nearly intercepting Jon Kitna on a third-and-11 pass from the Pittsburgh 17.

It should've been fourth down and time for a field goal attempt, but when Bengals guard Bobby Williams pushed Polamalu after the play, Troy pushed back. Bengals center Rich Braham got involved and Troy flipped the ball in his face in front of the official, who flagged the Steelers 15 yards.

Kitna followed with a touchdown pass to Houshmandzadeh for a 17-7 Bengals lead.

JOEY PORTER: I remember when Troy did that, but I'm not going to call the kettle black. I done lost it out there on the football field and they *always* had my back. It's OK if he lost his shit because it wasn't in a selfish way. Something had to happen to get him to that point. We had a pet peeve: never let anybody push you last. Never help anyone off the ground on offense, sure, but don't ever let them get the last shove, because when we're watching film and somebody pushed you last? You don't do nothing? We're gonna talk shit about that. Makes the whole defense look weak. So we were OK with that. It's just a mystique that we had. Don't fuck with us like that. We don't play those games.

The Steelers responded immediately. Roethlisberger hit Cedric Wilson with a 54-yard bomb to set up a 5-yard touchdown pass to Hines Ward and cut the Bengals' lead to 17-14 at halftime.

After the Bengals botched a snap on a short field goal attempt, the Steelers' defense took the game over. Kitna, who was 14 of 19 before Polamalu drilled him in the chest on a late first-half sack, completed only 10 of 20 in the second half as the Steelers surged to a 31-17 victory.

Polamalu got away with one more mistake. With 4:33 remaining, he made a diving interception of Kitna at the Pittsburgh 28. He ran four yards before lateraling back to Hope, who carried it 23 more yards.

The Steelers ran out the clock to advance to Indianapolis. But why the risky lateral when they were in position to seal the game?

HOPE: In practice, when either of us intercepted the ball, we'd always pitch it to each other. Against the Bengals, Troy grabbed an interception. He came all the way from the other side of the field and dove to intercept a dig route. Dives, makes the pick, gets up, makes a move. We practiced this so much that it almost became an instinct, and I yelled, "Troy!" He pitched it back. Didn't look where I was. Well, Coach Cowher was going crazy. Joey Porter's screaming. But Troy pitched the ball to me without even hesitating. I ran 20, 25 yards. We celebrated. When we got to the sideline, Coach LeBeau's fussing, everybody's fussing. Coach Cowher said "What are you doing?! You make one of the greatest plays and then you make one of the dumbest plays!" Troy said, "What do you mean? We do this every day!" Everybody on the sideline just died laughing because he was right. We practiced it every day for two, three years.

If the Steelers were going to pull this off, if they were going to the Super Bowl in Detroit, they would need to win two more games on the road. Only one other NFL team had ever won three straight road playoff games – the 1985 New England Patriots, who became Super Bowl lambs for the carnivorous Chicago Bears.

Twenty year later, it was a daunting task for the Steelers, but the second step on the road to redemption was the return their coach had promised to Indianapolis, home of the piped-in noise, the genius quarterback and the only AFC pass-rushing combo with more sacks than the Steelers' combo of Joey Porter-Clark Haggans.

In the Monday night loss to the Colts, the Steelers ran on their first seven first-down plays and 11 of their first 14. By then, the Steelers trailed the Colts 23-7.

The offensive plan needed a shake-up if they were going to pull off an upset as 9.5-point underdogs to the Colts in the playoffs, so the Steelers chose to open it up for Ben Roethlisberger.

"We talked about throwing on early downs that week, and Bill agreed it's what we had to do," offensive coordinator Ken Whisenhunt said. "He was good with being aggressive with it."

On defense, the Steelers wanted to make their pre-snap looks more difficult for the quarterback. The sound of Peyton Manning audibling after shouting, "Forty-three's the mike! Forty-three's the mike!" had repeatedly reached TV audiences during that Monday night broadcast.

BRYANT McFADDEN: Dick LeBeau came up with a great game plan. The Colts were strictly no-huddle, and Marvin (Harrison) and Reggie (Wayne) never switched sides. I was always the right corner in our sub-packages, so I was always on Reggie. Peyton Manning ran a not very fast no-huddle. He would look at the secondary specifically to see the movement, and call his audibles or checks based on what we were in. So Coach LeBeau wanted us to hold our movement until maybe seven seconds were left on the play clock, then roll into whatever we were playing. That way Peyton couldn't make another check because he was going against the clock. We had five sacks that day. Dick figured out what Peyton was doing after the first game and studying tape of their offense. It was one of the more strategic, innovative game plans I've ever been a part of. That's why we had so much success and dominated that 14-2 team. I think that Indianapolis Colts team might've been one of the best teams in NFL history to NOT reach a championship game.

BRETT KEISEL: Coach Cowher put something in late in our game-planning for us up front. He and LeBeau saw something and called it "Indy fire zone." Just a hardcore stunt from the weak side, that you line up looking like you're coming strong side, which we did a lot – brought pressure to the strength of the formation and we could at least come up there and stuff the run if they were trying to run to their strong side. We would line up that way a lot, but then we kind of flipped it for this game for Peyton, who was such a studious guy.

IKE TAYLOR: To me, it was just all about physicality. When you talk about the Steelers and the city of Pittsburgh, that's the only word you use: physicality. That's it. And that's mental. If you just talk to the old Pittsburgh Steelers in the '70s and how they played, their physicality was always mental.

DOUG WHALEY, *Steelers pro personnel coordinator (2000-09):* The Colts were an easy team to evaluate. They're a speed team headed by a guy who probably knows the offense better than the coaches. They're not a hard team to break down. They're a hard team to beat, but it can be done.

JOEY PORTER: Coach Cowher said, "Joey, don't say nothing about Indy." But I wanted to bait them into running the ball because we prided ourselves on being physical and we knew Indy was one of the best play-action teams in the world. Peyton Manning is going to hit you with the play-action and get Marvin Harrison by himself from an iso one-on-one. Shit, we didn't want to do that all day.

HOPE: We had the confidence to know we could beat them. We really believed it. And for the longest time their stadium was so quiet you could hear the calls from both sidelines.

The Steelers opened aggressively. After the first-down pass fell incomplete, Ben Roethlisberger hit Heath Miller on a play-action deep ball to beat Mike Doss for 36 yards. It set up a short touchdown pass to Antwaan Randle El for the early lead.

The Steelers scored on their third possession, too, thanks to a 45-yard yard pass to Hines Ward. Doss crashed into teammate Nick Harper to open it up for Ward, and a facemask penalty was added to put the Steelers on the doorstep for a short TD pass to Miller and a 14-0 lead.

The Steelers were pummeling Manning early, and then stiffened after the Colts had driven 97 yards to the half-foot line. A false start on third down hurt the Colts, and a goal-line tackle by Polamalu and Haggans forced a short field goal that set the Steelers' halftime lead at 14-3.

Polamalu nearly came up with a diving interception to open the third quarter, and a bit later noticed himself on the Jumbotron. He held up his ring finger to show Theodora – who was home sick – that he was thinking about her. It wouldn't be the last time Polamalu was featured on the Jumbotron in Indianapolis that afternoon.

He feigned a blitz on the Colts' next second-half possession that nearly resulted in two points, but James Farrior's end zone sack was ruled forward progress at the 1. A short punt set up a Jerome Bettis 1-yard touchdown run for a 21-3 lead late in the third quarter.

Manning rallied the Colts with a 20-yard pass to tight end Dallas Clark outside the right hash. He caught the ball at the Pittsburgh 30 and Polamalu was "picked" by teammate Hope and later "blocked" by a diving Farrior as the tight end completed a 50-yard touchdown pass to cut the Steelers' lead to 21-10.

The Steelers turned to their running game on their first possession of the fourth quarter, and converted a pair of fourth-and-1s before punting into the end zone with 6:12 remaining.

The Colts needed a miracle, and went right at McFadden with a 24-yard pass to Wayne.

However, the Colts' season seemed to be at an end when Polamalu, playing dimebacker, intercepted Manning by undercutting former UCLA rival Bryan Fletcher at midfield.

Game over.

Pack your bags for Denver.

Wait, what?

The play was being reviewed.

To all the world, it was an interception. After rolling on the ground with the ball secured, Polamalu did knee it out of his hand as he was getting up. But even though he recovered the ball, referee Peter Morelli reversed the call to incomplete.

"They're trying to cheat us!" Porter howled along the sideline as a nation of football fans shook their heads in disbelief.

LENNY VANDERMADE: That one sealed the game, but they said it was incomplete. I was so hot. That was an obvious pick. Troy collected all the balls he picked, and I told him he should have that one from Peyton Manning, too.

JUSTIN MYERS: Troy would never argue. He wasn't a talk-back guy. But he would get this look on his face like, "Really? You think you're right?" I saw him sitting there as they overturned the play. He kind of shook his head, gave that smirk, and I was like, "Oh, I know that face."

By that point he was so locked in. That he reacted without losing his temper wasn't surprising. But the smirk on his face told me that he knew he had just been wronged.

SALU POLAMALU: That just showed what Troy is about. He never complained. They had a camera on him, and when they made their final call he just put his helmet on and went right to the field. To me that was an example of a gentleman. Let the officials and all that do the talking, which they did, and later they said they made a mistake.

HOPE: Oh, my God. I was more upset about it than Troy was. He made an unbelievable play. Unbelievable.

CHRIS HOKE: Troy intercepted the ball. It would've ended the game. Troy had the mentality in any big game of "I want to make the big play." And he did.

PORTER: Coach Cowher knew they were going to overturn it. He had a feeling that they were going to rob us and he was doing what good coaches do: calming us down because he knew I would lose my shit if they took that ball away from us.

TROY POLAMALU: He was trying to coach ahead. He was doing his job. You always have to prepare yourself for the worst situation. He did that. But I was thinking, "What are you talking about? There's no doubt about it." But when he said that, it pretty much told me they're probably going to overturn this.

PORTER: I already had these conspiracy theories in my head about how the NFL wanted Peyton Manning to go to the Super Bowl so bad, and that was a clear-cut interception. In the timeout, Cowher's telling us to keep our shit if they overturn. I'm like, "Just go on down to the ref and tell him, 'Don't fuck this up.' Just tell them the real thing, what happened, that it's our ball." And they didn't. Now I'm so mad I can't speak. I don't have nothing to say. I just want to play now.

HOPE: (Cowher) said, "Well, I think we might have to go back. Get ready." And we were like, "How are you going to let that go down? There's clearly no momentum in the building. This is the only chance they have to even make it a respectable game, and you're cool with that?!" But he comes over and says, "We've got to go back out there." Troy was the first one on the field.

The Colts scored a touchdown five plays after what the NFL later admitted was the wrong call.

"The bad call made us play harder on that drive, but not as disciplined," says Hope. "We wanted to hurt somebody instead of playing technique."

Roethlisberger threw incomplete on third-and-6 and Chris Gardocki got off a 52-yard net punt as the Colts regained possession at their 18 with 2:31 left, now down only 21-18.

"Maybe we didn't do what we were supposed to do on that drive, but I remember the next series after that, when it got tight, we weren't going to let anything happen," says Porter.

Once again, with Polamalu threatening from the A gap, the Steelers got to Manning. Troy blitzed on first down to pressure an incompletion, and Porter got the sack on second down. Polamalu came up the middle on fourth-and-16 and Porter and Farrior shared the sack at the Indianapolis 2.

Game over.

Pack your bags for Denver.

Wait, what?

Bettis fumbled, Harper recovered, Roethlisberger tackled. Out came Manning with the ball at the Indy 42 with 1:01 left, trailing 21-18. He came right at the Steelers' rookie cornerback.

MCFADDEN: We weren't holding our disguise in the second half the way we were supposed to. Now, remember, I was the only rookie on our defense and I'm going against a potential Hall of Famer in Reggie Wayne in one-on-one opportunities, so of course Peyton's going to target me. I got tired of getting targeted. I was trying to hold my own. I was fighting. I was doing what I was supposed to do, but I kept yelling to Troy and Chris Hope and everybody else, "Man, STOP showing what we in! Hold your disguise! Do what Coach LeBeau told us to do!" They didn't just want to get in field goal range to tie the game, they were trying to score a touchdown and win, so I'm like "Aw shoot I know we're not disguising anything right now." We just lined up and it was all me. Those three or four plays, I literally didn't hear anything at all. It felt like I was on the football field by myself with no teammates, just me, Reggie Wayne and Peyton Manning.

McFadden broke up the first pass in the end zone. The next pass went to Marvin Harrison for 8 yards. McFadden broke up the third pass by nearly intercepting a poorly thrown ball. The final pass to Wayne also fell incomplete.

"I felt like I had been one of the guys by that time, but by the end of that game I was definitely with the in-crew," says McFadden. "Troy told me, 'Man, that's how you're supposed to step up. That's why you're out here with us.' He was telling me to believe in myself, and that's the thing about Troy: He always believed in himself. He never second-guessed himself. Ever."

Mike Vanderjagt, then the most accurate kicker in NFL history, came out to kick a game-tying 46-yard field goal, but wasn't even close. This time the Steelers could celebrate. They really were going to Denver.

PORTER: We had gone to a comedy show before the Indy game. Arnez J was at the Improv in Pittsburgh and he had this skit where it was like "You don't want none!" I don't know why but I thought of that in the locker room after that wild ride, that wild game. We win the game, Jerome's talking, and I was thinking man my big brother Jerome is always going with the political and saying something good, but I'm so fired up, man. We're going to the AFC Championship AND I'm still mad at the city of Denver because the last time I was there I got shot. So, I got this. "Man, they SHOT me in Denver!" I knew I would get the reaction I got from my guys, because I'm not making shit up. So they got mad at the Broncos like the Broncos had something to do with it (laughs). I turned everything into a Denver thing like the Broncos shot me and Denver has to pay for this right now. I'm going back and this time I got my whole team with me and there's going to be Hell to pay.

KEISEL: We knew that Denver was going to be a big mountain to climb. They had a really tough defense. But Peezy just made us laugh when he yelled, "That's where they shot me! Let's go! Who rides?"

TAYLOR: "Who ride?" "We ride!" "Who ride?" "We ride!" "Let's ride on three!" See, when Peezy spoke, and he spoke a lot, that shit came from the heart, and you felt it.

Most of the reporters at the Steelers' first-ever playoff win in 1972 missed the Immaculate Reception while en route to the locker room. It happened again in Indianapolis, where many reporters missed Jerome Bettis' fumble.

"I always shake my head at the guys who leave early, but I went down early this time," said one veteran Pittsburgh reporter. "I left right after Porter's second sack."

The reporter described descending a long set of stairways, and when he got to the bottom, he, along with several other reporters, saw Colts fans watching a TV in the hallway. Then those fans started cheering.

"What the heck's going on?" the reporter asked.

A fan told him the Colts had the ball at the 30.

"I looked and saw it was the *Steelers* 30 and I couldn't believe it. I asked another Pittsburgh guy what happened and he said he heard Willie Parker fumbled. I said, Willie Parker? Is Cowher NUTS?"

The reporter eventually got the facts straight.

"Now I know how the Chief and Cope and all those guys felt back in 1972," he said.

During one of the pre-game shows leading up to the AFCCG in Denver, TV analyst Jim Mora said the Steelers' most underrated player was Adam Smith.

Yep, the great Aaron Smith was so underrated you won't even know his name.

But reporters approached the Colorado Springs native anyway to discuss the mile-high air of Denver and how it might affect Bettis' asthma.

"The thin air is a myth," Smith said. "Now, if you were there about a week you'd notice the difference because your body's had time to feel the full-time effects of the altitude. But we're only going to be there 24 to 36 hours."

Troy Polamalu agreed. He had played in Denver as a rookie, and also as a junior in college.

"I've done elevation training in the offseason as well," he said. "I really don't feel the difference. I don't think it's an issue at all."

The Broncos had rushed for more yards than any NFL team over the previous five seasons; the Steelers had allowed the fewest rushing yards during that time. Would it come down to the Denver OL vs. the Pittsburgh DL?

"If it is, it's going to be a physical butt-kicking by our defensive line," said Doug Whaley. "Casey Hampton kicked Tom Nalen's ass for four quarters in 2003 and I don't know what's different except maybe Casey Hampton is a little bit better and Tom Nalen is a little bit older. I think it's going to start there, and once the Broncos can't run, which I don't expect they're going to be able to, certainly not to the degree that they are accustomed to, then Jake Plummer to me is Vinny Testaverde. I mean, he'll throw it to you."

The confident Steelers boarded their team buses and set out for Mile High Stadium at about 10 a.m. Mountain Time. Offensive line coach Russ Grimm, sitting up front, turned to offer some not-so-kindly advice.

"If anyone here is scared," shouted Grimm, "get the fuck off now!"

CHAPTER 15

GOING HOME

Hines Ward cried when he thought his team had blown Jerome Bettis' last chance to win a Super Bowl.

The beloved "Bussie" to his Steelers teammates, Bettis decided to come back for one reason – the 2005 Super Bowl would be played in his hometown of Detroit and this team had the talent to get him there.

The 33-year-old running back returned for what he hoped would be the perfect ending to a Hall of Fame career. And now the Steelers were one game away.

"Just get me to Detroit," Bettis told the team before the AFC Championship game in Denver.

But this week, the "Going Home" party was for the defensive linemen – Aaron Smith and Brett Keisel.

Perhaps no one was more excited about playing this championship game than Keisel, whose hometown of Greybull, Wyoming, is nearly 500 miles away from Denver but nonetheless thick in Broncos territory. Keisel had been led to believe he would be drafted by the Broncos in 2002, so he was looking forward to this opportunity to show them what they had missed.

"I wanted them to remember who I was," says Keisel. "And I was very motivated, as we all were in that game, to be one step away."

As a young special-teamer, Keisel appreciated that he was always on the field for the opening kickoff to chase away the butterflies. But with Kimo von Oelhoffen beat up, Keisel played early on the defensive unit and chased Jake Plummer out of bounds for a 1-yard gain that led to a Broncos punt on their first possession.

"I studied that play," Keisel says. "The tight end cracks down and they run a bootleg, where Jakes dishes it or runs for 40 yards. I prepared and then saw the play coming and was able to get out there and put pressure on him and get my first tackle. It was a big play in the game because field position flipped and we went down there and scored."

Hines Ward plucked a Champ Bailey deflection out of the air to convert a third down for the Steelers, and undrafted rookie Nate Washington converted the next first down. Washington then broke up an interception in the end zone to save Jeff Reed a 47-yard field goal for the early lead.

A Joey Porter strip-sack three plays later set the Steelers up at the Denver 39, and a 24-yard Ben Roethlisberger pass to Heath Miller led to a 12-yard touchdown pass to Cedrick Wilson to open the second quarter. Roethlisberger's pump fake on the TD pass caused the All-Pro CB, Bailey, to bite and the Steelers led 10-0.

The Broncos appeared stopped by Troy Polamalu's terrific open-field tackle on a third-and-10 pass to the running back, but Denver converted fourth-and-1 and drove for a field goal.

The Steelers, though, were unstoppable on offense. Roethlisberger hit Wilson for 18, and on third-and-10 threw a 21-yard strike to Ward. A screen to Antwaan Randle El behind Alan Faneca gained 10 more, and Bettis followed Faneca on a counter-power play for a 3-yard touchdown run.

Faneca took out three Broncos on the play to get Bettis into the end zone, where Bettis' beastly celebratory cries in the quiet stadium came through loud and clear back in Pittsburgh.

I was always trying to do more than my job," says Faneca. "If I can get a piece of someone else's guy, I'm going to do it. That was a fun game."

On Denver's next snap, Ike Taylor undercut Plummer's intended target and intercepted a pass to set the Steelers up at the Denver 38. Four plays later, Ward caught the back-breaking 17-yard touchdown pass that gave the Steelers a 24-3 halftime lead as they ran off the field to the sound every visiting team loves to hear: booing.

Chris Gardocki pinned the Broncos deep in their own territory with his first punt of the game to open the second half. It was nearly turned into points for the Steelers as Polamalu read a screen pass and came like a blur to upend Mike Anderson in the end zone for what appeared to be a safety.

The ball was spotted at the 1, from where the Broncos punted.

"He covered 30 yards in like 2.1 seconds in five strides," says Keisel. "It was a safety. It was one of those plays that not all of Steelers Nation remembers, but players who watched the game remember it."

The call was correct, actually, and the Broncos did cut into the lead with a touchdown pass in the third quarter. Anderson then ran for a touchdown to cut the lead to 27-17 with 7:52 remaining, and a Steelers three-and-out gave the Broncos the ball at their 20 with 6:12 left.

But it was Keisel's breakout moment as he sacked Plummer on third-and-3. As the Broncos huddled to go for it on fourth down, Porter said to Keisel, "This is the game."

Keisel responded with a strip-sack that was recovered by Travis Kirschke with 4:52 left. Roethlisberger ran 4 yards for the final touchdown and the Steelers were in the Super Bowl.

Back in Bill Cowher's only other Super Bowl appearance, in 1995, he proudly hoisted the Lamar Hunt Trophy for winning the AFC championship, wiped away tears and hugged Dan Rooney.

This time, Cowher passed along the Hunt Trophy as if it were a hot potato, and there were no tears. The goal was no longer just to get to the final game of the season, but to win it.

Cowher did hug Rooney, but instead of hoisting the trophy Cowher put up his index finger and said, "One more to go."

JOEY PORTER: I was on that field for that last fumble and LeBeau got mad at us for the first time. He cussed all of us out because guys were celebrating and the game wasn't over. But we just kind of knew we were going to Detroit.

CHRIS HOPE: That's the first time I saw LeBeau get upset. The game is clearly over after Keisel sacked their quarterback and we recovered. Myself, Tyrone Carter, B-Mac, Ike, we were dancing. Peezy's dancing, and we finally get Troy to come over and give us some. The minute he started dancing, Coach LeBeau cusses and starts chewing everybody out. "Have some class! Act like you've been here before!" I'm talking about going off, and McFadden, Tyrone Carter and Ike, those guys have a different kind of persona – very, very cocky. They were saying, "Man, forget that. This game's over. We're going to the Super Bowl. We're going to dance." And they danced and danced.

BRETT KEISEL: That was a career-changing game for me. My agent texted me after the game when I was on the bus, it just had a $ sign. As a seventh-round draft pick grinding it, I had taken a risk being an unrestricted free agent after the season – because the Steelers had offered me a deal before the season. It was a couple-year, backup-role type deal. "Or do you want to go out and prove you can start in this league and make starter-type money?" So it was a big gamble that year. It was a great gamble. Shoot. To make plays like that in the AFC Championship Game, then go to the Super Bowl, it was the greatest gamble ever.

PORTER: Troy made a lot of big plays in that game. He was all over the field. Cedrick Wilson also had a good day. It kind of shocked us because he got Champ Bailey twice, and Champ Bailey at the time was, well, he was Champ Bailey.

HOPE: Troy was in the zone in those playoffs. He made a pick against the Bengals. He made a pick against the Colts. He made two awesome plays on screens against Denver.

ALAN FANECA: I was crying in the locker room. Bawling. Everybody was so excited but I think I was the only guy crying. I was just so proud of the guys, so ecstatic. Having missed out a couple of times probably made me more emotional. I don't even know if we broke it down after that game. That visiting locker room is humongous. I didn't see the trophy presentation or anything.

PORTER: We got cheated in Denver, too. We did. I was on the loser of a couple AFC Championships before that and watched the other team celebrate on our field. That's *tough* to watch on your football field. But when we beat them, there was no stage. They just ran us into the locker room. My wife was at the game and I knew a lot of people up in the stands because I played at Colorado State, so you're looking for people after the game, trying to think who you're going to bring close to the stage with you. But, man, they treated it like a regular game. But we won and we were off to Detroit.

Prior to the season, Troy Polamalu had put together a study tape of the top safeties in the game. He watched every play from their previous season, and after the AFC Championship Game he approached Broncos safety John Lynch to tell him he was on the tape and how much he had inspired Troy.

"Troy has a respect for the game that's really unique," said Lynch. "He had no idea what that meant to me. Here I am in my 13th year, and he's telling me how much he respects me."

What did Lynch say?

"I told him, 'Go win the Super Bowl! You have no idea how much respect I have for your game.'"

Troy Polamalu, Jan. 27, 2006

Have you heard the Puhlahmahlu song?
TP: I've heard it. I think it's pretty good. I think Whitney Houston was originally supposed to sing it, but I guess Sesame Street outbid her.

Are you making that up?

Yes.

In the last game, you made two of the more athletic plays you ever made. Would you agree?

I don't know. I haven't really watched the game, to tell you the truth. I've moved above and beyond that.

You ought to see it. This one guy, No. 43, he's quite good.

I feel it all over my body right now. Trust me.

Is that pure instinct?

In some sense, yeah, but the defense allows me to just go out and be able to take shots and make plays like that, knowing I can trust the 10 other guys to have my back if I make a mistake.

Dick LeBeau was talking about all the different blitzes he has. Do you look forward to his game plans each week?

Yes. Actually it's very fun, very entertaining on our Wednesdays, our first meeting with him, just some of the things he does to free people up and get mismatches. It's pretty amazing the way he works.

What has your growing popularity been like?

It's a blessing in a way, but people come and go. Obviously you guys are going to be with what's hot, but a game from now, a week from now, I could be a distant memory. In some sense it doesn't bother me at all whether you guys are here with me or not because I know I'm not defined by prestige.

What does define you?

Me. Just me.

What do you take pride in?

I take pride in my life – my wife, my family. I try my best not to let football define who I am.

Does your wife watch more football than you?

She doesn't watch any football. She doesn't know anything about football, which is a good thing.

Why?

I don't want to come home and hear "Hey babe, you got smoked today. What did you think of that cover-2? Why did you let the quarterback look you off like that?" I'd be like, "Hey, come on, babe (changes voice) get in the kitchen and cook for me (laughs). No."

Are you the type of guy who has a trophy room or a football shrine in his house?

I do have a trophy room. It's in my attic in boxes.

Do you enjoy dealing with your newfound fame when you're out in public?

It's not really a problem. It's a blessing in a way as well; just to have this stage to hopefully be a positive influence on people. That was actually a goal I've always had and I prayed ever since I was little to be able to help people and to be a role model to people. So this role, this prestige, has provided me with that and it's a blessing in that way.

Does it ever overwhelm you?

It does become overwhelming. I can separate myself from football but it's hard for football to separate from me when I go home and I've got people coming over to my house for autographs and things like that. It's very hard for me to say no. I've never been an autograph person as a kid, never sought anybody's autograph or really got too much celebrity shock from anybody anyway because I never found value in that, so it's really different for me to be on the other end of it and to have people value signatures.

There's so much excitement around town. Will it help you guys to get out?

Pittsburgh, it's nice to be around here. Very seldom is everybody very happy like this, if ever happy like this. But it's been a very special winter for us as well. We've had good weather. We've been winning. It's very nice to be around here.

PORTER: We finally made it. We're taking Jerome to Detroit. The first week of practice was in Pittsburgh and the second week was in Detroit. I've never watched two weeks go by so fast in my life. Everything was a blur. The only thing that was in slow motion, something I really remembered, was us with the jerseys for Jerome. I made sure everybody had the No. 6 Notre Dame jersey. The plane ride was just amazing, to see everybody lit up like that. Get into Detroit, Jerome's parents' house, feeding us, coming together even closer as a team.

BRYANT MCFADDEN: The thing I loved about that Super Bowl run, we felt like we were the villains. We knew we were the underdogs because we were the sixth seed, but after we beat Cincinnati we felt like we couldn't have lost if we had six more games after Seattle. Some people debate me that I'm biased, but you cannot name me a playoff stretch like the stretch we had. We went through the top four or five offenses in the NFL, all on the road, with one neutral site. And we dominated. Cincinnati was one of the top four offenses. The Colts were 2. Denver was 7. And Seattle had the most yards AND most points in the NFL. They also had the Offensive MVP in Shaun Alexander.

FANECA: Jerome did have a party, but I didn't go. I didn't do a thing. I was there to win a Super Bowl. I stayed late at practice and didn't do anything. I got massages and chiropractic work all day long. I barely talked to my family. They would stop by the hotel for a few minutes, Julie included, and then they would go off. I told them, "See you all on Sunday." It was probably mostly me and the O-line guys who kind of hunkered down and just did our thing and were staying in the moment. The deal wasn't done for us.

HOPE: I've got a picture of our last practice. It was the DBs. I told somebody to snap the picture and we all jumped into character. We had a great week of practice. We enjoyed each other. We took pictures and went out to eat. There was no other way to end the season than to win the Super Bowl. We never even had a thought of losing the game, and I never had the thought to sit down and realize that it would be my last game as a Steeler.

BILL COWHER: We put in a defense the night before the Super Bowl and called it like 31 times, only because of a walk-through the day before when I saw a void. We really didn't have anything to stop a certain formation. Troy said, "I can do this," and I said, "No, no, no, I don't want Troy taking these kinds of risks against this football team. (Matt) Hasselbeck will rip us up."

We had a very smart defense. We had guys that understood their role. They understood the more you got comfortable with one another, you had each other's back. Guys took chances, that's fine. Troy was an integral part of that because you saw him do special things and then everybody else felt they had their specific roles. Joey got us going before games. James Farrior was the calm amid the storm. He got everybody lined up, made sure they did everything. Larry Foote was doing his thing; he got the last push in. Aaron Smith never came off the field. He knew exactly what to do, always. He was a smart, cerebral guy in the defensive line. Farrior was a smart, cerebral guy in the linebacker group. And really, Troy was a smart, cerebral guy on the back end. You had to have smart guys who could keep everyone else accountable at every level to do what we were doing. Pretty special group of defensive players.

HOPE: We had this thing called Hell No We Won't Go Friday and we would rebel against everything that was going on. Every Friday, all the DBs wouldn't warm up. We would stand on the line at the end, and Coach Cowher would be cussing. And we'd tell each other, "You'd better not move. You'd better not do as much as touch your toes." We did it the first week and Coach Cowher cussed but didn't get us to move. We did it the second week and he cussed and we didn't move. And now he just said, "All right, just go ahead and do it, but nobody over there better pull a muscle today!" We did that every Friday. Coach Cowher gave up on it. He couldn't control it. We were young and cocky.

COWHER: We put Troy on the injury report that week because he got shin splints. It was a Field Turf at Ford Field, and so they had us practice on that turf at the old Silverdome. They just put it in that week, and it has to really settle, and by the end of the week Troy had shin splints from being on that frickin' turf. I don't even think he practiced on Friday. A couple guys were complaining about shin splints, and I thought, "Oh, shit."

MIKE LOGAN: Suddenly they're telling me that I may have to play strong safety and play the dime because Troy was injured. I'm like, "What?" They said, "You might have to come in at strong, we're going to do some things with Tyrone (Carter) and mix him in, we're gonna move him." I had been back-up free safety and nickel, so I would have to re-learn that other stuff in a couple of days. I kinda got nervous. This is how weird it was: I was thinking I had an opportunity to maybe start in the Super Bowl, but I would rather have Troy in there. I actually skipped Jerome's bowling party to make sure I knew everything I needed to know in case I had to go in and play some different positions. I remember telling my dad it was the first time I had ever been nervous playing football. And it wasn't because we were in the Super Bowl. I asked our training staff for a progress report on Troy every morning. And Ariko (Iso) would say "Oh he's working out. He's moving better. He's doing all right." I said, "Put the Mr. Miyagi on him. Heal him up." When they finally said he was going to be fine, I let out an inside gasp, thank goodness.

KEISEL: I think it was the weird-ass routine he would always do with rubber bands and balls and all the crazy stuff he did. It's not made for a normal human being. I'm not really sure what caused the injury, but he wasn't 100 percent. A lot of people aren't at that point, but you find a way to grind it. Potsie played with one arm. He hurt his shoulder and came out with some weird neck roll.

COWHER: We practiced up there on Friday. We had a little walk-through on Saturday and that's actually when we walked through one play and realized, "Man, we don't have a defense for this." That's why I put a defense in the night before the game – in a ballroom at the hotel.

SHELLEY POLAMALU: On Sunday we were out at a tailgate party, and everyone had that Puh-LOM-a-loo song playing out of the back ends of their rigs. Every car had that noise. It was like an anthem. We heard it so much we were pronouncing it wrong ourselves. "What's your name?" "Shelley Puh-LOM-a-loo."

PORTER: This dude that knew Jerome was taking pictures before the game and we had these suits made. And I remember Jerome coming out the tunnel for the game. But the game itself was a blur. I went in confident that we couldn't lose. Everything was set up perfectly with Jerome being at home. Seattle was a good team but I felt confident we could beat them. Even the trash-talking I did before the game really didn't matter to me. None of that was planned. I didn't want that to really be the headline going into the game. But I did my job. I made the tackles I was supposed to make. We had a lot of different people show up. Hamp had a big sack, Clark had a sack, Ike had an interception. Guys were making plays all over the field. Willie had that big run. That's what I remember: living in the moment, playing the game and the party afterwards.

The Seahawks broke up a scoreless game late in the first quarter with a field goal, which was a relief to the Steelers. They nearly gave up a touchdown, but the back judge saw Darrell Jackson push Hope in before Jackson cut out. A late flag nullified the touchdown pass, forcing the Seahawks to kick a 47-yard field goal.

The Steelers didn't put a scoring drive together until midway through the second quarter. Ben Roethlisberger's 37-yard pass to Hines Ward on third-and-28 put the Steelers at the Seattle 3.

Roethlisberger's TD sneak was reviewed, and during the review Troy Polamalu was picked up by field mikes telling Cowher, "I'll take it over the top, coach."

JUSTIN MYERS: That's such a Troy thing. It's like, wait, you're on the 1, you're in the Super Bowl, you've got Jerome Bettis, maybe the greatest short-yardage back in the history of the NFL, and you're saying, no, give me the ball with no carries all year, let me jump over the top. And he was serious as a heart attack.

JAMES HARRISON: Everybody secretly wishes they were a running back, especially if you played in high school.

SHELLEY POLAMALU: I laugh, but that run when he evaded about 10 tackles, going back and forth, and then ran right over Carson Palmer, that was a remarkable touchdown. I read where a question was asked about the emergency running back, if they all got hurt or something, and the coach said Troy. That shocked me.

SALU POLAMALU: Well, like Old Man Rooney always says every time he makes a run like that, "I think we've got him in the wrong spot."

MYERS: I remember after he came home that summer and I asked him if he practiced that, was it in the game plan? Why did he ask his coach for the ball? And he said, "Well I told him a couple times I could do it." He had been trying to talk him into it.

COWHER: Oh, he wanted it one time just to be able to run an offensive play. I said, "You're such a pain in the ass. The closest you're going to get to the offense is if we do a kneeldown and you can go out there. That's your offensive snap. Just stand behind there in case there's a fumble." That was the closest he was going to get to touching the ball on offense.

Roethlisberger's touchdown stood, Troy wasn't needed, and the Steelers went into the locker room with a 7-3 lead thanks to some awful clock management by the Seahawks. They had the ball at the Pittsburgh 40 with three timeouts and 54 seconds left, but lost 35 seconds (to 0:13) on a 4-yard run with two timeouts left.

Coach Mike Holmgren took those two timeouts into the locker room after Josh Brown missed a 54-yard field goal.

FANECA: We didn't play well on offense in the first half. We were kind of lucky to be where we were. It definitely wasn't going to plan early on. We did have this little package of plays we were using to hopefully set something up, and it ended up working. That package was about the only thing going right for us. We had Randle El in the slot and we just wanted to make a couple yards. We knew if we could just keep making a couple yards – maybe 5, 6, 7 and steadily keep doing it – that they would slide over and honor El more. That's what we wanted them to do, slide the 'backers over and play more to El, so we could run the other way. And right away in the second half they did, and we checked to our play to Willie right off the bat. I remember getting down in my stance and I was like, "Holy shit, we're about to do it." Oh, man, it worked.

Willie Parker's 75-yard touchdown run, with key blocks by Alan Faneca, Max Starks, Heath Miller and Hines Ward, is still the longest run in Super Bowl history. It gave the Steelers a 14-3 lead just as the third quarter was starting.

The Seahawks missed a 50-yard field goal, and the Steelers were looking to score the crowning touchdown with a first down at the Seattle 11.

Jerome Bettis gained four, and was stopped on second down. The Steelers called timeout before the third-down play.

COWHER: It wasn't one of our better offensive outputs that game, but we had that game in hand and Whiz called a pass for Ben, and Ben was not – you could just tell from the very first series it was a little bit big for him at that time. And I said, "Man, just run the ball and kick

Troy Polamalu dresses as a sailor for Halloween.

Troy Polamalu and good friend Erick Stookey celebrate their hardware earned on the baseball diamond.

Troy Polamalu was the leadoff hitter for Doc's American Legion team.
(Courtesy *The News-Review*)

Troy Polamalu slides after scoring the winning run for Douglas High.
(Courtesy *The News-Review*)

Uncle Salu Polamalu holds the fireknife he used as a professional dancer. Note the hook on the end that was useful in war.

Troy Polamalu's cousin, Tafe'a, hangs out with Chef Salu on Mother's Day of 2011.

From left to right, the Polamalus (Saul, Shelley, Denise, Talati, Keneti and Diane) always support Troy.

Troy Polamalu lived in this house with close friends Carson Palmer, Malaefou MacKenzie and Lenny Vandermade during his days at USC.

USC safety Troy Polamalu outruns Penn State's Imani Bell as he returns an interception for a touchdown during the second quarter of the Kickoff Classic in August of 2000. (AP Images)

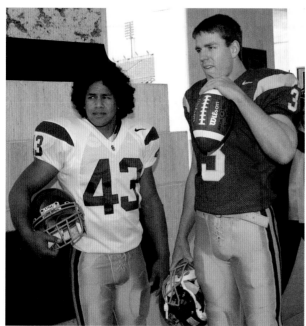

Troy Polamalu poses with his housemate and quarterback, Carson Palmer, outside the Los Angeles Coliseum in 2002. They would later face each other as divisional foes in the NFL. (AP Images)

USC head coach Pete Carroll walks with Troy Polamalu at a practice prior to facing Iowa in the Orange Bowl. (AP Images)

Pittsburgh Steelers head coach Bill Cowher welcomes recently-selected first-round pick, Troy Polamalu, at Polamalu's first minicamp in 2003. (AP Images)

Pittsburgh Steelers safety Troy Polamalu comes flying in to tackle Seattle Seahawks wide receiver Darrell Jackson during the first quarter of the Steelers' victory in Super Bowl XL. (AP Images)

Pittsburgh Steelers safety Troy Polamalu celebrates the Steelers' win against the Arizona Cardinals in Super Bowl XLIII with his son. (AP Images)

the field goal." It was 14-3, and if we kick a field goal it's 17-3 and they can't score two touchdowns. Well, he throws the interception in the end zone, they run it out 76 yards, and, three plays later, touchdown. So instead of 17-3 it's now 14-10. Now it's a ball game. We're going into the fourth quarter and I said, "Shit, if we had just run the ball."

FANECA: After Seattle scored, our backup center, Chukky Okobi, got hurt on the kickoff return and he was done for the game. I was the third option, the emergency center, behind Chukky. So Russ (Grimm) came up to me and said, "Hey, you've got to go get some snaps with Ben." And I'm like, "Fuck you, man, I'm not going to get snaps with Ben." He said, "No, just in case, man, you've got to go get some snaps." I didn't budge. I just stayed down there. Russ was on the headset and he turned around a few minutes later and he's like, "Get your fucking ass down there." So I go down there and I sit next to Ben on the bench, and Ben's like, "What's up, man?" I was never going down there to sit next to Ben during a game, so I'm like, "Chukky's hurt." And he said, "Chukky's hurt?" And I said, "Yeah, he's out of the game, so Russ wants us to get some snaps." And Ben instantly jumped up and was like, "Get the fuck out of here, man." I said, "Thank you. That was my same sentiment." Jeff (Hartings) had some knee troubles, too, and that was why Russ wanted me to get some snaps, because Jeff was banged up a little bit. During a TV timeout right after all this goes down, I was talking to Jeff, saying, "Dude, just snap the ball. I'll take care of everything else. Just snap the ball, man. I don't want to take my first live center snaps in the freakin' Super Bowl." He held it together. But, man, that stuff's like taboo. We practice a couple snaps and you know damn well what's going to happen. We both wanted to stay as far away as possible from that scenario.

The 16-yard touchdown pass to Jerramy Stevens not only brought the Seahawks to within 14-10, it brought the Steelers defense into a meeting on the sideline about how Stevens got open. The defensive backs and the linebackers began pointing fingers.

IKE TAYLOR: Troy don't usually say much. I think we all know that. But, when he talk, you listen. So we had a miscommunication on that Seattle touchdown. It was between a few guys on the linebacker crew and the secondary. We were arguing amongst each other. Well, Troy shut that shit all the way down. He said, "Now ain't the time, now ain't the place. It's time to close this chapter in the book."

PORTER: Potsie was mad because he said somebody didn't get something, and C Hope and Troy were like, "Peezy, don't you come down here with that shit!" I just stopped in my tracks and turned around. I was laughing in my head because I got exactly what I needed to know. If he's that damned mad about what happened, I know it ain't gonna happen again.

Troy's fiery sideline talk inspired Taylor, who intercepted Hasselbeck at the Pittsburgh 5 when Seattle seemed to be on the verge of taking a lead for the first time.

Ike's return, plus a 15-yard penalty, set up Antwaan Randle El's 43-yard touchdown pass to Ward, which gave the Steelers a 21-10 lead with 8:56 remaining.

TAYLOR: I dropped one, like I always do, in the first quarter. But we knew they liked to go two receivers side. The outside receiver did a 5-yard stop, and the slot receiver did a go. They knew we liked to play cover-3, and that's a cover-3 beater if the corner's eyes aren't right. I remembered that formation from the first quarter and I got the same call from Dickie and made the play. Same exact play. I just wound up catching it the second time.

The Seahawks got the ball back with 8:56 remaining, but a third-and-8 sack by Deshea Townsend forced a punt.

The Steelers got two first downs, the second causing the iconic first-down signal by Cowher, which essentially signaled game over. And the party for Championship No. 5 was underway.

Unless someone else wanted the ball.

With three seconds left, Roethlisberger ran back on the field with his running back, Polamalu, stationed several yards behind him in the greatest formation in football: a Super Bowl victory formation.

"There was no question we were kneeling," says Cowher. "I told Troy to get out there, and he loved going out there for that offensive play."

There was pure joy shining in the faces of the Cowher family on the trophy platform. The unfolding of it was beautiful.

If you fought back tears while watching the Cowhers deal with losing Super Bowl 30, you fought back tears watching his family experience the bliss of winning Super Bowl 40, too.

Bettis bade farewell to the game after pulling up his baby girl. If Cowher wasn't the Big Daddy of Steelers Nation on this night, Bettis was.

And then the newlyweds came up, Troy and Theodora. They took it all in, completely present in the moment, young and joyous in a glorious celebration of their first anniversary.

COWHER: The one moment I will always remember is being able to hand that trophy to Dan Rooney. That really meant a lot to me. Through 14 years of being there, the faith that he had in me, the support I got from that organization, from top to bottom, was unbelievable.

LOGAN: I got hurt right before halftime. Got caught in the turf and I felt it pop. I was in my ninth year, had one more year on my contract, and thought this might be it for me. So I started to take it all in. I really started embracing everything that went along with the Super Bowl, because I didn't know if I would be coming back. I was like, "Jerome's going to finish with a storybook ending. And me, the local guy who got to his hometown team, is going to finish on top, too." I stayed in the stadium for a long time. I remember picking my mother up over the stands to come down to the field and watch my kids make snow angels in the confetti.

FANECA: The stands were way above, and I was looking up for my family and I'm thinking Julie's going to kind of hang and then drop down. It was about an 8-10-foot drop, but she just totally jumps for it and lands right in front of me and pops right up, and I'm like "Holy shit, did you break a leg?"

LOGAN: That walk out of the stadium was a long one and I got to do that with my mother, who had bursitis in her hip. She was limping and I was limping, so we both hobbled all the way around to catch the bus. That was the most special moment in my career because my mother passed away a couple of years after that.

HOPE: I remember getting on the bus, and me and Troy really weren't feeling it because it was like, "This is what it feels like, but it's almost like we already were supposed to have done this." I don't know if you can feel what I'm saying, but it was almost like in college when we won the national championship at Florida State. It was like, "That was our goal. That's what we're supposed to do." The thoughts then automatically went to winning another one, and that's what my thoughts jumped to here, so we didn't really get to celebrate. That's why, I think, when you have a great team, a team that expects to win, you don't feel the win like you'd feel a loss.

MYERS: The Seahawks are kind of the Pacific Northwest team, so that was a weird day on air. I was hosting my show in Eugene and I remember Holmgren came out and said, "I didn't know we were going to have to play against the refs," and I went on the air and just ripped Holmgren to shreds (laughs). I wasn't the most popular radio host in the state of Oregon that day.

Seahawks fans – and many neutral NFL fans – bought the excuse by Mike Holmgren that poor officiating cost his team the game. Upon close inspection, only the 15-yard penalty on Taylor's interception return could be considered a missed call.

MYERS: I eventually got hired in Seattle and I was working for 710 ESPN, which was the Seahawks station. I went up there anticipating all these Seattle fans to hate me because I'm an Oregon fan, since Oregon-Washington is a huge rivalry in the Pac-12. But being a Steelers fan brought back 10 times what had been coming at me for being an Oregon fan, and I didn't see *that* coming. This was the year after the Seahawks beat Peyton Manning and won the Super Bowl, and I'm like, "Wait, you guys are still mad about 2006?"

It's still the third rail. That Super Bowl, they're so adamant they were screwed, but my theory is it's about two plays. One was the pass interference in the end zone that negated a Seahawks touchdown. The official whiffed on grabbing the flag and had to reach back again and throw it, so it looked like a late flag. And the other thing is Hasselbeck after the interception diving into a lead blocker, which is one of those technically legal things. But on the other one, the official whiffed and it looked like such a late flag that everyone assumed he saw what happened, the touchdown, and then threw it.

TAYLOR: After that Super Bowl, the parade downtown when Troy jumped out of the truck with the Lombardi in his hand, and the crowd caught him and waved him right back to the truck, that's one of my favorite memories of him. I thought, ain't this something? Man jumped off the float – *off the float!* – into the crowd. The crowd caught him and waved him back on the float. That's how much respect the city had for Troy. And that's how much he trusted the city.

CHAPTER 16

HOPE IS LOST

The great Pittsburgh sports writer Gene Collier used the term "walking hangover" to describe the Steelers' 2005 regular-season finale against the Detroit Lions.

Collier should've copyrighted the phrase for the entire 2006 season.

It's so often the case with defending champions, and this team lost hope before training camp: Chris Hope.

The young free safety had grown into the perfect complement to Troy Polamalu. But the fact that Troy was outrageously talented and would be up for a generational-wealth type of contract the following year caused the Steelers to shy away from giving Hope the money he eventually received from the Tennessee Titans on March 15, 2006.

Troy called his close friend as soon as he heard the news and the two talked for a couple of hours, shedding tears.

Troy wasn't quiet about his feelings, either. "I'm very hurt by it," he told *GQ.* "You spend so much time forming a relationship with somebody, and it's crazy how they can just be gone the next day. It's like losing a family member to death, because you'll never, ever have the relationship that you had."

That was just the start of this year-long hangover that ended with Bill Cowher's retirement.

The Steelers traded up in the first round for the second time in franchise history to draft Santonio Holmes, who spent as much time in the news for his poor decisions as he did on the field his rookie year.

Then, of course, came the motorcycle accident that almost killed quarterback Ben Roethlisberger. After Roethlisberger recovered, he went down with a bout with appendicitis right before the start of the season.

It was a long season, fraught with one seeming disaster after another, one question about Cowher's new residence in North Carolina followed by another question about Roethlisberger's future intentions on "crotch rocket" motorcycles, followed by another question about Holmes' next court appearance.

The other question was this: Could Ryan Clark, the man signed to replace Hope, beat out Tyrone Carter, Mike Logan and rookie Anthony Smith to become that all-important complement to Polamalu on the back end of the defense?

Polamalu, with 100, and Hope, with 97, finished third and fourth on the 2005 Steelers in tackles. They combined for 18 passes defensed, five interceptions, four fumble recoveries and two forced fumbles.

CHRIS HOPE: We were really, really playing at a high level. We were voted the most dynamic safety tandem in the league and we were still young. I guess that's where the disappointment, the letdown came. We were just about to become something, and it was over just like that. I didn't even get a chance to celebrate the Super Bowl. We got back to the hotel. My fiancée, now my wife, Linda, was on the bus with me, and Troy and his wife, Deshea and his wife. We were just talking and laughing and enjoying it. It still hadn't hit us yet. It was still surreal. We got to the hotel and had a team party. In the morning I did an interview on First Take on ESPN talking about the win. Next thing I know they're saying I'm the hottest free agent on the market! You don't really think about those things as a young guy. You're just playing the game. You never really focus on the business part; after you're drafted it's all football. So now the business side of it popped back up, and it was kind of tough for me because my loyalty and my friends – the guys that I bled with, cried with, rejoiced with – are all in Pittsburgh, and now I've got to make a decision. Do I stay or do I leave? And now you get into the personal part of what they think about you, and what they're willing to pay, and as a football player you never want to get in that part of it.

Hope spoke with Polamalu and Joey Porter about the negotiations. They told Hope they had been talking to Cowher "for hours about why we need Chris Hope to be here," all to no avail.

HOPE: Me, Deshea and Troy took a picture with our Super Bowl robes on after the game, and Coach LeBeau came over and hugged me and told me how much I meant to him. I guess he realized it was time for the team to make a business decision and there's a good chance I might not be back. He told me he loved me and said, "A lot of the success we had is because of you patrolling and controlling what's going on back there, you being the safety net, you making people right, and that you're just as important to us as Troy is, and I hope you're here, and I hope I'm here to coach you for the rest of my days of coaching." That stuck with me, to have so many people in that organization that really care about you as a person. It was hard to leave.

The players the Steelers believed were making "unreasonable demands" – as Omar Khan had said in August of 2005 – both left.

* Hope was replaced by free agent acquisition Ryan Clark and third-round draft pick Anthony Smith.

* Antwaan Randle El was replaced by first-round draft pick Santonio Holmes and third-round draft pick Willie Reid.

In Holmes, the Steelers got a fast, wiry, tough receiver who could catch short, deep, inside and outside, and was a dangerous punt returner. But in Holmes, the Steelers also bought trouble.

He was arrested for disorderly conduct in Miami at 3:30 a.m. over Memorial Day weekend. Those charges were dropped, but, less than a month later, the 22-year-old out of Ohio State was charged with domestic violence and simple assault in Columbus.

His girlfriend refused to cooperate, but the case dragged on throughout the season.

Just as the Cowher case did.

In March, the coach told Jerome Bettis that he planned to retire, and the running back who was carving out a niche in the media in his early post-playing days reported in August that, "This is the last year for Coach Cowher in Pittsburgh."

Cowher said it was all speculation and refused to further discuss the topic, but it raged throughout the season – even after Roethlisberger missed a car windshield by "three inches" and faceplanted on a city street while riding his high-performance Suzuki Hayabusa without a helmet on June 12. He underwent seven hours of surgery on multiple facial injuries.

The quarterback recovered from his accident and was able to resume the work at training camp, but the "walking hangover" lingered.

RYAN CLARK, *Steelers free safety (2006-13):* When I signed the contract and decided to become a Steeler, the first thing my wife said was, "I can't wait to meet the guy with the long hair. I bet he dances on top of tables at clubs." I didn't know Troy at all at the time. All I knew was the way he played the game. I thought he would be 100 percent different than he was when I met him.

IKE TAYLOR: Who's this new guy? Coach Cowher and Coach LeBeau said y'all heard of Sean Taylor, right? And we said, "Yes, sir." And they said this guy lined Sean Taylor and that defense up every play. "OK, coach, we hear ya. We need to see it." Then it was, "OK. We seen it. But can he hit?" Oh, Lord, why did we ask that? It's like we woke him up. Of course he could hit. But I don't think Ryan Clark wasn't R.C. until he got to Pittsburgh. Then he just woke up. The man had body count after body count. He ended up playing 13 years, an undrafted free agent who made the Pro Bowl.

Troy Polamalu, May 13/July 29, 2006

Will the character and chemistry carry over from last season?
TP: Yeah, but we lost a very, very important block of leadership in Jerome and Chris and Kimo and Antwaan. Those guys are big locker room guys. It will be tough to replace that. Their roles are very important, but from their personalities and the family that we created it's pretty much a death in the family because they'll never be back here and it's just somebody you'll miss. I don't expect the new people that come in to be funny like Chris, or loud and charismatic and caring like Antwaan. But new people do come through.

Will there be an adjustment for you with the new safety?
Yeah, there'll be a big adjustment. It's definitely different back there without Chris. Whether or not that'll be more successful or not, we'll find out.

Say the new safety takes time to learn the defense. How will that limit you?
It's not just understanding the defense, but understanding me. We got to a point where Chris and I didn't even have to talk. I got to do what I do and he just reacted to it. To form that type of relationship is tough, being how different of a safety I am.

When you do get out, what do you enjoy about Pittsburgh?
I enjoy fly fishing a lot. I learned that when I first came here. Other than that it's pretty hard to go out here without getting hassled too much. When I go out in California people couldn't care less, even if you're a Tom Cruise.

Is it tough being such a big celebrity that you can't go out?
It sucks in a way if you're eating dinner and people are bothering you, but it's beautiful in a way when there's a kid who has only five days to live and the biggest thing in his life is wanting to meet a Steeler.

Is your popularity here is due in part to the way you play?
I approach what I do in my living as a football player the way they do, in the blue-collar mentality. That term is thrown around a lot, but to say it and to live it and to experience it, even at a high-paying job like a football player, it's no different to a hard-working construction worker or a landscaper. It is a blue-collar mentality.

Does the training staff give you guidelines to follow during camp?
Not really, besides spreading their Gatorade propaganda. That's what it is: propaganda.

Troy's dig at Gatorade was the first of several over the years. Way too much sugar, says the former sugar addict.

The follow-up question was this: What should a young athlete drink?

Troy recommended organic orange juice, since it wasn't, as he said, full of sugar *and* pesticides. But Troy had an important addendum:

"Teach her the Jesus Diet," he said. "So many people worry about what goes into their mouth, when they should worry more about what comes out of it – the Jesus Diet."

Ben Roethlisberger had an appendectomy a few days before the Thursday night opener against the Miami Dolphins and missed the game. Brett Keisel said of Roethlisberger, "He's cursed," and the *Washington Post* ran a column on Ben under the headline, "Blindsided by Bad Karma".

Polamalu gave his take:

"Karma's a Hindu belief and a Buddhist belief," Polamalu said. "Jesus Christ said there's no karma anymore. He suffered everything for everybody. That's what my beliefs are.

"I really don't think it's up to you and I to understand. It's up to Ben to understand what's going on in his life. It's up to him to overcome these adversities that are set before him. If you look at anybody who's sick, any kid who's in the Make-A-Wish Foundation for example, it'd be hard to set those circumstances to your own life, but those aren't your circumstances. Those are that person's circumstance.   Everything is relative. So in this case it's up to Ben to really realize what's going on in his life and to set his priorities straight, or whatever it is that's in his life."

Charlie Batch stepped in at QB and led the Steelers to a 28-17 win over the Dolphins. Troy Polamalu's interception with 6:11 remaining and Miami down four sealed the win.

Polamalu hurt his right shoulder tackling Miami's "offensive lineman of a quarterback and their stud running back" – Daunte Culpepper and Ronnie Brown – then went up against 245-pound quarterback Byron Leftwich and 225-pound "scat" back Fred Taylor the next week in Jacksonville. The Steelers were blanked 9-0.

"That's what sucks," Polamalu said. "You just hope you can face a finesse offense every once in awhile."

They wouldn't find finesse in their next opponent. The Bengals had a 230-pound quarterback in Carson Palmer and a 235-pound tailback in Rudi Johnson.

Palmer was impressed by how his friend opened the season.

"Typical Troy, just making plays, being physical," said Palmer. "In my eyes he's the best defensive player in the game. He's more than just the best safety. He's the best defensive football player."

"Man, that's awesome," Polamalu responded. "He's probably the best offensive player in the league himself."

The Steelers led the Bengals 17-14 and were getting the ball back in the middle of the fourth quarter when the game turned in a snap.

Steelers announcer Bill Hillgrove: "Ricardo Colclough is back for the punt."

Steelers analyst Tunch Ilkin: "Uh oh."

Ilkin spoke, Larson kicked, Colclough muffed, kneed and kicked, and the Bengals recovered.

Palmer threw touchdown passes to T.J. Houshmandzadeh on the next two Bengals snaps, in separate series, and just like that the Steelers were 1-2.

The Steelers dipped to 1-3 in San Diego, but bounced back with a 45-7 rout of the Kansas City Chiefs.

Polamalu intercepted his second pass of the season against the Chiefs and returned it 49 yards to the Kansas City 33. Fifteen more yards were added when Chiefs RB Larry Johnson tackled Polamalu by the hair to save an apparent touchdown. Johnson then jerked him up by the hair after the tackle.

"The dude had hair!" Johnson explained after the game. "What do you want me to do? They said the hair is part of the uniform."

Said Polamalu: "If I'm hairless by the end of the season, it's a good thing."

SHELLEY POLAMALU: I thought that was pretty interesting, not just tackling him, but pulling him back up and hanging him in the air for a while. But I liked Troy's reaction, which was no reaction. It was first class.

TROY POLAMALU, *to Justin Myers:* I was just so happy I could actually take my frustrated running back bitterness out of me. To tell you the truth, I was just so happy to have the ball. As soon as I cut that corner, I just saw green. So I was trying to sprint to the end zone. But when I got tackled I didn't even feel it. I really didn't feel it. I didn't even feel the fact that he kind of gave me an extra tug. But the big story was how all my teammates saw it happen and ran over and tried to start fighting him, and I'm just like, "Dude, we got the ball back."

Troy Polamalu and Ryan Clark played their sixth consecutive game as the Steelers' safety tandem in Atlanta against Michael Vick, a quarterback who represented genius to young NFL players.

Vick had captivated the college football world from 1998-2000 as the strong-armed speedball who lifted Virginia Tech into its first and only national championship game.

Vick reportedly had been timed in the 40 at 4.25, and was clocked at 4.33 on the old, notoriously slow Indianapolis NFL Combine surface.

For comparison's sake, former Steelers quarterback Kordell Stewart ran his Combine 40 in 4.52.

Polamalu may have had that same sense of awe when he went up against the 26-year-old Vick in the seventh week of the 2006 season. Vick was in his physical prime but he hadn't figured out that Polamalu's appearance in the A gap was merely a disguise. Polamalu got back right before the snap and intercepted Vick 20 yards downfield on the opposite sideline. Polamalu undercut receiver Roddy White and intercepted the high pass. It led to a Hines Ward touchdown and a 10-7 Steelers lead.

"That may be one of the best defensive plays of the year," gushed TV broadcast analyst Phil Simms.

DICK LEBEAU: Troy is a master masquerader. He's tremendous. We try to establish parameters for our players. We don't want them to be frozen. We want them to create. We want them to deceive. But we don't want them to get so far off the diving board that they jeopardize the defense. Troy's parameters are a little bit wider than most of them because he's so creative. Again, he's introspective. He looks at his position. He looks at what the opponent would be looking at. All professional athletes, or at least in the NFL, study the game. To a certain degree they're film studiers. But not all can process what they're looking at and take it into the game and react to it as it's unfolding. Troy is probably the best I have ever, ever seen at taking knowledge that he has gleaned from studying tape and as soon as it happens in the game he can react to it instantly. It's one of the reasons that he plays so fast. He physically is fast. He physically is quick. But he can mentally convert what he has programmed his athletic system to respond to instantly when he's in the game. He's definitely the best I've ever seen at that.

There was Polamalu the introspective master disguiser. And then there was Polamalu the instinctive thoroughbred of an athlete. The latter came out in the fourth quarter with the Falcons ahead by 35-31.

They were looking to finish off the Steelers on third-and-6 from the Pittsburgh 8.

Vick attempted a pass that Brett Keisel batted back to Vick, who caught the deflection and headed for the left pylon. But Polamalu, playing in the middle of the front with a seemingly poor angle on Vick, put on a burst to run the QB down and push him out of bounds for no gain. It forced a field goal and kept the Steelers within seven points.

"That answered one of the questions I had today," Simms said in the booth. "If Michael Vick pulls it down, can Troy Polamalu get him before he gets around the corner? The answer is yes. In fact, he does it with surprising ease."

Play-by-play man Jim Nantz said, "Brad Johnson is the only quarterback to ever throw a touchdown pass to himself, and Michael Vick, for a minute, I thought he might get the corner there. But not with Polamalu."

CLARK: That's the most vivid play in my memory, Troy and Michael Vick basically racing to the sideline. I just remember thinking, "Gosh, I am such an inferior human." If Michael Vick takes off like that, your first thought is "Nobody's catching him." And if Troy takes off that way, your first thought is "He's catching whoever's running." Honestly, those are two of the greatest athletes I've ever been around, and I got to watch it first-hand.

The Steelers lost in overtime after Vick beat Polamalu, who blitzed off the blind side on third-and-9 at the Atlanta 45.

Vick juked Polamalu, rolled left, and threw for a first down. Four plays later, the Falcons kicked the field goal to drop the Steelers to 2-4.

RAY HORTON: There's another Troy play from that game that probably only coaches might appreciate. It's actually more of a Bill Cowher story and how much he respected Troy. We were playing cover-2 with Troy and Ryan in a half field. For some reason, Troy got a spidey sense and took off. Well, they threw a pass where Troy was supposed to be, and so Coach Cowher was yelling on the headset, "What's Ike doing?! What's Ike doing?! HE's supposed to be there!" It's kind of hard to correct Coach Cowher because he's almost never wrong. Coach Cowher understands football. So I calmly said, "No, coach, no, that was Troy." And he said, "No it wasn't, it was Ike!" I go, "No, coach, that's cover-2." And he started thinking and he said, "Where was Troy?!" I said "Troy blitzed." He said, "OK. Never mind." And that was it. Because he trusted him. That's what Troy had. Troy wasn't hundred percent correct, but he had the probability factor of about 96.7 percent. He was right so many more times than he wasn't.

Troy Polamalu, Oct. 25, 2006

Have you improved from last year?
That's tough to say. I truly believe within myself, and my wife would say the same – because I would say I'm only open to her about these sensitive issues – but I don't think so. Maybe a little bit, but not as much as I really want.

You don't watch football, but you like football, don't you?
Truthfully, I love life, and if you love life there's nothing that you can really find in life that could really disappoint you, whether it's something that you dislike or something that you like. That's kind of been my angle this whole year, and actually last year, too. The last couple years, I'm just loving life, loving everything and every part of it.

Was there a turning point in your life?
Not too long ago I started to really not care too much about winning or losing. My focus was all about having fun with my friends and making everybody happy. That's truly been my focus, and that whole playoff run was really fun because it was nice to see everybody else have fun, too. Just like now, it sucks because everybody's sad, because we've had such a bad start.

What does Theodora think of these ups and downs?
She doesn't pay attention to it. She doesn't care too much about football. She cares a lot about me. She's really worried about me when I'm out there because if I tell her, "You know, Theodora, this weekend is going to be a real physical game." She'll be like, "Oh, no, I don't want you to play." I'm like, "Theodora, you can't say things like that." But she enjoys some of it. Some of it's hard, too. It's hard for her to find friends that don't have an

angle for her, whether it's for tickets or autographs or something like that. *My wife doesn't read my stuff and I kind of like it that way. Is that something you maybe appreciate with your wife?*

That's exactly the same thing. The cool thing about it is she gets one comment after a game for me for football, and that's always really funny to hear. She'll say, "Gosh, babe, they scored three touchdowns on you today." And that'll be it. She may not know I wasn't even on the field, or I was on the field but maybe on the other side and it wouldn't be my responsibility, but it's like, "It's your fault, babe."

What did she say about your hair being pulled a few weeks ago?

She was really angry about it. Obviously I'm coming to the defense of the player, "Theodora, I'd do the same thing." But like I said, she's always worried about my health and welfare.

Now, do you take a Christ-like approach to a guy who pulls your hair?

I try to in everything.

How did you not get mad?

My mind was above. My mind was on God then. I was praising and thanking God for a gift like that (cradles imaginary football), "Thank you." Someone could've shot me in the back and I still would've run to the sideline. That's what's beautiful about it, and that's what taught me some great lessons: If you keep your eyes above on God, it's nothing if somebody grabs me by the hair or anything like that. There've been great lessons in life that happened to me like that. It's not only a blessing but a great lesson to me.

One of football's fiercest rivalries was all-square all-time at 11-11 when the Steelers traveled to Oakland to play the 1-5 Raiders.

The Steelers were 2-4 and on the road but were favored by 9 points.

That's how bad the Raiders were, but they never trailed the Steelers. Chris Carr's 100-yard interception return of a Ben Roethlisberger pass early in the fourth quarter was the crowning blow.

There was also something odd about the finish in "The Black Hole" as the Steelers drove inside the Oakland 20, down seven with less than two minutes left.

"I remember looking at the clock and it went from 1:50 to 1:20 in about three seconds, I kid you not," Polamalu said later in the week. "The only other person who saw it was Joey (Porter). We were looking at the clock and we were like 'What?' We both walked over to the ref, 'Hey, man, something's wrong with the clock.' He just shrugged."

The Steelers ended up losing 20-13 to fall to 2-5.

"I remember a couple Cowher outbursts, and one was when we lost to Oakland out there," says Chris Hoke. "He smacked that table so hard I thought he was going to break it, and he screamed, "I'M EMBARRASSED!"

The embarrassment for the defending champs continued the following week at home in a 31-20 loss to revenge-minded Denver.

The Steelers were now 2-6, but Cowher plowed forward, even as rumors of his impending retirement swirled.

"Let me tell you something," Cowher said. "Sports is a microcosm of life. You're going to have peaks and valleys. It's never as bad as it appears and it's never as good as it seems, and I truly believe that. How you deal with those circumstances speaks a lot more than the circumstances themselves."

"If you went back through some of the transcripts from 2003," said *Steelers Digest* editor Bob Labriola, "I'll bet you he said a lot of the same things. And with very little dramatic personnel changes, they won 26 regular-season games over the next two years and a Super Bowl.

Don't be surprised if it happens again."

After reviving the team with a 6-2 finish, for an 8-8 overall record, Cowher did retire. And Labriola went on to chronicle a near-precise prediction.

In a 24-20 win at Cleveland, Polamalu sacked QB Charlie Frye with a burst of speed that once again didn't seem humanly possible. And he read the next play and split the left side of the Cleveland line to tackle the running back after a short gain. On third down, Troy pulled up from a blitz and leapt at the perfect time to bat down a pass intended for Kellen Winslow.

The three-and-out in the fourth quarter allowed the Steelers to get the ball back with 3:06 remaining, and Roethlisberger drove for the game-winning touchdown.

Earlier in the game, Polamalu also saved a touchdown by running down wide receiver Braylon Edwards after a 63-yard gain, and then burst to tackle the Cleveland tight end after a 6-yard gain on third-and-7.

"I've been playing football a long time and I've never seen anyone make plays like he makes," Larry Foote told the *Post-Gazette's* Ron Cook after the game. "I'm seeing plays that I'll never see again."

"He's the best player I've ever seen at safety," said Winslow II. "He's on a different level."

"A gift from God," said Steelers defensive end Aaron Smith. "That's what he is, a gift from God."

There were a few more golden moments for Polamalu as the 2006 season wound down with wins over Carolina and Cincinnati and a loss to Baltimore. At this point, a consensus was forming that Polamalu was one of the best safeties in the league and he was named to his third consecutive Pro Bowl.

JOVON JOHNSON, *Steelers cornerback (2006):* In the first game I played, against Baltimore, we were playing cover-2. I was pressing the receiver and Troy was supposed to be the safety covering my side, but I looked over and he was in the box. I was waving to him – I didn't know if he knew what the play was – I was yelling at him, asking what he was doing. Well, they threw the ball, and I looked and saw Troy broke it up 20 yards downfield! When we got to the sidelines I told him he had me clueless. He told me not to worry about him.

CRAIG WOLFLEY, *Steelers Radio sideline reporter (2002-current):* Todd Blackledge always used to talk about the 7-yard walk, the most important walk for a quarterback. That was breaking the huddle, coming to the line of scrimmage, and viewing the defense from the back to the front. Where are the safeties? What's the coverage like? Linebackers? Defensive front? So one of the best examples, they were playing Cincinnati in '06 and Cincinnati was backed up inside the 10. They were huddling in the back of the end zone. I walked around and stood behind the back of the end zone to get the view. They break the huddle. The tight end goes right. They had two wide receivers. Troy was back where it looked like he would be in coverage over the tight end, about 15 yards deep. Carson was walking up, looking over, obviously he's looking for Troy. He goes under center and Troy starts to jog forward, and then he comes just behind Clark Haggans, the edge on my right, and Joey Porter was to the left. So Troy's about 2 yards deeper than Clark Haggans, and then he starts to jog laterally to the line of scrimmage. He's behind Brett Keisel, he's behind Snack (Casey Hampton), he's between Farrior and Foote, and he's going in-between these guys in the 3-4 base Okie. So he gets behind Joey Porter and then gets to the line of scrimmage outside Joey.

Now, Carson had broken the cadence off a couple of times while watching this unfold. Carson was just staring at him, rotating his head while following Troy. And Troy ends up finally at the outside behind Porter after starting 15 yards behind Clark Haggans, and I'm wondering if Troy's going to try to Superman him. Finally, Carson goes with whatever he's got called, and at the snap of the ball Troy zooms back and he's in cover-3 about 30 yards deep. How do you even begin to assimilate a play and try to run something when a guy's capable of doing that? It's one of the most amazing ways I've ever seen a player disguise his intentions.

BILL COWHER: To me, a multi-talented safety gives you so much more flexibility in a defense than a great corner. You can put a great corner on someone and forget about him, as we had with Rod Woodson. But you know where they're going to be. A team can stay away from a corner. Now a strong safety, you're not going to stay away from him. This guy can be disruptive whether he's in coverage, whether he's blitzing, whether he's doing things that create a little bit of indecision with a quarterback. That guy has a lot more ability to affect a game, to me, than a corner. A safety can disrupt from a disguise standpoint, from a blitz standpoint, from a coverage standpoint, from a run-support standpoint. He can create just a little bit of indecision in a quarterback and at the same time be the guy who can make plays because he's always around the ball and he's going to punch something out. I think Troy changed the game a little bit with his ability to disguise, his ability to anticipate, to take some chances, even though he understands where his responsibility is. Those guys, to me, a strong safety to me, can be a lot more impactful.

You're talking about the greatest player? No question Rod Woodson was just a special player at his position. It's hard to pick two, but I put both of those guys in the same breath. They didn't play the same position, but they had the same effect on the game.

Joey Porter didn't realize he was near the end of his time with the Pittsburgh Steelers in late December of 2006. Reporters didn't know, either, as they crowded around his locker before a game against the Baltimore Ravens.

But something was amiss. Reporters who had become accustomed to Porter's weekly outrage were wondering how he would react to the noxious cloud that overtook the group at the moment.

Do you expect Baltimore's trash-talking to be unbearable?

JP: Did somebody fart or something? Ooh, man, that's bad.

Yeah. It just broke up our talk with Ben.

Oh, wow (shakes head). Now, what did you say?

Since they've got the division wrapped up, do you expect their trash-talking to be unbearable on Sunday?
Aw, man, that smell's unbearable (shakes head again).
Do you need a signature win after a bunch of wins against backup quarterbacks of teams with bad records?
I don't know how to take that. Are you saying we ain't played nobody?
Certain people would say that.
I'm finished. I can't take it anymore. God, get me outta here.

It was a humorous end to a heroic stint in Pittsburgh. Porter finished his Steelers career fourth on the team's all-time sacks list with 60, was a three-time Pro Bowler, the 2002 team MVP and captain of the great 2005 championship defense.

He would return the following season and enjoy a big game as a member of the Miami Dolphins, and he returned to Pittsburgh in 2014 to coach outside linebackers for five seasons.

BRETT KEISEL: Peezy was such a fun leader. He had a certain mentality and a swagger to him and a certain chip on his shoulder that not a lot of players had, even in the NFL. And it was awesome to be around him because he put the uniform on and it meant something to him. He wanted to be the captain of a defense that offenses feared and to bring back that Steelers mentality they had in the '70s and '90s. As far as the hoo-rah speeches and stuff before games, it was awesome. Who ride? We ride.

JOEY PORTER: Pittsburgh is always going to have a huge part of my life. When Mr. Rooney and Cowher drafted me in '98, it changed my life forever. When I left the first time, it hurt because you put so much into being in one place, you want to be immortalized. You think you're going to play in the same city forever, and you want that. And then it didn't happen. That was the first time I learned about business.

CHAPTER 17

STATE OF GRACE

The high crimes and misdemeanors of a young Troy Polamalu are listed at the beginning of Chapter 2.

All but one.

His last one.

Troy was in sixth grade when he stole a Bible from a gift shop. He couldn't blame the mean streets of Santa Ana for this one because he had already been jettisoned to the serenity of Tenmile, Oregon.

Of course, that was Troy Aumua. That person officially metamorphosed early in 2007 into Troy Polamalu. He legally changed his name to the one he had been using since fourth grade to acquire a passport for his spring pilgrimage to the Greek Orthodox holy mecca of Mount Athos.

You may know of Mount Athos from the best-selling books *The Mountain of Silence*, featuring Elder Paisios, and *Counsels From the Holy Mountain*, featuring Elder Ephraim.

The latter is a book Troy kept with him throughout the 2010 playoffs. Ephraim is a Greek Orthodox monk from whom Polamalu seeks spiritual counsel in southern Arizona.

Paisios and Ephraim are the names Troy and Theodora gave their children, born in 2008 and 2010.

Mount Athos is known as "Holy Mountain" and has been occupied by monks at 20 different monasteries since the fifth century. Females aren't allowed on Mount Athos, in order not to distract the ceaseless prayer. Female animals are limited.

"The wisdom that you get from the people who you meet on these pilgrimages is truly amazing," Troy told *WHIRL*'s Leslie Hoffman. "It's very beneficial for your salvation, for your soul, for your spirit, for your relationships."

Troy and Theodora joined the Greek Orthodox Church in 2006. Troy even learned the Greek language in order to read the New Testament in Greek with Theodora. Troy explained to writer Gina Mazza Hillier that "Greek words carry emotions with them and I want to understand Scripture on this level with my wife."

According to those who played with Troy in high school and at USC, and who watched reams of tape on him, Troy didn't begin making the Sign of the Cross on the football field until 2004, his second season in the NFL.

"I'm asking for God's support in those moments – and in everything I do," he told Hillier. "Sometimes I'm just scared to do wrong. I wish not to do wrong."

Troy shed more insight into his spirituality in *GQ*:

* "With my life, there's no way that I could deny divine intervention. Coming where I've come from, the way that I've ended up at certain places where everything went just perfectly for me, whether it's here in Pittsburgh with a perfect defensive scheme, or the way it was at USC when Pete Carroll came in and just gave me the whole defense and allowed me to become a first-round draft pick. It's just beautiful the way it all worked out, and very humbling as well, because I see so many other, better, greater athletes than me on other teams. If they traveled this road that I traveled, I believe they could be more successful."

* "It got to a point in high school where I was almost constantly in prayer. Praying through the whole football game, praying through the meetings, praying as I'm driving – this constant conversation with God. Football was not, and is not, a sport to me. It's a spiritual battle. So it wasn't like after a play I would go, 'God! Why did I miss that tackle?' It was more like, 'OK, God, you've blessed me, and this is play, but I want to thank you so much for giving me the opportunity to play this beautiful sport.'"

Teammates, friends and family are quick to point out that Troy doesn't push his religion on others. He normally doesn't talk about it unless asked.

"There's a beautiful story of a monk who was very simple," Polamalu explained in the locker room. "He didn't know anything about Scripture, and then somebody asked, 'So what does he know about the Bible?' And he said, 'This guy lives the Bible. He doesn't need to preach it.' I think that would be the most elementary lesson that anybody would have to understand about the spiritual life, that it's one of knowledge. So I try to do it that way. My mouth gets me in trouble sometimes, too, so it's best to not talk too much."

CHRIS HOKE: You see this in professional sports, people want to talk and talk and talk like they're men of faith, and then their actions don't follow. Troy was a guy who showed you his faith by his works.

A rare Polamalu tweet in 2011 might explain why he had so little interest in discussing his life for a book <*shudder*> about himself:

"Those who live virtuously declare their small sins, & also their omissions, in order to avoid the glory that comes from men, & they conceal their virtues in order to safeguard their souls; lest they receive praise from men – when their virtues are discovered – & lose their zeal by becoming conceited. For just 'as wax melteth before fire,' so also the soul is paralyzed by praise; and loses its vigor."

– St. Synkletike

ED BOUCHETTE, *Steelers beat reporter (1985-current):* He had something religious hanging in his locker. I'd never seen anything like it. I was looking at it and he came over. He said it was a Greek Orthodox religious medal/icon, and he explained it to me. I didn't retain it, but he asked, "Do you want it?" I just said, "No, Troy. I'd never seen anything like it in a locker room. I was just interested in it." So he said to me again, "Do you want it? I'd like you to have it." I said, "Troy, really, no. You keep it. It's yours. It means something to you. I just was curious about it." OK, so the next day I'm interviewing someone else and I get this tap on the shoulder. "Here, I want you to have this." At that point I said, "Thank you, Troy." I gave it to my girlfriend and she cherishes it. It's hanging in her kitchen.

JUSTIN MYERS: Troy's kind of always in his own world – in a good way. We've talked about spirituality a couple of times and he's gone real deep into it, and I was just like, "Man, that's way too deep for me." He got real serious with religion and church when he went to USC. When we were in high school, he was religious. As a team we would pray, small-town stuff, but I didn't think it was the focal point of his life. When he went to USC that's when it really became, I think, his number one priority.

DARREN PERRY: He's very even-keeled and handles all the situations very calmly. Sometimes he'll give you this look like he's somewhere else. One time he got his bell rung and we didn't know whether he could go back in the game. Coach Bill looked over and said, "DP, is Troy OK?" I said, "Coach, quite honestly, Troy looks like that all the time." I didn't know if he was OK or not. I was just going to have to take his word because he's the same way all the time. I didn't know if he was in another world, if he was dinged, or if he was just being Troy. He ended up going back in the game

HOKE: He didn't go running around town chasing tail. He went home to his wife and children, the most important people to him. Those are values that don't come to everybody. The majority of time it comes through your faith. It keeps you grounded. And he was.

RYAN CLARK: I've never met a person like him. He's in some ways unfamiliar to me, because we aren't alike – even though we're super-tight. He has a level of self-deprecating mannerisms and a humility that's almost strange. He almost feels like he knows what he could be, from a negative standpoint. It's like he has a fear of "If I let myself be certain things" or "If I let myself feel certain things" or "If I let myself fall in love with certain attention, then I'll be someone I don't want to be." So I think he works extremely hard to be the other way. And it was weird because you end up kind of being his cheerleader. Whether it was Ike, me, Bryant, Deshea, we were always trying to convince him he was who we already knew he was, convince him to accept it.

The crazy part about playing with him was that we definitely put the responsibility of greatness on him, and expected it from him, but he never wanted the reward of that. The reward is admiration. The reward is compliments. The reward is players on your team doing special favors for you because they know in the end you're going to do something to help them get paid. He just never wanted those things. He wanted us to be his homeboys, his teammates, and that was that. I always thought that was just very strange, but also extremely unique and amazing.

Ryan Clark sat out behind young Anthony Smith the final four games of 2006, but Clark got a new lease on football in 2007 with the arrival of 34-year-old head coach Mike Tomlin.

The new coach had been recommended to the Steelers by Tony Dungy, who had been his boss at Tampa Bay. Dungy was a former Steelers player and coach who was now the head coach at Indianapolis, the new reigning NFL champions. His word carried weight with the Steelers.

After Ron Rivera fulfilled the "Rooney Rule" requirement regarding minority interviews, Tomlin entered the process late, but wowed ownership with his energy, enthusiasm and intelligence.

Chairman Dan Rooney and his son, team president Art Rooney II, also respected Tomlin's background as a cover-2 defensive coach. This is, after all, the organization that created, and won four Super Bowls with, that defense. They also felt that Tomlin was young enough to respect (and keep) his elder – coordinator Dick LeBeau – and smart enough to listen and learn from LeBeau, co-originator of Bill Cowher's 3-4 fire zone.

But could the youngest coach in the NFL ensure that franchise quarterback Ben Roethlisberger get back on track to fulfill his immense potential?

Roethlisberger endured his worst pro season in 2006, but ended by promising to work harder with his receivers in the offseason and return with a better grasp of the offense.

In his third season, Roethlisberger threw twice as many interceptions as he'd thrown in his first two seasons combined. He also flattened a two-year passer rating of 98.3 with a 75.4 rating in 2006.

A Super Bowl hangover can certainly devour a young star who had skyrocketed and then crotch-rocketed face first into pavement.

Another big question looming over Tomlin was what to do with Joey Porter? The defensive co-captain was turning 30, entering the final year of an expensive contract, was due a $1 million roster bonus in March, and his backup, James Harrison, was flashing immense potential as a blind-side pass-rusher.

Speaking of aging linebackers, co-captain James Farrior, the playcalling buck inside linebacker, was 32. He continued to play at a high level in 2006, leading the team with 154 tackles.

Also, young Troy Polamalu was approaching the end of his first contract, and renegotiating and extending that deal before the start of the 2007 season was a top priority for the Steelers, since he would surely draw massive offers should he reach free agency in March of 2008. Once the first game of the regular season is kicked off, the Steelers stop negotiating, per long held team policy. And if a player gets through that season healthy, he would be foolish not to test the open market.

The Steelers were making no secret of their desire to extend Polamalu's contract before the season kicked off, so the problematic monetary issues became Porter and All-Pro guard Alan Faneca, also entering the final year of his contract.

Porter was released on March 1, and within the week signed a five-year deal with the Miami Dolphins. A team that had fallen from fourth to 11th in the league in sacks had just cut its leading pass-rusher and emotional leader.

IKE TAYLOR: I thought the front office let him go because they thought Joey Porter would have more power over the team than Coach Tomlin.

BRETT KEISEL: It was James. James had come on as a player that was dominant. When he got his chance, he made something happen. If you put the tape on and run it, you could see that.

TAYLOR: I'm guessing. Put in there that I'm guessing, but I don't think I'm guessing wrong at all.

KEISEL: It's a business!

TAYLOR: Peezy wasn't tripping on no pay cut to stay in Pittsburgh. He always wanted to come back, even when he was at Arizona and Miami. He had to go to Miami because they paid him a whole 'nother big deal. But even though he went, he always wanted to come back.

KEISEL: We wondered who was going to be that next voice that Peezy was for us. Who's going to be that guy who stands up in front of the team and does the hoo-rah speech? Who keeps everyone together and isn't afraid to talk to players about some things? I think right away it was Potsie (Farrior), but that wasn't necessarily him. He got really good at it because all of us voted for Potsie for captain every year, because of the way he played the game. He united us. I think he took it over as kind of that guy and did an awesome job. Others stepped in. Aaron Smith stepped in as a voice – a loud voice. Aaron might not have done the hoo-rah speech before the game, but when he piped up everyone listened. Everyone respected him and followed him, because he was the yard dawg up front that beat a lot of people up. That's also when I started being more vocal. I remember Mr. Dan Rooney catching me one day when I was walking to my car. He said "I want you to be more of a leader. I want you to be more vocal. You're capable of it." That really meant a lot to me. I said that I have a hard time because of some of the great men in the building. He said, "Those great men respect you, too. It takes all of us."

The Steelers addressed the aging at linebacker by drafting a couple young linebackers early: Lawrence Timmons and LaMarr Woodley.

In the third round, the Steelers grabbed Mackey Award-winning tight end Matt Spaeth, who would complement Heath Miller the next several years as the "blocking tight end."

In the fifth round, the Steelers added a little-known cornerback named William Gay, who had been studying Steelers tapes for four years. He played in a similar scheme at Louisville, and on draft day exclaimed that the Steelers "have the best ways to disguise their coverages."

Gay's savvy soon became apparent as a valuable cog in the secondary for the next decade.

RAY HORTON: William didn't go to the Combine, so we could not draft him because we didn't have a physical on him. After we finished going through the reports of people we could draft, Kevin (Colbert) said, "Is there anyone else you want to talk about, Ray?" And I said, "Yes. There's this kid at Louisville I think would come in here and make our team and help us." I had made a cut-up tape of William Gay, and said, "They play our style of defense, blitzing and everything." I showed them some plays. There was one play where he would blitz like Deshea Townsend and he sacked the quarterback. "Here's our Sam fire zone. They run that." And later on in the game, he started the blitz, the quarterback saw him, he went back out of it and picked off the pass. I said, "This kid knows football. He's smart." Kevin said, "Well, we can't draft him because we don't have a physical. We'll go get a physical." So we brought him up and got a physical on him. We ended up drafting him in the fifth round and he played 11 years in the league. It was proof that when you're in the Pittsburgh Steelers organization, your voice matters. I've been places where the scouting department and the coaching department might as well be two separate teams because they don't trust each other; whereas in Pittsburgh, they do. And I think that's one of the reasons they're so good.

Troy Polamalu was on pilgrimage and missed the pre-draft minicamp, but he returned for OTAs in early May. At the same time, Alan Faneca, enraged about what he dubbed a lack of respect from the Steelers with their contract offer, declared this would be his final season with the team.

Troy's new contract was Priority No. 1 for the front office. So, from the enraged Faneca, the media herd bounced to the still-minded Polamalu. *Troy, have you gotten close to a contract deal?*
TP: No.
How hard are you trying?
TP: I've been up every night, you know, writing it up, typing it up.
Really?
TP: No. I have no idea.

Reporters didn't know Polamalu had just come off "The Mountain of Silence," and his brief answers and lack of interest in the contract negotiations – which his agent was handling – made little news. But, Troy did provide insight into the Steelers' coaching transition.

"I think it's troublesome, but I think it's good," he said. "I think it's good that everything is really shaken up and everybody's got to re-work and re-establish themselves. Whenever a new coach comes in you have to do this. I had to deal with it in college. We were all very wary about Coach Carroll and what was going to come about. Obviously, everything turned out pretty well for him and hopefully the same for Coach Tomlin."

An out-of-town reporter missed the interview and asked Steelers PR for a one-on-one with Troy after lunch.

The request was passed along to Polamalu, who showed up in the cafeteria. He told the reporter not to rush his lunch, that he would wait in the hall until he was done eating.

The reporter would hear none of it and left immediately for the interview. He came back a few minutes later shaking his head over Polamalu's courtesy, and asked, "Is that guy for real?"

On July 23, Troy Polamalu became the highest-paid safety in football by signing a $33 million contract extension that would keep him with the team through at least the 2011 season. The next day he reported to St. Vincent College.

The Steelers were playing in the Hall of Fame Game that summer, which meant an extra early start. No Hall of Fame Game participant had ever won a Super Bowl in the same season. Such teams endure a long training camp, particularly one in which a new coach is setting a tone. And Mike Tomlin – wearing long-sleeved black in 100-plus-degree heat indexes – was making his presence felt to the 2007 Steelers.

"That was pretty tough," coaching intern Levon Kirkland said after the first practice. "It kind of makes you wonder what the evening practice is going to be about. But, you've got to establish yourself as a coach. The players will respect that."

As for his all-black attire in the scorching heat, Tomlin said, "It's part of the mental warfare. I don't want guys coming to me talking about how hot it is because I don't care. I hope it gets hotter."

The first week was brutal, and when asked by a reporter whether he was going to "turn up the tempo next week," Tomlin stared in disbelief.

"If we increase the tempo any more, I expect the Baltimore Ravens to be on the other side of the line," Tomlin said.

Some of the other team developments:

* New offensive coordinator Bruce Arians began easing the fullback out of the offense, but he did take one more look at Casey Hampton back

there during the camp goal-line drill, much to Big Snack's delight.

However, Hampton was rocked by linebacker Clint Kriewaldt on his first and only lead-blocking attempt. Helmet knocked askew, runner tackled for a loss, Hampton finally admitted the job wasn't for him.

"That shit's a wrap, man," Mighty Casey said. "I've been begging to do it, but I don't think I can."

* Ryan Clark won his safety job back from Anthony Smith. Tomlin planned to alternate the two throughout preseason, calling them 1 and 1-A at the start of camp. But by the third preseason game Clark was nailing down the job.

"Ryan has been awesome," Tomlin said. "He has a passion for playing this game, and he plays it above the neck. His floor, if you will, is extremely high."

HORTON: Anthony was a third-round pick and Ryan was what I call a self-made man. He was undrafted. Nobody apparently thought he was good enough to play in the NFL, and he made himself. I love players like that because the game's important to him. He just said, "Hey, coach, you guys can keep putting me on the bench. You can try to cut me but you can't get rid of me." And I said, "Ryan, nobody's trying to get rid of you." He became one of our most valuable players.

KEISEL: LeBeau let our safeties and cornerbacks know that, "Hey, Troy's going to be kind of crazy, so you'll have to adjust." Especially Ryan. Ryan's job sometimes was nuts because Troy would do his thing and Ryan would have to cover for him, and he would sometimes make big plays while covering for him.

HORTON: In my eyes, Ryan Clark never, ever missed a tackle. That was what was so great about him and Troy. We could tell Troy, "Shoot your gun and go make a play" because Ryan would back him up and get the guy on the ground if he had to. But that's the mentality of Troy. Sometimes, in essence, when we're supposed to have two guys deep, or one guy deep, Troy would get an inkling – or as I called it "spidey sense" – and go, and it was OK because Ryan trusted that Troy was going to be right. It really was an unbelievable relationship with two guys that trusted each other. They always had the other guy's back. Now, for all these good stories, you can call Ryan Clark and he can tell you some "Oh boy!" stories about Troy. But Ryan and Troy were a great complement.

TAYLOR: Troy, Chris Hope, Tyrone Carter, Ryan Clark will all tell you this: Anthony Smith was probably our best safety, or would have been the best safety ever to wear a Pittsburgh Steeler uniform. If Smitty would've kept his head straight, he would've been Pittsburgh's best safety ever.

KEISEL: Shut up, Ike.

TAYLOR: Just ask Troy about Anthony Smith.

Troy was asked in 2007 which safety he preferred next to him.

"Whoever they have out there is going to be a great combination," said the athlete who could not tell a lie.

Polamalu was trying to abstain, but he finished his answer without incriminating Smith.

"Obviously, Ryan's a great safety," he said.

Clark not only became a championship and Pro Bowl free safety for the Steelers, he became one of Troy's closest friends.

CLARK: Among many other things, my relationship with Troy probably helped save my life. (Long pause) We had the first season and things were going pretty well for me, but Anthony Smith plays late in the season. He becomes somebody they really like, so I'm going to be in a position battle in '07. At this time Troy and I were cool, but we weren't necessarily close. One day he invites me over to work out in his garage. It was the freakin' longest workout ever, first off, so we're in there forever. But before we do it, we pray. I was like, "A'ight, if I gotta pray to work out, that's fine." I grew up with a very strict southern Baptist background. My mother's still in church every single day. So I sit down and eat with his family. He's telling me about being Greek Orthodox and how they pray, kind of how they worship, some of the strict pious fasting rules they have. I got really interested in it. So, my family and I would go to the monastery with him and his family. On the road, Troy and I would pray together. It was such a regimented religion, it was just awesome because you always knew how to pray, when to pray, what to be doing. I believed immediately that's part of what started to bring us closer, because I was so inquisitive about this and he loves sharing and letting you be a part of it.

Clark almost died during a game that year. In the sixth game, at Denver, Clark felt pain throughout his entire left side. He left the stadium for a local hospital, where he was diagnosed with a splenic infarction due to having the sickle cell trait.

"Sometimes when you go into a high-altitude situation, the trait actually forms into the disease and that's kind of what happened," Clark said upon his return to the Pittsburgh locker room later that season.

"My spleen wasn't receiving oxygen, red blood cells exploding, platelet levels low. It's a lot of things that go along with it."

He may have been home, but he wasn't well. Clark eventually had his spleen and gall bladder removed as his season came to an end.

"Playing in Denver was probably not the smartest thing," Clark said.

CLARK: When I got sick, I just remember how much praying he did with me, and for me. And on the other side of it, how much stronger my faith was, how much closer I was to where I needed to be spiritually because of that relationship. I could just remember not having fear during that time and being strong enough to think I was going to beat all that stuff, even though no one knew what was wrong with me. Part of that was because, man, we just dove into the word. On Saturday we would go eat together, come back to the hotel and do the meeting. Sunday morning, if it was a night game, we would wake up, go to church together, go to brunch, come back, go to the game. If we had time, we were spending it together. I think his unselfishness almost makes you ashamed that you aren't like that. The way that he gives to people, the way that he gives of himself, I think all of those things make a person better. It's part of why I believe he's blessed the way he is.

Under their new head coach the Steelers opened strong.

They crushed the Browns in Cleveland 34-7. Dick LeBeau celebrated his 70th birthday by putting his interior linemen in a fourth-man front to open the game. It surprised everyone, particularly the guy who was supposed to block Aaron Smith on the edge. Smith's third-down sack forced a punt and set up the first Steelers touchdown in the romp.

The defense would've given LeBeau a shutout for his birthday had James Farrior held onto a third-quarter interception. The drop allowed the Browns to score their only touchdown in the third quarter.

"Well, the coordinator didn't call too many good ones after that or they wouldn't have gotten in there, either," said the humble LeBeau. "It all works together."

The defense played even better the following week in a 26-3 win over Buffalo.

James Harrison survived a scare when he slammed his head into Casey Hampton's rear end. Harrison was taken from the field to an ambulance as a precaution against a neck injury. The new starting ROLB squabbled with paramedics, telling them he was fine, and later appeared on the sideline hoping to play.

"He probably slashed their tires so they couldn't go to the hospital," said LOLB Clark Haggans. "Whatever's mangled in the ambulance, I'm sure they can fix it and repair it."

The Steelers improved to 3-0 with a 37-16 win over the San Francisco 49ers, but suffered their first loss in Arizona 21-14. Polamalu played a terrific first half against the Cardinals, but was hurt while returning an interception in the second quarter.

Polamalu wasn't the only former USC Trojan to sit out the second half of that game. His former college teammate, Matt Leinart, the successor to Carson Palmer and a former Heisman Trophy winner, was benched for Kurt Warner, who rallied the Cardinals to the win.

Polamalu sat out the next game with the ankle injury, but the Steelers got LeBeau his shutout, 21-0 over the revenge-minded Seattle Seahawks.

The bye week allowed Troy to heal, but the Steelers lost in Denver 31-28 on the near-fateful trip for Ryan Clark. At 4-2, the Steelers went to Cincinnati with Anthony Smith starting at free safety.

"Make sure you have your mouthpiece in," the cocky second-year player told Bengals receivers Chad Johnson and T.J. Houshmandzadeh before the game.

"Chad told me he doesn't wear one," Smith said. "I told him he'd better start."

Smith proved prophetic when he belted Johnson over the middle and his gold teeth went flying.

Polamalu picked them up out of the grass and handed them back to Johnson, who then collapsed. The Bengals did, too, in a 24-13 loss to the Steelers.

Smith told the story of the gold teeth after the game, but when Polamalu was approached for confirmation, he said it was just a mouthpiece that he handed back to Johnson.

"But Anthony said – " the reporter countered before Troy cut him off.

"Well, why did you ask me then?" he snapped.

After a brief pause, Polamalu grew contrite.

"I just don't want to be a part of a big story," he said. "Sorry. Bad interview."

The James Harrison Show occurred the following week, on a Monday night, in a win over the Ravens.

In one of the greatest performances ever by a Steelers defensive player, Harrison recorded nine tackles with six QB hits, three-and-a-half sacks, three tackles-for-loss, three forced fumbles, a fumble recovery and an interception.

It was so shocking that it overshadowed Ben Roethlisberger's five first-half touchdown passes and a perfect passer rating in a 38-7 Steelers romp.

As a defense, the Steelers allowed the Ravens only 105 yards and five first downs. Even the offense smacked the Ravens around. Hines Ward drilled Bart Scott with a vicious block, and later knocked Ed Reed out of the game.

Scott was still yapping at the end of the blowout.

"He said he was going to kill me," Ward said with a big smile.

On Scott's radio show in Baltimore the next night, he promised to pay Ward and the Steelers back by the end of his career.

"Tell him to join the club," Ward said.

A win over the Browns was followed by a shocking loss to the New York Jets, before Joey Porter returned to Heinz Field with his new Dolphins team.

Porter made eight tackles and intercepted a pass in front of the Steelers' bench that ended with Porter howling at Mike Tomlin.

Porter's defense allowed the Steelers only three points, but those points were enough for the Steelers to win the "Muck Bowl" at Heinz Field 3-0 on a late Jeff Reed field goal.

The shutout of the Dolphins was the second for the Steelers that season, and both were accomplished without Polamalu. He sat out the game with a sprained knee, which also caused him to miss the next two games – a win over the struggling Bengals and an infamous loss to the undefeated New England Patriots.

Even without Polamalu, and of course Clark, Anthony Smith was feeling unduly confident about his team's chances in New England.

HORTON: I'll say one thing about Anthony: He had a lot of God-given ability. I think what happened, during that New England week, it was a big game, he was a young starter and the media asked him something about the game and they asked if you think they're going to win. If you go back and watch the video, he hesitated for a second because I'm sure he was realizing there was no really good answer. So he took the lesser of two evils and he said "Yes." They asked if he guarantees it. I think he got caught in one of those brain-synapse things where they're firing and it's like, "Dude, you just backed yourself into a corner and both answers aren't good." So, when he said yes, obviously New England used that, and when they picked on him with that flea-flicker, it was like, "Oh, see, look at Anthony! Look at Anthony!" To a young player, that can devastate you.

BRYANT MCFADDEN: We were surprised that Smitty came out and guaranteed a win. And then we were like, "OK, Smitty, if you're going to put it on paper, we're going to back you." I think the most critical part about that was Anthony Smith wasn't a household name. Any professional sport, if you're not a household game, most people feel you shouldn't make guarantees. Smitty was a backup who was starting.

HORTON: It's amazing you don't know what you have until you don't have it. Ryan missed some games and we kind of fell apart. He came back and, again, the rest is history with him and Troy and Ike, all my guys on that back end.

The Steelers – 10.5-point underdogs – lost to the undefeated Patriots 34-13 and fell to 9-4, only one game ahead of the second-place Browns. But the Steelers had the 2-0 series tiebreaker going for them, and Polamalu was set to return from his three-game absence to face Jacksonville.

It would be his fourth NFL game against Uncle Keneti coaching on the other sideline, and this would be Troy's best. He made 10 tackles, one of which set up a Steelers touchdown with his trademark burst from out of nowhere to tackle QB David Garrard a foot shy of the stick on a third-and-7 run.

On another play, Polamalu blitzed and pressured Garrard into hurrying a throw, then turned and sprinted upfield to make the tackle on the receiver.

However, the Steelers lost to the Jaguars 29-22, and it was Kenti's moment to shine. His running backs piled up 224 rushing yards, the most allowed by the Steelers in over a year – or since the previous time Keneti, Fred Taylor and the Jaguars played the Steelers and rushed for 240.

KENETI POLAMALU: The greatest moments for me, because I had to coach against him in the NFL, are when the coaches on my teams thought I might be upset by the things they were saying about him. "We gotta block this guy." "We've got to find him." "Find him!" I mean, he was such a focal point of every game plan. They would all look at me to see if I was mad about the way they were describing him, and believe me, we spent some time talking about him. The year I left Tennessee, the Tennessee coaches called me and said, "Aw, man, he made this play. He jumped over and hit the quarterback at the goal line!" I said, "Yeah, he does take a risk."

The Polamalus would compete against each other one more time – three weeks later in the playoffs. The result was the same. The Jaguars won and ended Mike Tomlin's first season on a sour notes.

This time, Troy – still limited by a sore knee – made only two tackles in a 31-29 loss.

A long season that began in the Hall of Fame Game, at a training camp in which the new coach admittedly overworked his players in order to set his tone, followed by injuries that knocked out key players such as Clark, Aaron Smith, Willie Parker and Marvel Smith, had combined to take a toll.

MCFADDEN: I was mad that we lost but we probably needed it. We were tired. At training camp we had like 15 straight days of two-a-days or something crazy. We were spent.

HOKE: I'm not so sure of that. There was a different way of doing business with Mike. It was actually more relaxed. Bill Cowher kicked our butts in practice, man. Mike T came in with the Tony Dungy way: get in and get off. But we won with both coaches, right? It was the core of guys that we had there. But the culture, in terms of the players and the locker room, didn't change much. We still had the same leaders.

KEISEL: Tomlin came in and put his foot down and let us all know what type of team he wanted, so I thought it was different. He had his own way. Meetings were different. I loved when he had Tomlin's News. Who's in the news? "Well this person got laid out," and he'd run the clip. You thought, "I can't let this happen to me." You didn't want to be in the news, and it became a fun thing for the team. He did it his own way, and when we went to training camp it was different. But he had to, looking back on it, do it that way. He had to show that he meant business. He knew he had a good team and he wanted to push us. He wanted to see what we were capable of. And he wanted to see what he needed as a coach to help us get to that next level.

MCFADDEN: The thing about BC, his training-camp practices were tough, but we knew we would get unexpected off-days, like movie days or he might cancel a morning practice, and those days were huge for us. With Mike Tomlin, we were hoping for those days. I remember Hines brought it to his attention in Latrobe and he just ignored it. There was bad weather one day, and we usually went inside to the gym. Well, Mike Tomlin bused us to the South Side. Oh my goodness.

"I think Coach Tomlin did an excellent job his first year. You can't say anything bad about him," Troy Polamalu said after the playoff loss.

"The whole year lasts from the first offseason all the way through the end of the second offseason: How we react to losing, how we react to a winning season, how we react to a Super Bowl win. It's all kind of like a career process. I have no doubt that Coach Tomlin is going to take us there one day."

CHAPTER 18

OH, YOU SUCK

Troy Polamalu didn't comment much on organizational business. For instance, he trusted the Rooneys in the hiring of outsider Mike Tomlin in 2007.

But Troy was clearly steamed about the departure of Chris Hope in 2006. He struck similar chords in early 2008 about the imminent loss of All-Pro Alan Faneca.

"I've never seen anybody show up and work like him every day and never complain," Polamalu said after the Steelers lost to Jacksonville in the playoffs. "He's really a leader on this team – whether he wants to admit it or not. I really hope we do something good for him because he deserves it more than anybody I've ever seen in this organization."

However, the Steelers would not keep Faneca, who signed with the New York Jets and played there two years before ending his career in 2010 with Arizona.

Although Faneca kept to himself and his position group as much as Polamalu kept to himself and his position group, there was great respect between the two Steelers leaders.

"Anytime you put positive people around you, or positive people are in your life, some of that rubs off, and Troy's one of those positive people," says Faneca. "Being on a football team and spending so many hours a day, all day long, so many months, especially those guys on defense sitting in the room with Troy, it's going to rub off. You can't see a guy that kind-hearted and genuine and not find a way to either consciously or subconsciously find a way to make that part of who you are or put a little bit of that into your life."

Kevin Colbert raved about the college crop of offensive tackles available in the upcoming draft, but after eight were taken in the first round, the Steelers chose a running back, Rashard Mendenhall, to complement Willie Parker.

In the second round, they drafted a tall receiver, Limas Sweed, whom they hoped would bring back some of the big-receiver magic Ben Roethlisberger enjoyed in his rookie season with Plaxico Burress.

Neither top pick, though, provided much help in 2008.

The Steelers signed free-agent center Justin Hartwig to compete with Sean Mahan, but center would remain a problem in the middle of a rebuilt line that had allowed 47 and 49 sacks the previous two seasons.

One other seemingly minor addition in free agency, Mewelde Moore, would prove to be the complement Parker needed as Mike Tomlin promised to continue to run Parker "until the wheels came off."

"I kind of said that tongue-in-cheek because he is our feature ballcarrier," Tomlin said as 2008 dawned. "Those guys do need their touches. When Willie runs the ball, we have a chance to win. Do we need a stable of backs? Absolutely."

Polamalu, meanwhile, underwent a clean-up surgery in his right knee while his Robin, Ryan Clark, was still recovering from the removal of his spleen and gall bladder.

Around the division, the second-place Cleveland Browns, whom the Steelers edged by tiebreaker in 2007, added one of the most talented interior defensive linemen in the NFL, Shaun Rogers, a former teammate of Casey Hampton's at the University of Texas.

"It's going to be ugly," warned Big Hamp. "That's my boy, and he's motivated and pissed off."

Hampton was asked whether the Steelers' new center might provide a counterbalance to Rogers.

Hampton just shook his head. "I'm telling you," he said, "it's going to be ugly."

It got ugly with Hampton, too, at training camp when Tomlin put his foot down after the just-married nose tackle performed poorly during the run test.

Hampton checked in at 360 pounds, 25 over the weight that would've netted him a six-figure bonus and 35 over his listed playing weight. So, Tomlin put Hampton on the physically unable to perform (PUP) list and made him train alone on a far field with assistant strength coach Marcel Pastoor.

Polamalu, along with Faneca's would-be replacement, Chris Kemoeatu, were also placed on the PUP list. This was done before the first practice to allow the team to activate the player – should his injury linger – during the season, rather than be forced to put him on season-ending injured reserve.

Not that Polamalu's hamstring pull was considered problematic.

Clark's weight had plummeted to 172 after his near-death experience in Denver, but he was back at camp at a robust 206 pounds.

"My wife's not into football," Clark said. "But this year, as I was training, and she'd see me gaining my weight back, she'd get so excited. She'd say, 'Baby, I can't wait for this season.' She even wanted to come to practice the first day. I told her I can't be the guy who has his wife at the first practice, so she should come to the second. She came out and smiled the whole time."

It was also the dawn of defensive coordinator Dick LeBeau's 50th season in the NFL.

Cut by the Browns out of Ohio State in 1959, LeBeau embarked on a Hall of Fame career as a cornerback with the Detroit Lions. He played 14 seasons there before beginning his coaching career with the Philadelphia Eagles' special teams in 1973. As defensive coordinator of the Cincinnati Bengals in the mid-1980s, LeBeau doodled the zone blitz defensive scheme on a napkin on a plane, and the following season it helped the Bengals reached Super Bowl 23. They took a dagger from Joe Montana's last-minute drive in losing 20-16.

The zone blitz (aka: fire zone) was designed to counter the run-and-shoot Houston Oilers, the divisional power at the time, and eventually became the central point of Bill Cowher's defensive scheme of the 1990s. It involves blitzing linebackers and safeties while dropping linemen into the vacated space(s).

Cowher, LeBeau and then-coordinator Dom Capers made the zone blitz a central part of the Steelers' 3-4 defense, and LeBeau refined it further upon becoming Cowher's coordinator in 1994.

LeBeau left in 1997, returned in 2004, and used Polamalu to further refine the defense he'd left in place.

After the 2005 championship, LeBeau was on his way to becoming an iconic figure in Pittsburgh, but he was more than that to his players.

RYAN CLARK: When I was sick, Coach LeBeau called my wife every day. He told her that he loved me, he loved her. For a guy going on 50 years to not just care about the whole defense and the numbers they put up, but to have that much individual care for one person is the most important thing any coach has ever done for me.

BRETT KEISEL: Every morning he told us it was a great day to be alive. He was always smiling, always happy to be here, always happy to see us. He was a father figure to all of us. We all kind of felt like he was our dad.

JAMES FARRIOR, *Steelers inside linebacker (2002-11):* I learned the defense with Tim Lewis, but when Dick LeBeau got here he was the originator so it really took hold and sunk in.

TROY POLAMALU, *to Justin Myers*: Coach LeBeau, in my opinion, supersedes even the Vince Lombardis of this game. Nobody has been part of this game longer than Coach LeBeau. He's checked the box in every single realm, and his influence on the game – with the zone blitzes and introducing the game to these really unique approaches from a defensive strategic standpoint – has made him an amazing individual. He doesn't yell, always calm, low key, thinks cerebrally about things, and then is just an amazing human being.

He played for the Detroit Lions with Dick "Night Train" Lane and they were really good during the same period of time Motown started to come up, so he bumped shoulders with Lionel Richie, Marvin Gaye, and he would talk about partying with them. Coach LeBeau has an album, plays the guitar amazingly every night. He's a scratch golfer, just a really talented, amazing human being. He would sing for us, tell us all these great stories, very philosophical as well. Definitely one of the greatest humans I've ever known.

LeBeau was asked at that 2008 training camp whether the Steelers could improve on their previous season total of 36 sacks, a low for one of his Steelers teams.

"The number that I really like is No. 1 in defense," LeBeau said, "and we've been that two of the last four, and one of the two that we weren't we were the world's champions. So those are the numbers that we're really focusing on, playing good effective defense. We led the league last year in (fewest) yards per pass attempt against us. It's the first time we've done that here, and you have to have pressure to do that."

To that end, second-year linebackers Lawrence Timmons and LaMarr Woodley were smashing and breaking things – loudly – at their second training camp. One poor undrafted rookie showed up the next day in a neck brace after a particularly violent encounter with Timmons during a backs-on-backers drill in downtown Latrobe.

LeBeau's hope for Timmons was that he would relieve Polamalu at the linebacker position in the dime defense, allowing the safety to play deeper on passing downs. That would take some time for Timmons to grasp, though.

Woodley, clearly a physical terror at 266 pounds, replaced Clark Haggans at the strong-side OLB spot opposite James Harrison. The pair would combine for 27.5 sacks that season to smash the team record of 24 shared by previous combos Kevin Greene-Greg Lloyd (1994) and Joey Porter-Jason Gildon (2000). The Harrison-Woodley record still stands after a ferocious assault by T.J. Watt and Bud Dupree in 2019 fell short at 26.

"Just look at James Harrison," rookie runner Mendenhall said after the goal-line drill at training camp. "You don't find too many college guys looking like that."

Mendenhall ran to the opposite side in the drill.

"How'd that work out for him?" asked opposite-side run-stuffer Aaron Smith.

It did not.

The Steelers' rugged men up front weren't the only defenders raising a ruckus at training camp. Anthony Smith, in his bid to hold his free safety job, lit up Hines Ward during a 7-on-7 passing drill.

"Are you out of your goddamned mind?!" screamed offensive coordinator Bruce Arians.

Smith was pulled from the field. He didn't start another game for the Steelers.

Casey Hampton was activated on August 10, but Troy Polamalu remained sidelined after aggravating his hamstring injury.

Did Troy pull it or tweak it?

"I don't know," he said. "I'll have to get our medical book to study the definitions of each."

Polamalu was scheduled for activation from the PUP list on Aug. 19 when the team returned to the UPMC Rooney Sports Complex on the South Side of Pittsburgh after breaking camp in Latrobe. In the meantime, Troy served the team as best he could during its Aug. 8 preseason opener against the Philadelphia Eagles.

A TV camera picked up Polamalu – with Hines Ward and James Harrison – as he brought water off the sideline to Santonio Holmes during a timeout.

Polamalu handed Holmes the water bottle and stepped back. Ward and Harrison laughed as the top came off and the contents poured onto Holmes' face.

Polamalu, the silent assassin, was already out of sight.

HINES WARD, *Steelers wide receiver (1998-11):* Troy's one of those guys who's so serious all the time but is actually a big prankster. He'll try to lull you to sleep and when you get there he hits you with the joke. That was a good one. Troy told him he had some magic juice that tastes real good. James said, "Oh, it tastes real good."

CHRIS HOPE: That's definitely one of his pranks. He would unscrew the top of the water bottle. "Want something to drink? Want something to drink?" And the minute you do, it's all over you.

MALAEFOU MACKENZIE: He's always been a prankster. Don't let that innocent nice guy fool you. He was one of the biggest jokesters at SC. Nobody suspects him because he's so nice. And that's the *problem*. That's the problem! Everybody suspects and blames guys like me or my brother-in-law, but little do they know it's actually Troy who's scheming everything.

MIKE LOGAN: Your first reaction is to go after the Peezys or the Jeromes, those types of characters on the team. That was the part of Troy's magnificent plan, that you wouldn't expect him to be that jolly or cheerful or that fun.

CHRIS HOKE: He'd roll up tape into a ball and stuff it in the trainer's horn so when he blew it during practice no sound came out.

DESHEA TOWNSEND, *Steelers cornerback (1998-09):* He's always untying shoes, hiding helmets. You have to be careful when you're around him.

Polamalu's best may have been the trick he pulled on Doug Legursky, a rookie offensive lineman in 2008. Legursky told the story to Ron Lippock in the book *Steelers Takeaways:*

"There was a line of urinals. I was standing there when Troy Polamalu came in and stood right next to me. Now, the guy code says you leave a urinal in between you when you can. So I thought it was weird. But what can I say? It's Troy Polamalu. Then all of the sudden I feel something splash on me. I thought he was peeing on my foot. I said 'Dude!' Then I saw he had a plastic Gatorade bottle that he put a hole in the top of and was squirting it at my feet. It was a rookie hazing move. Then he said in that sweet Troy voice, 'What were you thinking?' Hey, he was Troy Polamalu. He could have pissed in the middle of the locker room and no one would have said anything."

Upon his activation on August 19, Polamalu held a brief Q&A for reporters. In between a battery of questions that were answered with "I feel good" and "Whatever coach wants" were some interesting answers.

Why is James Harrison faster than you?
TP: Because I'm stronger.
How did you do in the camp softball game?
TP: I had to call my wife and tell her I went 0 for 4. She said, "Oh, you suck."
How did you get into shape?
TP: I don't know if I really focused on coming into camp in my best shape. My focus was coming into camp in good enough shape and to leave camp in great shape. That's the best thing for players. I think as a rookie it's hard to do that; I think as a veteran you have to understand that.
Are you more muscular?
TP: More fatter, yeah. Yeah, I'm bigger than I have been in the past. In the past I fluctuated. In my rookie year and second year I was around 215. In my third and fourth year I went down to 210 and even got down to 200. This year I'm probably about 215.

James Harrison had gone up against Browns rookie Joe Thomas in the previous year's opener and had a sack and led the Steelers in tackles. Harrison was preparing for another rookie in this year's opener against Houston. Duane Brown was the eighth tackle taken in the first round, one spot before the Steelers drafted Rashard Mendenhall.

"You figure they'll give him some help with James," LaMarr Woodley said with a Chesire smile.

That, of course, would help Woodley, and it did. He and Harrison combined for 4 sacks and the Steelers dismantled the Texans 38-17.

Harrison had three of the sacks. Woodley recovered Harrison's forced fumble, and Harrison rolled around end to force the interception to Woodley.

"Pick your poison," Aaron Smith said. "Their pressure was unbelievable."

"I told them at one point to let us make some plays," said Brett Keisel. "Woodley stole a fumble from me. I'm like, 'Come on dude, give us a little bit.'"

The hit of the game belonged to Ryan Clark. One series after leaving the field with an apparent injury, Clark returned to blow up a Houston runner and thus begin his bid for Comeback Player of the Year.

He was also a few days removed from his parents getting hit by another big hurricane – Gustav – down in New Orleans.

"They're OK," Clark said. "Their house burned down last month, so the hurricane wasn't a problem."

Say, what?

"At least they didn't have to batten down the hatches," Clark said with a forced smile.

Willie Parker rushed for 138 yards and three touchdowns, but there was bad news concerning the offense: Ben Roethlisberger injured his right shoulder when Mario Williams beat Chris Kemoeatu, tomahawked Ben's right arm, pinned it behind his back, and drove Roethlisberger into the ground and forced a fumble.

Roethlisberger returned for the next several series, but the right shoulder would bother him the remainder of the season.

The following Sunday, on a warm and windy night on the Lake Erie shoreline, Troy Polamalu made his first documented dive over the line. He appeared to have timed the countdown to the two-minute warning. The disruption was successful and resulted in a tackle-for-loss by James Farrior against the Browns.

Later in the drive, Polamalu preserved the Steelers' 7-0 lead by intercepting Derek Anderson, his old foe from Oregon 3A football, in front of the goal line to end a Browns threat with eight seconds left in the half.

Late in the fourth quarter, Anderson drove the Browns to the Pittsburgh 20. Down 10-3 with 3:24 remaining, Browns coach Romeo Crennel opted to kick a field goal on fourth-and-7.

The kick was good but the math wasn't. The Browns still trailed by four points, and Cleveland fans bitterly watched a 10th consecutive loss to the Steelers when Roethlisberger threw a game-clinching 19-yard touchdown pass to Heath Miller.

The Steelers were 2-0 and Polamalu was the AFC Defensive Player of the Week.

The 2008 season was coming into focus.

Troy Polamalu, Sept. 17, 2008

What were you trying to accomplish when you dove over center?
I don't know. Actually, I just saw that they were in a hurry-up situation and I expected them to do a quarterback sneak. We didn't have a defense called so I figured, you know, try to do something.
Did it have to do with the two-minute warning coming?
No, I'm not that smart. Charlie (Batch) actually asked me that, and I said, "Charlie I might run with that." But then I'd be lying.
Your next opponent, the Philadelphia Eagles, lost to Dallas on Monday night. Did you watch it?

No. Saw the score, saw the film, heard the breakdown.

What did you do instead?

My wife is pregnant, so maybe I was just running to the refrigerator and back.

The Steelers hadn't won in Philadelphia since the 2-12 Steelers beat the Eagles in 1965.

The 2008 Steelers were annihilated thanks to a horrific performance by the offensive line. The Eagles piled up nine sacks – eight of Ben Roethlisberger in addition to a safety on an intentional grounding penalty – in a 15-6 win over the now 2-1 Steelers.

It was amazing the game was that close, considering the Steelers converted only two of 13 first downs and only gained 1.7 per rush attempt and 3.6 per pass attempt.

Polamalu's eye-popping, one-handed, er, one-elbowed, diving interception of a Bryant McFadden tip to open the second half put the Steelers in great position, at midfield, to cut into the 10-6 deficit. However, the Steelers went three and out and never came closer.

"That was truly one of the greatest plays I've ever seen," said Dick LeBeau.

The interception in Philadelphia was the sixth-year safety's third in three games. While the offense was shaky, at best, in Philadelphia, the defense was shaping up to be LeBeau's finest.

IKE TAYLOR: I don't mean to be rude, but Dickie put in our head we don't care what the offense do. All we trying to do is give the offense the ball as many times as possible. That was our whole thing. That's why nobody talks to you about Ben. It wasn't that he wasn't special. Shit. Me and Ben were shuffleboard champions together. But Dick LeBeau just got it stuck in our head that we don't care what the offense do.

TROY POLAMALU: We definitely had it going at that period of time. I think if we would've known how special that time was, looking back on it, we would've taken better advantage of even being more successful. But all of us played such a huge, consistent role. We developed such a brotherhood, a bond that will last forever.

TAYLOR: Everybody was on the same page, and the same page was being ourself. When one person make a play, we all made that play. That was our motto. And I guarantee, in Troy's Hall of Fame speech, that's what he's going to say: "When one person made a play, we all made that play." That's a guar-on-tee.

MIKE TOMLIN: About the time I came on the scene, man, he was Troy (laughs). He had gone through the growing pains that young guys go through in terms of finding his process, his preparation process, his play demeanor and all of those things. He was an established Pro Bowl-caliber player by the time I got here. Obviously there wasn't a lot of discussion about trying to discover what it was I was working with, or his talents. More than anything it was just about figuring out ways to capture it and to highlight it and to continue to allow him to grow.

"I'll say this," offensive coordinator Bruce Arians told reporters Thursday after the Eagles loss, "If anybody is still trying to look for a story about Philadelphia, and who to blame, just spell my name correctly so Philadelphia can go to bed and that way we can get ready for Baltimore."

Arians did have one more question to answer, considering he had said in 2007 that Ravens free safety Ed Reed was the best safety in the game.

"Ed and Troy are ballhawks," Arians said. "I'm not going to say any more that Ed's better than Troy; I got a lot of crap the last time. Troy's better, all right? I'm keeping Troy. But Ed is great."

It was a debate that continues even after each was voted into the Hall of Fame on respective first ballots in back-to-back years, 2019 and 2020. Troy won this encounter as the Steelers bounced back from the Eagles debacle with a thrilling overtime win over the Ravens on a Monday night.

Polamalu made nine tackles and Reed made two. Polamalu even made a tackle with his back to the runner. He also broke up a key third-down pass.

Jeff Reed's 46-yarder in overtime – on the heels of a late timeout and attempted freeze by Ravens Coach John Harbaugh, during a kick that went through the uprights – gave the Steelers the win.

As Mike Tomlin jogged off the field, he hollered to Harbaugh, "You can't freeze a psychopath!"

The Steelers had trailed at halftime 13-3 when Ben Roethlisberger "cussed us out," according to tackle Willie Colon. Roethlisberger was outplayed by Ravens rookie QB Joe Flacco in the first half mainly due to three sacks of Roethlisberger and only one of Flacco. Those numbers more than flopped as the Steelers hounded Flacco with four sacks the rest of the way. The Steelers replaced Kendall Simmons with rookie Darnell Stapleton at right guard and kept Roethlisberger clean.

"Game changer! Game changer!" Max Starks shouted at Stapleton after the game.

"How DID you turn it around?" Roethlisberger asked Stapleton before shouting the question to the rest of the locker room.

"See what you started?" the quiet Stapleton said to the reporter. "You're getting me in trouble. You're a troublemaker."

Not everything went smoothly for the Steelers in the second half. First-round draft pick Rashard Mendenhall – making his first career start in place of Injured Willie Parker – had his scapula busted by Ray Lewis on the first play of the third quarter.

Mewelde Moore replaced Mendenhall, and Moore's 24-yard catch-and-run in overtime, on third-and-8, set up the game-winning kick by "The Psychopath" Reed.

If Moore's play wasn't the Steelers' biggest, James Harrison's strip-sack that allowed LaMarr Woodley's scoop-and-score in the third quarter was.

The other critical play was made by Polamalu, who came from the deep middle to break up a third-quarter pass at the sideline to Mark Clayton on third-and-9. The Ravens were leading by 10 at the time.

Polamalu was clearly coming into his own as a coverage safety with Lawrence Timmons playing Troy's old dimebacker spot on pass downs.

"That play showed the growth he's made," said the team's most tenured defensive back, Deshea Townsend. "Coming from the middle third to get to the top to break up that play was very impressive. He started on the other hash, and before the quarterback threw it he was already there to break up the play. We all know he can get down there in the line of scrimmage, but now he can get down the middle of the field if he needs to."

Onward and upward, as Dick LeBeau liked to say, as the Steelers traveled to Jacksonville for the ever-difficult road game following an overtime win against a hated rival on a Monday night.

But the Steelers had revenge on their minds against the Jaguars, who had knocked them out of the playoffs the previous year. And this time, the Steelers had run-stuffer deluxe Aaron Smith in the lineup.

Smith missed the end of the 2007 with a torn biceps and was a major reason the Jaguars rushed for 404 yards in two wins over the Steelers at the end of the season.

Smith was back, and rabbit's foot Chris Hoke was replacing the injured Casey Hampton at nose tackle. Hoke entered the game 12-1 as a regular-season starter.

The Steelers also had Moore running the ball instead of Najeh Davenport, who had replaced Parker in the 2007 playoff loss.

Moore started this time against the Jaguars and led all rushers with 99 yards. Jaguars star Fred Taylor was held to 19 yards on 10 carries by Smith, Hoke and Co.

Moore's 27-yard run late in the game set up Ben Roethlisberger's 8-yard touchdown pass to Hines Ward for the game-winner with 1:53 left. The Steelers headed into their 2008 bye week in first place at 4-1.

CHAPTER 19

EVERY BLADE OF GRASS

Five games into the 2008 season, Troy Polamalu spoke up.

The quiet voice inside the Steelers' locker room took on the NFL's new plan to fine defensive players into accommodating its definition of safe play during a mid-week mob interview before the game against the Bengals.

It was his most controversial interview ever, the first time he had really made waves, and Polamalu was so startled by the national reaction that he pulled back on interviews the remainder of the season.

Here's the best of it:

Troy Polamalu, Oct. 15, 2008

What's your take on all the fines? And have you ever been fined by the league?
I'm not familiar with the fines that are going on. I didn't know there were. Sorry.
Nate got one. Hines got one. Ryan got one.
Well, I think regarding the evolution of football, it's becoming more and more flag football, two-hand touch. We've really lost the essence of what real American football is about. I think it's probably all about money. They're not really concerned about safety, because people have been doing this for thousands of years (laughs) – no, for quite a few decades.
What is the essence of American football?
Besides mixed martial arts, it's the real gladiator sport. We go out there, really, at a high speed and we're just killing each other out there. You look at these guys who are dying at 40 and 50 years old and it makes you wonder how much this really takes out of you. I don't know. It just loses so much of its essence when it becomes kind of a pansy game, because when you see guys like Dick Butkus really raw, old school, pound-it-out

257

type of football players – those have become our football heroes, way up to the Ronnie Lotts, Jack Tatums. These guys really went after people. They were that way because the game was physical. They couldn't survive in this type of game.

They couldn't function?

They wouldn't have enough money. They'd be paying fines all the time, and then they'd be suspended for the year after they do it two games in a row. It's kind of ridiculous.

Knowing the risks, why do you do it?

I think it's fun. It's just the essence of what NFL football is. You don't want to get into a sport that loses that core mentality. It's like playing basketball: "Oh, you can't body somebody up. You can't touch them. You can only play defense from a foot out." It takes away from the real athleticism of the sport.

Have you been fined for anything this year?

No, thank God I haven't. I've been fined quite a bit in the past.

Doesn't your new commercial with LaDainian Tomlinson epitomize the gladiator element?

Kind of. It's showing things that people don't see on Sundays, the training. "The Destiny" is the name of the commercial. From a little kid you kind of dream, you look up to those people – the Dick Butkuses, the Jack Tatums, the Mean Joe Greenes, the Jack Lamberts, guys who did things after, who were ruthless. But like I said, it's lost that.

You don't do things after the whistle. When did you lose your ruthlessness?

Quite honestly, I'm not that type of player. For example, Joey (Porter) would be that type of player. And I loved that about Joey, that he was that type of player. If you take that away from us, we lose our identity. And with that, football loses its identity.

Speaking to not necessarily being foul or cheap after the whistle, but just playing hard –

I didn't mean being cheap. Not taking any crap. Know what I mean? Joe Greene wouldn't take crap from anybody. Do you know what I mean? Joey Porter wouldn't take crap from anybody. When people came to our field, they knew this was our home field. Nobody was going to mess with us. When Warren Sapp was trying to run between the Pittsburgh Steelers when they went down there at Tampa Bay, the Steelers weren't going to let that happen. That's the type of attitude that I think is really awesome.

Was there a Butkus in your childhood?

I was a Walter Payton fan.

Were you coached to be physical?

Oh, yeah. I had a couple players in my family. Our Thanksgivings were more physical than our Sundays.

Welcome to the Jungle, it gets worse here every day, particularly this day when the winless Bengals were blown out by the 5-1 Steelers 38-10.

Cincinnati rookie linebacker Keith Rivers felt as if all 38 of those points were bricks falling on his head after Hines Ward peeled back and drilled him in the chest. Rivers' head bounced off the turf and he missed the rest of the season with a broken jaw.

The hit cost Ward more money, and, in fact, resulted in a new rule – the "Hines Ward Rule" – the following season, outlawing blindside blocks into a defender's head or neck area.

Carson Palmer had been shelved for the season with a sore elbow two weeks earlier. Ryan Fitzpatrick replaced Palmer at quarterback and the Harvard-educated QB nearly had a lateral picked off by James Harrison.

The play lost 15 yards, and then the wave of pressure got to Fitzpatrick for seven sacks – two each by linebackers Harrison, Woodley and Timmons.

Polamalu left the game with what was believed to have been a concussion. This was always a touchy topic for Troy, who rarely agreed with reporters' counts of his past concussions, yet refused to put his own number on it.

That, coupled with the league talking to him about his "pansy" remark the previous week, caused Polamalu to promise reporters he was done with the national spotlight.

Polamalu was asked by a lone remaining reporter in Cincinnati whether – considering the fact his wife was pregnant – he was beginning to worry about his accumulation of concussions, no matter the correct number.

"I'll tell you because you're a nice guy," Troy said. "I have to trust the technology today. I don't know what that would have done for a guy like Mike Webster, but when they tell me there's been no cumulative effect, and I feel all right, then I have to believe them."

The entire team was rocked on Oct. 22, before a Week 8 matchup with the New York Giants, by a medical problem that had nothing to do with concussions or any other football injury.

BRETT KEISEL: It was a Wednesday morning. I'll never forget it. Aaron Smith's always the first one to work. Usually his workout is done and he's either in the steam room or ice tub when everyone else is just showing up. That day, when I came in, he wasn't there. It was weird. I went to (trainer John) Norwig and asked him where's Aaron.

He was working with some other guys and just said, "He's going through something." So, I went through my morning routine, got some breakfast, got a workout in and came back to talk to Norwig when the special teams meeting was going on, and he said, "Yeah, Aaron's son's been diagnosed with leukemia."

IKE TAYLOR: Smitty like Troy, man. Smitty don't say much, but he was one of the best defensive ends in the game. So when Smitty hurtin', we hurtin'. That's how we felt about each other. When something was going on bad at your house, it was going on bad at mine.

KEISEL: We didn't see Aaron that whole week. We were playing the Giants and we weren't sure if he was going to play. We were preparing for him not to play. It was scary. None of us knew what was going on, and then he showed up and said he was going to play. "I'll be there tomorrow." Not knowing any of the game plan; not knowing anything. Going through this mental tornado and emotional roller coaster with your only son in the hospital fighting cancer, it put things into perspective for us. He came and played and it was a super tough game, really physical. The Giants won the Super Bowl the year before. They were very, very good

Aaron Smith was introduced to a roaring crowd at Heinz Field that Sunday, arms flailing as he ran onto the field. The defense performed admirably in the loss, holding the Giants to six total points during three first-and-goal situations. The high point was a five-play stop for no points after a first-and-goal at the 2. The Giants finally broke through with their only touchdown on a fourth goal-to-go situation with 3:07 left.

They had the ball after replacement long-snapper James Harrison – in for injured Greg Warren – sailed a snap out of the end zone for the game-tying safety. The ensuing touchdown gave the defending champions a 21-14 win. Brett Keisel led the Steelers defense with 11 tackles.

KEISEL: That loss was tough because we wanted to win that game for Aaron, but you learn a lot from your losses. Sometimes after you look down the road years from now you go, "Oh, maybe there was a reason for that."

AARON SMITH: My favorite Mike Tomlin-ism is "Fight for every blade of grass." That one's special to me. That one reminds me of when Elijah was diagnosed that week and we had the goal-line stand. The whole week that line was going through my head, "Just give me a blade of grass to defend."

KEISEL: I'll never forget Aaron's speech to us on the D-line before that game, in tears, just "Let's go out and fight. Let's fight together." We all played tough in that game. It's hard to fall short but we used that loss to the defending champs as motivation. We knew we were going to have to really come together for Aaron, because he might not be at practice or around us all the time. We knew we had to support him when he was in the building and support him when he wasn't. So it became different for us. We were fighting for something other than just the football team and the glory of being champions. It was, like, we've got to get this family to Tampa.

Roethlisberger tore a ligament in his right thumb in the first half of the loss, but that didn't stop the Steelers from overindulging in their passing game when they traveled to Washington the following Monday night.

Polamalu had complained about the changing offensive philosophy the week of the Washington game – the day before the birth of his first son Paisios.

"They're winning football games the way we're supposed to win football games," Polamalu said about 6-2 Washington. "Running the ball and playing great defense, that's Steelers football right there and they've taken the mold of what we like to do to win and have done a good job."

After Willie Parker returned from injury, and carried 21 times for 70 yards in a game the Steelers dominated from the start, he picked up the baton from Polamalu.

"It frustrates me," Parker said. "I'm going to have to talk with coach. I'm not getting anything consistent going and that's all I want to do. I'm a running back. I want to run the ball. We've got to get back to Steelers football."

Even though Parker's 21 carries were a normal workload, the Steelers attempted more passes than runs in a 23-6 game with backup QB Byron Leftwich playing the entire second half.

"It's going to change," growled defensive line coach John Mitchell. "It HAS to change."

"It drives us crazy on the sideline," said Keisel. "Willie gains eight yards on first down and then we start throwing. No one understands it."

This was still five weeks before Mike Tomlin responded with his now-famous comment, "Every morning I come to work I walk past five Lombardis, not five rushing titles. The issue is winning."

The Steelers survived the continuing Roethlisberger shoulder issue in Washington, but lost to Peyton Manning and Indianapolis 24-20.

Despite saying that the bye week didn't soothe his aching right shoulder, Roethlisberger threw 41 times with three interceptions in the loss.

The Steelers were 6-3 but held the tiebreaking edge with the 6-3

Baltimore Ravens in the AFC North. The next two games against the Ravens would decide the division, and then the conference.

At a meeting the night before the Steelers' first blustery, wintry game of the season, Nov. 16 against the 7-3 San Diego Chargers, Mike Tomlin called on the "A players" – Troy Polamalu, Ben Roethlisberger, Hines Ward and James Farrior – to "step up," said Ward. "And we did that today."

The Steelers won the league's first-ever 11-10 game. It would've been 17-10 had the officials not erred in overturning Polamalu's return of a fumbled lateral on the final play.

That play only mattered to the gamblers. What impressed everyone else was a play Polamalu made that's still discussed today: his diving scoop of an interception off the top of the snowy grass on the game's first series.

Threatening to blitz off the defense's left edge, Polamalu turned at the snap and sprinted nearly 20 yards down the right hash, where Vincent Jackson was being hit by Ike Taylor. The ball popped up, Polamalu dove and made a remarkably athletic play.

The Chargers asked for a review – as the Eagles had on the previous, last, best-ever, diving, one-handed interception by Polamalu.

Both interceptions were inspected closely for the slightest evidence of the ball touching the ground first, or any kind of bobble. Both interceptions were upheld.

JAMES HARRISON: The play where he dives for the interception and literally scoops the ball off the ground was the most impressive play that I've seen. I saw on the replay that he got up under that ball and I said, "Oh my God."

DICK LEBEAU: That's the best one I've ever seen. Our guys up in the booth were saying he got it, and I said, "No, I was right here and he didn't get that ball." But he did. That was the greatest.

The scoop against the Chargers may have drawn gasps, but it didn't result in points as Jeff Reed's streak of 20 consecutive field goals, stretching back almost a year to a missed 44-yarder in the infamous "Muck Bowl," came to an end when he missed a 51-yard field goal at wind-swept Heinz Field. The Chargers answered with their only touchdown of the day.

The Steelers scored their first points early in the second quarter when James Harrison's strip-sack of Philip Rivers in the end zone was recovered by a Charger for a safety. Reed kicked a field goal at the end of the half and the Steelers went into the locker room trailing 7-5.

Another Reed field goal gave the Steelers an 8-7 lead to open the third quarter.

A goal-line stand by the Steelers forced the Chargers to kick a field goal to re-take a 10-8 lead with 6:41 left to play.

The Steelers started the game-winning drive from their 13. Hines Ward caught four passes for 42 yards to set up Reed's field goal with 15 seconds left.

Polamalu's scoop-and-score after the final kickoff was overturned – to the angst of "professional" observers – but regardless of the stricken score the Steelers improved to 7-3 and gained the head-to-head tiebreaker over the Chargers.

While Polamalu's interception drew the eyeballs, Harrison's strip-sack-safety and interception at the Pittsburgh 10 were the game's key plays. Harrison's 33-yard return set up the Steelers' late first-half field goal.

The big plays by Harrison and Polamalu reflected their duel for NFL Defensive Player of the Year. Both were making plays to either clinch or change games.

The questionable officiating decision that cost Polamalu the late, meaningless touchdown maybe wasn't so meaningless as Harrison went on to win the award.

After 10 games, the Steelers' defense was tops in the league in points allowed, yards allowed, run defense, pass defense, red-zone defense and fewest yards per play. It was all evidence for the argument that they really did have two legitimate contenders for NFL Defensive Player of the Year.

The Steelers won their second and third straight games by steamrolling the 1-8-1 Bengals, then clobbering the Tom Brady-less Patriots in Foxboro.

New England reporters said that Anthony Smith had guaranteed the win, again, but that wasn't actually true.

Pittsburgh's 970 sports-talk radio had interviewed Smith in the locker room during the lead-up to the game, and the now-benched safety said, "If we play like we've been playing, and our offense comes around and has a good game, and we're clicking on all cylinders, we're going to win the game."

The station interviewed Mike Tomlin the next night. Tomlin's response? "Why do you interview backup safeties?"

This time against the Pats, instead of Smith and Tyrone Carter patrolling the back end, the Steelers had Troy Polamalu and Ryan Clark. And without Brady, the Patriots started Polamalu's old housemate, Matt Cassel, at QB.

Why Smith DIDN'T guarantee a win would've been the better question.

The 9-3 Steelers rolled into December with a "five-star matchup" against the 8-4 Dallas Cowboys at Heinz Field.

The game featured another Defensive Player of the Year candidate in Cowboys pass-rusher DeMarcus Ware, setting up a game within the game between he and Harrison.

Ware seemed to have the advantage in opposing left tackles. Max Starks was playing well for the Steelers, but Harrison would be up against the more accomplished and decorated left tackle, 6-7 Flozell Adams.

Starks knew it wouldn't be easy for Adams.

"He has no idea what he's in for," Starks said. "I don't care how many times you go against DeMarcus Ware (6-4, 262) in practice, you can't prepare for a James Harrison-type of player because he's an outlier. You're not used to seeing that size, that power, that agility all compacted in there. He's definitely going to be a test for him because for taller players Harrison's a nightmare."

Ware had a strong game, but the 6-foot Harrison had a stronger one.

Each pass-rusher had a sack, but Harrison had three more tackles – one a stuff on fourth-and-1 – and his sack forced a fumble.

It was the Steelers' secondary, though, that won this game.

Polamalu got it rolling with an interception of Tony Romo on a pass to Terrell Owens on the game's initial third down. It gave Polamalu a league-high seven interceptions.

RAY HORTON: When we watched film before that game, I told Troy, "Terrell Owens will tell you what the play is. Just find out where he lines up." It was off his foot – if he was outside the numbers, if he was inside the numbers, if he was the No. 2 guy, or if he was the No. 1 guy. Well, he lined up one time inside the numbers, and when the ball was snapped, Troy went to exactly where Terrell was going and beat him to the spot, so T.O. stopped running because it was like, "Well, he's already there." Tony Romo threw the ball because he's expecting T.O. to be there and Troy picked it off.

The play resulted in a missed field goal and the teams remained scoreless deep into the second quarter, when Ike Taylor intercepted Romo at the Dallas 22. Jeff Reed's 24-yard field goal gave the Steelers a 3-0 lead.

The Cowboys tied the game at halftime and then scored 10 more points in the third quarter for a 13-3 lead.

Reed's 41-yard field goal in the middle of the fourth quarter cut the deficit to 13-6, and a Travis Kirschke sack got the Steelers the ball back with 5:10 remaining.

Ben Roethlisberger drove the Steelers 67 yards in eight plays to tie the game. The drive was capped by a 6-yard touchdown pass to Heath Miller with 2:04 to play.

Would there be overtime at Heinz Field?

No. Dallas had the ball, but two snaps later, in one of the iconic plays of the 2008 season, Deshea Townsend intercepted Romo and returned it 25 yards for a touchdown and a 7-point lead with 1:40 remaining.

The Steelers closed the game with hard pressure on Romo from Harrison and LaMarr Woodley to give them a 10-3 record heading into Baltimore.

LEBEAU: Troy approached me before that series and said they're hitting that tight end, give us something. I can't hardly think of one time he's approached me and wasn't right. So I gave them a call and the next series Deshea made his pick and took it down to score.

RYAN CLARK: Deshea and Troy, man, they did each other's jobs. They've been playing together so long, they were able to give a good look and disguise something else. Romo thought it was going to be a different play and they did a great job.

DESHEA TOWNSEND: It was a route they had been running all night. They had been working T.O. down the seam and press out with Witten. Coach LeBeau had a great call for that route and luckily they ran it into our defense. It was typical zone. We had been running a lot of man with it, but we saw how they were just pressing away from it. It gave us a chance to see the quarterback and react to the route and it worked out well.

TROY POLAMALU: I was actually hoping he'd pitch it back, but once I saw him dive for the end zone I was really happy.

Normally, Townsend would take the wide receiver – Owens – running the out, and Polamalu would handle the tight end – Jason Witten – running a curl. But LeBeau allowed them to decide on the field and Troy plotted to jump the out to Owens. The Cowboys instead threw inside and Townsend came off Owens to intercept the pass to Witten.

Touchdown. Game. Maybe even season.

"Deshea always gives the pre-game speech for the DBs," said Clark. "He likes to say that when one person makes a play, we all make a play – play for your brother. So when Deshea crossed that end zone, we all crossed that end zone."

Hines Ward gave the Ravens several opportunities if they A.) still wanted to kill him, as Bart Scott had threatened the previous season, or B.) wanted to collect a bounty by knocking Ward out, a Ravens strategy to which Terrell Suggs admitted earlier that season.

Ward caught eight passes for 107 yards, leading the Steelers to this 13-9 mid-December win at Baltimore that clinched the AFC North Division championship. And Ward didn't catch those balls along the sidelines, either.

One slant over the middle went for 21 yards, a crossing route for 30, and on the last drive Ward got the Steelers out of a hole with a pair of 13-yard catches over the middle. His 10-yard catch over the middle put the Steelers at the Baltimore 4.

Instead of getting their big payback on Ward, the Ravens were sucking wind. And on third-and-goal, Roethlisberger threw over the middle to Santonio Holmes, who got over the goal line by a single blade of grass for the game-winning touchdown.

The Ravens still had 43 seconds left with the ball near midfield. A 14-yard pass to Willis McGahee advanced the Ravens to the Pittsburgh 39. But two plays later, William Gay intercepted Joe Flacco's pass to Derrick Mason and the Steelers were division champions.

It wouldn't be the last the Steelers would see of the Ravens in the 2008 season.

CRAIG WOLFLEY: On the flight back me and Tunch were sitting in the back row, convict row. I was watching Troy. He came back where Casey Hampton, Brett Keisel, Aaron Smith and James Farrior were, and I just sat there watching them. They were enjoying each other's presence after a win, the talk that goes on, and I was smiling. Tunch turned to me and said, "You watch these guys and you know that they really love each other." And they did. They really loved each other. You can tell by the way guys interact that there's brotherhood, this unspeakable bond that goes beyond professional football. They really were a band of brothers. Is the culture different today? Maybe. I don't think it's anything where you sit there and say players are different now in 2020 than they were in 2010, or that they were in 1990 to 1980. It's reflective of the culture. Make your own judgment. What I do remember, from '05 to '08, those guys really loved each other.

CHAPTER 20

CALL DOWN THE THUNDER

At this point, the Steelers had played in six Super Bowls, each of them preceded by a win over the Houston/Tennessee Oilers/Titans during the regular season.

That made the Steelers' 31-14 Week 16 loss at Tennessee so concerning – at least to those who pay attention to insignificant minutiae.

The win gave the Titans a 13-2 record and clinched for them the No. 1 seed in the AFC playoffs. The 11-4 Steelers would be the No. 2 seed.

Man, did the Titans party it up. LenDale White stomped on the Terrible Towel and Jevon Kearse blew his nose into it as Keith Bulluck danced around both players.

CHRIS HOPE: It was my first game against the Steelers, and, man, my guys on the sideline did that stupid Terrible Towel thing. I saw one of the guys grabbing The Towel but I thought in my heart they weren't about to do anything like that. I really didn't pay it any attention, until I found out later what they did. I was upset. They were my teammates and I'm committed to them, but I was thinking the class that we showed wasn't represented well. We didn't handle that win like we knew we were going to win. It was almost like we surprised ourselves by winning, but it wasn't the Super Bowl. It decided the first seed but we could actually see that team again and we didn't need to give them any more momentum or bulletin board material than they already were going to be playing with. Me and Troy took pictures after the game. We exchanged jerseys. We're still friends. But, of course, after that game they were frustrated and we were excited. We shook hands and took pictures and went our way.

Steelers fans remember what happened to T.J. Houshmandzadeh and the Bengals after they abused The Towel in 2005.

They lost their quarterback in the first quarter of their first-round playoff game, lost that game to the Steelers, and didn't make it back to the playoffs again until Houshmandzadeh left in 2009.

Here's how the Titans would fare following their flings with The Towel:

* Lost their next eight games – including the first-round playoff game as the top seed – and didn't return to the playoffs until 2017.

* White fumbled in the red zone during the 13-10 playoff loss to the Ravens, was traded the following season and finished his career in 2010 on injured reserve.

* Kearse was benched and released in 2009, his last season in the league.

* Bulluck suffered a knee injury in 2009 and finished his career in 2010 with the New York Giants.

Still wanna mess with Myron Cope, fellas?

The Steelers finished the regular season by stomping a mud hole in the Cleveland Browns 31-0.

Despite their 12-4 record, the Steelers' offense finished 22nd in yards, the worst of all playoff teams. They were next-to-worst among playoff teams in offensive scoring – only 0.1 points per game better than the Miami Dolphins.

It didn't help that Ben Roethlisberger was still feeling the effects in his shoulder from the first sack of the season, and now he was missing two practices because of a concussion-causing last sack, by Willie McGinest.

The Chargers probably helped the Steelers' playoff path by upsetting the Indianapolis Colts in the first round, and now Philip Rivers and Co. would return to Heinz Field for another game in snowy weather. This game would be even colder than their earlier matchup. The 4:45 p.m. kickoff came in 28-degree weather, with a wind chill of 20 degrees.

Before the game, James Harrison became the NFL's first undrafted player to win NFL Defensive Player of the Year, and the fifth Steeler, joining Joe Greene, Mel Blount, Jack Lambert and Rod Woodson as Steelers DPOY award winners. Harrison's main thought seemed to be that Polamalu should have won the award.

"No," Troy said without hesitation. "The right guy won it."

Harrison's 16 sacks broke the team record, and his seven forced fumbles led the NFL. He also recorded a safety that was significant in beating the incoming Chargers in the 11-10 game.

The Steelers had played that game without tight end Heath Miller, who returned for the playoffs. LaDainian Tomlinson, the Chargers' future Hall of Fame running back, was out with a torn groin, replaced by speedy scatback Darren Sproles.

"I got juked out by him a couple of times in college," Polamalu said of the former Kansas State runner.

The referee in this game was Bill Leavy, who told Seattle reporters he loses sleep over his performance in Super Bowl 40, and Vincent Jackson did his Marvin Harrison imitation by beating Ike Taylor deep for a 41-yard touchdown pass on the Chargers' first drive.

These were certainly ominous signs, but Santonio Holmes answered with his own harbinger of things to come by returning the first Chargers punt 67 yards for a game-tying touchdown.

The Steelers lined up to punt on their next possession but called a fake on fourth-and-1. Upback Ryan Clark was stopped short, setting up a Chargers field goal late in the first quarter.

The rest of the game was all Steelers. They scored the next three touchdowns under a brilliant full moon and led by 28-10 after Gary Russell plowed into the end zone from a yard out early in the fourth quarter.

A Chargers touchdown pass made it 28-17, but Willie Parker's 16-yard touchdown run around right end put the game away.

The Steelers finished their 35-24 win, and the preparation for Steelers-Ravens III was underway. Parker outrushed Darren Sproles, 146-15, while Michigan linebackers LaMarr Woodley and Larry Foote paced the defensive effort with two sacks and an interception, respectively.

Brett Keisel took defensive style points, though, with his "Rowing down the Rivers" sack celebration in the fourth quarter.

BRETT KEISEL: Philip was such a trash talker. You play a lot of quarterbacks who don't say anything. Philip from the time he went to San Diego was lippy. They were a really good team, too. Had a lot of weapons. I thought I needed something else if I got a sack, because it's tough for us 3-4 linemen to get sacks. I needed something good.

DICK LEBEAU: Troy struggled a bit in that game. I think it was a calf issue. I'm sure that he went through some discomfort, but it is that time of year where, if a guy can go, they are going to go. And if Troy is on the field, we are not limited at all.

BRYANT MCFADDEN: To be honest, we were happy when we found out we had San Diego. Defensively we just shut them down. We were pretty confident about Baltimore, too. We knew what they were going to do and they knew what we were going to do. We just couldn't shoot ourselves in the foot, that's it. We felt we were the better team. Even if we both played as well as we could play, especially at Heinz Field, with the Super Bowl on the line, I mean, come on. We couldn't have screwed that up.

Ben Roethlisberger's arm was finally alive for the first time that season, and Super Bowl fever followed.

The feeling of "Yes, we can do this again" was suddenly evident, even in 76-year-old chairman Dan Rooney as he bopped around the practice facility with that Irish gleam in his eye.

Here we go, indeed, as the city of Pittsburgh came alive once again in the middle of January.

Historically, the Steelers were 2-0 in playoff games against teams they had beaten twice in the regular season, and those teams – the 1994 and 2002 Browns – spawned these 2008 Ravens. So, karma was riding shotgun with all of the palpable excitement.

Beyond the obvious excitement was the motivation of fear. The Steelers were 0-2 at Heinz Field in AFC Championship games. Hines Ward remembered watching opposing teams celebrate on their field. "It's something that stuck with a lot of our veteran guys," he said. "You *definitely* don't want to see Baltimore cheering on our field."

Even former Ravens coach Brian Billick predicted the Steelers would win and go to the Super Bowl.

"I thought Pittsburgh gained more from that bye week than any other team that had the bye," Billick said on *Mike & Mike in the Morning*. "They look healthy. Ben Roethlisberger looks healthy. Willie Parker looks healthy. That's as healthy as I've seen those two individuals and that team all year long. That bye week to me plays an even bigger factor now that Baltimore's had to fight through an additional game. They're playing in Pittsburgh. Pittsburgh looks on rhythm and healthy. They're going to be a formidable team."

Not only did the Ravens play an extra playoff game, but because a hurricane the second week of the season had rearranged schedules, they came to Heinz Field having played 17 consecutive weeks.

And the Steelers were gaining physicality as they ran the ball more. After compiling a 45-55 run-pass ratio throughout the season, they were 60-40 against San Diego as the offensive line was finally jelling in front of the healthy Parker, even while Roethlsiberger had the livest arm he'd shown all season, a fact he acknowledged at a press conference.

"The receivers tell me the same," Roethlisberger said. "We are close and hopefully it stays alive."

"This is going to be the highest intensity level we've seen this year, probably in my career," said Aaron Smith. "It's going to be an incredibly physical game."

"They put the extra offensive lineman in there so that they are big," Dick LeBeau said of the Ravens. "They have a big running back and a big fullback. They are a big, powerful team. It's a good thing in that Cleveland runs the same offense with the unbalanced line; so does San Diego. This is really the seventh time we have played this kind of offense, so our guys are used to finding the true center of the line and getting lined up."

Is everybody ready? Is Troy?

"Yes," Tomlin said on Friday. "As a matter of fact, he wasn't limited in any way yesterday. He had a pretty good day."

Carey Davis was also ready. The Steelers fullback blew up Ravens special-teamer Daren Stone on the opening kickoff to set the tone for the Steelers. It would last throughout the biggest play of Troy Polamalu's career and into the final moments when Ryan Clark sent Willis McGahee off the field on a stretcher.

RYAN CLARK: Yeah, I remember everything – up to a point.

KEISEL: Greatest home game ever. Like always, the game was a grudge match – physical, running the football, dink and dunk your way down the field and really battling for field position to just get points any way you can. Both defenses were super stout, super swaggy. You know when you're riding the bus to the stadium that day how you're going to feel the next day, but you can't wait because you know everyone's going to be watching.

On Sunday, Jan. 18, 2009, at 6:43 p.m. under cloudy skies with a wind chill of 15 degrees, the greatest game ever played at Heinz Field was kicked off.

On the first series, Hines Ward caught a third-and-12 pass over the middle and ran between colliding safeties Ed Reed and Jim Leonhard for 45 yards. It set up Jeff Reed's 34-yard field goal for a 3-0 lead.

Ravens rookie QB Joe Flacco struggled early. A three-and-out was followed by a two-and-interception, by Deshea Townsend, as James Harrison and LaMarr Woodley converged to hammer Flacco. That set up another Reed field goal for a 6-0 Steelers lead.

Ward limped off the field, and then limped back on, but Willie Parker was stripped by Ray Lewis and Baltimore had the ball at the Pittsburgh 43.

Instead of attempting a 51-yard field goal on fourth-and-1, the Ravens ran a QB sneak, and Polamalu came flying over the top at the snap and grabbed Flacco around the neck and shoulders as Casey Hampton clogged the middle. Flacco went down for no gain and three plays later the Steelers led 13-0 on a 65-yard Ben Roethlisberger touchdown pass to Santonio Holmes.

Roethlisberger escaped pressure, scrambled and got a block from Heath Miller on a blitzing Lewis before unloading the ball to Holmes. The Steelers' hustling tight end – who had lined up as a fullback at the snap – ran downfield to spring Holmes for the touchdown with a block at the Baltimore 15.

Miller had sprung the passer and receiver on both ends of the 65-yard touchdown pass for a 13-0 lead.

The Ravens got a 45-yard punt return by Leonhard to set up McGahee's 3-yard touchdown run and were back in it, down only 13-7 at the break.

With momentum and the ball to start the second half, Flacco ran an option/boot play that didn't fool Polamalu, who tackled the QB for a loss of eight. Troy then broke up a third-down pass to win back the momentum.

A couple of series later, Reed kicked a 46-yard field goal for a 16-7 lead late in the third quarter.

Miller set up the field goal with a 30-yard catch on second-and-24, and Limas Sweed – whose TD drop, (feigned?) injury and timeout caused the Steelers to not get off a field goal attempt late in the first half – broke up a sure interception to preserve this field goal attempt.

Mitch Berger shanked a punt of 21 yards – "That was almost a miss," TV analyst Phil Simms said of the Steelers' punter – to hand momentum back to the Ravens and they drove for a McGahee 1-yard touchdown run.

With 9:29 left in the game, the Ravens were within 16-14.

The Steelers tried to run from their own 41, but gained only a couple of yards, and Roethlisberger was sacked on third down by Terrell Suggs to force another Berger punt, which was returned to the Baltimore 39 with 6:50 remaining. But Stone – the Raven who had been blasted on the opening kickoff – was flagged for unnecessary roughness and the Ravens' possession began at their own 14.

Clark drilled McGahee low for a loss on first down, sending McGahee limping out of the game. Todd Heap gained 20 to give the Ravens a first down at their 32 with 6:00 left, still down by only two points.

A short Ray Rice run was followed by a LaMarr Woodley sack, and Flacco was looking at third-and-13 with 4:39 remaining.

He lined up in the shotgun, took the snap, looked right the entire time for Derrick Mason, and did not see a dropping Polamalu, who had lined up as the dimebacker in LeBeau's three-safety quarters package.

Seemingly from out of nowhere, Polamalu reached up for the pass, caught it at the 30, cut back across the field, and broke into the clear with 4:30 remaining. Number 43 got a block from Aaron Smith inside the 5, and hopped into the end zone to send the Steelers to Super Bowl 43 as Heinz Field was literally rocking.

Polamalu pointed up into the stands before proceeding to celebrate the greatest play of his football career with teammates.

When Troy makes a play, they all make a play.

JAMES HARRISON: We were all screaming "Troy go down! Go down! Go down!" He's like, "No, I'm goin' to score." Everybody was like go down and let the offense come in and kneel on the ball. Go down. That's why you see all of us running around like crazy trying to get a block. We're like, "Just slide on the ground!"

MCFADDEN: It was a gold call. That's when corners have trap technique on the No. 1 wide receiver. The nickel or dime would have a vertical hook on the No. 2 receiver. There were two half safeties, and Troy was lining up in the middle of the field as a freelance player. He was the dimebacker, but he was lining up in the middle of the field where the dime had no business being. He was actually lining up like a mike backer, but he was using his eyes because he knew exactly where he needed to go. Long story short, Troy ended up drifting in the middle of the field and you didn't know if he was playing a vertical hook technique or a middle seam type technique. He allowed Joe Flacco's eyes to put him where he was going to go.

Derrick Mason was running a curl or dig route and Troy came from out of nowhere. I think that play will always highlight who Troy was as a player.

HEATH MILLER: That's probably the signature play of his Hall of Fame career. A very timely play that probably only he can make.

CLARK: Troy's basically a linebacker in that grouping. That was always the really cool part about that personnel group; it allowed Troy to be close to the line. I don't mean this in a negative way, but less responsibility is always good for him. The less responsibility you put on him, the more he could roam and see. Joe Flacco drops back. Troy's the underneath defender and he just reads it perfectly. When he caught it – and this is how selfish I am – I was like, "Man, I could throw a block and it's going to be a legendary play." So, I run in front of him and hit the guy – and Troy goes the opposite way. So now, I'm not even in the freakin' final video of the touchdown. And then I remember going to hug him afterwards and I think he ducked me. I don't even think he hugged me back. That plays is part of his legend, but it was probably one of the more predictable things in life to us. There was no shock that Troy got a pick-6 to seal the game. That wasn't like, "Oh my goodness I can't believe he did it." It was more so like, "A'ight, 'bout time."

IKE TAYLOR: He just prepared. Troy remembered watching that same formation on tape. And he baited, he baited, he baited that curl route. I remember clearly. But all that was Coach Ray Horton, who really broke it down to us, like, "Football ain't hard, guys. Let me tell you about these offensive coordinators." Just like how these offensive coordinators like to say, "This is what Dick LeBeau likes to do on first, second, third ...," it's the same thing. And Coach Ray Horton wasn't lying.

COACH RAY HORTON: That's good to hear that. Ike even remembered my name.

LEBEAU: Heap was their great tight end and I had Troy in the game to match him because Heap's a tough match for DBs. He's big and has body position and he's fast enough to run away from you if you make a mistake. We were playing a configuration so that Troy could match him, but Heap blocked on the play, and Troy, with his ability to diagnose and his preparation from looking at the video, kind of lured the Baltimore quarterback into throwing the ball where he did, then he picked it. It was all Troy, realizing he was free to create and then creating.

MIKE TOMLIN: To me, the Flacco pick was the most memorable play of Troy's career, because of the gravity of the moment and the physical feel that the moment provided all of us. Um, the ground was shaking. That stadium was shaking.

MCFADDEN: That was the loudest I've ever heard Heinz Field. Out of all the big games, playoff games, rivalry games, anytime we played Styx, I never heard any stadium like it in my life. In college I played at Clemson's Death Valley, I played at The Swamp, I played at the old Orange Bowl with Miami when they were hot. I played in Seattle against the Seahawks and we know about the noise at their stadium. But that was the loudest I ever heard any stadium. And we felt everything that was being felt in that stadium. That's when we felt we were destined to win: With the backing we have, and how hyped everybody is right now, it doesn't matter who we play in the Super Bowl, we're gonna win.

LEBEAU: As I think back over the years, so many standout, critical plays come to my mind. But when they carry me out, the play that will be Troy to me was the interception against Baltimore to take us to the Super Bowl. Because that game had tilted. We had led by at least over one score for a large portion of the game, and all at once their offense got going and our offense was bogging down. They had gotten back into the game, then stopped us and took the ball over. There was no margin anymore and Troy took that ball back for a touchdown and it was Super Bowl for the Steelers.

CAMERON HEYWARD, *Ohio State defensive end (2007-10):* I was in my dorm room. The way he cut back on everybody, man. And you see so many different players getting out in front of him. That was really cool because it was all on the defense. They needed a stop to win that game.

LENNY VANDERMADE: I was in San Diego. Man, I just remember going nuts in my apartment, just running around going crazy. People in my complex had to be wondering what this dude's problem was. I was so happy for him. To have that big of a moment, to seal the game, I was so excited.

JUSTIN MYERS: I was watching that game at home in Eugene. I got to a point where I could only watch his games by myself, especially playoff games. I was going to curse and scream and yell at the TV too much. And I despised the Ravens. I despised every player on that team. I remember being on my couch when he made the interception to lock everything up, and I was just jumping up, running around, yelling curse words, yelling at Flacco, and getting a lot of odd looks from my dog.

SHELLEY POLAMALU: We were right here, at home in Tenmile. I thought it was neat that it was Piasios' first game. Troy was pointing to him in the stands.

SALU POLAMALU: That was the first time I saw Troy point into the stands like that.

CLARK: As for the hit on McGahee a little later, he was such a monster of a man, and I don't necessarily recall that. I just know I won because I got up first. I remember getting up and being super emotional and just loving everyone. I was doing a lot of hugging, a lot of telling people I love 'em and they're the most important thing in my life. I remember that part.

CHAPTER 21

SUPER BOWL 43

Bengals coach Marvin Lewis was at the Senior Bowl that week, and the Pittsburgh area native and former Steelers linebackers coach summed up the Super Bowl matchup between the Steelers and Cardinals as "Pittsburgh I and Pittsburgh II. Pittsburgh East and Pittsburgh West."

When Mike Tomlin was hired, two Steelers assistant coaches who were finalists for the job headed west after being passed over.

Ken Whisenhunt, the former Steelers offensive coordinator, took the head job with the Cardinals and brought with him OL coach Russ Grimm.

They were joined by special teams coordinator Kevin Spencer, wide receivers coach Mike Miller and defensive assistant Matt Raich. Whisenhunt also hired former Steelers ballboy Todd Haley to coordinate the offense.

The Cardinals signed former Steelers players Sean Morey, Tim Euhus, Rodney Bailey, Chukky Okobi and Mike Barr.

"When they played this game a year ago, the Cardinals did a great job against them," Lewis recalled of the 2007 Week 4 matchup. "They were able to protect, keep the ball off the ground, run the football effectively. Kenny made a couple of good decisions. They converted a fourth down. Now they're at the Super Bowl."

What also stood out for the Steelers in the 2007 loss to the Cardinals was the play of Troy Polamalu. His performance in the first half ranks among his best halves of football.

Polamalu forced Edgerrin James to fumble on the second play; knocked his former USC housemate, Matt Leinart, into throwing a short pop-up (that was dropped by James Harrison); hammered wide receiver Bryant Johnson into dropping a pass; and recovered a Larry Fitzgerald fumble before making a frenetic 13-yard return that required a Cardinals gang tackle to bring him down at midfield. Troy also tore cartilage in his ribs on the play and had to leave before halftime.

The Steelers held a 7-0 lead at the time, but Kurt Warner replaced Leinart at QB and tied the game early in the third quarter. Another Pittsburgh kid, former local prep phenom Steve Breaston, returned a punt 73 yards for the go-ahead touchdown, and James' 2-yard touchdown run put the Cardinals ahead by 21-7. They won 21-14, handing the Steelers their first loss of 2007.

Before the 2008 season, the Cardinals added a few more former Steelers in Keydrick Vincent, Brian St. Pierre, Clark Haggans and Jerame Tuman, thus setting up this Pittsburgh East-Pittsburgh West Super Bowl. Polamalu was asked prior to Super Bowl 43 what he remembered about the 2007 game against the Cardinals.

"I remember my ribs hurting," he said. "I remember it was really a highly emotional game, just seeing the coaches. You know, we really have that family mentality in Pittsburgh. We still talk to Joey and Chris Hope, and they still have their hearts in Pittsburgh. When you see coaches leave like that, there's still a little bit of animosity, probably for them, that they've left."

Dick LeBeau's 2008 defense led the NFL in fewest points allowed, and Gil Brandt, the former Cowboy VP of player personnel then working for NFL.com, proclaimed this defense better than the '70s Steel Curtain teams.

"What they have accomplished is unbelievable," Brandt said on Sirius Radio, reasoning that because scoring in 2008 was at its highest in 43 years – (there's that number again) – the average points per game allowed by the 1976 Steelers (9.8) wasn't as impressive as this year's average (13.9).

And, Brandt pointed out, 1970s offenses used only two formations as opposed to the countless sets that presently spread the field, and that defenses could jam receivers all over the field. Offensive linemen weren't permitted to extend their arms or use their hands to grasp (i.e. hold) as they are in today's game.

The 2008 Steelers also led the NFL in fewest total yards and passing yards allowed, and were second in fewest rushing yards allowed. They had come within 55 rushing yards of becoming the first defense since the NFL-AFL merger to lead in all four major categories, and they had gone up against five of the NFL's top 11 offenses.

"Before 2000, you're almost talking about a different game," says LeBeau. "Those numbers that our guys were putting up were 1960 numbers, really. It's remarkable what they were doing from a statistical standpoint. They weren't too bad from a won-loss standpoint, either."

LeBeau was at the peak of his Hall of Fame coaching abilities and had a future Hall of Famer in Polamalu as the defense's heart and soul. He also had the reigning Defensive Player of the Year in James Harrison, who was quite the interview topic leading up to Super Bowl 43.

JOHN MITCHELL, *Steelers defensive line coach (1994-19):* We cut James a couple times. He had no clue about professional football. He had no clue about our scheme. He was just a guy running around trying to be a special teams guy. Now he understands how important it is to play within the scheme. He knows the scheme a lot better, so it gives him an opportunity to go out there and make those kinds of plays. He's been around Larry Foote. He's been around James Farrior. He sees how these guys conduct themselves. He sees what professionalism is. A year ago he dressed nice, but when he travels this year he changes into a suit and tie. It shows his maturity from the time he's been here. Every game he's played this year, every trip, suit and tie. That goes to show you: When you're around good guys, it rubs off on you.

LAWRENCE TIMMONS, Steelers inside linebacker (2007-16): He does a crazy workout. Some days, he'll work out three times. That's unheard of. Real workouts. He'd spend like 10 hours at the gym. I've never seen that done before. I'd do two workouts with him, three or four hours. It was crazy. But I was in the best shape of my life.

At a podium interview a few days before the game, Harrison was asked by a political reporter what he would say to the President if he got to the White House. "I'm not going to the White House, all right?" Harrison snapped.

That ended his second media session of the week, and Harrison looked tired, as if he had just finished one of his legendary workouts. Reporters sensed he was finished and left him alone – with the exception of one, lone, familiar, sympathetic scribe.

James Harrison, January 28, 2009

Have you made a conscious effort to be nice?
JH: I'm trying. I'm trying my best. But it's kind of difficult when you don't like cameras in your face.
How much patience do you have left?
I've got enough to make it through this week. I stocked up on it before I left Pittsburgh.
Winning awards kind of leads to more interviews (points to DPOY trophy on stand).
Yeah, but I'll take this one home and let my boy play with it. He'll like it (smiling, finally).

Has DPOY sunk in yet?

No. I haven't had time to sit back and look at it and say, "Oh, I'm the Defensive Player of the Year." Maybe after the season's over. If we finish business here, it'll be great, but without the win here all of that just slips into the background.

Your former position coach, Mike Archer, told me Joey Porter and Jason Gildon took you under their wing when you started. How did that unfold?

Joey and Jason really treated everybody the same. It wasn't so much that they took me under their wing, they just let me feel like I belonged there. They didn't let me feel like I was one of the outside guys coming in. As far as Archer goes, that's another story in itself.

He wished you well.

It's great that he wishes me well (grimacing, again), but, like I said, that's just something else altogether.

RYAN CLARK: Troy's my guy. He eats too much, though. I used to always tell him, "You're the only Samoan in the league not playing D-line."

BRYANT MCFADDEN: Troy can eat. One of my friends from Miami owns a Caribbean restaurant. He sent me some food and I let Troy taste it, because I know Troy loves Caribbean food specifically. My guy sent me a red devil cake. If you know anything about Troy, he loves dessert. So Troy was like, "Mac, wow, where is this from?" I told him it's from one of my partners in Miami. He said, "Can he send some more?"

CLARK: Yeah, he found a spot. Monday night we sat in my room at the Capital Grille and watched *Soul Men* with Samuel L. Jackson and Bernie Mac. The next night, or Wednesday, he's like "I found us a Jamaican spot."

MCFADDEN: I said, "OK, I'll see if he'll send some up, but what do you want?" I was thinking he would take a little of this and that, but he ordered everything! "Could you have him send curry goat? Ox tails? Jerk chicken?" I said, "Troy, are you feeding a whole village?" He said, "No, I just love it, Mac." So I sent out a message to my homeboy and when I told him who it was for he said, "Yeah, no problem." So he shipped up a whole bunch of food.

CLARK: And he orders *everything* that he wants. It wasn't "I want this one meal." He wanted to taste a bunch of stuff, so instead of trying to find a smaller way to do it, he just ordered the actual full meals of everything. He and I go back to the room and we eat as much as we possibly can. And we ate a ton. But we had purchased so much food. He was walking down the hall knocking on everybody's door giving food away. Along with being an overeater, he was an overbuyer of food. I think sometimes his eyes were bigger than his belly. But, yeah, we definitely ate too much Jamaican food that week. And he has this crazy ability to adapt. I've seen him play at 190, and I've seen him play at 245 – in that Super Bowl.

MCFADDEN: Within the week Troy was ready to put another order in. I can't remember if he did. The thing about Troy, if he would've ordered again he probably would've been another 20 pounds heavier by Sunday.

CLARK: Yep, 245. Oh, he was the fattest. He was a true, true Samoan.

MCFADDEN: I saw Troy this past Super Bowl (54) in Miami and we got a chance to chop it up a bit. We did an interview, and then off the record he asked about the same restaurant. I was like "Troy, are you serious?" He was. "Yes, Mac, please. I have to get some of that. Can you set something up?" That tells you how much he loves food.

CLARK: He ballooned right after he retired. He was fat. We came up when my son was being recruited. We stayed with them in Pittsburgh before they moved. He was fat then. But then he got it under control. He looks amazing now. I'm happy for him. I don't want him to be the fat boy.

"I don't remember anything of that nature," Mike Tomlin said about any weight gain by Troy Polamalu.

Troy either hid it well or wore enough baggy clothing as he – and everyone else in the secondary – began focusing on Cardinals receiver Larry Fitzgerald, the pride of the University of Pittsburgh.

Fitzgerald ended 2008 with 101 receiving yards against New England and 130 against Seattle to finish with a career-high 1,431 yards on 96 catches and an NFL-high that season of 12 touchdown catches.

The rampage continued – even accelerated – in the postseason. Fitzgerald caught 6 for 101 with a 42-yard TD against Atlanta; 8 for 166 with a 29-yard TD against Carolina; and 9 for 152 with 9, 62 and 1-yard TDs in the NFC Championship Game against Philadelphia.

The Steelers were prepping Ike Taylor to "travel" with Fitzgerald in man-to-man situations. And of course they would play enough zone coverage to worry each of the defensive backs, as the Steelers lasered in on the great Larry Fitz.

LEBEAU: A wise man once said, "He who defends everything, defends nothing." That was Fredrick the Great, the unifier of the Prussian states. I think he knew what he was talking about. He had a pretty good competitive record.

IKE TAYLOR: We saw what Larry Fitzgerald was doing in the playoffs. He was breaking Jerry Rice's records for a playoff run, right? Couldn't nobody stop him. I don't care if you double, triple-teamed him, it didn't matter.

MCFADDEN: They were playing some of the best football of their lives. That playoff stretch by Arizona, they were unbelievable. So Troy was saying, "Just know your keys and when one person makes a play, we all make a play." That was the mindset the week leading up to that Super Bowl game.

TAYLOR: Oh, we were confident. You couldn't tell us nothin' man. We already won a Super Bowl, then we come back a couple of years later and we're right back in the dance.

MCFADDEN: We just wanted to finish the drill. Mike Tomlin told us that entire season that great defenses win championships. We had an historic run in '08 that led to a nice record and defensively we had some real nice numbers. When we got to Tampa, collectively we were like "We've got to finish the drill." Arizona didn't have a great record but their offense was great. They had a quarterback who's in the Hall. They had two receivers who I believe will be in the Hall. Definitely Larry Fitzgerald will be a first ballot, and I think Anquan (Boldin) will eventually get in. And of course Edgerrin James is going into the Hall this year (2020). So you're talking about four players on their offense who will have a gold jacket.

LARRY FITZGERALD, *Cardinals wide receiver (2004-current):* If you pull a name out of a hat on that defense, James Farrior, anybody, those guys are unbelievable. Not only are they an unbelievable talent, they play so well and hard for each other. When they make a play, they go to one another and congratulate one another. Brett Keisel had been playing great. All around, we knew it was going to be a dogfight for us to put something together, but we were confident we could do it.

TAYLOR: I couldn't wait to play him. I watched him go through the NFL. I watched that Philly game – because Philly also had a good secondary – and I was like, "Ain't no way. Ain't no way." But you kind of knew it. Shoot, he was right next door with the Pitt Panthers, so you saw it. Like, Fitz won't beat nobody deep. But throw that thing around his area code and he's catching it.

MIKE MILLER, *Cardinals WRs coach/coordinator (2007-12):* Troy, of course, was the guy in the secondary, but we thought we matched up well. We thought they were average players at the other positions.

I don't mean to offend people with that comment, but if you look at how those careers went, Troy was THE guy in the secondary. The thing the Steelers had was their front seven. They were monsters, every one of them. And they're all try-hard guys, too. They don't take anything off. They fight tooth and nail every play. So, you have Troy roaming all over the place and we just always felt, as far as game-planning, you try to get him to the middle of the field, deep middle, try to motion and shift where sometimes their rules take him to the center of the field, and then that way we got him away from the line of scrimmage. You remember Tom Brady taking advantage of that in some of those games when you could look him off and then you can go ahead and attack away from that action. So we felt good about doing that, too.

CLARK: I don't know if you recall this, but we were a solid defense that year (chuckles). Yeah, we were OK. And so Wednesday at practice for the Super Bowl we were picking the ball off and guys were not running it back hard. People weren't transitioning to offense. So, Thursday morning we come in and Coach LeBeau shows every turnover we practiced. And he shows those turnovers and he points to the person who got the turnover not running the football back. He points to the rest of the players on the field for not blocking and transitioning to offense, and he put an emphasis on it for the rest of the week.

RASHARD MENDENHALL, *Steelers first-round draft pick (injured reserve):* In the tunnel just before coming out, Troy pulled me aside and said, "Hey, I know this is tough, but you're going to be out there with us next year. You should've been out there with us this year." That meant so much to me, that a guy would stop and say something like that. That was a memorable time for me.

Before the game, Mike Tomlin gave Ben Roethlisberger a note that said, "Terry Bradshaw 4, Joe Montana 4." Tomlin listed the Super Bowls those QBs won and asked Roethlisberger, "Where do you want to fit in that group?"

Perhaps Tomlin sensed this was Roethlisberger's coming out party; perhaps the note had something to do with it, because Roethlisberger was far more calm than he had been in his first Super Bowl.

"Ben said the last Super Bowl he started nervous and stayed nervous the whole game," TV analyst John Madden said at the start of the game.

Bill Cowher had recognized this right away that day in Detroit. But this was a different Ben. On this day, on this grand stage, Roethlisberger opened with a 38-yard completion to Hines Ward out of play-action. He then found Heath Miller down the middle for 21 yards to the Arizona 1. Goal-line runner Gary Russell lost 4, Willie Parker gained 4, Roethlisberger scrambled for no gain, but appeared to have crossed the plane. However, the call – unlike the similarly close call against Seattle – didn't go his way and the Steelers kicked a field goal.

The Steelers got the ball back and this time put it in the end zone. A 25-yard screen pass to Santonio Holmes, a pair of 11-yard passes to Miller, a 7-yarder to Holmes and a 4-yarder to Miller set up Russell's 1-yard TD run and the Steelers led 10-0 behind their red-hot QB.

The Cardinals came back with a touchdown on their next possession. Kurt Warner threw to Anquan Boldin, who sprinted 45 yards down the right sideline to the Pittsburgh 2, from where Warner threw a 2-yard play-action TD pass to tight end Ben Patrick. With 8:34 left in the first half, the Steelers' lead was 10-7.

Linebacker Karlos Dansby intercepted Roethlisberger and the Cardinals had the ball at the Pittsburgh 34 with two minutes left in the half and were looking to at least tie the game.

Warner threw a third-and-10 pass to running back Tim Hightower for 10, and then hit Larry Fitzgerald over the middle for 12, Boldin for 7, Boldin for 4, and looking again for Boldin when ...

... James Harrison happened.

You know the story. The Steelers' right outside linebacker was supposed to rush as part of the max blitz, but he did a Troy, gave it some thought, and said, "Nah, I'm going to turn this game around."

Harrison dropped a few yards into the end zone, picked off the pass intended for Boldin, and returned it 100 yards officially for a Steelers touchdown. It's generally regarded as the greatest play in Super Bowl history, and so it follows that if the Super Bowl is the greatest game in football, Harrison's play was the greatest play in football history.

The return was the classic struggle of a man whose time was up, but who raged against the dying of the light.

Harrison wouldn't go gently into that good night. Oh, he was going down, that much we knew, but would he go down in the glory of the end zone?

Harrison might have had about a 1 in 1000 chance of making it all the way down the sideline. But he huffed and puffed as the defense rallied, just as LeBeau had stressed all week, and Harrison became the running back he KNEW he always had been. He trudged forward, the power of 3 x 3-hour daily workouts pumping his legs as bodies fell by the wayside.

Defensive teammates became offensive blockers as the Silverback took one last desperate lunge inside the 5 before he was brought down – just inside the end zone, and his team led, not trailed, at halftime.

Somewhere Jack Buck was shouting that he did not believe what he just saw.

Did Al Michaels believe in miracles?

"Harrison," exclaimed Michaels, the great play-by-play announcer, "runs through the entire state of Arizona to get to the end zone!"

CLARK: There's only one person on the team that didn't get a block, and that was Troy Polamalu.

HARRISON: Troy might've been on the far end.

CLARK: No, he's not there. Seriously. The only person who actually didn't get a block was T.P.

HARRISON: Noooo. I seen Troy.

CLARK: He just held his frickin' hand up in the other corner. Just terrible.

HARRISON: I seen him laying in the picture with his (looks at a photo) – no. Wait. He's standing up.

CLARK: Didn't even try! Didn't even give effort! I'm pretty sure he never even made it down there!

HARRISON: You're right!

CLARK: Man, it's gotta be his worst play ever. Least effort he's ever given, for sure.

HARRISON: Ryan threw like two blocks. The best block gotta be Woodley. Without that block, it's over. Yeah, that play ends right then and there.

CLARK: Everybody just sprung into playing offense, except for one guy. I guess he had made enough plays and we should forgive him.

Troy Polamalu was on the far end, but, after a late start, he did bolt for the body-strewn sideline and did make an attempt at a block behind the play.

Clark, meanwhile, stood over the gasping Harrison in the end zone and frantically waved to the Steelers' sideline for help.

BRETT KEISEL: James was straight – as we say in the business – blowed. He was straight up exhausted. Trainers were seeing to him. He was laid out, getting IVs. No one could believe it.

HARRISON: No question. No question. My wind was gone. I had two bags of IV on it. That run took it out of a lot of people (laughs).

KEISEL: We wanted to make sure he was all right because he laid there for a bit. But halftime of a Super Bowl is so long. It's like an hour, it seems, so you have plenty of time to go in there, kick your shoes off, relax, game plan, come back and kind of do your team hoo-rahs and then go out and play. Halftime's really surreal. You're sitting there in the locker room and you hear a show going on. You can hear it, like a muffled bass drum. It's weird kind of being the entertainment for that (laughs) but it's amazing. Every time I put my rings on to this day I think about it.

MIKE MILLER: Man, I'm really glad I recommended the Steelers sign James Harrison. He really proved to pay big dividends for me and my career.

LEBEAU: I'm not a collector of mementoes. I don't have very many letters. No magazine articles or stuff like that. I'm just not that kind of a person. But I went back and looked at that play again and again and again because I recognize that it's a rare play, and the background with which it unfolded, you know, with the importance of the game. You've got a 102-yard run with a linebacker, guys running all over the field making two, three blocks on the same play, and him jumping over people clutching for him, and maybe three or four different situations where would-be tacklers are literally inches from him.

When he first picked it off, I knew he was in the end zone and my only thought was, "We're out of this without giving up any points." And then I expected him to go down very quickly. There were a lot of Cardinals in the vicinity. But pretty soon you saw that helmet. They were down in the far corner from me, certainly not the best vantage point, but I saw that helmet still bouncing around over there, and then pretty soon it broke, and I thought, "Hey, we've got a chance here." And then our guys rallied and I could see some of the angles that our guys had. And then James made a couple of fantastic individual moves and jumped over a couple guys on the ground that might've tripped him up and he fell probably two inches into the end zone.

It's so Hollywood-ish that if you were in the movie business you'd say, "Get that out of here. A play like that could never happen." And yet, it did happen, and it happened at the most fortuitous time for us. I could not get myself to go on to the next series. I just kept running the play back. I can describe it to you pretty well. It was a relish. I guess you get a relish every now and then in your life.

KEISEL: Going into halftime everyone's hyped, but then we come out and it kind of stalled. They started moving it a little bit and scored. Then Larry's touchdown and it was like, are you kidding me? This is NOT happening. But, great finish. That's what great teams do.

After Bruce Springsteen finished his 12-minute set, the Steelers returned to the field with a strip-sack by James Farrior that was recovered by the replenished Harrison. However, the play was reviewed, reversed, and a punt set the Steelers back 31 yards to their own 18.

A couple of personal fouls by the Cardinals, a 15-yard pass to Santonio Holmes, a 15-yard run by Willie Parker and the Steelers were knocking on the door of a blowout. They had the ball first-and-goal at the Arizona 4 with a 17-7 lead and 3:32 left in the third quarter.

The Steelers sputtered, however, and Jeff Reed's 21-yard field goal gave them a 20-7 lead with 17:11 remaining in regulation. The Cardinals punted to start the fourth, but got the ball back at their own 13 with 11:30 left.

At this point, the great Larry Fitz had only one catch for 12 yards. The Pitt man who entered the game threatening to break all three of the primary NFL postseason receiving records, held by three different players, was being frustrated by Ike Taylor.

LEBEAU: He's going to catch more than that no matter what you're playing against him. You're not going to keep him down the whole game.

TAYLOR: Larry was so cool I couldn't even talk smack to him, He asked, "How your family doin'? How your kids doin'"?" I'm like, "For real, Larry? You're really gonna do this? For real, bro?" He played at Pitt, so it was just like "Hey, bro, let's get it, dawg." But at that point you knew it was just a matter of time, man. That boy at the time was the best player in the NFL, was he not? Shooo. Lord have mercy.

LEBEAU: We had treated him like you would a prolific scorer in basketball. Say a guy's averaging 40 points a game; you know he's going to get 18 or 21. You just can't let him get 45.

Fitzgerald got his 45.

Kurt Warner started the Cardinals' rally with a 13-yard pass to Breaston and an 18-yard pass to Jerheme Urban. Warner stayed hot, completing all eight passes on the drive, including 6, 22 and 6-yarders to Fitzgerald before throwing a third-down, 1-yard TD pass to Fitzgerald, who skied to make the one-handed, helmet-pressed catch over a smothering Taylor for a touchdown with 7:33 to play.

The Steelers went three-and-out, and back came the red-hot Warner. He completed two more passes for 34 yards, plus a personal foul on Taylor for slugging Anquan Boldin after a catch.

At the Pittsburgh 26, the Steelers got a reprieve when left tackle Mike Gandy was called for his third holding penalty of the game against Harrison, and the Cardinals eventually punted to the Pittsburgh 1.

Backed up on third-and-10, Ben Roethlisberger threw a 19-yard completion to Holmes, but Steelers center Justin Hartwig, flattened by linebacker Chike Okeafor, had grabbed the blitzer while falling, was flagged for holding and the Cardinals were awarded two points for a safety. It cut the Steelers' lead to 20-16, and Breaston returned the ensuing punt to the Arizona 36 with 2:53 left.

Too much time, the Steelers thought.

Two snaps later they were thankful for all of that time, because Larry Fitz struck quickly. He broke free from Taylor's jam and the two safeties bit on the slot receivers running outs on separate sides. Fitzgerald caught the short slant and sprinted through the parted middle for a 64-yard touchdown that gave the Cardinals a 23-20 lead with 2:37 left.

TAYLOR: Up the middle, up the chute, man. I figured that was going to fall on me. Regardless of what I did in the beginning, people always remember the last couple of plays.

JAMES FARRIOR: You couldn't talk to Ike at all. He thought he lost the game for us.

CLARK: It was Troy and I's fault. It's a two-man under and they ran a post-corner. Troy and I are the two deep defenders, and you're actually not supposed to try to cover that unless it's thrown. It's a late throw. You can read the quarterback and get to it. But because Troy and I both knew the formation and the tendency, we both broke on it early just out of anticipation. Essentially, when Larry Fitzgerald catches the ball, Troy and I should meet in the middle and tackle him. But because we both bit on those corner routes, we basically weren't even a part of the game.

TROY POLAMALU: When Larry Fitzgerald split me and Ryan, I just remember thinking, "Oh, that Jamaican food."

TAYLOR: If they said that was their fault, that was their fault. I ain't gonna take nothin' away from them.

CLARK: We just were both wrong. That happens sometimes. The way the defense is designed, the DBs up front who are covering are playing inside and underneath, so our jobs are high and outside. So as soon as we saw that break, we both went, which necessarily isn't wrong. It's not wrong. But it's also not going to help you make any play other than if that ball is thrown.

LEBEAU: I'm sure it was something they'd seen. We encourage our players to trust their instincts. Nobody's right 100 percent of the time. To me, the significant thing about that play was there was nothing like that the whole season, and usually you'll have five or six of those types of plays. So I'm proud of them even though they messed that one up.

MIKE MILLER: If you're going to live by the sword with how Troy can be – how they let him play by his instincts, and most of the time he's right and they're wearing two rings because of it – sometimes those kinds of plays are just going to happen. If that's the one play or three or four plays out of so many that get you, you live with it.

LEBEAU: Of course, our guys were a little bit down when they gave up the lead in the fourth quarter, which is something you never want to do, but I said "Get yourself collected and ready because we're going back out there. This game is not over." I really thought the game was going into overtime because I thought Ben would get us down there for a field goal. I hoped he would get us down there for a touchdown, but I felt pretty strongly that he would get us a field goal. I've seen it happen all year and our guys had to be ready to go out there and get the doggone ball if we lost the toss. The only time that I was concerned honestly was when we had 1st and 20 on our own 12.

"Who's laughing now, O-line?" Roethlisberger would famously crow from the podium a little more than 2 minutes and 37 seconds of game time later.

However, here was Roethlisberger, facing a first-and-20 from his own 12 following left guard Chris Kemoeatu's holding penalty.

The ghost of Alan Faneca didn't stop Roethlisberger, who hit Holmes for 14 yards, and then hit him for 13 more on third-and-6. An 11-yard strike to Nate Washington, a scramble for 4, and a second timeout was followed by the big play, a 40-yard catch and run by Holmes down the right side to the Arizona 6. The Steelers called their final timeout with 48 seconds left. Holmes, who told Roethlisberger at the start of the drive, "I want the ball in my hands no matter what, no matter where it is," had prowled the sideline prior to the drive shouting to no one in particular, "Time to be great! I'm daring to be great!"

Roethlisberger, with Hines Ward hobbled, stuck with the red-hot Holmes and threw to him in the left half of the end zone. But the high pass went through Holmes' outstretched hands as six seconds ticked off. Holmes walked back to the huddle and told Roethlisberger, "My bad." Roethlisberger countered with, "It doesn't matter."

It didn't.

HINES WARD: When it went through his hands, he said, "Fuck, I've got to make up for that." Then he went and made the greatest catch in Super Bowl history. But the play wasn't designed for that. Ben went through his progressions, they doubled me, we lost the flat, Santonio stepped up in the corner, and when Ben threw it, he just threw it to a point and Tone did a phenomenal job with the toe touch. Every day we practice that, dragging, getting your toes down. All of that went into that play. I can still see Santonio practicing, developing, working on getting those two feet in, making a great catch.

Holmes said later that "I definitely thought I lost us the Super Bowl," but on the next play he made the now famous toe-dragging, fingertip, Super Bowl-winning catch on the right sideline in the end zone. The pass was thrown perfectly, just over the outstretched arm of cornerback Ralph Brown and two other closely trailing DBs.

The catch by Holmes completed the touchdown drive, and the extra point put the Steelers up 27-23 with 35 seconds remaining.

Yes, 35 seconds remained with Hall of Fame QB Kurt Warner and Larry the Legend coming back on the field, and Warner didn't waste any time. He hit Fitzgerald for 20 yards and J.J. Arrington for 13. The Cardinals had a first down at their 43 with 15 seconds left as they used their final timeout. Troy Polamalu would confide later that he was worried about Fitzgerald making him a highlight for the rest of eternity. But LaMarr Woodley hacked Warner's arm as he was winding up to throw deep. The fumble was recovered by Keisel.

LEBEAU: We got to end the game with Woodley's great play. That was a great sack and it was recovered by Brett. It was a three-man rush so they had to keep going on that thing and the coverage was really good. Kurt actually held the ball quite a while on that and my whole objective that whole drive was to keep him from where he could reach the end zone, because that's the place where Fitzgerald excels the most, jumping up, and you just didn't want him having any shot at the ball in your end zone, so it was a huge sack by Woodley and a great recovery by Brett.

KEISEL: I laid there on the ground for awhile. I landed on that thing and I just laid there and went, "That's it! That's it! That's it!" James jumped on me and then kinda helped me up, and I just remember walking to the sideline, walking around in shock almost, because that game ended the way it did.

CLARK: It was the moment I remember the most. And it was fitting to be on the field when LaMarr stripped the ball. We were expecting a deep pass, a Hail Mary, so we were deep. And when LaMarr stripped it, I just took off running for the stands. Troy was chasing me and saying, "Bro, where are you going?" I said, "I don't even freakin' know. I'm just so happy because I was so scared!" I thought Larry Fitzgerald was going to jump over me and Troy's head and we would forever be immortalized. And he was like, "Bro, me too!"

LEBEAU: Troy told me exactly those same words. On the bus the next day going to the airport, Troy said, "Coach, on that last play, Fitzgerald was right here and Boldin was right here." He said, "I knew the ball had to be thrown right there." He said that he didn't want to be on ESPN for the next 20 years with one of them jumping up and catching the ball. As soon as he said that to me, I said to myself, that tells me that they wouldn't have caught it, because if Troy was motivated in that respect, he'd have found some way, the way Troy usually finds some way, of getting the dadgummed ball, of making sure either he got the ball or they didn't. But it's interesting what shoots through your mind while a play is unfolding.

CLARK: Things like that always made me feel good talking to Troy, because for me he was just this extraordinary talent, honestly just a freak of nature. But to hear his fears, to know he was super nervous all the time, to know that he feared failing and not being enough, I think all of those things humanized him so much to me. He was just like all the rest of us. He had those same fears. He had those same doubts about his talent. I always thought that was cool.

The post-game party rolled deep into the night. Mike Tomlin talked to Barack Obama early in the night, and now Tomlin had a Mr. Snoop Dogg in his ear on the stage of a room that was growing more packed with each beat.

Tomlin, with the curved bill of his ball cap covering his forehead and much of his eyes, just nodded as Snoop talked. Tomlin looked as if he was about to sing with the band as more players filed in and began hooting, as Snoop kicked off what surely would become a raucous late-night party for the Pittsburgh Steelers.

The small room was becoming a cramped room and no place for a middle-aged sports writer who spent much of the week following an Allman Brothers cover band at outdoor keggers in the Tampa area. So, I went outside for some fresh air and struck up a conversation with a rock 'n' roll DJ.

RANDY BAUMANN, WDVE DJ: I was smoking a cigarette and when I saw Troy, I quickly put it out. I remember having the feeling that I didn't want Troy to know I smoked because I didn't want him to be disappointed in me (laughs). But we were sitting there. It was really late. I want to say it was 3 in the morning. Troy and his family were a bit away, 100 feet or so. You and I were on a veranda BS-ing as the party was winding down. Troy said goodnight to his group and walked right over to us. It was kind of surprising. We were both watching him, thinking, "Is he walking over to us?" And we both kind of straightened up like the caddies in Caddy Shack at the pool.

He let out a sigh and said, "When did you think we were going to win?" I said, "Win what?" And he said, "When did you guys think we could win the Super Bowl?" He was talking about that particular team, and I said, "I didn't think this team was going to win the Super Bowl until you picked off Flacco two weeks ago." He said, "I thought this team was going to go 9 and 7. I told my wife we were going to go 9 and 7 this year. I did not think we were going to be a Super Bowl team."

Wex, you asked him about Fitzgerald's touchdown and he said he knew as soon as he lined up that was a touchdown because they were in the wrong defense, that they had it called completely wrong and he didn't think he could make it up. And then you guys talked X's and O's on that. I think we were both kind of so shocked that he was sitting there casually talking to us after having won the Super Bowl. And it was Troy Polamalu. It wasn't just any player. It was Saint Troy. Then he said how great it was to have won the Super Bowl with that group of guys and that team and how much it meant to him for Coach LeBeau to have won another one. He said, "I really feel happy for the city of Pittsburgh and all of the Steelers fans, because this means so much to them." And then he said, "Well, you know. You talk to them every day." I remember wondering, is this Candid Camera? Is this a joke someone's playing on us? How can he be that selfless? After he won, all he was happy for were other people: the city of Pittsburgh, his teammates. It was Troy, so it was completely genuine, but it was shocking to me that somebody was capable of being that happy for other people right after he had just won the Super Bowl.

CHAPTER 22

THE AFTERGLOW

It was the tail end of the team's post-Super Bowl party, and Troy Polamalu, who hated to watch or talk about football, was busy sating the curiosities of a couple of immature outsiders at 3 in the morning.

He had to make one more polite exchange before heading home.

A young woman had been waiting nearby, waiting for a break in the conversation. That's when she approached Troy to congratulate him and tell him that she was a big fan, always had been. And then she asked for a hug.

Troy smiled and said no.

The girl, a striking beauty dressed tastefully, tantalizingly, in light powder blue, dark hair and eyes, was shocked. She looked as if she had never heard that word in her life.

She asked again, stressing that she only wanted a hug.

"No," Troy said firmly, but, again, smiling courteously. "My heart belongs to another."

CHRIS HOKE: I love that! That's powerful! That's a guy you know you can count on, because of his values and his foundational principles. This is a guy you can count on at any moment, any situation, not just football, but life.

Polamalu also said during the post-game party that this particular team became closer than even the previous Super Bowl team, and he said that team was very close. He gave Bill Cowher credit for building the foundation before acknowledging that Mike Tomlin gave them the freedom to become even closer.

IKE TAYLOR: You are your coach's and defensive captain's personality. With Joey Porter and Coach Cowher it was the physicality, a we-don't-give-a-you-know-what attitude, both on and off the field. Even when we traveled. It was more relaxed. As long as your pants weren't sagging or you weren't looking straight ignorant, Coach Cowher wouldn't care how you traveled. Now, with Coach Tomlin and James Farrior, it was more business-minded. That's when people really got into the suits and all that good stuff. It was just two different personalities from the coach's personality and the defensive captain.

BRETT KEISEL: I love that "Tomlin only won because of Cowher's players" stuff. You can say whatever you want, but to lead a team, he deserves credit. To people in the building, it mattereth not. You've got to lead. A team needs direction and it needs people putting people in the right spot at the right time, making the right decisions at the time it's needed and knocking the door down when opportunity knocks.

DICK LEBEAU: We were coming off making the playoffs, then getting beat in the first round of the playoffs, and plus we'd gone through a transitional period with a new coach. You know you've got a pretty good football team, but for the year to go the way that it went you had to enjoy that as the most special year of your coaching career. I mean, if you took a defensive coach and said, "Coach, describe for me the perfect season," I would describe the 2008 year. Statistically, they led in everything. They put up numbers that go back to 1960, when teams ran the ball 70 percent of the time. And then have that team, coupled with a fighting competitive offense, win the Super Bowl, that would be my dream season. And then you would say, "But it could never happen. It's 2008. There's not going to be those scenarios." And guess what? It did happen. So for me to say that it wasn't the best year of my coaching career wouldn't do service to these guys and what they did.

TAYLOR: Dickie said he been coaching for 66 years. He's never seen, whether it's kids or adults, a group with a bond so strong as the one we had.

HEATH MILLER: Picking between the two championship teams is tough, but I would say 2008. Maybe that's because I had been around more. In 2005 I was a rookie flying by the seat of my pants. I was just taking it day by day. In 2008, I was able to sit back and appreciate it. Our defense was *soooo* good that year. No one could run the ball on them. It was almost like if they handed it off they could kind of keep it somewhat honest. And we were stopping that with a seven-man box continuously, which was amazing.

CAMERON HEYWARD: You could arguably say that defense was the best defense ever, besides a couple of drives in that Super Bowl. If they don't give that late one up, that is the best defense ever.

MILLER: In '05, my strength wasn't what it should've been by the time we got to the Super Bowl. I had just played twice as many games as I ever played in my entire life and by the time we got to Detroit, I was 245. I tried to work out that week and I was doing 225 just for a few reps and I thought, "This is depressing. I'll just save my energy for the game." I was the new guy, but the team was just so close. The chemistry and camaraderie made it so special. So many good leaders. Joey and those guys had been together so long. Jerome, Alan and those offensive linemen had played together for so long. It's a really tough call for me.

LEABEAU: Throughout 2008 you see where Troy goes from Point A to Point B and how many plays he snuffed out with his explosiveness, and how well Ryan Clark played, and how well Aaron Smith played. In years past Casey got a lot of notoriety and went to Pro Bowls. I didn't hear so much of that in 2008 because he missed the training camp. But Casey's unblockable in the middle of that defense. He was just a foundation for it. Guys like Deshea, who battled injuries, then accepted their role coming back, making key interceptions like he did down the stretch; those are things you will never forget. Our safeties, other than Troy, don't get a lot of notoriety but together they were head and shoulders the best tandem in the league. They just did it week in and week out, and that's one of the reasons our numbers were what they were. And then you've got Woodley and Harrison. They're a dream combination. From a coaching standpoint, you can't do anything but smile about that. And then you've got Larry and James in the middle. They're so smart and they just don't get fooled. People try to fool us because it's hard to go and beat us without fooling us because Aaron Smith and Casey and Brett Keisel are so good. Then you add Timmons running around doing stuff that he did for us. It was a dream season for a defensive coach.

Super Bowl 43 was cathartic for LeBeau. He had been the loser in similarly dramatic fashion 20 years and 10 days earlier, the Bengals' defensive coordinator when Joe Montana, an idol of Roethlisberger's, gutted them with an eerily similar drive.

Montana and the 49ers trailed the Bengals in Super Bowl 23 by three points with 3:20 remaining.

Roethlisberger and the Steelers trailed the Cardinals in Super Bowl 43 by three points with 2:30 remaining.

Both quarterbacks came out of the two-minute warning by converting third downs.

Montana overcame a second-and-20.

Roethlisberger overcame a first-and-20.

Montana hit Jerry Rice for 27 yards on a catch-and-run to the Cincinnati 18 after two Bengals safeties collided at the catch point.

Roethlisberger hit Santonio Holmes for 40 yards on a catch-and-run to the Arizona 6 after the Cardinals safety fell down at the catch point.

Montana hit John Taylor for a 10-yard touchdown with 34 seconds left for a 4-point win.

Roethlisberger hit Holmes for a 6-yard touchdown with 35 seconds left for a 4-point win.

LEBEAU: Don't think the irony of that was lost on me. Coach Whisenhunt and I are good friends and I did not want to talk to him for a while. But when I did, I told him, "I know how you feel because I've been involved in one that we lost exactly the same way, and the sun will still come up, and you'll still be coaching football." It's just a tough pill to swallow. They say things balance out if you stay around long enough. Well, I had to stay around pretty long. I'm glad it came back.

KEN WHISENHUNT, *Cardinals head coach (2007-12):* Obviously you're excited because we'd just made a play to take the lead, especially when we were down 20-7 with not a lot of time left in the game. You're very happy about that, but you look up at the clock and see there's 2:30 and realize that's a lot of time, especially with their quarterback and their weapons. So when we got it to first-and-20 on the first play, you're encouraged because that's not something that's easy. But as Ben scrambled and made some plays and made some throws, and they got over the 50, then you're hoping for a field goal and maybe go into overtime. Obviously it didn't work out that way. It was a tough series.

LEBEAU: The whole thing had an eerie context to it. Probably it's a little ironic that you would remember that Montana game yourself, but I thought of it instantly.

WHISENHUNT: It wasn't a slow death because you were caught in the moment of trying to be successful. It was a slow death at the end because it took so long to find out if that play was good, and then you had only 35 seconds to score a touchdown, so that was the game.

LEBEAU: I don't think they should have to defend anything about what they did. Our guys just made the one extra play when it mattered the most. They were a very good football team playing its best football at the right time. They certainly did a great job competing.

WHISENHUNT: Mr. Rooney wrote me a letter. He said, "Your team played very well, congratulations on your accomplishments this year." It meant a lot to me. It's very classy. Not surprising.

TAYLOR: When I think back on our playoff run that year, I think about Coach Ray Horton. He broke football down to the least common denominator. So simple, man. So, so simple. Coach Ray Horton, when he became the DB coach, he'd say, "Cornerbacks, safeties: Respect and watch tape on a wide receiver or tight end, but we're playing the offensive coordinator." What you mean, coach? "Offensive coordinators aren't going to change. They're going to run this on first down, this on second down, this on third down. They'll go with the formations that they like to use. These are the same routes, the same concepts, different formations. It's a high percentage they like to run this formation on first down; it's a high percentage they like to run that formation on second and third down. Now, Ike, if they see you off coverage, and they're looking in the middle of the field and see one safety, they're going to throw a right down pass. Be aware of that. Safeties, the more we can disguise and move at the snap of the ball, the more we can confuse the quarterback." When I say this man broke that shit down to the least common denominator, that's exactly what he did. He wanted us to respect who was in front of us, please do, but we're always going against the offensive coordinators. They'll never change.

RAY HORTON: Oh, for sure. And I had a room of players: Ryan Clark could be a coach if he wanted to; Deshea Townsend is a football coach in Chicago; Ike was on the NFL Network; B Mac's in the media; Troy was an executive in the AAF, could be in the NFL or doing very well on Wall Street. I had some phenomenally smart players who made it easy because I love the X's & O's of football. For me, they're my kids. And when you watch your kids execute a game plan, that's what it's all about. It was a pleasure. It was so easy coaching those guys because they worked hard and they got it. I look back to Ryan Clark in the playoff game against Baltimore in Pittsburgh when he hit Willis McGahee so hard they were going to change another rule.

Or, you go to Troy's play in the Indianapolis playoff game. Troy picks a ball off, rolls on the ground, gets up and runs. There are so many phenomenal plays for me in my short time there in Pittsburgh. It was unbelievable the players that we had.

And the organization – I don't know how many times coaching we were sitting in meetings after practice watching film and it was 5:01, 5:02, and Mr. Rooney would walk through the halls and start shutting down the lights, and we would have to say, "Oh, we're still in here, Mr. Rooney." And he'd just look and say, "You shouldn't be. Go home." In the old days, they probably went home at 5 because there was no film. So when you say it was a family organization with the Rooneys, that's what I mean. It was kind of like last man out turns out the lights.

TROY POLAMALU: He's Papa Rooney to everybody here. He's very close to a lot of guys. You can walk into his office and say "What's up?" to him. There's really no formality with him. Obviously you have a level of respect for him. But he's great. He's the best out there for sure.

TAYLOR: So picture Papa Dan growing up in Pittsburgh with the old Steelers helping him on train rides with his schoolwork. That's what started it. And everybody knew soft-spoken Dan Rooney could cut you like a blade with words if he needed to. But he never needed to because when he talked, everybody listened. "Oh by the way, my door's always open. Anytime anybody wants to come talk to me, I'm not more important than you." Ain't that crazy?

HORTON: I was coaching with Cleveland later on and we happened to be playing in Pittsburgh. I came up behind Mr. Rooney. He could've just said who's that guy? Who was that defensive backfield coach seven years ago for me? But he turned around and said, "Oh, Ray, hey, how you doing? We miss you. We love you." That's the Rooneys for you.

CHAPTER 23

BEEN NICE WORKIN' WITH YOU, DAWG

Troy Polamalu made his fifth consecutive Pro Bowl following the 2008 season. He was able to play, since it was the last Pro Bowl held *after* the Super Bowl, and he was lined up next to his old running mate Chris Hope. The safety tandem from the Steelers' first championship of the decade was reunited not just in Honolulu, but in the AFC starting lineup.

CHRIS HOPE: Troy likes to laugh and have fun, and we had a game where anytime you would get comfortable on the sideline, like taking a knee or something, we would almost crook each other by the head with a wrasslin' move. I would be taking a knee on the sideline and he would come out of nowhere, put me in a headlock and roll me over. Now, I hadn't played with the Steelers in a few years and we go to the Pro Bowl together. In the last conversation we had on the phone, before I signed with the Titans, he told me, "Man, I'm going to miss you, brother, but we'll be teammates again." When I got off the phone, I never really took to heart what he was saying, but I guess he was telling me I'd go to the Pro Bowl one day. The first Pro Bowl practice, I'm sitting down getting ready to stretch and here he comes and he puts me in the headlock. I said, "You've got to be kidding!"

The two Pro Bowl safeties would see each other again in the next game that mattered that calendar year. For Hope, it would be one of the most productive games of his NFL career. For Polamalu, it would be one of the greatest single quarters of his.

But a single quarter would be all.

Bryant McFadden considers himself the Steelers' lucky rabbit foot. He was drafted in the second round in 2005, and the Steelers won the Super Bowl. He was installed as the starting outside cornerback in 2008, and the Steelers won the Super Bowl.

He lockered near Troy Polamalu, watched over Troy's lit candle display, his prayerful moments, was even invited into Troy's adjoining locker "apartment complex" – often assigned to Pro Bowl veterans in the corners of the Steelers' locker room – and watched Troy blend up his green drinks. A few years earlier, one of these drinks gagged a struggling Alonzo Jackson, who was game to try anything to get better.

"Uh, no, those things didn't look good, didn't smell good," said McFadden. "I always say, if it doesn't look good in a cup, I shouldn't put it in my body. But I probably should've drunk whatever it was Troy was drinking. He was always doing the right thing."

As so often happens to Steelers who find themselves at a position that includes a key veteran such as Ike Taylor, only one can be afforded. When asked about the status of McFadden, the 27-year-old soon-to-be free agent, General Manager Kevin Colbert said, "He's a priority. But we know we can't keep this whole team together."

Then McFadden was gone. The Arizona Cardinals – replete with coaches who knew his work ethic and had just watched reams of his tape, and were then beaten by him in the Super Bowl – made a short-but-large contract offer that well-stocked Super Bowl champions can rarely match. McFadden signed a two-year, $10 million contract with the Cardinals, and William Gay stepped into the Steelers' starting lineup.

The Steelers still employed 34-year-old Deshea Townsend as their nickel back, and began looking into a fourth cornerback to develop. They drafted Keenan Lewis in the third round, 12 picks after they had drafted one of his childhood friends from New Orleans, Mike Wallace, a wide receiver with 4.31 40 speed. At training camp, Taylor would call Wallace fastest receiver he had ever covered.

In the first round, the Steelers drafted a hard-working, high-character defensive lineman named Ziggy Hood. The only other rookies who would prove beneficial over the long haul were seventh-round tight end David Johnson and undrafted guard/tackle Ramon Foster.

The Steelers sustained a bigger loss than McFadden during this period. Chairman Dan Rooney was nominated by President Barack Obama to become the United States ambassador to Ireland on March 17 and moved his office overseas on July 1.

"He's with us in spirit," Mike Tomlin said as the defending champs opened camp in 2009. "He told me this is the first start of training camp he's missed in 68 years. I'm missing him, but I'm sure he's missing us more."

As for Polamalu, he was experiencing trouble in camp with a calf muscle that tightened on him.

On a positive note, defensive coordinator Dick LeBeau was nominated by the Seniors Committee for induction into the Pro Football Hall of Fame. His 62 career interceptions in 14 seasons with the Detroit Lions certainly qualified LeBeau, but he believed his name was being rekindled due to the success of his current championship defenses. After all, as a player, he had once been cut by the Cleveland Browns.

DICK LEBEAU: There's a great story there. Paul Brown is an Ohio guy and he had some friends in my hometown (London, Ohio) and they had a men's stag night at the golf course and they asked him if he would speak there. He acquiesced, and during his speech – it was kind of a question and answer thing, several years after I had finished playing – one of my friends stood up and said, "Paul, you've got a great coaching record and you're supposed to be a master of personnel, and yet you let Dick LeBeau go and he played 14 years in the NFL, and when he finished he was third in all-time interceptions. How could you let him go?" Paul didn't blink an eye and said, "Oh, I cut a lot better players than LeBeau." So, that's how I got cut by Cleveland.

Casey Hampton, Sept. 1, 2009

Here's one for you, big guy. Someone from NFL Network is reporting the Steelers are going to cut you.

He was serious?

It's all over the internet.

Really? Are they going to cut me today?

Well, before the season starts.

I guess I'm on the bubble, man. But I'm workin' hard.

Didn't you say after the last preseason game you've never been on the bubble?

There's a first time for everything.

Do you have a comment on getting cut?

No, man (begins laughing). What do you want me to say?

Is it laughable?

Hey, man, you never know. It could happen to anybody. I'm not exempt.
You don't seem worried.
No, man. I'm pretty sure I could make another team (raucous laughter).
You're playing up to your old standards, aren't you?
I'm doing all right. Just trying to win another Super Bowl. That's my main
thing, man. Trying not to be complacent like we were last time and trying
to show these young guys how to work.
*When you get cut, the Lions would be first in line to claim you. How would
you win the Super Bowl?*
Nah, if the Lions pick me up on waivers I'll retire (laughs). I ain't going there.
Not to be with Larry Foote?
I'll retire. I'm not going to the Lions. I don't care. Foote's my guy, but I
can't deal with 0-16.
James Farrior: You going to the Lions, man?
CH: Yeah. Didn't you hear? They say they're going to cut me before the
season starts. That's the rumor going around.
JF: Been nice workin' with you, dawg.

MARCEL PASTOOR: Oh, man, Hamp's laugh. You didn't know what the
conversation was but when Hamp would start laughing you would
start laughing and you don't know why you were laughing, because he
had that big, belly laugh – no pun intended – but it generally put you
in a good mood. I can hear it right now. It puts a smile on your face.

Casey Hampton made the team, but they may as well have cut another
of their stars, Troy Polamalu. The hero of the previous season's AFC
Championship Game and the 2008 first-team All-Pro strong safety was
hurt early in the opener when he tried to pick up a blocked Tennessee
field goal attempt during the Steelers' 13-10 overtime win.

A Titans player – 280-pound tight end Alge Crumpler – fell on
Polamalu's extended left leg, at the side of the knee, and he left the
game in the second quarter. The injury not only disrupted Polamalu's
season, it ended an incredible first game.

"I don't know if a guy can make the Pro Bowl after the first quarter
of the first game of the season, but it may have already happened,"
broadcaster Al Michaels said with 1:38 left in the first quarter.
Polamalu made two of what Mike Tomlin calls "splash plays" in the first
quarter, and a couple of other plays that were fairly outrageous as well.

On the first, Polamalu bolted into the Tennessee backfield from 14
yards away to upend speedy halfback Chris Johnson for a 2-yard loss. The

broadcast crew timed the 14-yard burst in 1.8 seconds.

On the second splash play, Polamalu jumped to pull in an interception with his extended left hand on a deep Kerry Collins pass to 6-foot-3 receiver Kenny Britt.

What Polamalu did in both extremes – against the run behind the line of scrimmage at one goal line, and downfield on a deep pass to a receiver at the other goal line – is what the Steelers would miss from their injured safety through much of 2009.

"Troy's range," said defensive coordinator Dick LeBeau. "It just hits me whenever a play's breaking. He always shows up."

On a third play in that opening quarter, Polamalu ran down Johnson – he of the NFL Combine-record 4.24 40 time – from the other side of the field to knock him out of bounds after a 32-yard gain.

The ridiculous Bill Leavy walked off 15 yards for a late hit on Polamalu even thought it appeared Johnson was off for a long touchdown run, and, only at the last instant, crossed the sideline in mid-air as Polamalu barreled over.

Later in the drive, Polamalu flashed his Hall of Fame-level closing speed to break up a third-down pass and force the Titans to settle for a 37-yard field goal attempt, which they missed. So instead of Johnson breaking free for an 89-yard touchdown run, Polamalu held them without a point, even with the poor call by Leavy.

It was an eye-popping show put on by the 28-year-old Polamalu in the opening quarter of the season. It naturally inspired this question:

Would we ever see the likes of such a player – in his athletic prime, with the fresh legs that come with playing in an opener – again?

BRETT KEISEL: It was getting to the point that when you watched him you would see he was at a different level, just a different type of freak. A lot of those plays were instinctual, especially going over the line of scrimmage, him reading the play and being like, "All right I'm going to shut this down right here," and he'd slip over. When he did something like that, when none of us were even out of our stance, and he would already have him on the ground, it was like "K, thanks, Troy, you saved me a body bash there."

HOPE: He came up and hit Chris Johnson for a 2-yard loss when Johnson looked like he was getting ready to go for 50 yards. Then a little later Chris reversed field and Troy came from out of nowhere to take his feet out from under him. If Troy doesn't do that, Chris Johnson is gone for 90. Then he made a one-handed interception. He was playing lights out football until he got hurt. I saw him in the tunnel after the game to see if he was all right. Alge Crumpler is a great guy. He called me and he apologized to me and he told me to apologize to Troy for him. It was a very hard-fought game. Both teams lost some people that day.

Polamalu didn't finish the first half, but his six tackles led the Steelers at halftime. He underwent an MRI and the sprained ligament (MCL) in his left knee was expected to keep him out 4-6 weeks. He was replaced by 33-year-old Tyrone Carter.

The injury to Polamalu – the cover boy that season for the historically jinxed Madden video game – got the Steelers off to another rocky defense of a title in spite of the win. In holding the team with the best record in the AFC the previous season to 10 points and 320 yards, the defense was off to a great start. But injuries wracked the unit so badly that by the end of the season Tomlin was praised for calling an onsides kick in order to *preserve a late lead* against the Green Bay Packers.

Without Polamalu, the Steelers lost to the Chicago Bears and the Cincinnati Bengals before surging with a five-game winning streak.

Polamalu rejoined them for three of those wins, against the Browns, Vikings and Broncos, but he was injured again in the Nov. 15 loss to the Bengals that dropped the Steelers to 6-3.

RAY HORTON: A couple of games in that stretch stuck out in my head, as far as me giving him information and him using it. One, we were playing the Bengals. The team had brought in an extra lineman to be a tight end. In theory, the lineman could go out and catch a pass, but never did. I told Troy, "When this guy comes in, it's not 100 percent run, which you would think, but when it is a pass he never goes out." And he goes, "Never?" I said, "Troy, he *never* goes out." He goes, "OK." He just filed that away. Well, during the game, he took off and blitzed. I was up in the booth and I called down to talk to him on the phone and I said, "Troy, what are you doing?" He said, "Well, Coach, you said he never left for a pass." I just hung up the phone because he was right. That. Is. Him. I don't know how many times on fourth-and-1 he would jump over the center and hit the quarterback on the quarterback sneak and stop him. He would blitz. People just thought he was guessing, and I used to tell people, "If you run something one week, you better not run it from the same formation because he'll get you." He was just remarkable.

The other instance occurred when we were playing the Vikings in Pittsburgh and he saw a formation and said, "Hey, Coach, if Minnesota does this, can I do this to counter that?" I couldn't OK Troy doing something when it wasn't his job, so I went to Coach LeBeau and said, "Troy saw this. Can we do this if we get that?" Coach LeBeau just looked at it and said, "Sure. Why not?" And doggone it, in the game Minnesota gave us that formation and Troy took off and blitzed and made a tackle for a loss. Big play in the game. But it was all on football IQ. One of the smartest guys I've ever seen in a room.

AOATOA POLAMALU: What was I most proud of? You kidding me? He made me famous! I'm just so proud of him, not just as a football player but as a man. But I was at the Cincinnati game in 2009. My son Maika was being recruited by Pitt, which was playing Notre Dame so we went there to visit, and went to the Steelers game on Sunday. Troy got hurt, had to go to the hospital, so Theodora and Paisios went to the hospital. Maika and I were still at the game. We got back to the house; he looks at me and said, "What did you see?" I said, "We didn't see anything. You got hurt." There was one point in time where I think the defensive line for Cincinnati was causing some ruckus, but that's all I said to him and he said, "Oh, OK." We didn't talk about football much. Keneti and I don't talk about football much. My family doesn't talk about football much.

"We didn't see anything. You got hurt," might be one of the more apt descriptions of Troy Polamalu and the Steelers yet. Another apt description came from Casey Hampton, who was asked about the player on defense with the best closing speed. Hampton called Polamalu 1 and Lawrence Timmons 1-A.

"With Timmons," said Hampton, "when he's closing like that, he's made a mistake and he's just trying to get to his guy."

Timmons was still growing into his role, and was also in and out of the lineup that season with an injury. Polamalu was hit and miss, for instance limping off the field after an interception against the Browns.

LaMarr Woodley was also struggling with a hamstring issue and, worse, Aaron Smith was lost for the season with a torn rotator cuff. The defense was taking some serious body blows.

Polamalu reinjured his left knee in the 18-12 loss to the Bengals, but Tomlin said two days later that it was a different ligament (PCL) that was strained this time.

Troy Polamalu, Nov. 19, 2009

How did you hurt your knee Sunday?
I have to refer all knee questions to Coach Tomlin.

Even that one?
All of them. I'm sorry.
Did you know it was hurt as soon as it happened?
(Laughs) I love how you guys try to snake your way in there. I'm sorry. I can't.
They taught us snaking in the third year of journalism school.
(Laughs).
Marvin Lewis said it was a couple series before he realized you weren't on the field. Do you think that's ever the case?
(Shrugs shoulders).
The way you were playing, you looked like you were completely over your first knee injury. Is that how you felt going into the game Sunday?
Yes, each week it's been feeling better and better.
Then how frustrating is it to have another injury?
Is that fourth year journalism school?
Is there any frustration?
Of course. I want to play football.
Your old college teammate, Matt Cassel, just told us that you were really outgoing. When did that change?
(Laughs).

The injury wasn't deemed serious at the time, but Polamalu was done for the season. It would be explained a few weeks later that the injured PCL wasn't as limiting as had been his injured MCL, but the weakened PCL was a bigger threat to Polamalu's long-term health.

The Steelers were done, too. The home loss to Cincinnati was the start of a five-game losing streak. A wild win against Green Bay begat a three-game winning streak, and the Steelers finished 2009 at 9-7 and out of the playoffs.

Polamalu and the Steelers would bounce back in a big way in 2010.

CHAPTER 24

HE'S NOT SUPERMAN, HE'S TROY

It was April, 2010, the first day of Organized Team Activities, or OTAs, on the South Side of Pittsburgh, and Mike Tomlin was angry. He was looking directly at a couple reporters standing along the far sideline.

"I told you I don't want those assholes NEAR this practice field!" Tomlin shouted to the new PR assistant, Ryan Scarpino, while pointing at us.

So, *that's* how it's gonna be after an unsettling offseason.

Ben Roethlisberger was accused of sexual assault. Santonio Holmes was traded for a song. Troy Polamalu was recovering from injury and wasn't present. President Art Rooney II declared that the running game must improve its ranking of 19th in the league in 2009. It was all kind of ugly, and Tomlin seemed determined to make it uglier.

The coach walked over to us, every reporter bracing for confrontation, but he broke into a big smile. Tomlin shook hands and asked about our families.

So, that's how it's gonna be.

In the spring of 2010, Tomlin no doubt had his hands cut out for him, as Hines Ward liked to say. The coach had to re-channel his team's energies back to the present in order for the future to look a lot better than last season's 9-7 finish without any playoffs.

The Steelers were still considered – and paid like – a Super Bowl team, as long as Roethlisberger could overcome the four-game suspension that remained even after allegations had been dropped; as long as Polamalu, the team's spirit, the heart and soul of the defense, could return healthy; and as long as the offense could get back to running the ball, at least more than 42 percent of the time.

In 1991, Chuck Noll's last year as coach, the Steelers run-pass ratio was 43-57 and they went 7-9. In 2003, the Steelers' last losing season, the run-pass ratio was 44-56.

Those had been the previous low ratios for a franchise storied in running the ball – until 2009.

But here was Polamalu on the field, on June 11, not yet running full speed, but present for the final voluntary workouts after leaving San Diego and his routine with Marv Marinovich.

Polamalu told a mob of reporters that he wasn't too concerned about the progress of his left knee.

This reporter arrived late, so Polamalu accommodated a request of a one-on-one. After it ended, Polamalu said, "Now can I ask a few questions?"

He asked for an opinion of the Steelers' pass-first philosophy, which he had begun to question in 2007. And he nodded along with my opinions that, 1.) Improving the run game doesn't mean harkening back to the Kordell Stewart era for quarterbacks; and, 2.) The game is cyclical and once teams overdraft DBs and small LBs to defend the pass, a power team will rise up and dominate.

Polamalu agreed, and went further.

TROY POLAMALU: We look at teams with all of those receivers on the field and have always believed the solution is to blitz them and attack the source. It's usually successful. Really, the only time it didn't work at all was the 2004 AFC Championship game against the Patriots. No matter what we called, or how many players we blitzed, they kept just enough blockers in to pick it up. It happened on every single play. They were perfect. Before we found out what had happened, we thought they had gotten into our playbook. I never experienced anything like it before or since. I walked away from that game thinking Bill Belichick was the greatest coach the game had ever seen.

Of course, Bill Belichick and the Patriots organization were later accused of illegally stealing signs. The evidence involving games against the Steelers went as far back as 2002, thanks to testimony by Patriots fullback Marc Edwards.

The NFL eventually came down on the Patriots, but destroyed all of the evidence. Five years later, the league punished the Patriots for deflating footballs. That was – we in the conspiracy business believe – done to placate teams such as the Pittsburgh Steelers and players such as Troy Polamalu.

Clearly, it did not, and never will, placate anyone.

RYAN SCARPINO, *Steelers PR assistant (2010-16):* I first started in April, 2010. Even though I was born and raised in Pittsburgh and watched these guys play growing up, I never, ever was taken aback by anybody. And they still had some big names. Not just Ben, but guys like James Farrior, Hines Ward, Aaron Smith, the guys playing when I was in high school and college. So I knew of them and it's kind of like, "OK, they're humans. They're just players." But I tell you this: The only person who was above that was Troy. I don't know how to describe it other than obviously you look at him as an amazing football player, but what a great person, what a great human being. And this is no disrespect to anybody else on that team because they had some great people, but Troy was always a peg above them and I can't explain why. It's almost like he was this supernatural being. Even though I went on to watch him for years play in front of me, and I don't know if it was because he was so humble and quiet, but being around him always felt different from being around other players. He just had this presence. I felt like I was in the presence of something greater than a football player.

Troy Polamalu was a slice of grace, which was something that 2010 Steelers team needed in the worst way – along with a quarterback for the first four games to replace the suspended Ben Roethlisberger.

They also needed a center to begin piecing together a sturdier run game, and a receiver to replace Santonio Holmes, who came to the organization the same way he left it – troubled. The Steelers traded Holmes for a fifth-round pick from the New York Jets. The Steelers used that fifth-round pick to re-acquire their "lucky rabbit's foot," Bryant McFadden, from the Cardinals, and with him received a sixth-round pick.

They brought back Larry Foote, Antwaan Randle El and Byron Leftwich, who was targeted to play quarterback those first four games. The local folk were also down on Roethlisberger. Some in the media – even those who write books – advised that the Steelers trade him. This kind of behavior was unacceptable, right? If they had to give Holmes away, couldn't they get a cache of picks for a franchise quarterback?

When the question was put to the team's "supernatural being," Polamalu provided his customary touch of grace.

"There are a lot of great examples of guys who are just really good guys, like Peyton Manning and Tom Brady," Troy said at the time. "But there are also great examples of what Ben is going to be able to do and just show how much he can turn his life around. To me, that can be an even better example. Right now he's going through a tough time not being here, but it's going to be even a better example to show how he comes back. And I hope people will appreciate that process."

On draft day, the Steelers not only re-acquired McFadden for Holmes, they used the Cardinals' sixth-round pick to draft wide receiver Antonio Brown out of Central Michigan.

New WRs coach Scottie Montgomery proclaimed Brown "an unbelievable player!" But the receiver also brought with him his own baggage after growing up sometimes homeless on the notorious streets of Miami's Liberty City. Soon after joining the team, Brown took public shots at veteran cornerback Keenan Lewis.

"Keenan is a second-string DB and I've been catching a lot of balls on him," Brown after a spring practice. "I'm sure he doesn't want a young guy coming in and exposing him."

And so it began.

Not all the news was negative that offseason. The Steelers did re-sign Ryan Clark after nearly losing him to Miami in free agency. And they extended the contract of the great Casey Hampton. The best news, though, was that revered defensive coordinator Dick LeBeau was going into the Pro Football Hall of Fame and the Steelers were shutting down camp to attend the induction ceremony.

"This is going to be the first time he's ever missed a practice in his entire career," said Polamalu. "What better blessing from God: All right, here's your first real opportunity to miss a practice."

Troy Polamalu, August 6, 2010

How did you spend your summer vacation?
I spent most of it training. I usually try to spend most of it surfing or cross-training, doing some other stuff that's fun, but this year is so important I really wanted to make sure I did everything I could to prepare.
Are you feeling the aging process at this point?
I could say that, yeah, the soreness is lasting a lot longer, but I wouldn't say I'm feeling older at all. I'm not even 30 yet, so I don't think I could even use that as an excuse.
You have one child and another on the way. How has fatherhood affected you?
I'm starting to understand what makes it so great. My son's getting older.

He hears music. He's dancing. It's really becoming a fun relationship with him. Like my wife sending me videos. That's what's great, I guess, about today's technology: I can actually talk and see video on the phone with her and see my son making faces at me, actually saying words to me, like saying "da-da" and pointing at the phone.

So you haven't ignored technology completely, have you?

No. I've been trying to get rid of my phone and all these things for so long, but my wife says I have to keep it for us.

You've called this the longest offseason. Were there benefits to it?

I learned so much more by not playing than I did playing last year – first and foremost as a human being, how to appreciate things, how to appreciate each opportunity of the health that we have, and not to take things for granted. The other thing, as a football player I was able to see the game from a different level. For one, it's amazing to me: I'll see somebody like Larry Fitzgerald or I'll see a game on film and I just kind of amaze myself because I'm like, "How in the world do I ever go out there and play this game? These collisions are so hard." For one, you kind of respect the game in that way. For another, you see from a coach's perspective how offenses attack and you see the chess match much better because I'm seeing the game plan, thinking about calls, what we could've done better or why Coach LeBeau made a particular call. Learning from that perspective is an awesome experience, too.

You consoled Rashard Mendenhall in the Super Bowl tunnel. Did you ever have a moment like that, when someone inspired you?

Probably the most traumatic experience to me was my rookie year. I didn't fit into the team at first. The team had a much different personality my rookie year than it does now. I replaced a veteran who had been here a long time, and I didn't have a very good rookie year. Then, I used to like read papers and stuff like that. I remember – it might've been like Week 4 or something like that – we had the paper and I picked it up and it was calling me a draft bust, or something like that. Some guy named Jim Wexell wrote it (laughs).

Really?

No (laughs).

I've written some dumb things. That's possible.

No. But all I saw was "draft bust" and I remember we just canceled the newspaper, like "forget it, no more newspapers." And later in the season, it might've been like Week 12, Mr. Rooney walks up to me and says, "Troy, don't worry about what's written in those newspapers, you're doing fine." But I thought, "Oh great, what are they saying now?" That offseason I went directly to California with my trainer and I literally was on chicken breast, broccoli and olive oil all summer long. There was nothing that was swaying me. My wife and I would go to concerts and we would leave early to train in the morning. So I would say that whole experience really was important, where at first I was contemplating "Man, is this really for me? What is this game about?" Then I just told myself I was going to give it everything I had. I approached my whole offseason in that way. Thank God I'm still here now.

SCARPINO: I seldom approached Troy to do an interview, because he never did production meetings. "No thank you." But I remember this time, like, "Troy, hey, I know you don't typically do these, but Pat McManamon from Cleveland wants to talk to you. It's not about football." And he said with that soft voice, "OK." I told him that Pat wants to talk about his spirituality. "Great," Troy said. We were in the back of St. Vincent and it was after dinner, and you know how players use the other entrance. It's not a good spot for reporters to wait for players, especially after practice. But Troy got off the golf cart and I was the only one there with Pat. I introduced them and Troy grabbed his hand and said, "Yeah, let's go." And they disappeared into that tranquil, wooded area behind the cafeteria where the monks are. I don't know where they went. I just assumed everything was good.

There was also the saving grace of an improved running game. The Steelers bolstered their offensive line with a highly prized rookie and a proven five-time Pro Bowl tackle.

The rookie was LaShawn Maurkice Pouncey, the first center chosen in the first round by the Steelers in 69 years. Over at right tackle, the Steelers added massive 35-year-old Flozell "The Hotel" Adams on July 29 after Willie Colon tore an Achilles' tendon.

Adams, according to Steelers scouts, had plenty left after being cut by the Dallas Cowboys in a salary cap move. The only problem was that he had spent all of his 12 NFL seasons at left tackle. The move to the other side of the line wouldn't be as easy as many assumed.

Veteran defenders agreed that the Steelers' run game was on the verge of making a comeback.

"I see a lot of toughness," said James Farrior.

"We're running the 9-on-7s at least two, three times a week. We ran it maybe once last year," said Aaron Smith.

"Pouncey's real good. He's got what it takes," said Casey Hampton. "He's up there with Hartings, ain't no question about it."

Of course, the defense was setting the tone at training camp. Smith would race Farrior to wherever the ball was placed on a "river side" change. Sometimes Brett Keisel beat them both. The racing set a tone and established a great practice pace. And coaches love when the biggest and best players, in particular, work the hardest.

With Polamalu running without a hitch, the defense allowed only three meaningful touchdowns in the first four games. The Steelers just needed a veteran QB capable of managing the offense. However, Byron Leftwich was hurt in the preseason finale, and his backup, Dennis Dixon, was hurt early in the second game. Charlie Batch, fourth in the pecking order, finished the run.

HEATH MILLER: We went 3-1 when Ben was suspended. We beat the Falcons when Troy picked off Matt Ryan at the end of the game on the sideline. Dennis Dixon was the quarterback and he got hurt.

RAY HORTON: I loved that play against Matt Ryan and Atlanta. We were playing cover-2. He and Ryan Clark each have a half. Well, Troy started to go towards the middle of the field because he kind of knew what the play was. This is late in the game. And then he took off and went to the sideline and picked off Matt Ryan at the sideline. Unbelievable play. Nobody else is going to make that play but him.

RYAN CLARK: Atlanta was throwing deep outs. And the way that we ran a certain coverage was Troy would be playing the hook position and then someone else would be playing curl flat. So someone else should be responsible for running underneath, say, the deep hitch or the out. We had gotten it early on in the game, he's like "Man, if they throw it again I'm going to get it." And he said next time he would call the invert, which meant he would switch responsibilities with a certain guy. And, so, they switch and he actually does pick the ball off.

Everybody was always asking me, "What's it like playing with him? Are you nervous? Do you know what he's doing?" I don't always know what he's doing, but I always know he studied it, he's thought about it, and then he did it. He wasn't just guessing. I just remember that play vividly because in order for him to be there, he had to actually change the call.

Polamalu jumped in front of the same down-and-out pass Falcons QB Matt Ryan had been throwing to Roddy White all game. The interception occurred at the Atlanta 31 with 1:40 left in a tie game.

White finished the game with 13 catches for 111 yards, and he'd been targeted an additional 10 times. He was just about all Falcons coordinator Mike Mularkey had left in his arsenal after the Steelers effectively took tight end Tony Gonzalez and running back Michael Turner out of the game.

Polamalu was the main cog in the Steelers' defense of Gonzalez, but he grew bored with that role.

"He was on the sidelines wanting to get more involved and wanting to roam a little more rather than be locked down on Tony," said Brett Keisel. "Finally, Coach made a call and Troy made a great read and a great catch."

Coordinator Dick LeBeau made the call that either Polamalu or Will Gay could jump the out route run by White, as McFadden dropped into a safety-type position.

"I asked Willie Gay if I could have it," said Polamalu. "And he said yes."

It was the same option LeBeau gave his defensive backs two years earlier, when Deshea Townsend also agreed to let Polamalu have the outside receiver. This time it was Polamalu jumping the route, and he dragged his feet for the interception.

"I'm a lot smarter when he's in there," said LeBeau.

"I thought I made a pretty good throw," said Ryan. "Against him, you have to be perfect."

Farrior said that after the interception Polamalu went to the sideline and said a few prayers of thanks. But Keisel heard Polamalu say something else.

"*I'm the greatest safety of all time!*" Keisel roared. "No, I'm kidding. He didn't say that. He didn't say anything. He never does. He's the type of player that just lurks and waits for those types of situations to make a huge play in the game."

MILLER: Troy had such an uncanny feel for the game. He wouldn't be able to do all those things if he didn't have a group of guys around him who had the equal amount of experience to be able to change things like that on the fly, whether it's a Ryan or a Deshea or an Ike. Those guys played together so long they could communicate those things on the fly and it could work seamlessly.

CLARK: We want it to seem to the offense that it's what we planned on, kind of like organized chaos. They see us bouncing and moving around and they may think to themselves, "They don't know what's going on." But they may not know we're moving on this side because we feel the play's going to the other side and that's where we'll end up.

MILLER: Next game was Charlie Batch against Tennessee, and in that game was one of the times Troy jump over the line. That was against

Kerry Collins. Vince Young got hurt and Kerry Collins came in and Troy jumped over the line.

AOATOA POLAMALU: I was talking to Kerry Collins one day on the field at Penn State, and I looked at him and he looks at me and said, "You know, that nephew of yours, I never saw him. Never saw him. I turned around and he was already on top of me." I said, "Yeah, it surprised the hell out of me, too." Kerry said he looked up at him and said, "What the heck was that?"

TROY POLAMALU: I can honestly say there's been one time in eight years when I just did whatever I wanted to do on a play. That was this one ... it was a complete guess. The rest of the time I have a responsibility. Now, if I can see that there's no threat in my area of responsibility, that's where the creativity comes in.

It was the third instance of Polamalu timing a leap over the line of scrimmage to either stop a quarterback sneak or indirectly blow up a play. In all three instances, the offense was stopped for no gain or a loss.

Against the Titans, with Collins in for Young and set to attempt a QB sneak into the end zone from the Pittsburgh 1, Polamalu flew arms first over the top of the line with perfect timing to drop Collins for a loss the instant he received the snap.

Collins did throw a touchdown pass two plays later, and the Titans recovered the onside kick, but the Steelers held on for a 19-11 win.

Earlier in the game, Polamalu stopped a Titans drive with an interception in the end zone, his second pick in as many games.

MIKE TOMLIN: Those short-yardage moments really eloquently describe what you suggest with the "no, no, no, YES" concept, because, man, there's a lot of risk in that. You've got to get to a certain speed and you've got to have a certain amount of momentum to dive over these big men, and you've got to anticipate it. And there becomes a point of no return. I think those are the no, no, no moments when he's already started to take off and the play clock is down inside of 5 and he's picking up speed and he's getting close to the line of scrimmage and something is going to happen.

KERRY COLLINS, *Titans quarterback (2006-10):* I looked up and all I saw was hair in my facemask.

CRAIG WOLFLEY: Who could've ever equated him with Superman going over the top? How do you do that? How do you have the balls and the timing to pull that off? To me, that was one of the most mystifying things. There's no margin for error. And he nails it.

Polamalu has attributed his "spidey sense" to all of the practice reps he took during his formative years with the Steelers. Craig Wolfley, the Steelers Radio Network sideline reporter, believes that, combined with his meditative sideline pauses, allowed Polamalu to see the play before it unfolded.

WOLFLEY: Mushin is mind/no mind. It's when you stop the self-chatter. The Americanized version of it: It's the zone. People talk about letting the play come to them; some people just have it. I think Minkah Fitzpatrick is someone who's going to be very much like that. Some guys I've known who were tremendous athletes but they just couldn't get outside the norm. Very strong players, but once the X's and O's start moving they lost their minds. They couldn't seem to adjust, be creative, understand the flow of the game. Troy was all about flow. For years I trained in jiu-jitsu, and Rickson Gracie, one of the earliest of the jiu-jitsu masters from the Gracie family coming up from Brazil in the '80s, he used to say you've got to flow with the go. It's a very descriptive term that means you just turn off the chatter and do it. And that's what Troy, in my most humble estimation, is. The boundaries that contain a lot of other players are defined by "You're the free safety." "You're the strong safety." "You do this." "You do that." Troy really exploded all of that.

Recall that Troy's cousin Tafea, or Brandon, the cousin in Tenmile closest in age to Troy, referenced Troy's interest in Rickson Gracie as a teen.

WOLFLEY: Good. So there's a connection right there. A guy like Rickson Gracie really makes me think about Troy because Rickson was always about "I'm ageless, I don't discuss my age, I flow with the go," and how jiu-jitsu is a lifestyle and a discipline. It's not what you do, it's who you are. That's kind of how I view Troy. Troy was more than a football player. But his ability to disengage from the chatter on the sideline allowed him to just relax, and you could see him controlling his breathing, his emotions. He would just start to settle in. Other guys are up and down, moving around and stuff, and Troy is just (pause) chilling. And then he'd have a few words maybe with Dick LeBeau and, boom, he's right there, he's paying attention, he's focused and then he would return to that same sort of seminal moment that he always returned to where he was just kind of into himself. And it wasn't anything where he was "Om, Om," that sort of stuff. I think he reviews and he takes it in, but he's learned the essence of not confusing himself with a lot of self-chatter.

TOMLIN: I wasn't about to say whoa to those kinds of things. No, I think that as a coach, you realize when you're in the presence of the things that you can't capture, things that are not coachable, and you try to work at ways to enhance it, to assist in the utilization of it. But more than anything I think you appreciate it. I think experience has allowed us to have that perspective.

CLARK: He's just special, man. He moved in a different way. He thought in a different way. I just remember we're playing the Bengals, and Carson Palmer actually didn't throw this ball because he knew Troy was going to pick it. We were in cover-2, which means both Troy and I have a deep half of the field. We studied it all week and we kept telling each other if we get duce left or duce right twin, this is what we're getting. And in that coverage, the corners are actually the people who can make a play. So, I'm on one side with my corner and I'm telling him what to watch for. I looked at Troy and he isn't saying anything. And I know he knows it. I know he knows it's coming, because we talked about it. But he didn't say anything, because to him, if the quarterback reads the coverage and knows that the corner is going to do a certain thing, if he moves or does anything, the quarterback's reading it. And Troy's thought was, "He thinks I'm supposed to do A, and if I do B he's going to throw the ball right to me." That was just the way he thought. My thought was to tell the guy who's responsible what's coming. Troy's thought was "I know what's coming so it's time for me to go pick this ball off."

MILLER: The whole first part of the year that Ben was suspended the first four games, the defense was awesome and Troy was the leader, making incredible plays.

BRETT KEISEL: He wanted to be special, and he wanted to make special plays on Sunday, so he would prepare that way. It didn't just happen.

DICK LEBEAU: He's inquisitive; he wants to know about everything. The aspect that allows him to be a great player is the competitiveness, but the thing that marks his character I think is his inquisitive nature and his thirst for knowledge.

Perhaps that's why Polamalu might even ask a sportswriter for an opinion on why the Steelers aren't running the ball the way they had.

Of course, a return to the basics without the Nos. 1 and 2 QBs no doubt made Polamalu happy. With Dennis Dixon and then Charlie Batch at QB, the Steelers' run-pass ratio in the first quarter of the season was 58-42, a 180-degree change from 2009.

Led by Rashard Mendenhall and the improved offensive line, the Steelers averaged 4.3 yards per carry and were 3-1, the only loss by three points to Baltimore on an 18-yard pass with 32 seconds remaining.

The Steelers went 3-1 in the second quarter of the season, too, including a win at Cincinnati. With Roethlisberger back, the run/pass ratio evened at 50-50 through those four games.

The best news for Polamalu was the birth of his son Ephraim in between the Falcons and Titans games.

On a down note, defensive end Aaron Smith was lost for the season with a torn triceps, although Tomlin would keep him on the roster in the hope Smith could perform a Rod Woodson and return if the Steelers were to play in February, the way Woodson's 1995 Steelers had.

Also, James Harrison was fined $100,000 for separate hits on Mohamed Massaquoi of the Browns and Drew Brees of the Saints. The first involved the offensive player lowering his head while Harrison was already in motion, and the second was ticky-tack, no doubt due to Harrison's reputation.

Harrison went to New York to talk to the commissioner while Polamalu simply said of the league office, "They're wrong."

Did he care to expand?

"I don't care to expand," Polamalu said, but later added, "I don't think (punishment) should be just totally based on what two or three people say who are totally away from the game. I think it should be some of the players that are currently playing."

On the field, Polamalu was trucked by his good friend Domata Peko, who attended the same high school in American Samoa as Troy's Uncle Salu.

Peko, a defensive lineman for the Bengals, was playing fullback at the goal line when he crushed Polamalu, and for a moment it didn't look like Troy would get up.

Some friend.

Yeah, that's what I told him," Polamalu said. "'Uso' is how you say brother and 'us' is kind of short, so I said, 'Hey, us, you gonna do that to me?' He said 'I'm sorry' and then turned around and started celebrating with his teammate."

Polamalu added that he was fine.

"Sometimes it looks like you're hit really hard but you don't feel anything. That was one of those hits. My ego felt it."

The third quarter of the season got off to a bad start with a loss at home to New England, but once again the Steelers went 3-1 through the stretch – including a win at Baltimore.

Polamalu strained his right Achilles' tendon in the loss to the Patriots. This problem had been foretold in Steelers mythology when Polamalu was held by his heel while being dipped in the River Styx. But Polamalu wasn't ruled out by Tomlin, and in fact intercepted his third pass of the season in a 35-3 blowout of the Oakland Raiders.

"We started off real slow," said Polamalu, "but when we started running the ball, controlling the clock, keeping their defense on the field, and getting our energy back, that's Steeler ball and we executed our game plan today."

The defense allowed only 182 yards and sacked Raiders QBs six times. Farrior led the way with eight tackles, two tackles-for-loss, a sack and an emotional surge.

"Potsie was out of his body today," said Hampton. "The coaches were in the huddle trying to talk, telling us to calm down and this and that, and he was over-talking them. He was just into it. I think everybody fed off his energy today."

"And those weren't normal tackles," said Chris Hoke. "He was putting the helmet on 'em."

"I was just so fired up I couldn't help it," said the normally "chill" Farrior.

LARRY FOOTE, *Steelers inside linebacker (2002-08, 2010-13):* See, that's a misconception with Potsie. He's not as rambunctious as me or Joey or one of those guys, but when he gets mad, he lets it out. I've heard him say some stuff to the referees, and they're surprised because he catches them off guard. They let him get away with stuff me and Joey could never get away with. He's one of those sneaky bad kids. One time he got a personal for sticking his middle finger up at the fans. Ryan Clark was hurt – it was in Cleveland – and the fans were clapping and he stuck his middle finger up. One time he kicked a lineman and got caught. Another thing no one knows is that he got hurt in both Super Bowls. Everybody just paused for a second, especially the first one when he had to go in for a shot. The coaches and me we were scrambling on the sideline trying to see what I know and what I don't know. In Tampa he got hurt again. I don't know if he got a shot, but it was questionable whether he'd go back in. He didn't miss any plays either time, but he scared us a little bit.

At Buffalo, Polamalu made four tackles and intercepted his fourth pass of the season as new teammate Shaun Suisham kicked four field goals in a 19-16 overtime win.

Polamalu's diving interception of a deflection at the goal line with 2:51 left to play temporarily preserved a three-point lead, but the Bills got the ball back thanks to a holding penalty on left guard Chris Kemoeatu that negated a third-down conversion.

Polamalu broke up the Bills' first-down pass by nearly breaking Stevie Johnson at the catch point in the flat. But the Bills eventually kicked a 49-yard field goal to send the game into overtime.

The Steelers won only after Johnson dropped Ryan Fitzpatrick's 40-yard pass in the end zone. Suisham – signed after Jeff Reed was cut following a missed 26-yarder against New England – kicked the 41-yarder to win it.

Polamalu recovered a second-half fumble before his interception, and the big hit no doubt had spooked Johnson. Troy nearly had another interception in breaking up a first-down pass in overtime.

"Man, he made significant plays and timely plays," Tomlin said. "That's what we've come to expect from him. A guy who didn't practice much during the week, he's always ready to deliver for his teammates."

As the Steelers prepared for the Ravens in the battle between 8-3 teams for first place in the AFC North, Polamalu was still missing practices with his sore Achilles' tendon, McFadden was struggling with an injured hamstring, Harrison was still getting fined (total of $125,000 for the season) and Roethlisberger was limping around the locker room on a sprained foot after taking several cheap shots from the Bills. As has been the case throughout much of Roethlisberger's career, the big QB was left unprotected by officials who saw that he could withstand brutal, late and cheap hits from defenders.

The following Sunday's game at Baltimore was the essence of this fierce rivalry, another bloodbath. Literally.

It was Roethlisberger continuing to play with blood pouring out of his nose. It was Heath Miller taking a vicious, concussive blow to the head. It was Terrell Suggs hanging on to Roethlisberger as the big QB pulled out of Suggs' grasp just enough to get off "the incompletion of the year." It was Polamalu getting that "spidey sense" and blitzing and hacking Joe Flacco's arm for the big, late defensive play.

It was another three-point game, this one won by the Steelers 13-10 in an epic, bruising, bloody football war.

It was the game Troy will one day tell his sons to watch. It was the game Theodora will one day forbid her sons to watch.

First Quarter

* What does a referee think when he sees a quarterback get up with a crooked and bloody nose? Does he think he may have missed something?

That's what Roethlisberger asked referee Terry McAulay as the QB trotted out for his second series. In the first series, Ravens nose tackle Haloti Ngata punched Roethlisberger through the facemask and broke his nose.

"I asked him if he saw the blood," Roethlisberger said. "I'm not one who cusses at the refs or anything, so I just asked him if he saw the blood from my head. His response was, 'He was just trying to tackle you.' I just let it go at that."

Second Quarter

* What does a defensive coordinator do on third-and-15 with the Ravens in field goal range and holding a 7-0 lead? Dick LeBeau asked Coach Ray Horton, who dialed up a cornerback blitz. Ike Taylor took the Ravens out of field goal range with an 11-yard sack to force a punt.

Third Quarter

* What does a mother at home do when she watches her beautiful boy take yet another brutal blast in the head? Heath Miller's mom no doubt left the room instead of watching replays of Jameel McClain knocking out the Steelers' tight end on a pass over the middle.

If you felt sick watching L.T. v. Theisman, you felt sick watching this replay, perhaps even sicker when the Ravens weren't penalized (McClain was fined $40,000). Miller would miss the next week's game with a concussion.

Fourth Quarter

* What does LeBeau call as the clock's winding down with only 3:22 remaining and his team trailing 10-6 on second-and-5 as the Ravens approach midfield?

That really shouldn't be a question. Polamalu – one of six rushers in a risky, cover-zero blitz LeBeau had just installed for the game, which had resulted in two goal-to-go incompletions in the third quarter – came flying off the edge to hack Flacco's arm and cause a fumble. LaMarr Woodley returned it 19 yards to the Baltimore 9 and the Steelers were goal-to-go with 3:13 remaining.

Bonus question

* What does a TV announcer call a first-down play that had the unblockable Suggs hanging onto Roethlisberger's neck as the QB escapes just enough to throw the ball away? At a time when the Steelers absolutely could not afford to lose yardage?

"The incompletion of the year," said Cris Collinsworth.

Two snaps later, on third down, the Ravens blitzed and Roethlisberger hit his hot receiver, Isaac Redman, on a slant out of the slot. Redman broke two tackles on his way to the end zone to put the Steelers in first place with a 13-10 win.

"They could play this one 16 times," Collinsworth crowed to a Sunday night audience, "and I'd come to them all."

Mothers and wives might not agree.

SALU POLAMALU: To me that was the No. 2 play by Troy in his career, both against Baltimore. And even the Ravens, when their defense was on the sideline, they could see Troy cheat up on the line and they yelled and the quarterback never saw him coming. That's what Suggs said. Suggs played against Troy at Arizona State.

TERRELL SUGGS, *Ravens pass-rusher (2003-18)*: We let one of the best safeties in the National Football League run scot-free and hit the quarterback. You've got to question what we were thinking there. What were we doing? We all know when you see 43 at the line in the four-minute offense, he's coming. It's just like, "Man, I hope we got a plan," because it just didn't feel good when I saw that hair at the line of scrimmage.

WOLFLEY: Watch how Troy sugars it. He's off the ball. He and Lawrence Timmons are both sugaring it up. Timmons goes strong side and Troy comes weak side. James Harrison goes to the inside and Troy waited for Flacco – who was looking over the defense – to turn his head. When Flacco looked away, Polamalu sunk down to the end next to Harrison, and then comes off the ball in such an explosive manner and tomahawks it and Woodley picks it up. It was all part of him being able to sugar, or disguise, what his intentions were, and then being able to execute it with timing and explosiveness. It's remarkable, just remarkable.

LEBEAU: That play by Troy was critical to our season. Think about it. I mean for us to get the home field and all the things that ensued along the way to the Super Bowl, you can go back to that play. And that play was all Troy. He just timed it. It was just a dinky little quick-out pass. I'm sure their quarterback's thinking there's no way anyone can possibly get to me before I throw this ball, but Troy is so much faster than anybody else.

The Sun of Baltimore awarded it the Worst Play of the Ravens' 2010 season. "No play changed the Ravens' Super Bowl fortune more than this one," wrote Jamison Hensley.

Yet, LeBeau, who had just installed the blitz, which worked all three times he called it, wouldn't take any of the credit.

LEBEAU: Because it would be nothing but bullshit. It was a critical situation in the game. There wasn't much time left and we were trailing. We had to get the football, and, again, do I have enough things that I can call that will let our best guys try and make that kind of a play? It was no great call. It was a great, great play by Troy. I put our fastest guy trying to get around the corner. Hell, if they could've handed the ball to the fullback Troy would've made the tackle, but you have to have some luck in this, too (chuckles). They happened to be throwing it and the quarterback had his back to Troy. Troy's timing was perfect. It could not have been better.

RAY HORTON: Coach LeBeau would call the game, always, and he had great instincts. But I do remember on a crucial, earlier third down, when LeBeau was kind of talking out loud, "What should we call?" We had a defense that was a very unusual blitz where the weak corner came. The quarterback almost never sees the guy because he's coming from his blind side. And the ball happened to be on the correct hash, on our right, the defense's right side. I looked down real quick and said, "Run weak cobra right." That stood for weak corner coming with cover-6 behind it. I just said, "Run weak cobra. Flacco's never seen it." And I'll be doggone if the play didn't come wide open. Ike was the right corner for us and he got the sack.

Ray Horton raved about Ike Taylor's year-long performance after the win over the Ravens, and agreed he should be considered for the Pro Bowl.

"If you think Nnamdi Asomugha out in Oakland plays good ball, then this guy's playing the same thing," Horton said of Ike. "Guys don't throw at him anymore. He picks the ball off when they throw it to him.
He's always on their top guy. He's doing a heck of a job with everything we want: tackling, covering, and being responsible, accountable."

Horton called the question "very astute," but on the other hand disagreed with the same reporter who asked about Polamalu's performance, which resulted in Troy winning AFC Defensive Player of the Week.

"I know you guys think he had a great game," Horton said as the Steelers prepared for the Bengals. "I don't."

Horton pointed out that Polamalu's decision to blitz Flacco on a third-and-15 pass in the first quarter resulted in Anquan Boldin's 61-yard catch that set up a touchdown.

"The thing with Troy, I kind of compare him to Reggie Jackson," Horton said. "Reggie had a lot of home runs, but he also had a lot of strikeouts. Troy, you have to let him be creative, and we do. He's a special player and you can't deny that, so he has a lot more freedom than you would give somebody else. But he's not Superman, he's Troy."

HORTON: Troy made me a better coach because some guys don't process information. Some guys don't use information. Some guys don't want information. He did. So when you put all those hours in just to find where T.O. was standing; Was he outside the number? Was he inside? Did this lineman ever leave? What did they do from this formation if the quarterback comes out to his right? Those kinds of things meant something to Troy. They did to me also as a player. For me, in the coach-player relationship, he made me better, not the other way around.

CHAPTER 25

SWEETNESS

On the field against Cincinnati, Troy Polamalu was his usual self with two interceptions, one of which he returned for a game-tying touchdown.

In the locker room, Polamalu was also his usual self, bemoaning his mistakes, in particular a wild lateral while returning his second interception.

In fact, he apologized, and at one point had to fight back tears.

Reporters, of course, wanted to know about the touchdown and beating Carson Palmer again for six.

"I don't know," Polamalu said in such a hushed tone one would've thought the Steelers had lost to the Bengals instead of winning 23-7.

"Let's just focus on the negative," he said before smiling.

There hadn't been much negative, even through the last four games:

* Polamalu returned an interception 38 yards to snuff out an Oakland rally;

* He recovered a fumble and later intercepted a pass at Pittsburgh's goal line to hold off Buffalo;

* In Baltimore, his late fourth quarter strip-sack turned the game, the division and ultimately the conference around.

* Throw in his 45-yard pick-6 Sunday against the Bengals and Polamalu is the common thread in the Steelers' four-game win streak.

Polamalu's first interception against the Bengals came out of a cover-2 shell. Receiver Terrell Owens ran a skinny post that Polamalu jumped at the Cincinnati 45. It was yet another interception off Palmer, his old college roommate, and, as he had in 2004 during his breakout moment in the NFL, Polamalu took aim at Palmer near the goal line.

"I wanted to see Troy bowl him over again," said James Farrior.

It wasn't that extreme. Palmer clipped Polamalu near the Cincinnati 5 and he needed to dive over the pylon for the tying touchdown in the second quarter. This time, the interception itself was more artistic.

"In cover 2, it's really hard for the safety to get underneath that play," said Steelers reserve safety Will Allen. "A skinny post is designed to hit in between the linebacker and the safety. It's designed to hit right behind the linebacker, so he just jumped it. If you decide to go get the pick, you'd better get the pick or a knockout hit or break the pass up. That's the gamble he took and he made a good play on it."

Polamalu aggravated his injured ankle on the dive for the pylon but stayed in the game, albeit hobbled.

He wasn't too hobbled, though, to read Palmer for another interception in the fourth quarter, Troy's sixth of the season.

"No one is playing as good as Troy Polamalu in football right now," Mike Tomlin said after the game.

Tomlin was asked about the ball Polamalu nearly lateraled away after the second interception.

"Ask Troy," Tomlin said. "He'll be available after he washes his hair."

Notoriously slow and forever last out of the shower, Polamalu emerged clearly upset. His errant lateral was recovered by teammate Bryant McFadden at the Pittsburgh 12 with 1:52 remaining in a game the Steelers were winning easily.

"First and foremost, I want to apologize for that play at the end of the game," Polamalu began. "It was incredibly arrogant and selfish. I represent something bigger than myself – my faith, my family and this team. I'll try to never let that happen again. It was just a very arrogant play."

What happened on your touchdown?

"It was a good call by coach. I was just doing my job."

How do you explain making game-changing plays in back-to-back weeks?

"I would definitely say the play of this game was LaMarr's interception."

How do you explain your two interceptions for touchdowns against your friend Carson Palmer?

"He's scored a lot more touchdowns than me."

After another question, Polamalu turned away to fight back tears. He re-composed himself and wrapped up the interview by crediting the run-stopping of the defensive line and the pressure by the linebackers.

BRETT KEISEL: Troy was just trying to share the love a little bit with the lateral. He's so used to having the spotlight I think he was trying to let someone else take it to the crib.

MARCEL PASTOOR: I know that LeBeau, even at practice at times, was never a fan when someone would do that. "Don't do that in the game," he would say. "Risk versus reward. It's never worth the reward because the risk is so high if you give the ball back to them."

CASEY HAMPTON: Coach Tomlin congratulated him, but LeBeau, man, he wasn't happy and told Troy about it. Troy came down by me and he felt bad. He was saying, "That's not me." But Troy's a fun guy. He made a mistake, so I said, "Just go apologize, man. You don't have anything to worry about." So he went up to him and the next thing I know they're hugging.

DICK LEBEAU: If Troy makes a mistake – and he rarely does – he doesn't get over it easily. So, I think you were all seeing that character portrait there of what makes him tick and why he's so good. Troy's about as close to perfect, I think, as a football player can come, from a coach's standpoint. He's an absolute joy to coach. But none of us are perfect. We're all going to have plays when we don't do what we want to do, and that was one of them. I can't think of another play, anything close to that, from Troy, but that's what makes you love Troy. You never know what you're going to get. He can come up with some pretty bizarre things sometimes.

It's seemingly a Samoan trait that they famously hate to disappoint those they respect. In the book *Tropic of Football*, author Rob Ruck quoted one of the top coaches on the island, Gabe Sewell, this way:

"You're taught from when you're little, that when you leave the island you're taking the name of the family, village, and religious community with you. You carry the hopes and dreams of the whole island. You know your parents and grandparents are constantly praying for you to succeed. You cannot let them down."

It's also a trait of Polamalu's to win AFC Defensive Player of the Week. He was so honored for the second consecutive week and fifth time up to this point in his career.

Polamalu missed the next two games – a loss to the New York Jets and a win over the Carolina Panthers – with what Tomlin called "a strained Achilles' tendon," but Polamalu explained that it was actually a strained muscle near the tendon.

The win against the Panthers improved the Steelers' record in games missed by Polamalu over the previous two seasons to 6-7. In the same time span, the Steelers were 15-4 with him.

If Troy could skip the awards portion of every regular season, he would. But in this one – with two awards being presented in one day – he had to get up and speak.

Troy entered the media room with the same disdain he probably held while approaching similar podiums at Douglas High and the University of Southern California.

Polamalu intercepted another pass in the finale against the Browns, giving him seven to match his career-high from 2008. Many of those were game-changing or game-ending, so Polamalu had every reason to expect the Steelers MVP award.

If he could credit his offensive line, as he had in his very first interview with *The News-Review* of Roseburg, Oregon, he would have. But this time he just washed his hands of the entire concept of football MVP awards.

"If I was ever a coach," he said, "I wouldn't ever have an award like this because it's such a team sport."

Then he received an award that figured to please him. Not only was the Walter Payton Man of the Year Award named after Troy's football hero, it honored charitable works. However, Polamalu isn't so easily defined.

"I don't really know what to say about any charity award," he said from the podium. "I don't think people do it so much for any type of recognition, so it's kind of uncomfortable winning anything like this."

After so many hours of community service and charitable works, Polamalu has preferred, and often requested, anonymity about his visits to places like Pittsburgh's Children's Hospital, where his time and loving input have become legendary.

LEBEAU: He's a great sharer of his time, a devoted father and husband. But many of his things he even goes painstakingly out of the way to make sure it doesn't become public. He doesn't want that aspect of it. He goes over to Children's Hospital every week almost, but he'll go through the side door. It's just part of his nature and he's a very considerate and caring man, and I think it goes very perfectly with a soft-spoken somewhat introspective nature. I would never call him introverted, but he is introspective.

CRAIG WOLFLEY: On Fridays he would visit Children's. When they brought special needs people in, he was always one of the first. I always thought he truly understands that strength is for service unto others, and I really appreciated that about him. There's a quote I heard that goes, "Nothing is as strong as gentleness; and nothing is as gentle as true strength." I learned that years before, but Troy really depicted that. He has the ability to reach out to those who were less fortunate, to those who were suffering, and put a smile on people's face. That always spoke to me as someone who's incredibly strong, because he knew that the strength and the gifts that he had were also for enriching other people's lives.

RANDY BAUMANN: The amount of nurses at Children's who have told me how often he came there; every time we were there for a radiothon they would tell Troy stories. He was there all the time. It's just him. He's a genuine guy, and there are few of them. I've been told not to mention it on the air, not by him but by whoever was telling me the story, Michele Rosenthal or Jaime Greenwald (Steelers community relations managers). I just know he's famously private about that kind of stuff. Again, one of the last selfless guys. That's why that post-Super Bowl story always blew me away. When every other dude was in there high-fiving buddies, he's outside telling us two doofuses how happy he was for the city of Pittsburgh.

RYAN CLARK: The Baltimore trip was just one example that comes to me. Like I said, we had a strange habit of getting too much food most times. We actually stopped in Baltimore. They have a pretty high homeless population, and we stopped and he got out of the cab and gave our food away. For him, it wasn't really anything he thought about. We had; they didn't. So he gave.

RAY HORTON: There are a ton of stories about his generosity off the field. I think he would be embarrassed for me to say what all he did for people. He was just a humble man. There's one small story I can share that doesn't involve his service but kind of provides some insight into Troy. It gets cold in Pittsburgh. Some of the players had a box, a suite, at the stadium. He did not at this time, early in his career. Theodora got cold and wanted to go inside and sit in someone's box. Troy said, "Well, no, you can't do that. The Steelers were gracious enough to give us two tickets. You sit in my seat outside." But that's how he believed life was. These are your seats and you sit in them outside in the cold, even though someone you know is warm and has nice food. That really is him.

CLARK: Theodora's the same way. Some people say they'll give you the clothes off their back. Well, we know instances where there have been less fortunate people visiting the Steelers, or them doing community service, and people would say, "Oh I love that jacket," and she literally takes it off of her back and gives it to people. That's truly not only Thea's heart, but Troy's heart. That's who they are as people. I think the world of her. She's super dope. She's actually really good for him, too, because their personalities are different. But they balance out. It's a beautiful union. His career is as much about her as it is about him. And she would've felt the same if he was Troy Polamalu the garbageman. I think that's the special part of it. She's going to love that man no matter what. And, trust me, he ain't the easiest to deal with, so God bless her heart.

KEISEL: You know how they say charity begins at home? Well, home is the locker room for us and Troy was so fun to have in there. I think one of the reasons we were so close as a team was because of the way Troy interacted with everyone. He was kind and humble with everybody. Always treated people with the same respect, whether you were a starter in the Pro Bowl and played right next to him or someone who just got there the day before.

JAMES HARRISON: Me and Troy had a lot of in-depth conversations where we've talked about life and just basically everything outside of football when I either had things I wanted to express or wanted advice on, and then get his perspective. Troy is *that* person. And he's going to give you an honest opinion, whether you want to hear it or not. That's something that you've got to respect. He's not going to give it to you raw like I would. He's going to give it to you in Troy fashion, but it's going to be honest and real and he's not going to say what it is that you want to hear. Or what you *don't* want to hear.

KEISEL: If you went up to him and asked him to sign something for your grandma, or your sister who just gave birth and named her son Troy, he would do it without question. I think that's why everybody loved him so much and why fans voted him their favorite player – and not just Steelers fans, NFL fans.

HARRISON: No, I couldn't give you examples, because it's not like I'm coming to him with, "Hey what should I do with the grass on the lawn?" It's not like I'm coming to Troy with BS. It's in-depth. It's personal. It's close.

KEISEL: It's just the way he was. And then, snap! Opening kickoff happens and he turns into this crazy animal who's flying around and his hair's all over the place and he's making these plays that no one's ever seen made before from the safety position. And then (snaps fingers) you meet him on the street and he's got his hair tucked up in a bun or under a hood and so gracious. It was awesome to be a part of it, to be in the locker room with him, to learn from him.

HEATH MILLER: Troy's personality was so laid back and he was always calm in practice and around the facility, so calm and collected. But if you pay attention you could see how obsessed he was with being the best, being the greatest he could possibly be. He obviously had that fire and the heart of a warrior.

The Steelers and Ravens both finished 12-4, but the Steelers won the AFC North Division by the divisional tiebreaker and were the No. 2 seed in the AFC playoffs behind the 14-2 New England Patriots. That provided the Steelers, and Troy Polamalu, a much-needed bye week to rest injuries. Troy had been hobbled with his ankle injury since the loss to the Patriots on Nov. 14, and was still limping around the practice facility throughout the bye week.

The Steelers would host the highest remaining seed the following week, so when the wild-card teams both upset divisional champs Indianapolis and Kansas City, that meant Heinz Field would host World War III against the Ravens.

The first-team All-Pro safeties of the Steelers and Ravens became an early storyline for the game since Ed Reed, with eight, and Troy, with seven, were 1-2 in the NFL in interceptions. Oddly, Reed to this point in his career had only one career interception and two other passes defensed in nine games against Ben Roethlisberger.

Not that Big Ben was gloating.

"I just know where he's at," Roethlisberger explained. "People might sit there and say he's a non-factor, but that's probably because I didn't give him a chance to be one."

"A ghost?" asked Steelers receiver Mike Wallace as he recoiled at the question. "I see Ed Reed everywhere. I see him the whole time. That's one guy who you wouldn't want to call a ghost. It may seem like he appears out of nowhere but that's the guy you have to know where he's at at all times."

Polamalu, on the other hand, had already wrecked two monumental Steelers-Ravens games, and that season had one fewer interception but one more touchdown and 26 more tackles than Reed. Both had one forced fumble and one fumble recovery in 2010.

Throughout the entirety of their first-ballot Hall-of-Fame careers, Reed's from 2002 to 20013, Polamalu's from 2003 to 2014, the statistical comparison (courtesy of *ProFootballReference.com*):

* Reed 1 ring, 9 Pro Bowls, 5 first-team All-Pros, 646 tackles, 6 sacks, 64 interceptions, 24 forced & recovered fumbles, 9 defensive TDs.

* Troy 2 rings, 8 Pro Bowls, 4 first-team All-Pros, 783 tackles, 12 sacks, 32 interceptions, 21 forced & recovered fumbles, 5 defensive TDs.

LEBEAU: I don't think there's any question that Troy's better. Now, I may be somewhat prejudiced, but I'm talking about from the standpoint of everything that he can do. I don't think there's a safety in the game that can match him. I think Reed's a wonderful safety. He's a great interceptor. He has great speed. Troy is so much more impactful in the running game. He just shows up all over the field. There's arguably no safety that can do everything, ever, the way Troy can do it. I think Reed has so many big plays because when he gets the ball he's hard to get on the ground, too. They're both safeties who if you're playing quarterback against them you want to know where they are. But the nod goes to Troy in my mind because of his overall versatility. I mean you don't see Reed blitz that much. You can blitz Troy. You can blitz him 10 times a game because he's more than 200 pounds. He'll hold up. If he's got to get an offensive lineman, he'll hold up on him. I just don't think there was anybody that can match his versatility in any way shape or form. He's the best.

DENNIS THURMAN, *New York Jets secondary coach (2008-14):* They're different. I say that with the realization they had tremendous similarities in that they were always around the football. Both of them were pretty good special teams players, blocking punts and things of that nature. They both got interceptions. They both caused fumbles. They both were good blitzers when called upon to do it. It's hard for me to separate, but there was not a doubt in my mind that when their careers were over they were both going to be first-ballot Hall of Famers. They both are where they deserve to be.

CLARK: Ed Reed and I grew up about 15-20 minutes from each other and we both graduated in 1997 from high school, the top two safeties in the state. His coach made him take a visit to Tulane and my coach did as well. So now I'm in the back of the bus with Ed Reed and he goes, "Where are you going to school? Have you made your decision yet?" And I said, "I'm leaning toward LSU." He said, "I'm going to go to Miami." I said, "Man, you know what? I'm *definitely* going to LSU then," because I was just scared he was going to LSU. I knew we both couldn't be there. I always just had a great admiration for him. I think he's the best deep safety to ever play football, and he was always like that. I would get two interceptions, return a punt for a touchdown and rush back to my mom's house so we could turn on Friday Night Football and I could see if I was the Defensive MVP or Player of the Week, only for Edward Reed out of Destrehan to have three interceptions, throw a touchdown and return a kick and win the award. I just think he's always had something that other people don't, but the difference between him and Troy were Troy's physical tools. Troy also understood the mental part of the game and was instinctive and all those things, but he had physical tools that stood out. Ed never really did. He just made plays. And so I think those guys are very different. I think Troy could do more. I think Ed could do one thing better than anyone who's ever done it.

THURMAN: Troy made so many plays against us when I was with both Baltimore and the Jets. Dick LeBeau did a phenomenal job. The Steelers did a great job with Troy and how they used him. They took advantage of all the different things he could do. Just remember that you can't coach the things Troy and Ed did. Anybody that says they can is lying to you.

Dennis Thurman had earlier compared and contrasted the abilities of his former teammate Ronnie Lott with Polamalu. Another of the all-time great safeties to consider is Sean Taylor, who lined up next to Clark in Washington from 2004-05.

Taylor was murdered in his home by a burglar at the age of 24. Clark wore Taylor's No. 21 ever day at Steelers practices to honor him.

CLARK: Troy is the best player I've ever played with; Sean is without a doubt the most talented person I've ever played with; Ed is just special. It's almost confusing to talk about Ed because you see some of the physical limitations, and then you look at the output. Those things honestly don't match up well. I believe that Sean was possibly going to be better than both. He just was different. He had all of that Troy stuff, except Sean was 6-2. And he was probably better in the deep part of the field, just because he was a little bit more patient. Troy's not the most patient football player of all time.

HORTON: The greatest safety of all time? Hmmm. That's interesting. I think if you go in generational – or 10-year – spots, you go back to Troy and Ed Reed, but they played different positions. They couldn't do what each other did. Troy couldn't return punts like Ed Reed did, but Ed Reed can't blitz and be disruptive like Troy. So, in the latest generation it's Troy and Ed, but at different positions. Then you move back a generation and go to Ronnie Lott, Steve Atwater. You move way back to Roger Wehrli. I don't want to say who's the best of all-time because the game changed the position. There are no more fullbacks on the field and the tight ends are like wide receivers. So if you just go in 10-year blocks, it's easier to say who's the best of the decade, and there was no question it was Troy and Ed Reed during their era. They were both phenomenal players. As for Sean Taylor, it's hard to project because his life was cut so short. I've been around the Redskins a while and his aura, legacy and presence are still there.

TROY POLAMALU: Ed was the kind of guy that broke down the barriers of taking the top off defenses, with Rodney Harrison being able to be the most universal safety in the sense of being able to play man-to-man in the slot when he was in New England, of playing the deep halves, with freeing up and playing the run as well. If there is any safety that I really admired the most, it would have probably been Rodney Harrison.

The Ravens/Browns had not beaten the Steelers in three previous playoff games and that didn't change this time. After falling behind 21-7, the Steelers rallied for a 31-24 win in their first playoff game of the 2010 postseason.

It made Ben Roethlisberger 9-2 in the playoffs, and it made Heath Miller 8-1. Miller was one of the Steelers' top players on this Saturday evening. He caught a team-high five passes. They added up to only 39 yards, but one was a 9-yard touchdown catch early in the second half that put the Steelers back in the game at 21-14.

Miller's blocking was also critical, whether he was out in front of screens, blocking Terrell Suggs one-on-one, or making the key kick-out block on Suggs that allowed Rashard Mendenhall to run 14 yards off left tackle to set up Miller's touchdown catch.

James Harrison was one of two Steelers defensive stars. He sacked Joe Flacco the snap following Miller's touchdown, then pressured Flacco into an incompletion on the ensuing third down.

The other Steelers defensive star, Ryan Clark, intercepted the next Flacco pass to set up the tying touchdown pass to Hines Ward.

The Ravens' offense after Ward's TD continued to self-destruct. Flacco fumbled the snap and Keisel recovered to set up the Steelers' go-ahead field goal.

In eight offensive snaps, the Ravens fumbled twice, threw an interception and punted as their 21-7 halftime lead turned into a 24-21 deficit with 12:15 left in regulation.

The Ravens regained their composure and drove inside the Pittsburgh 10, but Anquan Boldin's drop in the end zone on third down forced the Ravens to settle for a short field goal to tie the score with 3:54 left.

The ball was now in Roethlisberger's hands, and he converted a third-and-10 with a 12-yard pass to Ward. A sack brought up third-and-19, but the key play of the game, perhaps the key moment of wide receiver Antonio Brown's rookie season, came next. Roethlisberger heaved a deep ball to the rookie, who streaked past cornerback Lardarius Webb and secured the catch by pinning the ball to his helmet as he ran out of bounds at the Baltimore 4 for a 58-yard gain.

A defensive hold moved the ball to the 1, and on third down Mendenhall scored the game-winning touchdown with 1:33 remaining.

"They keep asking for us and we keep putting them out of the tournament," Ward said after the game. "They're going to be ticked about this for a long time."

"We're both good football teams," Flacco told *The Sun* of Baltimore. "But the bottom line is they're better at winning the game right now than we are. We're just not there yet."

The AFC Championship game was not the expected rematch with the Patriots. They were stunned by the Jets 28-21 in Foxboro.

"Oh, man, it felt great to beat the Patriots," says wide receiver Jerricho Cotchery. "The emotions ran pretty deep, because the Patriots talk slyly. They're not perceived as a big trash-talking team, but they do it in different ways. They blew us out on a Monday night and there was a lot going on between the two teams, so after that playoff game all of the emotions just poured out. Bart Scott was the spokesman for our emotions that day."

Forty days and nights had passed since the Patriots bombed the Jets 45-3 on a Monday night, so the emotional outpouring after the playoff win was understandable. The Jets had beaten Peyton Manning and the Colts in the first round, but for these guys it was ALL about beating the Patriots.

"All we hear about is their defense. They can't stop a nosebleed!" Jets linebacker Bart Scott screeched into an ESPN microphone immediately after beating the Pats.

"They're the 25th defense in the league and we're the ones who get disrespected!"

Scott was asked about the Steelers. "Can't WAIT!" he said, and it became the Jets' battle cry.

Until they fell behind 24-0 in the first half at Heinz Field.

The Steelers had outgained the Jets 231-50 in the first half and allowed them only one yard rushing. Perhaps it was the spent emotion; perhaps it was the 5-degree wind chill that Sunday night down by the rivers.

"Those emotions weren't there in that first half against the Steelers," says Cotchery. "The second half, those emotions started to pick back up, but it was too late."

On a sour note, the Steelers lost rookie center Maurkice Pouncey – their best lineman – for the rest of the season with a high ankle sprain during their opening drive. The crowd chanted his name as he lay on the ground. They picked it up again as he was helped off.

Ike Taylor's strip-sack of Jets QB Mark Sanchez for a Will Gay scoop-and-score late in the first half appeared to have put the game away, the Jets' field goal right before the break notwithstanding.

Maybe the Steelers got too warm at halftime; maybe they started looking at the Super Bowl. But the Jets stormed back.

Five plays into the second half, Taylor fell down and left old friend Santonio Holmes wide open for a 45-yard touchdown pass.

Casey Hampton, in the midst of one of the best games of his career, fought back to dominate a goal-line sequence. The big nose tackle defended the last blade of grass in stopping LaDainian Tomlinson on fourth-and-1 early in the fourth quarter. However, Ben Roethlisberger fumbled the next Doug Legursky snap. Roethlisbeger fell on it in the end zone for a safety and the Jets were within 24-12. The Jets took the ensuing kick, converted a fourth-and-1, and a third-and-4, before Sanchez found Cotchery open in the end zone for a 4-yard touchdown pass as the Jets closed to 24-19 with 3:06 left.

They didn't get the ball back, though. Roethlisberger hit both Heath Miller and Antonio Brown with 14-yard passes, the latter on third-and-6 to set up victory formation. And, yes, Troy lined up in the backfield. He didn't get the ball, but he did get another trip to the Super Bowl.

"Can't WAIT to get on the jet!" Ryan Clark shouted on his way to the locker room in stealing the Jets' rally cry. "Can't WAIT!"

Polamalu couldn't wait, either. His ankle felt better against the Jets than it had in two months. The Steelers' driving spirit would be 100 percent for the challenge of facing the vaunted Green Bay passing attack in the Super Bowl.

RYAN SCARPINO: Leading up to Super Bowl 45, my first year there, we got Troy to do this photo shoot. It was a Super Bowl promo done at the team facility. It was Troy, James Harrison and James Farrior. FOX was super happy he was doing it, but they had to do full uniforms, which sucked because you've got to put the pads on, and it was right after practice and James Harrison was getting antsy about it. "Where's Troy? Where's Troy?" And Troy comes in and asks the equipment guys for a razor so he can get a quick shave. Harrison hears this and just gets up and leaves. "I gotta go." So he took off his uniform and left. At this point we've got Farrior, Troy, and Troy's going to shave. Lawrence Timmons was around so we grabbed him and he did it for us. But the one time we got Troy on board, he wanted to be professional about it. He wanted to shave. That just goes back to who he is.

That's what the first week of the two-week wait between conference championship and Super Bowl is about: performing the tedious tasks. The coaches install the game plan, the PR department gets its most important shoots done, and the media provides a rough analysis to fans before the true focus turns to the day-to-day countdown from the game site, in this case Dallas, Texas.

In this rough media analysis, the concern for the Pittsburgh Steelers was whether they could defend Aaron Rodgers (101.2) and the Packers' quartet of talented wide receivers: Greg Jennings (76-1,265-12), Donald Driver (51-565-4), James Jones (50-679-5) and Jordy Nelson (45-582-2).

Even though the Steelers ranked high in the key pass-defense indices (first in yards per attempt, second in passer rating and yards per completion), Troy expressed concern at the start of the playoffs because, "I think we had a more complete defense in '08. I think we were a lot better on the back end."

Also looming in the backs of Steelers minds was the wild shootout with the Packers the previous season when Mike Tomlin had so little confidence in his defense's ability to stop Rodgers that he called an onside kick with the lead and 3:58 remaining.

The Packers recovered, but scored too quickly, and Ben Roethlisberger pulled it out with a TD pass to Mike Wallace at 0:00 to win 37-36.

"In the words of a great philosopher, Bartholomew Scott, neither one of us could stop a nosebleed," Ryan Clark said.

Polamalu didn't play in that 2009 game. Neither did Bryant McFadden. Players such as Joe Burnett and Tyrone Carter took their places before being released, and William Gay was struggling at the time.

"It always comes down to the secondary for me," Polamalu summed up. "I would say that if I was a coach. I would say that if I was a defensive lineman. Because if we tackle well and not give up big plays, then we give our team the best opportunity to win the game."

That was the challenge if the Steelers were to win Lombardi No. 7.

CHAPTER 26

FEBRUARY FOOTBALL, PART III

Super Bowl media week is drudgery for players, and media, but oftentimes it becomes humorous, even if it's the dark humor of James Harrison.

Asked about concussions by a reporter, Harrison said it's the risk he takes because he loves his job.

"Don't you love your job?" Harrison asked the reporter.

"Yeah, but I don't get concussions in my job," the reporter said.

"You will if you ask another question like that," Harrison said.

Everyone chuckled, except, of course, Harrison.

Troy Polamalu's descent into frustration with the media occurred in three steps:

What do you think about the weather?

I was surprised when I opened up the curtain and saw all this snow on the ground. It was like we were back at home. Usually the Super Bowl is in a warmer environment, but I guess they'll have to deal with this in New York.

What are your feelings on winning NFL Defensive Player of the Year?

I felt nothing. ... There are other guys more deserving: Clay Matthews, James Harrison might be the best candidates. Ed Reed, Julius Peppers, all these guys are great candidates. I think they're probably more worthy of the award than myself.

In your rookie year, was it the freelancing that your coaches didn't like?

I did absolutely none of that. I don't know where people come up with this "freelancing" but I didn't have the flexibility then and there was no way I was going to push the boundaries then, either.

DICK LEBEAU: Well, to a certain extent we fostered that a little bit. I liked people to think maybe that Troy wasn't anchored. Perhaps it would open up a couple more avenues for him to attack. He does have parameters. He is a team player. He is blessed to have Ryan Clark beside him who gives Troy more freedom to create because Ryan is so rock solid and has a concrete knowledge of what the defense is supposed to be doing back there that he can back up any move Troy makes. I think together they're a perfect combination. But, no, I don't think any player wants to be known that way. That does smack of a selfish aspect and not playing team football and not taking care of your job first and then going to help the team win. When you look at the record over the years at how many impactful plays he has made, it would be very difficult to criticize his approach to making them.

TROY POLAMALU: I don't know any other way. Coach LeBeau has pretty much been our only defensive coordinator since I've been here. You don't sit there and tell Albert Einstein how to write out his equations.

LEBEAU: With the tremendous statistical base that our defenses have put up here in recent years, you couldn't just let someone "freelance" with a secondary that wasn't structured and making sure that their part of it's taken care of first. I think that's all you need to say to defend the fact that people think he's just running all over. He's not, or there would be more big plays against us. And we have one of the top records in the league since he's been here of not yielding big plays. Sure he's not perfect. None of us are. But he does a very good job of making sure his side of it's taken care of and then going to create.

Of course, during Super Bowl week the oddball questions come up. Troy was asked about soccer, his hair, his hair vs. Brett Keisel's beard, his favorite TV shows, on and on. And then someone asked him a question that lit him up: What's driving you?

TROY POLAMALU: I've experienced what I've seen in my teammates' eyes and how much they enjoy the experience of winning. I would love to see them happy and to get their fulfillment from that. I think people are motivated by different things, and I don't spite them for that at all. A large part of people's identity is winning this game. Forever, whenever you're introduced as somebody in a football setting, you're introduced as a Super Bowl winner. I would just like to see my teammates be happy.

BRETT KEISEL: It's the joy you get out there on Sunday, because there's so much work that goes into preparation, and there's so much criticism, and the minute details that go into it throughout the work week, as far as where to be, where to fit, what nuances we're doing this week, and how close you need to be attentive to those details to make it roll into the game on Sunday. So there's a lot of work that goes into the week and a lot of build-up. And then when Sunday comes around, and you're prepared, and you look to your left and you look to your right and you see your guys, you're free. You're free to go a hundred miles an hour to unleash everything. There's no letting off the quarterback. There's no letting off the guy coming up and just touching him on the hips. NO. You light him up and you make him feel you. You make him feel the Pittsburgh Steelers. That's what we all loved about Sundays. There wasn't any holding back. It was FREEDOM!

TROY POLAMALU: Our strength has never been in our talent. It's always been in our virtues of hard work and most importantly our camaraderie, our humility and how we respect the game and respect our opponent. That's something that youth can never have. It takes a lot of experience, a lot of chemistry, a lot of life experience to have that.

KEISEL: When you get the play-call, you have seconds to line up right, 11 guys lining up right, and if they put someone in motion you all have to make that motion adjustment, you all have to be on the same page whether it's hand signals or just a look. You all need to be on that same page on the nuances of the defense so it fits. You know, that LeBeau defense is like a jigsaw puzzle. If one of those pieces is out, it's not going to roll together. If it all fits together, there is not a place for anyone to advance the ball. So that's what made everyone so happy when it was successful.

CHRIS HOPE: I heard Troy's speech about winning Defensive Player of the Year. He said, "It's 11 guys' trophy. There are two or three or four other guys on this team that could've won this trophy. I didn't win this trophy." So he's never taken the credit, and it made it so much easier for me to genuinely love him and then genuinely play hard and be satisfied. I didn't tolerate his success. I celebrated it with him.

RYAN CLARK: I was sitting downstairs in the restaurant when I saw it go across the screen that he won the NFL Defensive Player of the Year. I called him, and like most superstars he doesn't really answer his phone very much, so then I texted him, "Congrats man you deserve it. I love you." And he was like "Well, that's our award so let's go try to win this trophy." I think that is the most amazing thing about him. He can do all these great things on the field and you'll never hear him talk about it. That is not what he's concerned with, individually winning awards. He is about team. It's great to be around a player like that with such humility, with no ego.

Clark showed little ego himself as the drudgery of answering the same questions every day marched them closer to kickoff. Finally, when asked how the Steelers could stop such a vaunted passing attack, Clark just shrugged as if he had no clue.

"We're just going to give up," he said. "We're just not going to go. We're underdogs anyway. They are better than us at every position it seems, so we've decided to come to Dallas, buy the tickets, sit in the stands and watch them scrimmage."

"Nah," he said. "We're going to play, man. We feel we have a good enough team to win the game. You don't get to the Super Bowl being a bad football team. They're the hot team right now. They're the team, quote-unquote, nobody wants to play, the team that everybody thinks is going to win, and that's fine."

MIKE TOMLIN: That week was just about a group that was seizing their moment. There was a great deal of confidence and singular focus that you felt within and around the group in that week leading up to the game, and obviously Troy was a central component of that. It felt really normal.

It was only abnormal in that the Steelers lost, but what will stick with them forever is how close they came to winning, even on an off day and with Aaron Rodgers red hot. After James Farrior pressured the Green Bay QB into a third-down incompletion on the first series, Rodgers led the Packers to a 21-3 lead.

The first touchdown was a perfect 29-yard strike to Jordy Nelson down the right sideline over solid coverage by Will Gay.

The second was a defensive score by the Packers. Third-team nose tackle Howard Green bull-rushed left guard Chris Kemoteatu back into the end zone and hit Ben Roethlisberger's arm as he was throwing deep to Mike Wallace. The ball fluttered into the arms of Nick Collins, who returned it 37 yards and ran over Kemoeatu at the goal line for a 14-0 lead.

The Steelers answered with a 33-yard field goal, but Rodgers – set up by another interception of Roethlisberger – scored again on third-and-1 from the Pittsburgh 21. It was another perfect touchdown strike – this one between coverage backer Farrior and safeties Polamalu and Clark in their cover-2 – to Greg Jennings for a 21-3 lead.

The Steelers responded before halftime and regained momentum. Roethlisberger made an off-balance throw and Hines Ward made an off-balance 8-yard touchdown catch with 39 seconds left in the half to cut the deficit to 21-10.

The Packers committed three penalties in their first five plays of the third quarter and the Steelers were able to get within 21-17 when Rashard Mendenhall scored from the 8-yard line.

Shaun Suisham missed a 52-yard field goal, but the Steelers continued playing strong defense, stopping Rodgers and the Packers on all four third-quarter possessions.

The Steelers had the ball at the Green Bay 33, facing a second-and-2, as the game turned into the fourth quarter. The experienced Steelers figured this was their time to strike, and called on Mendenhall to run behind pulling H-back David Johnson. But Johnson missed his block on Clay Matthews, who didn't miss Mendenhall. The linebacker belted the running back hard enough to force a fumble, which the Packers recovered, and Rodgers made the Steelers pay. He found Nelson over the middle and Nelson kept running until Polamalu pushed him out of bounds at the Pittsburgh 2, a 38-yard gain.

LaMarr Woodley's sack of Rodgers gave the Steelers a bit of a reprieve, but on the next play he found Jennings in the end zone for what proved to be the backbreaking touchdown.

Jennings, without a cornerback over him as the first of two slot receivers on Rodgers' right, easily got by the linebacker and then lost Polamalu, who guessed Jennings would cut inside. He cut outside and was wide open for the 8-yard touchdown and 28-17 lead.

The Steelers came back with an 8-point play. Ward's 15-yard catch set up a 25-yard touchdown pass to Wallace, and Antwaan Randel El took an option pitch for the 2-point conversion to make it 28-25 with 7:25 left. Green Bay answered with a field goal for a six-point lead to put Roethlisberger in another last-drive Super Bowl scenario.

Pushed back via penalty to his own 15, with 1:59 left, Roethlisberger started with a 15-yard pass to Heath Miller, followed by a 5-yard pass to Ward. But then the QB went away from his two veteran receivers and threw two deep incompletions before throwing incomplete to Wallace on fourth-and-5, and the Steelers walked away with their second Super Bowl loss in eight organizational trips.

Some blamed Mendenhall for the fumble. Some blamed Polamalu for the Jennings touchdown. Some blamed Kemoeatu for the pick-6. Some blamed Johnson for missing the block on Matthews.

TROY POLAMALU: Toughest loss I've ever had.

SALU POLAMALU: I was in the hospital so we didn't get a chance to go. I watched the replay. They were watching Troy. Troy was the key in all the passes that Green Bay had, from what I saw. I could tell he was frustrated because he couldn't get close enough. I talked to him and he said "I'm so disappointed in the game."

AARON RODGERS: He's the guy that you have to be aware of, where he's at all times. He's a great player, had a great season, but guys have to respect where my eyes are looking so it was important to me to use good eye control on the field and not stare anybody down because he can cover a lot of ground quickly. And when he was down in the box, we made sure he was picked up in the protection schemes. A couple of times when he came on blitzes, we adjusted the protection to make sure we had him picked up because he's a very talented blitzer. And when he's high, a deep safety, you just have to make sure you are good with your eyes.

TROY POLAMALU: Their last touchdown was completely my fault. Earlier in the game they ran Jennings down the middle and I was anticipating that same pass play and I guessed wrong.

LEBEAU: That wasn't Troy's fault.

GREG JENNINGS: It was a corner route. I had a corner route the entire time and they dropped me and let me run free the play before. They dropped me on another corner route and we came back to it and scored on that play.

LEBEAU: I thought that if we could keep their points down around 17 or 18 that it would give us a very good chance to win. One of their touchdowns was an interception return, so we were close. Was it our best game? No. But it was not our worst game, either. We had a chance to win it in our last possession. We kept the game in balance. I don't think any of our guys played poorly. But I don't think it was our best played game.

SALU POLAMALU: I thought Troy's injury wouldn't let him stop and turn as well, and his reaction time was hurt because Rodgers was so accurate. And that lineman, Kemoeatu, looked bad in the beginning of the game. What was he doing backing up on the blocking scheme in the end zone? He wasn't thinking. And I was disappointed the way they ended the season on the final drive. You've got Heath and you've got Ward. Why was he trying to go to the young guys? What were they thinking? On fourth down you go to the player who carries your team. What was he thinking?

HINES WARD: That's a story for another time.

HEATH MILLER: I can't remember a lot about that game. I know that we were kind of taking over, then the turnover, and then Aaron Rodgers made some unbelievable throws, and that was a wrap. It was disappointing. You remember the ones you win, but the ones that you lose eat at you forever.

HOPE: Troy was hurt. He still wasn't 100 percent. His ankle was messed up. When your game is built on speed, you still have to find a way to be effective. If your game is one-dimensional, you have to find another way of doing it. And Troy can do that. But again, people were looking for him to make a game-changing interception. Sometimes being in that position, you don't get a chance to do that. I face this a lot. The more I learn about the game, the more I have to slow my game down to not take away a play before I know it's going to happen, because if you take it away before it happens they're not going to throw it. And when you're in the post, it's hard to turn it on and get involved in the game. That's why it's important with guys like him to get more in the box, get more involved in the game, so now the game just comes to you and you feel like it's a natural reaction, as opposed to being in the post not getting any action, taking away the deep ball, not having a chance to get hit or not making a tackle for three or four series, and then now you need to make an open-field tackle and you haven't hit anyone since pre-game warm-ups. So for a guy like Troy, his game is built around being involved, even if he's being crack-blocked, even if he has to jump over a lineman and roll. Those are movements and flow that gets his juices flowing. And I think with his ankle, with his Achilles, and being in the post the entire game, it was more of a safe-playing Troy than a playmaking Troy.

KEVIN COLBERT: He was healthy. He practiced during the bye week. Previous to that he was only practicing on Fridays. He was not physically impaired. To blame any one play in a six-point loss is kind of narrow-minded anyway. You win as a team; you lose as a team. We weren't good enough as a team. To pin it on any one play or any one player is very narrow-minded.

LEBEAU: He was flying on the field. I'm used to seeing Troy. I know how Troy goes from point A to point B. I don't really need a medical report. I can tell. And I thought that he was covering everything by that time. I thought he was pretty close to 100 percent, and definitely in the Super Bowl he was moving OK.

TROY POLAMALU: It was the best I've felt probably since the middle of the season.

BRYANT MCFADDEN: It's tough to spot any NFL team a nice lead, but it's tougher to spot a guy like Aaron Rodgers.

TOMLIN: Aaron Rodgers was unconscious. Just some of the throws he made in that game were those world championship, legacy-producing, life plays. We were just on the wrong side of it, unfortunately.

MCFADDEN: I had the luxury of going to the Super Bowl almost every other year. So I didn't know how hard it was to get to the Super Bowl. And then when we lost, it's like, I don't want to go if you have to experience that.

CHRIS HOKE: I remember sitting at my locker looking around and everybody was sitting at their lockers just bewildered. Didn't know what to say. We were like, "We lost? We lost the Super Bowl?" We were supposed to be out there celebrating and we just couldn't believe it. We never thought we'd ever lose the game. I didn't really break down and get emotional until I got back to the hotel room.

COLBERT: On the way back from the game, Troy and Theodora were sitting in the row ahead of us with their two little boys. Casey Hampton's right next to him. Again, we just went through a horrible defeat and everybody was feeling down. But it was kind of neat. Big Casey was making these funny faces trying to entertain Troy's kids. It was a neat moment from a perspective of feeling horrible. It was a light moment and it just showed the camaraderie that group has. You know how a guy like Troy and his family can influence a guy like Casey. There are so many different moments like that.

TROY POLAMALU: I've never had a defeat like this in my life, but I think this is a great spiritual lesson. When you kind of put your whole life into something, this is not a game to us, this is a lifestyle. It's a big part of our life and all of us are going to be challenged, the way that we forced a lot of other people to be challenged by winning two previous Super Bowls. It's just important for us to rebound, take this loss. It's incredibly humbling. God willing, in some way we'll be benefitted by this.

CHAPTER 27

HE MEANS THE WORLD TO US

KEVIN COLBERT: Monday, the day after, was abysmal for everybody. For us, in the personnel department, our scouts flew in Tuesday night and we started our draft meetings on Wednesday. We watched the Super Bowl game film right away. You have to do that right away and move on. That's one game to add to the evaluation for the season. But you can't dwell on it, especially when you enter into this phase of the year. You're behind so we have to make up for lost time and, quite honestly, I'm glad we had to make up for lost time because it took your mind off it.

Kevin Colbert attended the NFL Draft Combine a few weeks after the Steelers' first Super Bowl loss since 1996. His team was picking 31st, and the front office also started contract negotiations with Ike Taylor, Will Gay and Willie Colon, who were due to become free agents in a month.

Colbert mentioned that the Steelers wanted to get something done with 26-year-old LaMarr Woodley, but didn't say anything about the other key defender who was entering the final year of his contract, 30-year-old Troy Polamalu.

As for the upcoming draft, *Pro Football Weekly* predicted left tackle Derek Sherrod to the Steelers, but a sports writer from Columbus, Ohio, had someone else in mind.

MARCUS HARTMAN, *Ohio State beat reporter:* Cameron Heyward would be perfect for the Steelers. He's really powerful and can get under a lineman and take him where he wants him to go. I think he'll be a great 3-4 end for a long time, one who is more of a playmaker than the average 3-4 guy, but not enough of one to play 4-3 end. So to a team at the end of the first round like the Steelers, that makes a lot of sense to me. He would be a great value pick there.

Heyward was known to Pittsburgh reporters, who had watched his late father, Craig "Ironhead" Heyward, star at the University of Pittsburgh. Cam spent much of his childhood in the Pittsburgh area and was a Steelers fan.

When the Steelers did in fact draft Heyward, he would talk about his deep respect for his father throughout his distinguished career as an All-Pro tackle and perpetual defensive captain.

The Steelers did lose one of their more underrated coaches, Ray Horton, who moved on to Arizona to become Ken Whisenhunt's defensive coordinator. The Steelers replaced Horton with Carnell Lake, their former strong safety whose All-Pro career caused the Steelers to seek out Polamalu in 2003. Eight years later, Troy was preparing to take his talents to the south beaches of American Samoa.

SALU POLAMALU: Junior Seau was the first really popular Samoan player. The Throwin' Samoan (Jack Thompson) was popular. Tuiasasopo. Manumaleuna's dad used to play for Kansas City. Now they've got a different generation and every kid involved with sports has long hair like Troy. They all are like Troy. They wear his t-shirt, jersey. He's very, very popular in Samoa.

BRANDON POLAMALU: He's the Manny Pacquiao of Samoa. He's adored. He's adored for the person that they see and the things he does for community, and that's huge. He's not just a jersey. He's giving back to the community in all these ways. It's not just Samoan communities, but all kinds of causes. And he's always speaking with humility and representing himself in a way that you can perceive as no other way than positive. Then of course the way he plays the sport, with great sportsmanship and great passion. But, yeah, when you walk into a Samoan community, it's huge, and it's getting bigger as he starts to participate with stuff back on the island.

SALU POLAMALU: He donated $100,000 of equipment. That's why the governor invited Troy and that's why Troy's taking all of us.

SHELLEY POLAMALU: With all the help of those going he's putting on a football camp.

SHAUN NUA: I thought it was just football but it went to a different level, to educate people, to help medical people. Troy is trying to help out as much as possible with the main issues there. For example, diabetes is a huge issue where we're from, and Troy is doing everything he can to educate the people there and send medical people to help. He goes beyond just football. He's dedicating a lot of his time and money to helping them.

TROY POLAMALU: It was in late June, early July. It lasted a week. The genesis of it started when we donated the uniforms to each high school with Nike. People close to me said "Their football could use some help" as far as IQ. So we came up with an idea to have a camp out in Samoa.

RYAN CLARK: As soon as we got there the whole island was at the airport. We met the first lady, the governor, you take pictures, do interviews. Then when we walked out we were escorted to our cars like we were the Beatles or the Jacksons. It was crazy.

TROY POLAMALU: It was life-changing definitely on my part, for my family and my children to be able to experience where I come from. And hopefully it was on their part because of all the life experience. It wasn't just me who was over there: Rey Maualuga, Malaefou MacKenzie, Domata Peko, Reagan Maui'a, Vince Manuwai, Deuce Lutui, Ryan Clark.

KENETI POLAMALU: The first day they put pads on, they wanted to kill. We had to spend half the time talking about safety, making sure they do it right. And then the Nike shoes that Troy gave them, they didn't last because their feet are wider since they're barefoot all the time in Samoa. The dirt, the grass, and then the rain, the weather, those shoes were beat. They looked pretty for the mainland here; we have nice turf and manicured lawns and practice turf that a lot of these kids play in. I'm not saying all of them are like that, but in Samoa those shoes didn't last because they were just ripped up, so he's hoping that maybe Nike or a shoe company can come out there and have Samoa as not only their test ground but to build a shoe that will fit these guys.

TROY POLAMALU: We were on a good field. We were at the main stadium. But the other high school field, from hash to hash, from 20 to 20, was lava rock. I'm not talking about patchy lava rock. I'm talking red middle of the field. But also during the camp, guys were playing barefoot. One guy was in socks. Very humble beginnings but they definitely appreciate the little things. They definitely use everything they've got and appreciate it.

CLARK: I'm teaching 14, 15-year-old kids how to backpedal. You could tell they have a lot of talent, just no coaching. And no matter what you said to any kid the answer's always the same: "Yes, coach." I could've asked them to run through a wall. "Yes, coach." No matter what I said it was the same thing. I went hoarse every day because it was that much fun and we got to put that much into it and we got to spend that much time with the kids. As a people, you saw how appreciative they were. For Troy to go back and have a heart for that and to do that, it was really amazing.

TROY POLAMALU: We want to be able to provide for them also through football, and also – football being our foot in the door – a higher education. By the same token, we also have to keep our traditionalism. It's fine to go either way, because you don't need higher education. If the land gives you everything, what do you need? Right? But then if you want higher education, you've got to be able to do A, B, C and D to be successful in the Western world.

CLARK: That's a big thing, education, basically to educate these kids and get them to the point where they can communicate and be successful in more than football. Troy preached that to them every time we talked – it's not about success in football, it's about finding other ways if you want to get off the island.

SALU POLAMALU: When I was growing up that was just a dream. My only way out was scholastic, military. That was it. Every Samoan kid has that dream now. That dream became very popular because of all these athletes.

ROB RUCK, author *Tropic of Football*: Sport is this story that Samoans have used to tell about who they are to the world. Football and rugby for independent Samoa are the two things people around the world know about Samoans, who are a tiny group of people. Sport has become very important to their collective self-identity, their collective self-esteem. Their ability to create this trans-national community that transcends village, island or even independent vs. territorial Samoa, and it's in large measure because they're the most extraordinary micro-cultural sporting excellence I've ever seen – at least in a team sport.

TROY POLAMALU: Samoans by nature are fishermen, are hunters, are gatherers. This is pre-Colonialism, when we were completely independent. But we were also warriors. We were also fighters. No wars are to be fought anymore and you see a lot of Samoans falling into three areas: 1. We go into the military – we have the highest casualty rate in the U.S. military; 2. We also have the highest percentage of making it to the NFL, so we have two ways of expressing our inner warrior-ism; but, 3. A lot of them fall into gangs and gang violence in Southern California and Utah. So these are ways we express our inner warrior. That's from the psychological perspective.

RUCK: Since World War 2, American Samoans have been forced to encounter U.S. culture. That's been devastating. World War 2 changed the dial. It's grim. Football emerges from the late '60s on and it cultivates discipline, toughness, physical culture, a warrior's psyche. What does that contribute to? It contributes to sacrificing your body and your mind. And Troy's an example of that. I mean, how many concussions did he have? Plus, even though football becomes a way off the rock, when these kids get to junior colleges and other colleges in the United States, they don't have the aunties and uncles, reverends, everybody, the principals who keep them in line. That's really tough. Only about 55,000 people live in the territory, so more Samoans in the NFL like Troy were born and grew up in the States. But the Samoan-American community has also shown those signs of duress. When it comes to income, educational attainment, problems among youth, it's very high, as it is in any socio-economic group, but particularly for second-generation kids growing up.

KENETI POLAMALU: There is still peer pressure. Gangs are still going on today. When you're a bigger kid, people try to get you to their side, to make sure that they're the cooler group or that will fight any group. And me being my size, and my aggression, it ended up I was going that way. But I had enough. Hey, I came here to get a college education. That was my parents' goal. It wasn't just to graduate from high school, it was to graduate from college. And football, sports happen to be a tool that can help. We didn't have the money to pay for me to go to school, but America was kind enough to have this athletic scholarship thing that we can take advantage of.

NUA: It's not a poverty place. It's almost the opposite. It's a place where before processed food came it was still rich with coconut milk and fish and all these foods. Now, McDonalds is there and it's a deadly cycle. Troy's trying to figure out a way. You always want people to be farmers and fishermen but at the same time it's a struggle. If you're not a farmer or fisherman, you become fat and diabetic. Everybody's trying to teach the happy medium.

TROY POLAMALU: It's so simple there. It's so beautiful. Everything that you ever need God gives to you. Everything's there that you can live off the land so easily and it's beautiful. What's also beautiful is island time is so much slower. People always say that island time is slow because you never bypass the process. When you're hungry, you drive up and go to McDonald's and buy a No. 1 and then you eat and you're done. There, traditionally, you have to go find the fish, you've got to cook it, you've got to prepare the umu – or the traditional way of making food there – so you never bypass the process. Also, you don't sit in front of the TV and vegetate. That's the beautiful things about Samoa and our culture.

RUCK: I was only in independent Samoa for a week and it's gorgeous. Here you've got this thin island that shoots up out of the sea slathered in green. I've sat on the beach, half in the water and half out, and just looked. And yet, there's a certain depression that affects the culture. There are not a lot of opportunities on the island. You can get a good job with government. You don't want into the tuna cannery.

The big tension is: For all the success in sport, the group as a whole, with socioeconomics and educational attainment, is not prospering. The American territory is a food wasteland, ironically, despite the fact it shouldn't be. It should be just the opposite. It once was. People feel they have to leave to get anywhere in life – although a lot of them come back.

TROY POLAMALU: We have a pretty big family title that was offered to me. It's an incredible responsibility but it's also something that I feel that I'm almost motivated to do, just because we're losing a lot of our traditionalism and I love our traditionalism and I want to instill that. But, it's such a huge responsibility. I don't know if I could have that. And it's a tremendous burden. Great leaders kind of look at these things as tremendous burdens and I don't know if I could sacrifice time and my family for that.

KENETI POLAMALU: My Uncle Koke, who was the matai of our family, passed away. Troy knew my older brother Salu didn't want the title, and I don't want to go back and live there, and he's thinking, "Uncle, I think I might take that title." And that's a big title now. It's the chief of Manu'a, which is the original island. That's where everything starts. That Pomele title, it's the orator and is very respected. Any time there's a Samoan gathering, wedding, funerals, doesn't matter, they are always the lead into whatever has to be done. He doesn't have to live there, but he has to be there for functions. He would've never thought of that if he didn't do this trip, but I think it's really turned him a little bit.

NUA: Junior Seau and Troy are similar in many ways because of the game of football, but Troy really made an effort to go back and learn about our people, about our culture, how we lived back in the day, what we look like now. I don't remember Junior Seau coming to Samoa when I was a kid, even though he was my first idol. Troy took it to a different level as he was coming to learn about us and help us. We saw a side that we're like "Wow, this guy never really grew up in the islands but that's exactly what an island boy is like." It's what our parents and our grandparents have taught us to be like. Troy and Junior are very, very special people that represent us, and especially in the athletic world. But Troy has definitely taken it to a different level where you have body, mind and spirit, and how he can represent us in a special way. It's almost like The Rock, who's doing all this stuff with the movies. Troy is still the one people look at as a complete role model. Junior gave us the intensity, the work ethic. Troy gave us the spirituality, the thinking, the mental part of it, the emotional part of it, especially how he handles himself. He's inspired each and every one of us in different ways. It's just amazing how huge of a platform he has, still has, and how he's taking advantage of it and inspiring our people. So he means a lot. He means the world to us.

CHAPTER 28

BOLT FROM THE BLUE

The Steelers came within a touchdown of winning a third Super Bowl in six years and Troy Polamalu was the reigning NFL Defensive Player of the Year. But all was not well. The Steelers, Polamalu, and even the league, with its Collective Bargaining Agreement expiring, were at a tipping point.

The Steelers' defense, the prime mover behind the team's outrageous success, was aging and management was determined not to hang onto players too long. That was one reason why the great dynasty of the '70s landed with a thud in the '80s.

Polamalu was a bit of a concern for upper management. He was turning 30 and was playing one of three positions – along with nose tackle and buck inside linebacker – deemed not only critical to the scheme's success but worthy of concern due to the physical toll exacted from those players.

Polamalu's contract had one year remaining, he was coming off a lackluster performance in a Super Bowl loss, and had missed 13 of the last 32 regular-season games with injuries. But his presence in the locker room, his popularity with fans and his status throughout the rest of the organization were at an all-time high.

CAMERON HEYWARD, *Steelers defensive end (2011-current):* Of course I was a Steelers fan before I came here. My brother was, too. He had a Fathead of Troy in his room. That was the oddest thing (laughs). But when I first came in, Troy was one of the first guys to introduce himself to me. It was after practice. This was a very personable guy. He went out of his way to be there for younger guys. The humility always showed.

RYAN SCARPINO: Troy heard I used to work at a restaurant and he asked me one Friday before practice if I could get him a table that night. It's no longer there but it was very popular, four stars, and if you didn't have a reservation on a Friday night you likely weren't going to get one. But it's Troy Polamalu, so I texted the chef and he said, "We're booked." I was like, "I know, but it's Troy Polamalu. I am not messing with you. Do you really want to tell Troy Polamalu no?" He said he'd see what he could do, and I'm sweating out this practice, thinking, "Oh my God I can't tell Troy no." I couldn't let him down. Then my boss texted me and said, "Hey, we're all set." So Troy and his wife go in that night and apparently they have a great time. My boss texted me that everything was good. The next day I see Troy. "Hey, Troy, did you enjoy everything?" And from down the hall he said, "Scarpino, it was bomb!" I will never forget hearing that. My boss said he was the nicest person you could imagine. He didn't ask for anything special. They came in, no one bothered them, and you would've never known a Hall of Famer was in. I know that made my boss's whole career.

HEYWARD: Troy's a big foodie. He's always like, "Hey, try this." I remember he would have this rainbow cake and Theodora would cut it up and pack it for him. He would give it out on the plane, and I was like, "What is this? This is ridiculous." He would just pass it out to Hamp, Keisel, everybody, and they were all like, "Oh my gosh this is so good!" I was a rookie so I'm the last guy to get a piece, and sometimes I wouldn't, but when I did get a piece I was like "Oh, man, this is good!" Theodora would make turkey sandwiches. Troy was known for passing out food on the plane. It was ridiculous.

LONI FANGUPO, *Steelers defensive lineman (2012-13):* Troy truly had a fat man's heart for roasted pig. I invited him over to my apartment once for roasted pig – a woman in the elevator recognized him and literally just froze solid. I think she almost passed out!

BRYANT MCFADDEN: Every Thursday after practice we would stay back and watch tape together and cater in food. That wasn't really about watching extra tape, it was about us being together, communicating. Then some of the linebackers would join us to watch tape, but also because we had nice food catered in.

BRETT KEISEL: He had all the DBs together and he would get things catered and go somewhere. I remember all those guys having so much fun, and some of us would sneak in there and get food.

HEYWARD: That has definitely been passed on. Now I make my regular appearances in the DB room, grab me a plate.

KEISEL: The D-line was super tight and we started doing that ourselves, but we never shared. We can put some food down, believe me.

MCFADDEN: The guys in the secondary didn't just have a working relationship; we had a for-real relationship. If you're part of a team, part of a business, there are a lot of employees who only see each other when they're inside the building. We talked outside and hung out. Even to this day, there's a chat of 15 to 17 of us. And we saw the results on the football field because of how much we were around each other and loving each other and knowing each other. That was togetherness and that goes back to the mantra: When one person makes a play, we all make a play.

HEYWARD: One time we were on the road and Troy was telling me about winning the Defensive Player of the Year and losing the Super Bowl. He was mad at himself because he felt like he was being selfish winning the award and not winning the Super Bowl. That astounded me. To feel like you cheated others because you – won an award? It was just unheard of.

Theodora, in late July, was planning another massive feast back home in LaJolla, California, to honor her husband for a successful first camp in Samoa, congratulate him on finishing up his bachelor's degree in history at USC and wish him off to the late-starting training camp in Latrobe.

Troy finally had time to finish that degree because the NFL was on lockdown during the renegotiation of the Collective Bargaining Agreement. The Steelers were the only team to vote against the ratification, and they did so unanimously, but like a bolt from the blue the CBA was agreed upon by the rest of the league and camp began immediately, so Troy missed the feast.

Another proverbial bolt from the blue struck that summer when James Harrison, in an interview with *Men's Journal*, trashed some big names, including quarterback Ben Roethlisberger. Harrison's primary target, though, was commissioner Roger Goodell.

"We were the best team in football in 2004, but the Patriots, who we beat during the regular season, stole our signals and picked up 90 percent of our blitzes," Harrison told reporter Paul Solotaroff. "They got busted for it later, but, hey, they're Goodell's boys, so he slapped 'em

$500,000 and burned the tapes. Was he going to rescind their Super Bowls? Man, hell no!"

On Polamalu, Harrison was almost reverential. "He's the one guy in football I respect absolutely, 'cause he's spiritual and lives it like he talks it."

Harrison later contested the critical remarks made about Roethlisberger and the two players walked out to their first practice at St. Vincent College holding hands.

Roethlisberger, a newlywed, wore Max Starks' jersey number at the time to make a statement to the team, which had released Starks right before camp after his weight had ballooned.

On reporting day 2011, the Steelers re-signed Ike Taylor, and a week later renegotiated the final year of LaMarr Woodley's contract into a six-year deal worth $61.5 million.

Polamalu was happy for the 26-year-old Woodley, and said all the right things, but Troy wanted his contract extended. He knew the Steelers would end any negotiations once the plane departed for the opener and he wanted to end his career with the team. After the final preseason game, he walked into Art Rooney II's office to remind him of that objective. Polamalu was healthy and showing well in preseason games, yet the Steelers had not talked to his agent at all. Polamalu was told at this impromptu meeting that after Woodley, the Steelers weren't going to renegotiate anyone else's contract.

This surprised Polamalu, and the surprise turned to anger two days later when they signed 25-year-old Lawrence Timmons to a $50 million contract extension.

That same day, an earthquake registering 5.8 on the Richter Scale rattled the Steelers' practice facility on the South Side of Pittsburgh. Some in the building thought it was a passing train. Brett Keisel joked that Casey Hampton was doing jumping jacks. But it just might've been the anger of Polamalu finding out the Steelers had just extended Timmons.

Troy stormed into the Steelers' front office area and circled the group of secretaries stationed in the common lobby of the front offices as if incited by Kevin Arbet or Keenan McCardell. Polamalu realized he needed to calm down and turned back towards Dick LeBeau's office to seek counsel.

LeBeau did calm him down, a bit, before Polamalu went into Rooney II's office. That's when the Steelers began talking in earnest. A four-year deal worth $36.5 million was eventually reached at the airport before the opener in Baltimore. Polamalu was once again the highest-paid safety in football and the Steelers released a photo of him signing the contract and smiling. But on the inside was a resentment that Polamalu would harbor through the day he retired.

A 35-7 defeat at the hands of the Ravens didn't get the Steelers' defense of their AFC Championship off to a good start, to say the least. The Steelers also lost Bryant McFadden with a recurring hamstring injury.

MCFADDEN: I just fought through it and played as long as possible before checking out of the game early in the fourth quarter. I missed five or six weeks and the defense was playing pretty well. I never really got back to being as healthy as I was before the injury. It was around Christmastime when Troy decided to write me a letter. Man, that letter was unbelievable. The future Hall of Famer, a guy I looked up to not just as a football player but a person, was saying the same things about me that I've said about him, how he admired the way I handled the adversity I endured the entire year. The guys in the secondary knew how disappointed and hurt I was about not being able to get back into the lineup. It seemed like I was being pushed to the side, put on the backburner. But I kept quiet. I handled myself as a professional as best as possible, and Troy acknowledged that – as did a couple other guys who talked to me, but Troy put it in writing. I still have the letter – handwritten, and pretty good handwriting. He told me he admired me, and there were some other things which I won't get into but he basically said how much he appreciated knowing me. I really was shocked.

In Baltimore, the Steelers allowed the Ravens to rush for 170 yards, or 22 more than the Ravens had gained on the ground in three games combined against the Steelers in 2010. Ray Rice led the way with 107 yards to become the first to rush for over 100 yards against the Steelers since ... Ray Rice in 2009.

Rice also kneed Troy Polamalu in the throat for no apparent reason and pulled his hair at the bottom of a pile. Writers didn't see what Rice had done and asked Polamalu later why he flashed his temper in the scrum. Troy smiled and said, "They were talking bad about our reporters."

The agitated Steelers returned the following week with a 24-0 shutout of Seattle on the heels of Warren Sapp's infamous critique that the defense was "old, slow and it's over" on *Inside the NFL*. Individuals drawing most of Sapp's criticism were James Harrison, Hines Ward and Troy Polamalu.

"They've been saying that for four or five years about our defense," said Dick LeBeau. "It's like the guy that got up and said 'This could be the last day of my life.' Sooner or later you're going to be right. But they ain't right yet. I wouldn't kick any dirt on us."

The Seahawks were playing in their second season for Troy's former college coach, Pete Carroll, who had won two national championships and played for a third during his nine-year stint at USC. But Carroll and the Seahawks ran into Polamalu and the Steelers at the wrong time. The Seahawks converted only 17 percent of their third downs, rushed for only 31 yards, and gained only 164. They didn't cross midfield until 10 minutes remained in the game. Carroll could've ended the shutout with a 43-yard field goal late, but had the Seahawks go for it on fourth-and-8, and they failed.

The Seahawks lacked receiving threats, so Polamalu moved up in the box and played a strong game. He was all over the field in leading the Steelers with six solo and eight total tackles. He also had a sack, but was a count too quick in jumping a route and just missed a pick-6.

Was the defense's performance the proper answer to the criticism?

"No," said Larry Foote. "Like Mike T said, that stink gonna be with us for half a season at least."

"If you don't approach each game humbled," said Polamalu, "if you don't approach each game with focus and urgency, we can see what can happen to us."

Next up were the Colts and Kerry Collins, a QB Polamalu timed at the snap like no other. This game was no different. On one pass play, Polamalu broke from 15 yards deep and ran past the line at the snap to bat a third-down pass. He also scored a touchdown on a 16-yard fumble recovery of a Harrison strip-sack in the fourth quarter. But neither of those plays was his best in the Steelers' 23-20 win – according to Ryan Clark.

"The one he missed was my favorite play," Clark said of a Colts running play that actually went for a touchdown. Polamalu nearly intercepted the handoff.

"I would've just tackled the runner," said Clark. "But to be such a playmaker, have such confidence in your abilities, that you feel you can actually reach out and grab the ball – and that's why it was a great play; that's why it was awesome because it's so Troy. I didn't even see what happened. I said, 'What happened Troy?' He said, 'Well I saw the ball and I thought I could grab it out of his hand.' To think that way and to be that type of playmaker, that's the only way you get an opportunity to make the plays that he does."

"I think the last two weeks Troy's been very, very impactful in our defense," said LeBeau.

What about those eight defensive starters age 30 and older?

"You guys spin it how you want it," said Polamalu.

Bill Cowher predicted on his pre-game show that the Steelers would lose to the Texans, "But, J.B., this is still a good football team," he added. "And they will win the AFC North."

Cowher was right on at least the first count. The Texans beat the visiting Steelers 17-10 as Arian Foster rushed for more yardage – 155 – than any back against the Steelers since Curtis Martin had 174 in 2003.

Foster carried 30 times for those 155 yards, 42 of which broke a 10-10 tie with the winning touchdown on a cutback run through Woodley and Polamalu early in the fourth quarter.

Offensively, Roethlisberger was sacked five times and the QB needed crutches to leave the stadium. The Steelers addressed the problem on their offensive line two days later by re-signing a slimmed-down Max Starks to play left tackle. He started the next game, a 38-17 win over the Tennessee Titans. Even with a sprained foot, Roethlisberger was sacked only once and threw five touchdown passes.

The Steelers improved to 4-2 the following week by beating the Jaguars 17-13. Chris Hoke filled in at nose tackle for Casey Hampton, improving his record to 17-1.

"Let's be clear that I don't think it's because of me," said Hoke.

"He's so humble," said Brett Keisel. "Go up and ask him his record, he'll be like, 'Oh, I don't know (pause) *17 and 1!*'"

The win also improved the LeBeau-coordinated Steelers to 12-1 against rookie quarterbacks as Polamalu was up to his old tricks against Jacksonville.

The Steelers had just extended their lead to 17-0 in the second quarter and the Jaguars were putting together their first quality drive of the game with a second-and-6 at the Pittsburgh 24. Polamalu timed the snap and hit rookie QB Blaine Gabbert just as he was throwing off a one-step drop. Polamalu pulled Gabbert down to force a wild incompletion as the center and pulling left guard collapsed onto Gabbert with him.

By now, Polamalu's teammates had become accustomed to such eye-popping timing and intuition, and only James Farrior gave Troy a slight hand slap.

Of course, the play was noticed in the TV booth.

"Is he offsides?" analyst Dan Fouts asked as he examined the replay. "Nope. Just perfect."

The first half of the 2011 season ended with much more promise than it began. First of all, James Harrison was voted the NFL's meanest player and Troy Polamalu the nicest in a poll of players taken by *SI.com*, so clearly the universe was back in proper working order.

At Arizona, Antonio Brown, Mike Wallace and Emmanuel Sanders began to emerge as an explosive trio of receivers in a 32-20 Steelers win. The group with the self-ascribed nickname "Young Money Family" combined to catch 15 passes for 266 yards and two touchdowns.

Tight end Heath Miller, who came out of Virginia with the media-concocted nickname "Big Money" – and pleaded with Pittsburgh reporters not to use it – caught four passes for 59 yards including a 12-yard TD catch to get the Steelers off and running to the win.

Next up were the 5-1 Patriots, a team that's perpetually bedeviled the Steelers, LeBeau and Polamalu. The Bill Belichick/Tom Brady Patriots were 6-1 against the Steelers.

RODNEY HARRISON, *Patriots safety (2003-08)/NBC analyst:* They love the fact that Troy freelances, because 90 percent of the time he guesses right but a lot of times he guesses wrong. The Patriots actually game-plan to attack Troy Polamalu. The Patriots are not afraid of Troy. They'll go at Troy and force him to stay disciplined in coverage.

BILL BELICHICK, *Patriots coach (2000-current):* At times it looks like he might be a little out of position, or maybe it's not even his play to make, but he just has the speed and anticipation to get to a point on the field where the play is. Again, whether that's actually his responsibility or not, he just can feel it coming and anticipate it and his awareness is outstanding. He has tremendous speed and burst and hitting ability. You have to be aware of him on every snap.

TROY POLAMALU: For sure I've had difficulty against Brady. He's won quite a few games against us. What he forces you to do is really be on your keys because he's able to see mistakes, and a lot more clearly than most other quarterbacks – I would say almost any other quarterback. As far as freelancing is concerned, I think that's a common misconception. I have a role in the defense like anybody has.

Dick LeBeau had no comment after the Steelers' 25-17 win over the Patriots, making the game his comment.

"Talk to the players," he said.

The Steelers' defensive coordinator had promised after Brady carved up the Steelers for 350 yards and 39 points the previous year that, "I hope we do get him again. He is a great player but he'll not do the same thing."

LeBeau believed in his players then, and everybody at Heinz Field on Oct. 30 saw why. His defense held the Patriots to a season-low 17 points and 213 yards, and Brady to a season-low 198 yards passing.

"Today we played more man than we've ever played against any team," said Ryan Clark. "I was in the middle of the field one time and I usually look in and say, 'OK, I'm going to go to the guy I'm scared of the most.' And I looked at them and said, 'Well I'm not scared of nobody.'"

Ike Taylor had the difficult task of covering Wes Welker. Taylor, primarily an outside corner, spent much of this day inside with the shifty, savvy Welker, who caught six passes for only 39 yards. Welker would finish the 2011 season with 122 catches and 1,569 yards.

Of course, much of the credit for the defensive success belonged to the offense for possessing the ball 39:22 of the 60 minutes.

"We played three plays in the first quarter," said Clark. "Brett Keisel looked over to me and said, 'Hey, man, I can take this.' I said, 'Yeah, I can play five more years if we play three plays every quarter.'"

"That's our formula to winning," said Polamalu. "It's always been our formula to winning."

The Steelers played without James Farrior and James Harrison, and then lost LaMarr Woodley to a hamstring injury. Woodley had sacked Brady twice and was on his way to a third when he went down as if shot by a sniper.

At that point in the season, Woodley had nine sacks. In his career to that point, Woodley had 53 sacks in 61 starts (counting playoffs), or 0.87 sacks every start.

For the next two-and-a-half seasons, after the injury, the newly signed $62 million man would muster only 0.33 sacks per start before he was released.

The momentum from the satisfying win couldn't be sustained, however. The following week the Steelers lost to the visiting Ravens 23-20.

Leading 20-16 with 2:37 remaining, the Steelers had a chance to extend their lead with a 47-yard field goal attempt, but a delay of game penalty (with two timeouts left) caused Mike Tomlin to send out his punt team, and the Ravens responded with the game-winning touchdown drive.

Joe Flacco hit Torrey Smith on a 26-yard touchdown pass with eight seconds remaining for the gut-punch to the Steelers, giving the Ravens a season sweep of their rivals and a half-game lead in the AFC North.

Polamalu injured a rib during the game, but played the following week in Cincinnati in a critical 24-17 Steelers win that dropped the Bengals to 6-3. The Steelers headed into their bye week 7-3.

In his first start at the Kansas City quarterback, former Pittsburgh high school star Tyler Palko threw three interceptions in a 37-3 loss to New England, after which his coach, Todd Haley, said, "Yeah, and oh, by the way, in your second start you have to play Dick LeBeau, Troy Polamalu and James Harrison."

Palko was game and played a solid if unspectacular game. The former Pitt QB, who had forced Flacco's transfer from Pitt to Delaware, was throwing into the end zone in the final minute before Keenan Lewis' interception secured a 13-9 Steelers win.

Palko was throwing against a Troy Polamalu-less secondary at that point. Polamalu left the Sunday night game after smacking his head on the knee of tackle-turned-fullback Steve Maneri, a 290-pound reserve lineman who had caught a pass in the flat during the game's first series. Polamalu tried to get off the ground but went back down before trainer John Norwig could tend to him. He was held out of the remainder of the game because of "concussion-like symptoms."

Polamalu, of course, lobbied to return to the game – "He always does," said Mike Tomlin – and was cleared to return the following week.

Before the injury, Polamalu had timed another snap to disrupt Palko, and once again timed it perfectly. It occurred the same weekend as a college linebacker, Arizona State's Vontaze Burfict, looked foolish in crashing through an offensive line, clearly offside, in an attempt to imitate the Steelers' star safety.

HEYWARD: The first time it happened when I was on the field, it was Andy Dalton that Troy grabbed out of the snap. I thought it was Larry Foote or Lawrence Timmons behind me, but it was Troy jumping over me, and I'm like, "Troy, let me know." (Laughs) "Troy, I have contain on this. Would you give me just a little inkling of what you're doing? I'll get out of your way. We don't both have to be in the same gap." His response was, "I want to make it look like I wouldn't be coming." Even though I knew that Troy liked to take risks, I was still surprised when Coach LeBeau would go up to him and question what he was doing, and how Troy would say, "I saw it on film." I guess just about everyone's had those conversations with him. He was always accountable, though. He was the firestarter and it was up to us to put out the flames if needed.

Polamalu returned for a special teams-fueled 35-7 thrashing of the Bengals and was asked afterwards if it was "a statement game."

He talked instead about how stacking wins was more important than posting one big blowout win, but the reporter pressed. Finally, Troy just said, "I really don't even know what a statement game means."

A few days later, during a short week in preparation for a Thursday night game against the Browns, news came down that Chris Hoke would undergo neck surgery and join Aaron Smith on season-ending injured reserve.

As championship-level leaders such as Smith and Hoke contemplated retirement, Antonio Brown was becoming part of the next wave.

Coming off his 60-yard punt return for a touchdown to break open the Bengals game, Brown clinched a 14-3 win over the Browns with a 79-yard catch and run for a touchdown with 2:52 left. Brown finished the win over the Browns with five catches for 151 yards, a then-career high.

In that game, Harrison decked Browns QB Colt McCoy in the chest as McCoy stopped what had been an open-field run to throw a pass. Harrison drilled McCoy in the facemask with his helmet and was suspended for the following week.

Polamalu intercepted his 28th career pass to move into a tie with Jack Lambert for ninth place on the team's all-time list. Polamalu was fortunate to have a friend such as Ryan Clark to make the interception possible. Earlier in the game, Clark put Polamalu's shoulder back in place on the sideline.

"He told me to pull it," Clark said. "I looked around to make sure nobody was watching – I forgot about the camera – and I pulled it. People have been tweeting me about it. I guess it's a big deal, but for us, I mean, it was just my brother asking me to do something, so I did it."

Sounds like something Lambert would've done to stay in a Browns game.

Of course, it's unlikely that Polamalu would drink a six-pack of beer and play the Browns again the next day, as Lambert had once offered.

The Steelers went to San Francisco without Harrison or injured center Maurkice Pouncey, and with Ben Roethlisberger immobilized by a foot injury. They lost to the 49ers on a Monday night 20-3.

A couple of power outages at Candlestick Park allowed the suspended Harrison to speak out on his Twitter account:

"If I can't play then can't nobody play – Lights Out!"

Roethlisberger couldn't. Or, better put, he couldn't play very well with his sprained left ankle. He threw three interceptions and was sacked three times in the fourth quarter, one of which resulted in a fumble to set up the 49ers' clinching touchdown.

The 10-4 Steelers bounced back to pummel the 2-12 St. Louis Rams 27-0, during which former Tampa Bay safety John Lynch, the TV analyst, shared these hard truths:

* "James Harrison's not a dirty player. He just hits everyone harder than most people."

* "Troy Polamalu's not only one of the great safeties of all-time, but in my mind one of the greatest football players this league's ever seen."

* "Polamalu and Ryan Clark are providing the best safety play in the NFL. Both players should make the Pro Bowl."

Clark and Polamalu would finish the season 1-2 in tackles for the Steelers, and both made the Pro Bowl, the first for Clark and seventh straight for Polamalu.

The Steelers finished their season 12-4 by beating the Browns 13-9 in a game marked by the 1,000th – and final – catch by the great Hines Ward.

The Steelers were tied with the Ravens for first place, but the Ravens owned the tiebreaker, meaning the Steelers would play in the Wild Card round at Denver, where Ryan Clark could not play, and neither would Maurkice Pouncey, Cortez Allen or Mewelde Moore. LaMarr Woodley did play but was still hobbled by his hamstring injury. Starting running back Rashard Mendenhall had recently joined Aaron Smith and Chris Hoke on injured reserve.

Also, running backs coach Kirby Wilson had been burned badly in an early-morning fire at his home. It was a pale imitation of the Steelers team that went to three Super Bowls in the previous six seasons, and, in a bolt from the blue, they were eliminated by QB Tim Tebow on the first play of overtime.

It was a play oddly foretold by Mike Tomlin at the TV production meeting. Tomlin was asked by play-by-play man Jim Nantz the night before the game whether he would take the ball if the Steelers won a coin toss in overtime.

"You know you are going to get a touchback in the thin air," Nantz told Tomlin. "The odds are you're going to get a punt and all you have to do is get a field goal."

"No way I'm doing that," Tomlin said. "I'm not putting my whole season at risk and giving the other team the football, because if one guy busts an assignment and in one play they go 80 yards and a touchdown, my season is over. I'm not going to let that happen. I'm taking the football."

Tomlin added, "I'm not going to put my season on the line for a 1-play, 80-yard touchdown pass."

Guess what happened?

A 1-play, 80-yard touchdown pass.

Denver won the toss and elected to receive. Shaun Suisham kicked it into the end zone for a touchback, and on first down the Steelers appeared to come with an all-out, cover-zero blitz. Tebow, whose longest TD pass all season was 56 yards, hit Demaryius Thomas, who might still be running.

Game over.

Tomlin said it wasn't a cover-zero (zero defenders deep), that the corners were supposed to "invert" with the safeties.

Another problem was Polamalu's study habits. Ray Horton had talked about how he and Troy would mine tape for "hundred percenters," and encouraged Troy to realize these in real time. The Broncos had a "hundred percenter" in which they ran the ball every time a particular wide receiver motioned into "crack" blocking position at the point of attack.

At every instance throughout regulation, this "hundred percenter" remained such.]Realizing this, Denver coach John Fox in overtime called for the motion, but followed by a pass. It's why Polamalu was out of tackling range on the 80-yard catch and run by Thomas.

Clark, of course, wasn't deep because Tomlin wouldn't let him play in Denver, where he had almost died in 2007. Clark's replacement, Ryan Mundy, didn't exercise the patience of a veteran and jumped at the play-action fake.

Will Gay backed off the ball as an inverted safety, but Ike Taylor didn't. He pressed Thomas at the line, got beat by a step, was shaken while trying to tackle, and Thomas went 80 to make a soothsayer of Tomlin as the 2011 season came to an abrupt end.

CHAPTER 29

COMMIT ALL YOUR ATROCITIES AT ONCE

A dozen players participated in the first three Super Bowls in which the Steelers played this century. After the 2011 season, changes were afoot and by the time of the April draft, five of them were gone.

Chris Hoke was the first to go, retiring in late January, 2012.

Bryant McFadden was released in early February.

On March 2, the Steelers released Hines Ward, and on March 3 they released Aaron Smith and James Farrior.

Brett Keisel heard the news about those final three cuts and took his dog for a walk to let off steam. A skunk sprayed the dog, which seemed like a perfect metaphor for the mood around the team.

It was a bleak time in Pittsburgh. Fans reminisced mainly about Ward and how he once caused the girl friend of an opposing safety to beg for mercy; how he deflected a pick-6 away from Champ Bailey in the AFC Championship Game and held on for a first down, even though John Lynch had delivered a head shot that would've landed James Harrison in prison; about how Ward once scored a touchdown in front of the Dawg Pound and, while wearing his dazzling smile, turned his back and kicked up dirt like a dog covering his crap.

Ward, Smith and Farrior were cornerstones. Their stories are still being told by the two Lombardi Trophies they brought home.

Renewal came as always with the April draft, and the Steelers got a gem when David DeCastro slipped to pick 24 in the first round.

DeCastro was a consensus All-America guard at Stanford, and when offered numbers 61 and 66, he chose Alan Faneca's 66, which seemed appropriate. The new guard brought an old-school mentality that would've fit the previous decade's Faneca-led O-lines, and DeCastro won the starting job at right guard almost immediately.

Protecting Ben Roethlisberger was the primary agenda of a franchise which punctuated that particular mandate by firing offensive coordinator Bruce Arians, who favored deep drops that got the quarterback hit, and hiring Todd Haley, who was tasked with implementing a quick-hitting offense.

DeCastro was a rock, but he wasn't the most enthusiastic interview and sports writers wondered whether the guy would ever open up. He did sidle up to one reporter in the cafeteria who was watching ESPN highlights of the Stanford-Oregon game, one of which won every Pac-12 title from 2009-15.

"Do you guys hate Oregon?" DeCastro was asked.

"Yeah," DeCastro said. "But the team we really hate is USC."

DeCastro wasn't surprised that Troy Polamalu once had a problem with Stanford.

"Yeah, we bantered about that a little bit," DeCastro says with a laugh. "But he grew up in Oregon and I grew up in Seattle so we bonded more over the fact the Pac-12 got so little respect outside of the West Coast. He came up to me the first time I was in the locker room and introduced himself with his soft-spoken voice. Didn't say much, but his aura spoke for itself."

Troy's aura, his personality, was once defined by former USC teammate Lenny Vandermade as "more of an O-lineman's mentality. O-linemen are like mules. You can whip 'em, you can drive 'em, you can give 'em a hard time and they'll keep showing up. That's Troy's mentality."

DeCastro picked up on it right away, agreeing with the assessment of both offensive linemen and why Troy fit in with them.

"That's the way we are," he says. "We're the pack mules. We just put our head down and keep going. You wade through the shit. Even when it's good you just keep your head down and move. That's the best way to be an O-lineman. And it's true, Troy never had any arrogance about him. He always carried himself with the utmost humility. Obviously he didn't need to have arrogance because his play spoke for itself. Everyone respected him. But, yeah, I like that definition of his mentality."

Polamalu introduced himself to another rookie, fourth-round pick Alameda Ta'amu, with a phone call on draft day.

"Polamalu represents the Polynesians, particularly on the West Coast where most of them stayed," Ta'amu said that day. "When he called me I didn't think it was him, but then you hear his voice and you remember those commercials. 'Hey this is Polamalu!' I couldn't believe I was talking to someone so many Samoans look up to. I couldn't hold it in. I had to tweet about it."

Tweeting was how athletes were beginning to communicate directly to fans. That had its upside, but social media was becoming a nuisance to teamwork, as many of the stars of the previous decade would soon find out.

A new wave of young leaders was moving in, and years later some would label it the "culture change." Antonio Brown was part of the new wave. As Mike Wallace held out for an extension of the final year of his rookie contract, the Steelers turned to Brown, who still had two years left on his rookie deal.

Brown was showing superstar potential, but he let it go to his head. Ryan Clark couldn't help but notice. "You're going to create a monster," Clark warned Steelers coaches as the team negotiated with Brown. Later, during the first practice of the 2012 training camp, Clark and Brown fought.

Clark didn't like what Brown was saying to Dick LeBeau, nor did he appreciate Brown yelling "Don't touch me, I'm the franchise" to the defense.

A bigger fight – or series of fights – broke out two weeks later on Family Day. This time it was Brown and Ike Taylor, who had been covering Brown most of camp.

The two had consistently pushed and shoved and talked trash to each other during scrimmages, and fisticuffs finally erupted after Taylor dove over Brown for an interception in the end zone.

Tempers calmed and the team came together at the end of practice. But a second fight erupted following the huddle, and Brown and Taylor had to be separated by general manager Kevin Colbert.

With Clark inciting the pair, Taylor and Brown squared up for a third fight, but Troy Polamalu stepped in and calmed Brown as they walked off the field.

DAVID GILREATH, *Steelers wide receiver (2012):* One story I remember well was about Troy Polamalu in training camp. There was a big fight between the wide receivers and defensive backs. A big brawl. As everyone was fighting I heard this real quiet voice behind me saying, "Scottie (Montgomery, WRs coach) - nobody's safe Scottie," just in this real quiet voice in the middle of the brawl. I still laugh thinking about that.

BRETT KEISEL: A.B. was just turning on the greatness juice and we were a hardened, veteran group, and we wanted to be respected and talked to as such, especially our leader. You never said anything to or about Dick LeBeau. Ever. You just didn't cross that line. It would happen other times, maybe LeBeau would say something about the defense in the course of a play during training camp and someone would pipe something back to him. Whoa, it was like getting swarmed by a bees nest. This was a similar situation. I think LeBeau was trying to break it up and Antonio took offense and said something back, and, yeah, those boys are going to snap.

RYAN CLARK: He said something to Coach LeBeau during practice the day he got his money. We were doing one-on-ones and I believe it was Keenan Lewis who was getting a little handsy with him. And he's like "Don't touch me. I'm the franchise." Cussing people out. And Coach LeBeau tried to stop him, tell him, "Hey, man, that's not what we do here, it's not that type of team, not the type of practice." And he screamed and cursed at Coach LeBeau. We just all pretty much lost it.

GILREATH: And then the next play Troy flies in and hits the running back and knocks him out. That's when I knew he was the real deal.

CLARK: The rest of the practice was just intense. I'll be honest, I forgot that we were playing our own team. Troy sacked Ben that day. He took him to the ground. The fact that Troy was with me on that day made me feel better about it, because I know he's not one to be quick to react. But that was who we were, at least defensively. We always felt that if there was ever a game that we had to face our offense, they would be in a whole helluva lot of trouble. So for us, it was time to prove it. I think that day just triggered that in us, like, all right, y'all wanna see? You think you're the franchise? You think this new contract makes you more important than the men who play on the other side? And the man who calls the plays? We'll see. What was crazy is nothing was said about it. Like, Troy didn't come to the sideline and say, "When they call cover-3 I'm going to blitz and if I get to Ben I'm going to throw him to the ground." He just did it. The emotions were high.

JAMES HARRISON: Our brotherhood was stronger than the game. It was stronger than the organization. We cared about each other. And the fact that we cared about each other made it mean that much more to you to go out there and do the things necessary for all to succeed, for your brother to succeed. And when you truly care about that individual, it's a lot different. That's how it was with Dick LeBeau. You had love for Dick LeBeau. It was love. You're not going to let anyone talk bad about him.

KEISEL: I remember reporters asking me, "Is this a new culture?" We would never admit that during that time. At least I never admitted it. I didn't want to feel like our identity had changed. I didn't believe that in such a short amount of time that thing could switch like that. But, it had. I mean, I feel like it really changed early on. When you lose a mountain like Aaron, who was dominant for so long and such a fixture that really didn't get the credit for how dominant he was, and you lose your captain, Farrior, who makes all the playcalls, who does everything on defense, and we've got new guys coming in on offense, you could just feel things changing. There just weren't the same guys around all of the sudden. How could we keep the standard the same? We all struggled to have that feeling of dominance again because it wasn't there. It was hard to swallow that.

CHRIS HOKE: Our defensive line had a certain culture, and when you start losing those leaders, and your leaders become Antonio Brown, Le'Veon Bell, that's when the culture changes. The culture changes when Hines Ward leaves, right? And that's around the time when Aaron Smith and the older guys – me, Keisel, Casey – left. Those are four guys who had been around for a decade-plus and did it a certain way. Luckily the defensive line room had Cam Heyward to carry the torch. It wasn't like that in the receiver room.

CAMERON HEYWARD: I was so fortunate my first two years because I literally just shut up and listened. These guys had been to the top of the mountain and back, so I wanted to just pick their brains. These dudes had won Super Bowls and played in multiple Super Bowls. But guys change. I don't know if it was necessarily a culture change. I always thought our culture's been strong. It gets tested.

KEISEL: Call it culture change, call it rebuilding, just know that it's hard to get old in the NFL. It's hard to get old and not be able to move like you once could and not be able to make the plays that you once made. But it is unavoidable.

HOKE: The game's changed. Not just the culture. The game's changed. It's become more about me, me, me. Social media's changed the game. Ugly. Social media's changed life in an ugly way.

HARRISON: Even when Jason Gildon was there with Joey Porter, it was a brotherhood and guys cared about each other. Nowadays, it's more about the likes and the follows. Social media has killed the game. It's killed the brotherhood of the game.

MARCEL PASTOOR: Social media has definitely hurt this. Growing up, you're a sports fanatic. You remember watching your heroes. You talk about Heath and Hamp and Troy, you're talking about great athletes on the field. If these guys had social media, well, I would like to think it wouldn't have changed them.

HEYWARD: The culture only works when you're winning. You're not able to foster that unless you're winning. But I think we have a good stable group right now (2020). I feel like Pittsburgh has always been the place where if you do the right things and you're able to accomplish what you want on the field, you can keep that group together and build that culture. I think we're stepping back in the right direction in that approach.

Columnist and talk-show host Joe Starkey was one of the top chroniclers of Troy Polamalu throughout his career. He did a probing interview of Polamalu in June of 2012, and the safety bemoaned the loss of so many stalwart players. "More than any other year, the face of this franchise has changed," Polamalu told Starkey. "We lost a lot of great leadership."

The two went deeper into a variety of topics, but leadership was the critical theme for the 31-year-old Polamalu in 2012.

Yes, he showed up for OTAs in possibly the worst shape of his playing career – overweight and stiff in the spring of 2012 – but he showed up, and that was a first for him since 2008.

"It's my turn to be around the team a little more," Polamalu said after Mike Tomlin asked him to come to the volunteer workouts.

By the start of training camp, Polamalu was in better shape. He took off his last few pounds by playing soccer in the mornings with a group of kids, and would run sprints after practices as one of the last to leave the field.

Polamalu was the NFL's Most Liked Player, according to a fan survey done by *Forbes* magazine. And he could still play at a first-team All-Pro level. After being so honored for the fourth time in 2011, Polamalu was graded by *Pro Football Focus* as having had the Nos. 2, 3 and 7 top coverage games of 2011 by a safety, and the Nos. 1, 2 and 8 top games in run defense.

Polamalu was clearly a team leader who was still playing at an elite level. Only Hampton and Keisel had more tenure with the Steelers.

Here's Polamalu in the summer of 2012 on a few important topics:

Leadership:

"I wouldn't say that I was asked to be a leader, or that I am a leader at all. I don't think that I've really changed my role within the team. I came to OTAs but there shouldn't be any big deal made of the fact that I came to practice (laughs). But, I don't think I've changed at all. I haven't made it an effort to be vocal or anything like that. I think more guys have been asking me for advice, and I give them as much as I can."

Conditioning:

"I guess if football was played in the spring I would be in shape then. But it's not. Football's played in the fall and the winter. I could probably work out twice as hard in the offseason and no body fat would come off. When you get toward football season, my body starts really adjusting and starts having a certain energy to get in shape and the fat burns off easier. It's because I've been doing this since I was in fifth grade."

Older and slower:

"I'm starting to wonder who's actually old and slow, because from the starting defense of our first Super Bowl, it's only me and Casey left. Maybe when we're gone we'll be young and enthusiastic."

Popularity:

"I wouldn't care if no one remembered me after I'm gone. I really wouldn't mind living a life where I go unnoticed in everything and anything I do."

MYRON ROLLE, *Steelers safety (2012)/neurosurgeon:* I met Troy at Chris Hope's wedding while I was with the Titans, then we reconnected with the Steelers. He started asking me about the Rhodes Scholarship and some of the things I studied, and I got into some of those more metaphysical issues and the conversations took off after that. I loved spending time with him. He would bring up a topic, "Myron, what do you think about existentialism?" "Myron, what do you think about universal truth vs. relative truth?" And we would get into it a little bit before or after practice. Yeah, he has a wonderful mind. He's brilliant and I loved talking to him because he always gave me his true, strong opinion. It wasn't jaded one way or the other, nor did he bend it because I may have felt a certain way. I appreciated it. I think we both grew and our ideologies both developed by doing that.

PASTOOR: When we would stretch, before Hamp came over to stretch, Troy would sit there on his I-pad, or his I-touch, or one of the original I-phones, and we would search Wikipedia on the most random thing we could pick out. When was Buddhism created? Something like that, something completely off the wall. Religion was always a good question, but we would always try to learn something new for the day. Later in his career, when maybe our eyeballs were telling us he was slower, he was able to study more and watch film more. Towards the end of stretch he would be talking about if they do this, I'll do this. And he would be watching film on his I-pad instead of Googling. But that goes with most of the guys who are elite athletes or 10-12 years into their career. They just figure they may not have that step they used to, but if they can lean a little bit this way they can make up for it. He was still a big kid, though. When I was stretching Hamp, Hamp would be on his back looking around to find out where Troy is because Troy's either going to come up and give him a wrestling move, an elbow drop, or just come up and scare him.

The Steelers were in revenge mode for the opener in Denver, but the extra motivation didn't help. Neither did the infusion of youth on defense. Ryan Clark didn't travel to Denver and James Harrison was out with a knee injury, so seven new defenders cut the age of the starters from the previous season by 41 years. But it didn't help against Peyton Manning in a 31-19 loss. Manning's 129.2 passer rating would be the best of the season against the Steelers.

In a theme that would be repeated throughout the season, Heath Miller was the Steelers' best player. On the first snap he drove linebacker Wesley Woodyard into the dirt, then was asked to block Von Miller one-on-one, and did. Heath caught four passes for 50 yards and a touchdown, including conversions on third-and-18 and third-and-7.

The Steelers' "dink and dunk" offense of Todd Haley's design got off the ground the next week in a 27-10 win over the Jets, allowing the

Steelers to utilize the passing of Ben Roethlisberger while possessing the ball and running clock, which allowed the defense to rest. But another disastrous loss at Oakland and a loss at Tennessee left the Steelers 2-3, and Troy Polamalu once again was hobbled with a calf issue that was becoming an annual issue. He missed Games 2-3, returned for Game 4, but hopped off the field in the first quarter and was on the shelf until Game 12 at Baltimore.

By that point, the Steelers were coming off a loss to the 2-8 Browns and, at 6-5, had fallen three games behind the Ravens in the AFC North race.

Polamalu didn't discount the basic sports physiology that says the right ankle/calf problem developed through compensation from the left knee injury back in 2009. But he wasn't about to adjust a training regimen that was built around the principle of strength emanating up from the foot – even though lower leg injuries had become his primary struggle throughout the back half of his career.

PASTOOR: I agreed with his philosophy to an extent. I thought the barefoot training was great. I know he wore the five-finger Vibram shoes for a long time and did a lot of his training that way. But as far as conditioning and on-field work, what's the difference in our sport vs. basketball? We wear cleats. If you want to be a great football player – and I agree there is so much intrinsically on the feet itself and the actual grabbing and using your toes efficiently, and the arch of your foot in supporting – but if you're not actually putting cleats on and running in the ground, your posterior chain's going to fail, meaning everything on the back side: glutes, hamstrings, calves, Achilles.

Hindsight's 20-20, so you can ask whether more offseason training in cleats would've changed the results. You want to say yes for your own mentality of strengthening and conditioning and the years of being in the business. Then again, you don't know. Anything can happen at any given time, and usually there's a cause and effect, whether it be from a nutritional value, a supplement value, a physical value, biological. The thing is, a rope is only so strong for so long. If it's a bull rope and one thread comes off, it's not a big deal. But as that rope starts dwindling and the strings start coming apart, that rope isn't a rope anymore.

Polamalu returned for a 23-20 win over the Ravens that kept the Steelers in the race for a wild-card berth. Charlie Batch, the 38-year-old backup, started in place of the injured Roethlisberger and directed the win.

Once again, the game ball went to Miller, who dove and reached for the pylon with the ball to score the tying touchdown in the fourth quarter. It's become the iconic play of Heath's great career. The Steelers got the ball again and drove for a 42-yard field goal as time expired.

The 7-5 Steelers were alive – for a week.

Ike Taylor was the NFL iron man at cornerback, having played 135 consecutive games, but the streak came to an end when he broke his ankle against the Ravens.

Replacing him against the San Diego Chargers was Cortez Allen opposite regular starter Keenan Lewis. Curtis Brown replaced Allen as the nickel back, DeMarcus Van Dyke became the first sub, and the Steelers promoted Josh Victorian from the practice squad.

It wasn't exactly LeBeau, Lem Barney, Yale Lary and Night Train Lane back there. Both Brown and Victorian were victimized by Philip Rivers in the Chargers' 34-24 upset win at Heinz Field. Brown was benched during the deciding 17-play Chargers drive that put them up 20-3 in the third quarter, and his replacement, Victorian, was beaten for the touchdown that ultimately knocked the Steelers to 7-6.

The Steelers remained in the thick of the wild-card race, but the vibe around the practice facility was anything but "Here we go!" as the team faced its December homestretch.

"Look back behind you," said Maurice Matthews, the personable cook at the UPMC Rooney Sports Complex. "Look back over where you were sitting and tell me this: Where are the pretty media ladies?"

The media tables were instead populated by pot-bellied, middle-aged white men gasping and wheezing over their lunches. They were Pittsburgh's sports writing fraternity in late 2012.

"This time two years ago," Moe said with a sweeping hand, "this place was full of beautiful news babes. Now, this."

It was as good a barometer as any as to how well – or poorly – the club was doing.

"Ain't that the truth," said Moe.

Troy Polamalu was back flying around the field in Week 15, looking like the Polamalu of old, but the Steelers lost in overtime to the Dallas Cowboys.

The offense was still struggling under Todd Haley, and it bottomed out the following week in a 13-10 loss to Cincinnati that effectively ended the Steelers' season.

Roethlisberger was critical of the playcalling after the loss to the Cowboys, but came back two days later and apologized to Haley, Mike Tomlin and Art Rooney II. After the loss to the Bengals, Roethlisberger blamed himself for throwing a pick-6 for the Bengals' touchdown at Heinz Field.

Roethlisberger wasn't helped by the loss of Heath Miller, who suffered a devastating knee injury while blocking in-line during a run play just before the two-minute warning of a tied game.

Miller was helped off the field by Brett Keisel and assistant trainer Ryan Grove and was finished for the season. He ended with a team-high 71 receptions and career highs in yardage (816) and touchdowns (8).

A few days later, teammates voted Miller the Steelers' Most Valuable Player for the season. There was even thought in some corners that Heath could win a humble-off against Polamalu.

That had been heretofore unheard of to those who covered Polamalu since his arrival in Pittsburgh. But even Troy thought it might be true.

Troy Polamalu, December 27, 2012

Why is humility so important to people like you and Heath?
Oh, man. I don't know if it's a syndrome or a cancer but there's kind of an uprising of a more egotistical, ego-centric athlete in sports, the selfish athlete who's looking out for himself and is money-centered, really avaricious. Heath would be better to talk to about this. Heath to me is someone who's innately humble. He doesn't struggle to be humble.
How important is humility to you?
Well spiritually it's obviously very important, but it's important in sports that everybody has a role, and sometimes you humbly have to accept it as a follower. Sometimes you have to humbly accept it as a leader. A lot of guys I think struggle with it but I always think, "Well, what is it that drives you to be better?" What drives you to be better is you understand that people are better than you, and that's a point of humility. That's what makes you work harder. That's what makes you study harder. But

when you let arrogance seep into your game and say "I'm the best," then you don't struggle at getting better at all, which in turn doesn't help anybody on this team.

Was there a turning point for you in this regard?
I don't know. It's innate within our culture to be humble all the time, especially in the youngest of the children in both my family and my adopted family. But, I don't know. It's not only humility. It's also meekness and just being reserved within yourself.

Heath is special in that regard, isn't he?
Yes. Heath is humility in its purest form. He's just a naturally humble guy who from the outside doesn't look like he struggles with it.

Do you?
Oh, yeah. If people could read my thoughts they would say that I'm probably the most arrogant guy. Self-deprecation, they say, is a great spiritual exercise when people start puffing you up. That's why I don't read the paper or anything like that. I don't like to read things that are good or bad about myself because they both affect me.

You hate giving speeches after winning awards, and Heath is like that. His mother said he tanked being valedictorian in high school when he found out he had to give a speech.
(Laughs) In orthodoxy I read a lot of stories of saints, and that's like a story from a saint. You hear of a saint that's got the most beautiful voice but won't sing because he doesn't want to be praised for it.

Doesn't God want you to fulfill your talents? Doesn't that please God?
How can you know God without having a humble disposition or humility? In that sense, that's what I would feel God wants, that sort of relationship. And how can you know that without humility? And if you sacrifice something that's your greatest gift, as God sacrificed, that's the ultimate act of humility.

HEATH MILLER: Years ago, someone showed me that interview, so I know what you're talking about. But wouldn't that be the perfect answer from the guy who's really the more humble? (Laughs) I was so fortunate to come to a team with so many guys that I could look up to, who I felt were great players but more importantly were great people. And I would say at the top of that list was Troy. For him to be such an unassuming person, such a normal guy on your daily interactions that you would never realize how great he was on the football field until you saw him play. For me that was something I always admired about him. It was something I always looked up to and tried to emulate. How would Troy handle this situation? So, for me, the comment he made was probably the exact opposite because he was the one I was learning from. Obviously, I have a similarly quiet demeanor. I don't like a lot of attention. That's not comfortable to me, as a person, but in the NFL it's quite easy to start to think highly of yourself. So, to stay grounded and to watch someone who's the best player – one of the best players on our team, probably the best safety in the league, probably one of the best defensive players in the league – and to see how he stays grounded, with the graciousness that he has, was just awesome for me to see.

BRYANT MCFADDEN: That's a really good question: Who was more humble, Heath or Troy? Well, I played against Heath in the ACC every year, and Heath never said anything on the field. He was just quiet. I was like, "How can a guy be so good and not say anything?" Then, when I met him in person in Pittsburgh, the same thing. He just went out and did his job and didn't say anything. He had that little fist pump when he made a good play, and that was it. (Sigh) You have me right there. Who's the most humble? I'm going to have to agree with Troy, that it was Heath.

PASTOOR: I talk to my kids about this. They're younger so they only know Troy off the field. But I tell them Troy is no different than Heath Miller and Larry Fitzgerald. If Heath scores – like that ridiculous touchdown he scored against Baltimore where he's literally parallel to the ground and he gets up and he's excited and he tosses the ball to the ref – Heath would show his excitement for a split second but then it's done. He's back to being Heath. Heath was the godfather. Nobody messed with Heath because Heath's never showed anything. I'm going to agree with B-Mac. Heath was more humble. But the only reason we honestly say that is because if you were good with Troy, he would show personality. Heath had personality, but he just didn't show you that.

HEYWARD: This is a story Troy probably wouldn't want me to say, but we were playing the Bengals and it's chippy and they're doing stuff after the play, and Troy doesn't usually respond. This one time Troy responded and went a little bit extra with Domata Peko, and Troy got a free shot. Everybody knows Troy as being quiet and reserved, but he hits him and Peko's like, "Troy, you're better than that." I remember talking about it with Troy after and he said, "Yeah, I had to have some words with myself because that was out of character." That told me a lot about Troy's humility.

MILLER: Oh, of course, Troy had a bit of an edge about him. Yes. But I think everyone who plays football has to have a little bit of an edge. It's not a natural thing to put your body through what we did to play. And I think his edge comes from his passion for the game, his passion for his teammates, and his passion for wanting to be the best. That's what you saw on Sundays. During the week you had to watch closely to see it. That's one of the things that I admired so much about him.

CHAPTER 30

WOE TO THE MONK WHO BECOMES FAMOUS

Troy Polamalu made the first interception of the 2012 spring OTAs after showed up in much better shape than the previous spring. The rest of the team couldn't say the same.

The Steelers lost five of their last seven games in 2012 and had anything but momentum going into 2013. A Week 4 trip to London was viewed as a massive distraction in their attempt to dethrone the Baltimore Ravens as not only divisional champs but world champs.

The Steelers lost two more mainstays from their great defense in James Harrison and Casey Hampton.

Harrison was released by the team as it struggled to get under the salary cap. That was also the reason given for why the Steelers re-signed backup nose tackle Steve McLendon instead of Hampton after his contract had expired.

Childhood friends Mike Wallace and Keenan Lewis also left in free agency. Wallace had stamped his release the previous summer when he turned down the contract offer that Antonio Brown accepted. Lewis, the starting cornerback opposite Ike Taylor, was deemed expendable because of the potential of young corner Cortez Allen.

Heath Miller was walking without a limp in the spring, but still had a long way to go before his knee would be healthy enough to play.

Ryan Clark was also coming off an injury. He suffered a severe quad contusion in the final game of 2012, but returned in 2013 as a first-time captain.

RYAN CLARK: After the last game in 2012, I had to stay in the hospital overnight, so our kids stayed with Troy and Theodora. We have three kids. The next day, she doesn't even bring them home and they stay another night. Then they come home and they have all of this stuff, all of these bags of clothes and different things. We asked them what happened. She ended up taking my kids shopping. While they were shopping, they would say, "Hey I would love to get that jacket for dad for Christmas." She buys the jacket for me, too, and so my kids come inside with all this stuff and we're like, "No no no no no, you can't do that, no Thea." She was like, "No, this is family. This is what we do."

In the draft, the Steelers took an older, lighter and slower outside linebacker in the first round – 24-year-old Jarvis Jones, who weighed 20 pounds less than LaMarr Woodley and at 4.92 in the 40 was possibly two steps slower. But the Steelers struck gold in the second round with running back Le'Veon Bell. He impressed the defensive players early in training camp.

"He's the real deal," said Taylor. "We've already got Red(man), Dwyer. We know what them boys can do. Le'Veon has the size of both of them, got feet like Jerome, and he's got power like Red and Dwyer. Every time he runs and somebody gets some kind of contact on him, he's still falling forward. With his agility, that's a good mix."

Polamalu reported for training camp in even better shape, and was enthusiastic about the progress made on his problematic right calf after working with new therapist Alex Guerrero, who would go on to some degree of infamy in New England as Tom Brady's personal therapist/coach/guru. Guerrero attacked the scar tissue in Polamalu's right calf and Troy was pleased with the results.

"They are most definitely a thing of the past," Polamalu said of the leg injuries that caused him to miss 22 games in the previous four seasons. And he was right. Polamalu would play in all 16 games in 2013 and returned to the Pro Bowl for the eighth and final time. Which isn't to say the year went well for the team.

The Steelers lost five of their last seven in 2012, all four preseason games in 2013 and the opening four games of the 2013 season. That added up to 3-13 over their last "full season" of ball.

Was the ride over?

"The screen and the running game are ruining the team! You had better address it!" shouted a man with a thick British accent from the back of a tour bus to Stonehenge. It was directed at a reporter who had mentioned the name Todd Haley to his wife.

With London calling it this way, imagine the talk shows back in Pittsburgh!

The Steelers fell to 0-4 with the 34-27 loss in London to the Vikings, who sacked Ben Roethlisberger five times and got a 70-yard touchdown pass from quarterback Matt Cassel and a 60-yard touchdown run by Adrian Peterson.

"We're the worst team in the league," said Roethlisberger.

DAVID DECASTRO, *Steelers guard (2012-current):* Now, 2013, that year sucked. It sucked. I'd like to forget that year. It's tough starting 0-4. You just put your head down and keep coming to work and try not to lose faith. That's easier said than done. I've had a couple four-game losing streaks. Not too many but they're not fun. It's tough but that's part of being a professional. As you get older you've been through it before so you know how to handle it. You keep giving the same effort no matter the record. That's what makes you a professional. You watch leaders and how they handle it. We still only missed the playoffs by six inches, right? A missed field goal.

Mike Tomlin made three lineup changes after returning from London. He moved second-year offensive lineman Kelvin Beachum to left tackle in place of Mike Adams; Cameron Heyward to left defensive end in place of Ziggy Hood; and Will Gay to the cornerback spot opposite Ike Taylor in place of Cortez Allen.

The moves, along with the return to health of Heath Miller, helped the Steelers settle down and win two of their next four.

The team also became accustomed to life without injured starters Maurkice Pouncey and Larry Foote. The latter problem was helped by moving Troy Polamalu back to dimebacker in sub-packages.

The Steelers ran off a 6-2 second half to finish 8-8 for the second consecutive season.

DECASTRO: Just sticking with it. The attitude remained professional. That's the thing with the Steelers; no one gives up. There's a lot of pressure in the city but I think that's good. It's a great place to play, knowing people care. You go to the grocery store and get yelled at about what happened on Sunday, but it's great being in a city like that. You know they're watching and I think everyone takes pride in that.

JERRICHO COTCHERY, *Steelers wide receiver (2011-13):* I've been around total chaos, and this organization was far from that. Total chaos is losing games and also dealing with drama. And at other places you don't just have one story flying around, you have multiple stories flying around and guys can't stop talking about any of it. They talk about it in the locker room, they talk about it around the lunch table. That's chaos that enters the room, and everybody's on everybody's mind. But I didn't see that in Pittsburgh. Not even at 0-4. Guys were just like, "We've got to work. We've got to get better." Even after getting blown out in New England (55-31), guys were the same way, "Get back to work."

CLARK: Guys made plays. Troy was phenomenal down the stretch. Cameron Heyward played a huge role up front in stopping the run and also pressuring the quarterback. Look at things Jason Worilds was able to do. I think people grew into their roles and kind of came along into what the 2013 Pittsburgh Steeler defense needed from them. And that was a process for us, with losing Larry and trying to figure out where to plug guys in. We had our ups and downs. It wasn't the dominance you're used to seeing from us, but it was good enough to win a lot of games down the stretch.

A couple of Polamalu's more spectacular plays occurred against Cleveland. Troy was blocked on a blitz, turned around, saw the running back had the ball, stripped it and recovered it to set up a field goal before halftime. Troy's strip-sack of Brandon Weeden in the fourth quarter sealed the 27-11 win.

Against Miami, Polamalu returned an interception 19 yards for a touchdown that gave the Steelers a 21-17 lead in the third quarter. He came close to making another classic Polamalu play by bringing out a missed 52-yard field goal from deep in the end zone. The Dolphins forced him to lateral, and then tackled Taylor across midfield at the Miami 41.

"We were an ankle tackle away from some open grass and a probable touchdown," said Tomlin.

CLARK: You're talking about Troy. For somebody that was human those would be great plays, but for him that was nothing. It's sad to say, but I think we've gotten desensitized to it. If another guy makes one of those plays, you think it's amazing. If another guy jumps over the line for the first time, you think it's amazing. We've seen him do it five times. If another guy scoops the ball off the ground with one hand, in the snow, we think to ourselves, "Oh, I can't believe that person made that play." If Troy does it, you shake his hand, pat him on the helmet, sit down with him and pray.

The 7-8 Steelers entered the final game of the regular season against the visiting Browns needing a win to finish among five teams tied for the sixth and final playoff spot, and then they needed a lot more help. But one by one, things were falling into place:

* The Steelers smothered the Browns, 20-7;

* The Bengals defeated the Ravens;

* The Jets won at Miami.

That evening, all the Steelers needed was a Chiefs win in San Diego. Troy and the defense's two captains were asked if they would watch the game:

"As soon as you guys quit asking me questions," said Brett Keisel.

"No, my son's in the championship game of a basketball tournament," said Clark.

"Ah, no," said Troy.

They missed anguish and more poor officiating from Bill Leavy. The Chiefs missed a 41-yard field goal that would've sent the Steelers to the playoffs, and Leavy "kicked" two calls. He negated a Chiefs touchdown in overtime by declaring that forward progress had stopped, when it clearly had not. And on the missed field goal, seven Chargers lined up on one side of the ball, an illegal ploy. The Steelers were told to expect an apology from the league.

But there would be next year, and the aforementioned defensive leaders fully intended to return. Only Ryan Clark would not.

CHAPTER 31

THE LAST RIDE

Before Ryan Clark left in free agency in March of 2014, he told ESPN's *First Take* that he knew "guys on my team who smoke (marijuana)."

Some of that has come to be expected of athletes coping with pain. Clark guessed that was the reason, but he never would've guessed the athletes were coping with pain on their way to the airport for a team flight.

Clark didn't know LeGarrette Blount, who signed after Clark had left. But Clark no doubt recognized the name Le'Veon Bell in news reports that he and Blount were pulled over in a Pittsburgh suburb for smoking on their way to the airport for a preseason game in Philadelphia.

That game would be remembered for more than the hijinks of the "Doobie Brothers," as Troy Polamalu's career wound down with his first and only season as a Steelers captain.

RYAN SCARPINO: I was at the team dinner scrolling through Twitter and I was just like, "Ah, here we go." I remember wondering how you can do that and get on a plane and not be able to smell it, but, hey, man, that was above my pay grade.

BRETT KEISEL: Yeah, that was just what the hell.

CAMERON HEYWARD: That was the game Troy called everybody out. We were losing to Philadelphia. Man, they blew us out. It was a preseason game but Troy called everybody out: "We've got guys from all over. Ohio State, all these different places, and we're just not getting the job done, Coach LeBeau." And when he went that route, I was like, "Oh, yeah, we've got to start stepping it up."

SCARPINO: The actual game was an escape from the PR nightmare of having your star running backs pulled over on the way to the airport.

But the Eagles were just going up and down the field on the first-team defense. It was just a bad, bad night for the defense, and you know how important that third preseason game is; the first team gets its reps. It was really hot and humid, just a bad night. And LeBeau was talking to the group, and you could tell that the defense just wasn't interested. I remember looking over because I always stood by the phones and that's where the defense was. I saw Troy out of the corner of my eye pick up a helmet. I don't even know if it was his helmet, but I had never ever seen him this mad. I think Willie Gay grabbed him, but he was going to swing this at somebody. I don't know who he was going to swing it at, but he was just so pissed. I don't know if it was because people weren't listening to Coach LeBeau. I think he was just pissed in general.

Right before they went on the field for the next series, he was in a group with Cam Heyward. Troy started pointing and poking in people's chest and was like "You're Cameron Heyward! You're from Ohio State!" And he was going down the line calling people out. Preseason or not, this dude does not care. He has one standard and that's excellence at all times. Cam was in the league a couple years and he was always a leader, but Troy was still the man and he was calling it out. "You're Lawrence Timmons! You're from Florida State!" I was like, damn, this guy. Nobody said a word during this. They just took it. This dude was not having it.

The Eagles led 17-0 at halftime and put their second team on the field for the second half. The Steelers continued playing their first-teamers, and the Eagles scored touchdowns on their first two possessions to increase their lead to 31-7. The final score was 31-21.

David Johnson tore an ACL in the game, too, but it wasn't a complete disaster for the Steelers. During the playing of the national anthem, Mike Tomlin looked across the field to the Eagles' sideline and noticed a 6-9, 300-pound defensive end with his hand over his heart singing proudly.

When Captain Alejandro Villanueva was released a few weeks later, Tomlin and the Steelers swooped in, claimed him and moved him to offensive tackle. Tomlin later cited seeing Villanueva sing the anthem as the genesis of his interest. Villanueva became the team's starting left tackle just over a year later.

The Steelers had bigger problems with their defense. Even Polamalu expected the coaches to point at him for the unit's failures in Philadelphia.

"I expect to get yelled at," a nervous Polamalu said before entering the meeting room for film review. "I spent the whole yesterday telling myself, 'Listen. Be humble. Get better.'"

That kind of accountability caused teammates to vote Polamalu defensive captain a week later.

CHRIS HOKE, *Steelers DL coaching intern:* He got more vocal late in his career, more so on the sideline. Something would happen, we'd give up a drive, and Troy would go over and do his little prayer first and then come down the line and say stuff. He was more encouraging than anything, and people would listen. Sometimes guys would come down and yell and scream and you would just kind of look down at the ground. But when Troy talked, you listened.

HEATH MILLER: He felt he needed to do that as we got older. It was what the team needed.

DAVID DECASTRO: He was similar to the Heath Miller type – quiet and his aura spoke for him. I always respected that. I'm not much of a talker, either; the play speaks for itself. A guy like that is not going to give you the big rah-rah speech. That's not their personality, but he was well-deserving of being a captain. Everyone respected him and the way he played the game, and ultimately that's what matters when you're captain: How you played the game.

HEYWARD: He was slow to speak but quick to hear. He was a guy who always gauged the room. He led by example most of the time but there were times he had to step back and talk. I watched, listened and learned, because to have that approach was different for me. I've always been the guy who has to be more hands-on sometimes. But there are times I feel I had to learn from Troy in that approach and just let things play out a little bit. You can't always have an answer for everything.

IKE TAYLOR: You know, wise men, all they do is listen. They barely talk. But when they talk, they're dropping gold nuggets. That's Troy. When Troy talked, everybody listened, including the coaches.

CRAIG WOLFLEY: The greatest thing that stands out about Troy is his humility and his commitment to being a humble servant of others. You don't find that with the players today. People just don't have that attitude. I'm sure the whole Hall of Fame thing, deep down in, if you ask him, he might say "I'm not worthy of it."

SCARPINO: The team was getting younger in 2014. Ryan Shazier had his music up and Troy walked over and turned it off. Mark Kaboly wrote about it. Troy was doing an interview and Shazier was a rookie and he had his music really loud. Ben had shut it off before. But Ben's in the far diagonal corner from Troy, so Troy stopped his interview, walked over and just turned it off. He walked back over like nothing happened. Troy was older and Ryan was a rookie, so Ryan knew no more music.

MARK KABOLY, *Steelers beat writer (2003-current):* I was talking to Troy and boy they were playing some music. It was Shazier's rookie year and he was four or five stalls down. Troy couldn't hear, and in mid-sentence said, "Excuse me." He walked over, brushed right past Shazier and just turned down the music. He came back and said, "OK, where were we?" Shazier looked around and said, "Whoa, he shut down the club." It never happened again. A couple years later they brought in some defensive lineman from the Chargers. Not Cam Thomas. It was that really bad defensive end they signed for a year, right around that era, a real slap-ass. He was a little bit too excited to be there, and he was blasting music until Ben came over and just shut it down. Shazier looked at him and said, "Don't worry, buddy. I've been there before."

SCARPINO: There was absolutely a change in that locker room. When I came there in 2010, they had those vets. Maurkice Pouncey was a rookie in 2010 and now he is that leader. 2014 is when there was a change. Once the young defensive backs were taking pictures with their shirts off and Troy said, "Hold on a second I have to take my shirt off for a picture." He was being sarcastic, of course.

KABOLY: We heard a bunch of commotion in the middle of the room, where all the defensive backs and linebackers took their shirts off and were posing for a picture. Troy said with that soft voice, "Excuse me, but I've got to take my shirt off and pose for a picture." He deadpanned for about 30 seconds and started laughing. He didn't go over.

SCARPINO: The locker room was totally different than it was and he was poking fun at his own teammates. None of those young defensive backs had ever won anything and we're talking about a two-time Super Bowl champion, future Hall of Famer laughing at how his own group was behaving. He was so sarcastic. His presence was supernatural, so when he made a joke like that it was extra funny because you didn't expect it. He had great timing. Not only could he time a play, he could really time up a joke.

KEISEL: Troy never came off as the typical captain type. He has great ideas, but he likes being his own guy.

MIKE TOMLIN: We never needed more from him in that regard because we weren't devoid of leadership. Sometimes, when you're devoid of leadership, you're looking for it. That's when you may ask somebody to be something they're not, or move outside their normal personality. I never felt like we were a group that was devoid of leadership, so you appreciated the uniqueness of his personality.

That year, 2014, may have been the first time they actually were devoid of leadership. As Brett Keisel had said, a primary reason behind the team's closeness "was because of the way Troy interacted with everyone throughout the locker room."

Troy wasn't the boss. He wasn't the captain. He was more of the team spirit. Both Judaism and Christianity define the Holy Spirit as "the small, still voice for God." That sure sounds a lot like Troy Polamalu.

Can that term be used so casually about a football player?

Can we ever so humbly call Troy the Steelers' Holy Spirit?

MILLER: Oh, I think that's spot on. As Troy got older, he didn't mind speaking up, and when he did everything fell silent and everyone hung on every word he said, and rightfully so. Even though he wasn't a visual leader, he was the heart and the conscience of the team and he had the respect of everyone in the locker room, coaches included.

KEISEL: He had a way of just keeping things real and understanding how to prepare. He did it first with the DBs.

HOKE: Troy really was a calming voice. He gave us confidence, because we knew that when Troy came on the field, man, you couldn't help but be confident. You had Troy Polamalu on your side! Right? And so it brought a lot of peace and comfort and kept you calm – exactly what the Holy Spirit does. So, if you want to look at it that way, absolutely.

WOLFLEY: When you say the Holy Spirit, if you're talking the practical realities of what I believe personally as a man who follows Jesus, no. He embodies and carries in him the Holy Spirit as a believer and follower of Christ. If that's where you're going with it, yes. If you're talking about what he kind of epitomizes – well, that's an interesting question. He's an encourager and a multiplier of men. He multiplies everybody around him. He doesn't do it in ferocity and fierceness of a Joe Greene back in the day, but he's a multiplier in the back end of the defense and the front of the defense by his enthusiasm. And he's one of these light guys. Some guys have a darkness about them, menacing and mean, and some guys are the shining kind who draw that which is around them. He did embody a very sensitive spirit about him, and I think so much of that has to do with his walk with Christ.

KEISEL: Probably one of my favorite stories about him, in 2014 we were struggling a little bit, getting older, and we had lost a game. We flew home and I asked a few guys to come over to my house and have a fire and chat about what to do here because we have some problems. How are we going to lead us past this? Troy came over, along with a few of the other leaders on the team. We're sitting around the fire saying we've got to do this, we've got to do that. Troy stood up and said, "We've got to honor Al." I didn't know what he was talking about. Honor Al? He said, "We really need to honor Villanueva." We had just got him, and it was like, "What the heck are you talking about?" But we said, yeah, because things were serious at the time with guys going and fighting overseas in battle. We thought about Al and how he got in there and didn't say much and had been in some serious battles where a lot more was at stake. Even though what we did was important and valued and was our livelihood and our jobs, it happened to be November, Salute To Service Month. So our motive was to unite our team. We went in the next day and talked to Coach Tomlin and said we wanted to bring the team together and say we want to win this next game for Al. And he did. The next game was the Titans.

Troy Polamalu described his duties as captain this way: "The best thing that the captain can do for any team is be the player that they need him to be, and that's always been my focus."

They also need to knock on Mike Tomlin's door at times, and that's what Troy and Brett Keisel did prior to the Steelers' trip to Nashville. They asked Tomlin if he could bring along a member of the practice squad, Al Villanueva, a former Army Ranger who had been awarded a Bronze Star Medal for rescuing wounded soldiers while under enemy fire in Afghanistan.

It was the first Monday night after Veterans Day, at Tennessee, where the Steelers beat the Titans 27-24 to improve to 7-4.

Polamalu didn't play in the game. He was out for a second consecutive week after Ravens running back Justin Forsett had pinballed into the back of his leg.

However, Polamalu was there to perform his duties as a captain.

"Troy gave Al the ball and said thanks for everything," says DeCastro. "Troy definitely has a soft spot for the military. He made some good friends with some Navy SEAL buddies who I've gotten to meet through him. He's always had a lot of respect for veterans."

The Steelers were adding leadership and losing troublemakers at the same time. Keisel had been signed over the summer at the last minute – at the airport, in fact, on his way to sign with Bruce Arians and the Cardinals – and he, Polamalu and Ike Taylor helped convince the team to re-sign James Harrison.

The offensive line was also coming to life as it responded to the high-level coaching of Mike Munchak, who had been hired in the offseason. The team did lose one of its "Doobie Brothers," LeGarrette Blount, after he left the field in Nashville before the game ended. Blount hadn't touched the ball in the game and left during "Victory Formation." Blount was released the next day, and his loss would be felt in the playoffs.

As for Harrison, he had retired after his 2013 season in Cincinnati, but re-signed after Jarvis Jones broke his wrist in Week 2.

Harrison walked around the locker room to re-acquaint himself with teammates. He even went into "Kicker's Corner" and said hello to veterans Greg Warren and Shaun Suisham. When first-year punter Brad Wing said hello, Harrison said, "Fuck you." Harrison then found his new locker and faced a media throng.

"All right, what lies do you want me to tell you?"

That's when it became official: James Harrison was back.

KEISEL: Yeah, I was in his ear a lot. He had been a rock for us for so long. When he was on the line, he was a force. And when he wasn't there, it was different. It was tough to replace a guy like that, so when we had the opportunity to bring him back, to solidify that position a little better – a LOT better – I wasn't going to let it slide. I called him at four in the morning after Jarvis broke his wrist. We were rushing the passer and he got turned around. His hand hit my knee and the wrist broke. So I felt bad, and called James.

The out-of-shape Harrison played 27 snaps against 0-3 Tampa Bay, but the Steelers lost 27-24 after Mike Glennon threw a deep slant to Louis Murphy, who ran past Polamalu to the 5-yard line.

The 41-yard play was a "failure at all three levels," said Mike Tomlin. Polamalu took the blame for the third level. He was the center fielder in cover-3 and Murphy angled past him to continue the big gain. It was becoming obvious that while Polamalu could still come downhill with speed and abandon, his deep coverage skills weren't up to his standards.

But Polamalu needn't have taken blame for an offsides penalty on which he appeared to mis-time the snap – a rarity in his career.

Early in the third quarter of a tied game, Tampa Bay tried to get off a quick snap after converting a third-and-10 pass to Vincent Jackson, who appeared to have fumbled.

The fumble wasn't called and Tampa hustled to the line on first down to snap before a review could be called. Polamalu saw what the Bucs were doing and timed a burst through the line to blow up the play. The play was whistled dead and he was flagged for being offside.

The Steelers also had 12 men on the field, so Polamalu couldn't accept all the blame even if he was in the wrong.

Was he in the wrong? To just about everyone, it appeared he had been.

"Was I really offside?" Troy asked with a bemused smile after the game.

It was assumed he had been, but the look on his face said that he thought otherwise.

He was right. When slowed down, the tape showed Polamalu had in fact timed it perfectly – again. He actually spooked Glennon into fumbling the snap, which Polamalu recovered.

WOLFLEY: No kidding! That actually doesn't surprise me, because that's what a Hall of Famer's capable of. Troy is much like Dermontti Dawson. They changed how the position was viewed. Dermontti was the first center that they pulled. Nobody did that. And Troy changed the game from his position.

JUSTIN MYERS: If I may disagree with the "Oh, Troy revolutionized the position" argument. Well, no, he didn't, because nobody else is going to be able to do that. Ever.

Other than allowing Murphy to get past the cover-3 umbrella as the center fielder, Polamalu played an exceptional game. While he appeared stiff during practices the week before games in 2014, his athletic ability showed up every Sunday.

The loss was followed by a 4-1 Steelers run that was capped off by a 43-23 win against the Ravens, the game in which Polamalu injured his leg. He missed the next two games, including a loss to the 1-8 Jets.

Ravens coach John Harbaugh mocked the Steelers' loss to the Jets to his own team in the Ravens' post-game locker room. "That team beat us last week. OK. Then, they went out and got their ass kicked this week."

Tomlin wouldn't comment, other than to say, "If we do what we're supposed to do, and they do what they're supposed to do, we'll see them again. Maybe we can settle it in '15. We'll see."

"Are you sure he has to come back this week?" Drew Brees asked about Troy Polamalu. "He doesn't look any different from when I first saw him on film 10 years ago until now."

You may recall that, in 2003, the first game-wrecking play of Polamalu's NFL career occurred against Brees, causing Brees to be benched and possibly causing the Chargers to draft Philip Rivers five months later. Now, Brees was complimenting his fellow aging vet as that vet was making the finishing kick of his Hall of Fame career.

Polamalu returned from his sprained knee along with Ike Taylor, who had missed eight games with a broken forearm. Ryan Shazier was also returning. The first-round draft pick with Polamalu/Taylor-type of elite speed had missed two games with a sprained ankle.

IKE TAYLOR: Shazier was a Troy kind of guy. You couldn't keep him off the field. Couldn't hold him back. They had to let him go through his learning curve on the field, because those kinds of guys come around every blue moon. Regardless of whether they're rookies or four-year guys, you've got to play them. Regardless of whether he's a first rounder or third-rounder, you couldn't leash him. They had to let Ryan Shazier play football.

Taylor was burned by Brees and Kenny Stills for a 69-yard touchdown pass that put the Saints ahead 28-13 late in the third quarter. Brees' fifth touchdown pass of the game gave the Saints a 35-16 lead early in the fourth. It was enough to withstand a late Steelers rally in a 35-32 Saints win.

Taylor took the blame, but was encouraged because he felt he had knocked off the rust of the past eight weeks and was looking forward to the final month of the season.

But at Cincinnati, an 81-yard Andy Dalton bomb to A.J. Green, over Taylor, spelled doom for the 34-year-old Steelers cornerback. Taylor took himself out of the game. He knew he was finished.

TAYLOR: A.J. Green beat me on the touchdown and I wasn't mad. That's why I was like "Oh, hell, I ain't going back in." Coach T said, "What do you mean?" I said "I'm not mad. I lost the passion. I'm not pissed off like I should be." And Kevin Colbert came down and asked why I wasn't in the game. "It's a wrap for me. Football's over with." He said, "What do you mean football's over with?" I said, "A.J. just beat me and I'm not mad. That's not going to be good for me or this team or this organization." I gave everything. That made it easy for me, babe. I wasn't fighting it.

Green finished with 11 catches for 224 yards, third-most yardage ever by a receiver against the Steelers. Taylor had been fighting through shoulder, forearm and knee injuries, and the bomb to Green was the final play of Ike's career. He was inactive throughout the remainder of the season.

The Steelers did beat the Bengals 42-21. Then they beat the Atlanta Falcons 27-20 and the Kansas City Chiefs 20-12.

Against the Falcons, Devin Hester caught a touchdown pass against Polamalu that brought criticism from the media and fans, but it was a perfect pass from Matt Ryan against which Polamalu had no chance.

If Polamalu wasn't becoming the fans' whipping boy, Dick LeBeau was. His unit would finish 2014 ranked 18th in both points and yards allowed. His pass defense ranked 27th in yards allowed and 28th in opposing passer rating. The 98.3 defensive passer rating ranks as the highest in team history.

To end the win over the Chiefs, the Steelers lined up in victory formation not with Polamalu stationed as the deep running back, but with Antonio Brown.

"Yeah," Polamalu joked after the game, "just wait until we fumble and he has to make a tackle. You'll see then."

The Steelers finished the regular season with a hard-fought win over the Bengals to win the AFC North championship. But running back Le'Veon Bell took an open-field helmet to the knee from safety Reggie Nelson and would miss the first round of the playoffs against the Ravens.

Outlined against a pitch-black January sky, the Four Horsemen rode again. In dramatic lore they are known as Da Beard, Swaggin', Troy and Coach Dad. These are only aliases. Their real names are Keisel, Taylor, Polamalu and LeBeau ...

Apologies to Grantland Rice, as well as Craig Wolfley, who before the game had dubbed these four legendary Steelers "The Four Warhorses Of The Playoff-alypse."

Their glorious run had come to an end following the Steelers' 30-17 playoff loss to the Ravens. Le'Veon Bell's replacements – Ben Tate and Josh Harris – weren't up to the task. They combined for 44 yards on 14 carries, forcing Ben Roethlisberger to attempt 45 passes in trying to rally the Steelers in the second half.

With the Steelers trailing 13-9 early in the third quarter, James Harrison attempted to close the gap by rolling around the Ravens' left tackle and homing in on QB Joe Flacco, as Flacco wound up slowly. It appeared a classic Harrison strip-sack was imminent – until the Ravens' left guard turned suddenly and gave Harrison a hard shove. Free, Flacco threw an 11-yard touchdown pass to give the Ravens a 20-9 lead from which the Steelers couldn't recover. It was the Steelers' first playoff loss to the Browns/Ravens.

Keisel didn't have anything to say as he cleared out first. He had been on injured reserve with a torn triceps tendon, but had played well, and after his injury maintained a rugged rehabilitation program. His only answer when asked about a possible return in 2015 at the age of 37 had been, in the weeks leading up to the finale, "We'll see."

Like Keisel, Taylor didn't dress for the game but said goodbye afterward. "I'm very fortunate to have played 12 years," he said. "I got an opportunity to win two, been to three. Got an opportunity to have three contracts, so money ain't the issue. This ain't nothing but the love right here. I'm so glad I made that decision to take a pay cut, because there ain't nothing better than being a Pittsburgh Steeler."

Polamalu was the last player to leave the shower and appear at his locker. Except for a crowd of faceless microphones and cameras, Polamalu was alone. He spoke so slowly and softly that sadness couldn't help but permeate the air.

Was this the 33-year-old's last game?

"Time will tell," Polamalu said, the first of four times.

Is that a reasonable question to be asked?

"Yes, it is," he said.

Polamalu also believed – "absolutely" – that the Steelers were headed in the right direction. It was a hopeful comment, rife with the positive energy for which Polamalu had become known, the reason why he had become the conscience, the soul, the Holy Spirit, if you will, of the organization.

But the reply also reverberated with sadness at the realization that Polamalu likely wouldn't be a part of that future.

"Those who have tackled a cyclone can understand" was how Grantland Rice finished his famed column.

Those who have watched one for 12 years can, too.

KENETI POLAMALU: I was in Pittsburgh for the Ravens playoff game. I didn't know it was going to be his last game, but I felt it was getting near the end so I wanted to be there. After the game we went to a soul food restaurant somewhere in Pittsburgh. It wasn't an area where you go, a popular restaurant area, but his teammates came, the security of the Steelers came. We all went. And then on our way home, he had packed all of the leftovers. While he's taking me back to my hotel room, he's stopping at every corner and feeding people on the street with the food. This was after a game. People were rushing off, but that's just the way the kid is. And he was hurt. He was hurt, lost a playoff game and didn't know the outlook for his future. That's a tough time, but here he is. The kids are in the back seat with Theodora and all of the sudden we're stopping. People are saying, "Hey, great game, Troy!" And he's handing out food to people on the street.

CHAPTER 32

A LOSS IN THE FORCE

Ike Taylor knew he was done during the 2014 season.

Dick LeBeau knew he was finished when the Steelers tried to kick him upstairs into an undefined advisory position. He called a familiar reporter in his hometown of London, Ohio, to let him break the news. LeBeau ended up with the Tennessee Titans.

Brett Keisel knew he was done the day before the start of free agency in March of 2015. That's when the Steelers released him with a year left on his contract. On the same day, Kevin Colbert told the team's website, "We do not have an update on Troy Polamalu or his contract status. We will continue to communicate with Troy and his representatives regarding his future."

The Steelers had already decided that Troy would not be back, but were waiting for their star safety to make the decision himself, whether he wanted to retire, find a better deal elsewhere or allow the Steelers to release him. Colbert, Mike Tomlin and Art Rooney II had met with Troy in February to tell him of those options.

MIKE TOMLIN: It's just the law of the jungle. It is an ecosystem that we're all a part of. Difficult decision, but they're always going to be difficult because there are men on the other end of those decisions, men that you admire and appreciate and respect. Man, he exemplified all of those things. The player's well being is obviously a part of those decisions as well, the health of the player and things of that nature. So, there were many layers to it, probably more layers than can be outlined in a setting such as this. But just rest assured that it was very difficult, and appropriately so.

MARCEL PASTOOR: As most of the guys in the league do, you get to a point later in your career that soft-tissue injuries occur more often. You also worry about the impact that certain people are taking. The helmets are getting safer but there are still concussions. Even in today's protocol, you try to catch the concussions and soft-tissue injuries. There comes a point in time, too, where "I just want to play." Guys have to be honest with themselves. From Troy's perspective, we do have film on it, and there are a handful of soft-tissue injuries that kept him out. At about three-quarters throughout his career, there were stretches where he would play two, three games, he would be out two, three, he would come back for a couple. And the soft-tissue injuries just started to pile up and the body starts to break down. God, Ike went however many games as a corner without any injuries and then he gets hurt and then he has another injury after that. Once that wheel falls off, the other wheels try to catch up and sometimes you just can't keep it there.

Troy thought it over long and hard. He initially felt he could put together his greatest offseason, get into the best shape of his life and prove everyone wrong. He wasn't happy with how all of it was going down.

Then one day he realized it was time to be with his family, and he made the decision to retire on April 9, 2015.

Similar to what his mentor, LeBeau, had done, Troy broke the news to a reporter with whom he had developed a close relationship.

TROY POLAMALU: I had a conversation with the Steelers. They just kind of said, "Troy, you need to retire." This was about a month and a half after the season. I said, "I'm really not sure if I want to retire or not." I walked out of this meeting really disappointed because they kept saying they were going to cut me or I was going to retire.

I had walked into the meeting just to talk to Kev, and then I was going to talk to Mike, and then all of the sudden I was confronted. I talked to Kevin for 15 minutes, then Mike walks in and then Art walks in and it's like, aw, man, I've got all three coming in telling me I need to retire, blah, blah, blah. So the decision came down to: Do I want to play somewhere else? Do I want to move my family somewhere else? Because I know Pittsburgh is not an option. And I don't know if I want to go back to Pittsburgh anyway because Coach LeBeau's not there. That's what made it a tough decision, because in truth I didn't feel wanted anywhere. After walking away from the meeting with Mike and Art and Kevin, there was no way they could recover from what they were saying. Kev says I'm old and slow. I said, "I agree with you. I don't have my speed. I don't have my explosion." But then I called Coach LeBeau right after this meeting and was like, Coach, this is what happened. Coach LeBeau had already been fired. He said, "Troy, that's nonsense. Don't believe any of that stuff. You've still got so much game in you. You're still great at all these other things," which he named. It led me to research and start talking to other teams, and Marvin (Demhoff, agent) had reached out to a bunch of scouts and a few head coaches and GMs. What it came down to, it didn't matter what team it was. It didn't matter how much money they offered. It was all about the situation with my family. Do I really want to move and break up their lives that I've been living for the last 12 years? Do I really want to get up and move to New England or Tennessee or wherever? And I think at this point it wouldn't be worth it.

There had been a report that Theodora had asked Troy to retire. Troy said that wasn't the case, and that the answer to his six-week question of whether to retire or play elsewhere came to him while he was in church.

TROY POLAMALU: It's all about my family. As soon as the season was over I had a chance to enjoy my family on a level I never had. It was awesome. Like for some reason I felt I had a pressure off of me. I had thought in my mind I'm pretty much retired and I just had less stress, because if I'm in the first year of a five-year contract and it was the fifth year of my career, I'm telling my wife I can't pick up the kids at school, I've got to train. In fact, I never really did pick them up from school or take them to school. I had never gone to Disneyland with them, nor did any of these things with them. So I had a chance to pick up my children from school, take them to school, spend real quality time without the added stress in the back of my mind. I was like, "Man, this is awesome." After experiencing that, I think that was probably the best sign that it was time for me to retire. (Theodora) hadn't said anything about it. She was the most supportive person. I would ask her, "What do you want me to do? What should I do?" And she was like, "Troy, I'm not here to tell you what to do. I'm here to support whatever decision you want to make."

Polamalu did seek outside counsel about playing elsewhere, and was bothered by feedback suggesting he should retire in order to preserve his legacy.

TROY POLAMALU: First of all, I don't care about a legacy. Second of all, I play the game because I enjoy it. That's the reason to keep playing. If I'm in my fourth year, fifth year, even my tenth year, I'm playing in Alaska if I had to. I thought this would be more black and white for me, in terms of today is the day. It wasn't, and that was kind of the sign for me to say, "Whoa, maybe you shouldn't play anymore." What I do know about this game is it takes a lot of commitment just to be an average player.

I've always told myself I wanted to retire from football at age 33 and play 12 years. I'm 33. Obviously the significance is Christ being 33; 12 years, 12 apostles. I'm not superstitious by any means, but I always thought if I played 12 years and retire from football at 33, and give my life and give my body and give blood to this game, I think that would be a pretty significant landmark in my life. So the big question becomes: What am I going to do now? The best I can do is make up for lost time, and that's with my family. Thank God that football has provided me the ability to be able to just sit back and see what the options are and what to deal with. I definitely want to be the best father I can possibly be.

With that, Troy Polamalu called Dan Rooney to inform him he had retired.

BILL COWHER: It was interesting to hear Brian Billick talk about Troy. He mentioned a story where he was on the sideline screaming at Troy after Troy had tackled one of their guys on the sideline, and he asked Troy in the heat of the moment, "like a petulant child," his words, but he asked, "Do you just hate us? Is it just me?" and Troy responded "No sir" and went back to the action. Billick completely calmed down after the exchange and was a bit in awe. If there was one player that Billick wished he could have coached, it was Troy.

CARNELL LAKE: Strong safety is a demanding position in this defense. LeBeau used to call me the clean-up guy. Everybody would take care of their gaps in front of me and then the ball would wind back to me and I'd clean it up. So after a while it does wear on you. But I played here 10 years. Troy played here a long time. Donnie Shell, my predecessor, played a long time. So I think it depends on the player. I think Troy was more instinctual at the position than I was, maybe because he played it longer than I did. I just started playing it when I got to the pros. My first few years, I was just learning how to play defensive back. Troy came in ready to go and he developed since. Fortunately for me and for Troy, we were able to get into a defense under LeBeau that allowed us to thrive. I really started to take off once LeBeau came here as my defensive backs coach. I think one of Troy's biggest assets is his ability to see offenses and be able to read on the run. He's got great vision. You don't want to stymie that. You just had to maybe pull the reigns back a tad. But once he got the concepts down, he was off and running. It really was amazing to see.

BRETT KEISEL: It's actually a proud thing for me to have gone out with LeBeau, Ike and Troy. Being able to be there together for that long, none of us wanted it to end. Nobody wanted the magic to stop. Nobody wanted the feelings to end, going into work and being around your best friends and game-planning and motivating your team and working out. I don't think any of us really had the desire to go play somewhere else, or try out with another team. For me, it's kind of special to go out with those guys because I know what all of them brought to the table. I know how hard all of those guys worked behind the scenes to be their best self. I know Ike's playing streak and how many games he started in a row. I know how great Troy was and how great Dick LeBeau was, both Hall of Famers and rightfully so. It's really surreal for me to be a part of this all. It's almost like the dream where once you get done playing you definitely miss it and you want to be back in it, because it's what you did for so long and it becomes who you are and it's hard to roll into everyday life without ball. But, so grateful for it. We accomplished so much in such a short amount of time that really we go on to this next phase of our young lives already with this monument behind us that we've climbed, stuck our flag in the ground, and walked off the other side with our feet up. It's a proud, proud thing for me, something I don't take for granted.

I say all the time that life is all about timing, and it was the timing of all of us being there together during that time, of all of us buying into the team and not our individual growth and not our social media growth and all the other distractions out there that the players have to go through. It was about appreciating and enjoying our time and maximizing what we could do in that time.

CAMERON HEYWARD: There are a couple of things I've taken from Troy. When we needed him most he was able to step up, whether it was jumping over the pile and stopping them for a fourth-down loss, or coming up with a fumble, or a sack-fumble in the AFC Championship Game. But it wasn't just the player that was great. The thing that separated him was his accountability. You look back at that 2010 team, or 2008 team. There were so many great players. Troy was responsible for a lot of the havoc but it was never like one guy flourished and everybody else suffered. Because one guy flourished, everybody else flourished. I love looking back at that ESPN The Magazine photo of the whole team. Everybody knew Troy was the guy, but it was more than just him.

JOEY PORTER: It's his personality. It's his play. It's his natural like of everybody. Until you wrong him, you can ask him for anything. Nothing's too big. Never going to say no on an autograph, or if you ask him to make something, to be there. He's going to make it and he's going to be there. He's everything you're looking for in a friend, a brother, a teammate – all of that. He and LeBeau kind of walk the same path. Those are the two most humble, gracious people I've ever met. That's why I've never heard of anybody that doesn't like Dick LeBeau. You're a bad person if you don't like LeBeau. You're a bad person if you don't like Troy. You might have football reasons for not liking him, but you've got to tell me what did he ever do to you for you not to like him.

RYAN SCARPINO: I just remember feeling sad when Troy left. Even though he didn't say much, he was just so very positive to be around. He made jokes. He made you realize he is human. He's just like us, even though he doesn't appear to be us. I just remember feeling sad when he left. Same way with Heath. When I left before the 2017 season, a lot of the guys that I came in with were gone. Those guys had this presence. Like Heath. Like Troy. These guys going, that's a big part of that locker room and a big part of that team's history. Gone.

RANDY BAUMANN: Troy's really one of my favorite people of all-time. He's legit. There are so few people you can say that about.

PASTOOR: He was so regimented from a training standpoint. You knew what time he was coming in to work out every day. We're used to practice at 1:15, and you know at 12 when the DBs break their meetings, Troy's not going to lunch. Troy's going to come in and get a workout, he's going to stretch, and when I'm done stretching him he's got 15 minutes before practice and he's out on the practice field. After practice, he's out there catching the long ball. No surprise that he's playing the deep half and he can cover the entire field, not just half of the field. It's because he practiced it continuously. But I'm telling you, if Troy wasn't on his regimen of having his shakes and having his meals at certain times, that dude could put on weight in a minute. That's why Cam and Ray (Jackson) and Troy and I are still on a group text and we joke around every time Troy has another birthday that we're going to send him another cake. Instead of four cakes, we'll send him five cakes because we know he can put 'em all down. That dude can flat out eat.

RYAN CLARK: The simplicity of Troy's goals is what allowed him to achieve such amazing things on the football field. My goals changed every year. At the beginning of my career it was just make a team; then it was become a starter; then it was be a Pro Bowler; and then it was be a captain. All of these things that were very tangible were important to me because as an undrafted guy that was the only way to know if I was being accepted. Whereas it always seemed that Troy's goals were much simpler. They were about him and the way he went about his work. And I think in trying to make sure you just played hard, trying to make sure you were accountable, those things don't just make you a good player, they make you a great teammate. And by doing those things and having that focus, the bigger things happened because of how talented he was.

MIKE LOGAN: I could say so many things. He really helped me out. I went through a rough period after my transition from the league. I went through a lot of personal tragedy and personal stuff. Just him reaching out and letting me know that he's there, that he's praying for me. The way I reacted to those things was because of my observation and interactions with him, how to carry yourself and handle yourself and use your faith to get through some of those things. Without that, I can't say that I would be in the position that I'm in now.

IKE TAYLOR: It was probably later, after my career, when I really leaned on Troy. For me, it was more my anger management. Troy helped me. I had a bad temper. A bad temper. BAD temper. From being around him so much I kind of took on his temperament in adverse situations, because he was always calm. So before he did any kind of act, he put a lot of thought into it. I was doing more acting than thinking about my consequences. So Troy helped me think before I would act. When Troy did say something, our lectures were real. When he talked, you couldn't say nothing but, "You right."

BRYANT MCFADDEN: Troy always taught me that you don't necessarily have to tell people how good you are. Troy taught me that whenever you're around a good individual, you feel it. If you've ever talked to Troy, he never said how good of a person he was. He never said how good of a player he was. I think the humility that he has displayed throughout his career, throughout his life, is the most important thing he's taught me.

PORTER: He made you change the way you treated people. You didn't really act a certain way around Troy. Let me say that. You didn't curse around Troy, because he didn't say it a lot, right? I have an X-rated story, then I have a PG story, and if Troy's sitting there I give it the PG version. That's how he makes you feel. Hey, he's heard enough X-rated because he's been in locker rooms so many times, but there are times I just tell a different version because he's there.

TOMLIN: His passion, love, respect and appreciation for the game were always on display, and that made him a no-maintenance guy. The splash plays will be remembered. The splash plays will be the highlight that they show when they talk about the impact of his career, the fingertip interception in the snow in San Diego, all of those things, but what really stands out to me are those seemingly mundane football plays that he made really unique by doing unique things like an angle tackle where he exploded and was absolutely the fastest guy on the field. His recognition and execution of a routine football play was something to really appreciate if you were a lover of football. That 1-yard tackle on the perimeter where he really came from out of nowhere, those are the things that I remember, man; those seemingly mundane plays that he made special because of his recognition, his calculated risk-taking, and his burst.

MIKE MILLER: You have one of the greatest safeties ever, and you've got a pass rush, so it was, as we say, a Steel Curtain. It was so hard to run on those guys. And if you should happen to get through the second level, you've got this maniac running and flying and just going to knock you into tomorrow, and if you want to try and run by him, good luck with that, too, because he could run. Pick your poison, but you don't want to go at 43.

SCARPINO: You always knew Troy would get in the Hall of Fame, but it still didn't take away from the moment. Of course, he's so humble. I joked on Twitter about Alan Faneca, that Troy probably said, "Put Alan in before me." That's who he was.

PORTER: He's the best football player I ever played with, and I've played with some great ones. I can easily say that.

MCFADDEN: The similarity you could see between Michael Jordan and Troy was their will to win, preparing themselves to always be in a position to win. When people see Troy play, they don't see the prep that leads to the success on Sunday. I had the opportunity to see the extra study time, taking down notes, doing things on the practice field to get a feel for whether they will work on Sunday, and then finding little nuances from certain quarterbacks that can put him in positions to be successful. I think that was one of the more incredible, insightful parts of that doc was listening to MJ and the way he strategized against opponents. He was talking about Byron Russell, how he saw on tape he was a heavy-foot guy, and how if he leaned one way, he was just going to lean. That was very impactful. He wasn't doing it because he was the best athlete, he was doing it because he was the best athlete and was also prepared above the shoulders. Troy was just like that.

LENNY VANDERMADE: Oh, I absolutely do see a similarity with Jordan. But Troy's style is a little bit different. I do see that there is a price to be paid to be a leader, to be great, and Troy paid that price. I can vouch for that a thousand times over. I think there was loneliness for Troy, too. He's better, and we all saw that, and so he had to separate himself a little bit. Now, I think the way he went about getting guys to play better, to step their game up, wasn't like Jordan's where he would call guys out. I mean, Troy would, but not to the extent to where guys seemed to hate Jordan. Troy would do it in a more encouraging way. Now, he would be firm. He obviously has the Kevin Arbet story, when he got in his grill, and he got into a couple other guys' grills. But then he would also explain to you why he did it, and he would always bring it back around, help guys understand why he did things. He wasn't doing it to be liked. He was doing it out of respect and just holding guys accountable.

TOMLIN: There was a clarity in Troy's life and in his game. It really was about that. He felt that. He was never distracted by peripheral things, the past, or the potential for the future. He's just a guy that cherishes moments, and you felt that. But you felt that in life, in the way he lives out his life, also in the same ways that you do in terms of his ability to capture a moment or you felt his presence in the game.

I think clarity in the midst of clutter is what those personalities are able to capture. It allows him to rise up in moments. The moments themselves are seemingly not too big for him. Those are the cliches that those of us who get to witness it use, but the reality is that they're not distracted by clutter, whether the clutter be circumstances of the gravity of the moment, peripheral things, sub-plots, etc. They're able to pull out what is significant, what is urgent, what is important and perform in the midst of it.

KEISEL: Reporters always ask us how we feel, what was going through our minds, how did we make that play. And we always said, "My team. My team put me in position." Because we worked together. You heard that with Troy immediately after he found out he was going into the Hall of Fame. He said, "This is an honor for my team."

That was the blessing of being in there together. Our team was a bonded, united team, and it wasn't just a bunch of good guys being together. They were bonded and united and great. And they were a cast of characters from all over America, from Colorado to California to Louisiana to Texas to Wyoming to Oregon – all over, and from different backgrounds, from all different walks, and united, and are now forever brothers. Forever. They're going to be remembered for what they did in Pittsburgh in, really, a short amount of time. And that's cool.

CHAPTER 33

IN THE MOMENT

Troy Polamalu wanted me to put off writing this book until he did something important with his life.

Like Bill Bradley?

Someone had mentioned Bradley, the former basketball star turned U.S. Senator, but that suggestion was usually met with guffaws by those who know Troy.

Politics? Nah, not Troy.

Politics might be something Theodora would pursue one day. She at one time was interested. Troy, though, might better be suited for helping to revive Samoa, training young athletes in a holistic fashion, or perhaps even making a movie with his friend, Steelers minority owner and producer Thomas Tull.

Of course, that would all have to wait until Troy finishes raising his two sons, and then maybe not until he's finished weeding his garden back home in Southern California.

Troy had once thought his future was in Pittsburgh. After his last game he said, "I'm a yinzer through and through. My boys go to school here. I'm going to be struggling through the winter like most of us who live here."

But he moved his family back where the weather suits his bones, back to Southern California, and he got back into shape, whipped up a garden and began the grueling travel circuit known as youth sports.

JUSTIN MYERS: He's just a full-on dad and husband. He is devoted now to his family, and he loves it. It's kind of the perfect ending. Just work, do all this crazy work, travel, time, and then now just kind of sit back and do what he wants to do. Every time I talk to him it's always about his kids. He's always asking about my family and my mom and dad, always wants stuff from back up in Oregon, but for him he's a soccer dad.

TROY POLAMALU: I've wrestled with my competitiveness all my life, so you'll appreciate this story: Paisios was six and he was playing soccer and another boy kept knocking him down and taking the ball. I pulled him aside and said, "Paisios, I know daddy taught you about sportsmanship, but sometimes you have to push back. It's OK. It's part of the game." And then he went out and knocked the boy over and took the ball. The boy was on the ground crying, and they stopped play, and the coaches and the officials came running over. Paisios started crying himself and he pointed at me and said, "HE told me to do it!"

HEATH MILLER: (Laughs) I've heard that story. There's another funny story: We moved to Virginia, and this other family had moved in from northern Virginia and eventually the lady found out that I used to play for the Steelers, so she came up to me during one of my son's soccer practices. One of her sons is on the same team. She said, "Oh, I remember we played a team from Pittsburgh and there was one of the boys, his dad played for the Steelers." She didn't know the guy's name. She thought he was a running back. Immediately I'm thinking it was Troy's kids because I know they're around the same age as mine and they played soccer. She was like, "Man, his kids were so physical. They were beating our kids up." (Chuckles) She said, "They had long and frizzy hair and they were so rough." I'm like, "I think I may know who you're talking about."

The Polamalu boys, Paisios and Ephraim, first made their presence felt at the Steelers' 2012 training camp. They showed up to watch practice, but really didn't watch too much of it. The toddlers darted around showing off their quick-twitch to mom, who had her hands full keeping them nearby.

Brett Keisel was standing nearby when I told him that in 10 years or so I would go watch them play high school ball for Pine-Richland.

"Yeah," Keisel said, "But they'll probably end up going to school in L.A." Keisel paused and said, "And I'll probably go there to watch them."

TROY POLAMALU: Maybe it was a sign for me to retire when I chased my kids around and couldn't catch them. Time for me to retire, or a sign for them to start training to begin maximizing their potential (laughs). It reminds me of me growing up. Once I got into open space – I've got 12 aunts and uncles and I'm the only one who, and I don't know the politically correct term is, but I was beaten up by all of them. But if I got into open space, there was no way they could catch me. My children are like that.

KENETI POLAMALU: His boys are just as athletic as Troy. Yes. Yes. Oh, yes. And the crazy part is they are in *everything*. This is something that Troy never had. Those kids get their dad full-time. They don't have to worry about whether dad has to go away for a job. He is right there for them. It's a beautiful thing.

SHAUN NUA: I disagree. They're not AS good athletically. I think they're going to be better because Theodora's side of the family is just as good as Troy's. She has two brothers who were drafted by the NFL – Alex and Khaled. So I think they're going to be better, and I've seen it firsthand. When we went to Samoa, I saw those kids run around and I was like "Wow!" The real question is: Do they have Troy's composure and mindset? There are a lot of athletic people out there. Athleticism-wise, they're going to be better than Troy. If I'm still a coach in a couple of years I'm going to offer them a scholarship right away (laughs).

TROY POLAMALU: Paisios and I are a very similar personality because he has that sort of free spirit. The difference is he's got parental supervision. So I realize in my mind what I'm trying to contain. My Uncle Keneti said it to me best: "Troy, Paisios is a lot like you. He's a free spirit. If you try to contain him, you may hurt him. The only difference is these days are a lot different than the days when you grew up."

IKE TAYLOR: Paisios, he's real good in soccer. He's *really* good in soccer. His youngest, Ephraim, he's OK in baseball, but I think they're going to finally let the man play football because he's a real live – (chuckles) his young one's going to be a handful – he's a real live Samoan (laughs). Real. Live. Samoan. He's gonna be one of those dudes you don't want to mess with, ever. (Pause) Ever.

MARCEL PASTOOR: I saw some pictures of Troy after he retired, and he was big, yes, but he's doing well now. Now that the boys are a little deeper in sports and he's getting a little more active in his life again he's doing better.

KENETI POLAMALU: Troy's a little more of a deep thinker now, because he has a lot of experience. But he's still a very humble young man. I can see him wanting to do something big to help mankind, oh, yeah, but I think the frustrating part in politics is they all speak out of different sides and Troy is just an honest person. He's doing a lot of good things in Samoa right now. I mean, it's unbelievable what he's doing, but he's not going to tell anyone. I was just telling one of my running backs: a sweet potato never has to say that he's sweet. That's kinda how the kid is, you know? He just does it. Right now he's training a couple Polynesian kids, teaching them some of the things that he did. He said, "Just be on time because my time is valuable with my kids. I don't want any money. All I want you to do is share it with the other Polynesian kids." So he's teaching them everything that he experienced in his training and nutrition, things like that. He does a great job of that.

LENNY VANDERMADE: I just don't see the politician part. I think Troy would be a great coach if he ever decided to get into it, just because of the way he talks to people and the way he gets his message across. He's demanding yet he still cares and empathizes with people, and I think people react well to that. I know one thing; he's trying to be the best husband, the best father. He wants to be there for his kids, especially since he wasn't there early in his playing career. That's something he talked about when he got out, that he always wanted to put time towards his family. He didn't want to take away from that. But I think he has so much knowledge with his diet and training, I think at some point there might be a future in that.

CHRIS HOKE: I texted him. I would run into him from time to time when he still lived here. But it's hard now. Since he retired he doesn't show up for anything. I hope they have the Hall of Fame Game. Hopefully we're going to have a party with all the guys who played with him. I tell you what, that was a special group. It really was. I don't know if they'll be able to do that again. Nowadays, with the kind of players coming out, I just don't know if you can get a group like that together again. It was a special time.

JUJU SMITH-SCHUSTER, *Steelers wide receiver (2017-current):* I met Troy when I was in high school. There was a Polynesian game he came to. He was one of our guest hosts and he talked to us. He told me whatever I need, let him know. It was so nice of him to do that because I idolized him. My mom and dad came over from Samoa. I played rugby for six years, but took the football route because of the scholarship. I went to USC to be the next Troy Polamalu. Sometimes I think about what would've happened if I had stuck with safety, especially now that I'm here in Pittsburgh.

TAYLOR: I have Troy in my will. If something ever happens to me or my son's mom, Troy's next in line for my son. That lets you know how much I care and trust Troy and Theodora. I asked them about it and they were all in.

MIKE LOGAN: My daughter's a sophomore at Eastern Kentucky on volleyball scholarship. When she was little she was on the field with me after the Super Bowl making snow angels in the confetti. Now she's dealing with sports the way we all did. She's been moved to a position that suits the team more than herself and she isn't getting as much acclaim. I tell her the things I've learned, things I've learned from Troy. Yeah, don't doubt the everlasting effects of Troy Polamalu. Like I said when he made an impact on my life, I truly meant that. When I was inducted into the West Virginia Hall of Fame, I talked about Troy and the impact he had on my life, and I said it's everlasting because there are times when you're going down that backsliding trail and I think about the example he set to get me back in line. I'm glad that I have that. And I'm glad that I have that when I'm lacking, or receiving too much and not giving. I think about him. I think about my brother Troy and I say this is how he would carry himself and still be able to have that joy and make quirky jokes and be full of laughter and smiles. I really, really honor who he was to me as a friend and as a teammate.

PASTOOR: He treated your kids like his kids. He's going to come up and give them hugs and give them kisses on the belly, kisses on the neck and make them laugh. Cate was almost two years old and we were at Paisios' birthday at the children's museum. I can't find Cate anywhere; Troy's walking around with her like it's nothing. He's having fun with her. That was the kid in Troy.

TAYLOR: Ivan Jr. will be 14 this year. He's ranked in the state of Florida as one of the Top 100 best athletes. He plays safety and receiver. Troy came down to see him play. Just ask Troy about him. Matter of fact, ask Kevin Colbert about him. I don't want to sound like that dad, but he's special. He's watched Uncle Troy on *YouTube*. He knows everything about Uncle Troy. When Troy saw him play, he said, "His mannerisms are all yours, Ike." He said, "It's unbelievable how this dude walks, talks, thinks and acts just like you." But he's a superior athlete to me, and his mom does a great job telling him if you can outwork your dad, it's a wrap. That's what I instilled in him. He's an honor roll student. He's respectable. He gets up every morning and runs two miles before he goes to school. I tell him all the time, you make being a dad too easy, bro. And he's a team guy. He's only 103 pounds but he comes downhill and lays guys out. That's what Troy couldn't believe.

MYERS: I don't know how often he comes back. Last time he came back was when Salu died. I think that was the last time I hung out with him back home, two years ago I think. His Aunt Shelley still lives in the same place, and his cousin Brandon – he now goes by Tafe'a, his Samoan name – moved into the house where their grandma used to live. Polamalus are still out there on the spread in Tenmile.

BRANDON POLAMALU: I see Troy leading a very simple life. He's going to be a family man always, a man of faith first and foremost. He loves surfing. He's always going to be doing his charities and giving back. But if you're asking me what I see him doing with his time, whew, I don't know.

NUA: Pittsburgh is huge in his heart as well. He loves that city. He always talks about "I got drafted by a city with a rich culture of work ethic, blue collar." He loves it. Everything worked out perfect. And now we're all going to be in Canton celebrating it.

BRYANT MCFADDEN: I really hope we all get a chance to go to Canton to share that moment, not just with Troy but with Bill Cowher. He drafted me. To see those guys go in along with Donnie Shell; and man I wish they would stop playing around with Alan Faneca and keeping him waiting on the wayside.

Polamalu was elected to the Pro Football Hall of Fame in 2020, the first year he was eligible. He was voted in along with his first Steelers coach Bill Cowher and Donnie Shell, the hard-hitting strong safety from the '70s glory days. The ceremony was postponed due to the coronavirus pandemic and as of this writing is scheduled to take place in summer of 2021.

KENETI POLAMALU: I don't know who'll present him. He luuuuuvs Coach LeBeau, and his wife. They're very, very close. Whoever it is, he has well earned his spot and I could never be more proud, because not only just as a football player, just the way he is, everything he's doing and continues to be.

TROY POLAMALU, *to Justin Myers:* Honestly, man, I just felt unworthy. I felt unworthy in the sense that I didn't grow up watching the game and being a big fan of the NFL. As I started to learn more and more about this game and saw how other football players, Hall of Famers, how much the game really meant to them, I felt unworthy because I just played the game because I loved it.

I didn't really seek out any sort of these awards that some players really enjoy. So, I felt unworthy because I've seen guys like Deion Sanders, Mean Joe Greene, guys who really put significant stamps within this game as a football player but also as kind of the whole body of work in the sense of doing the media, all of these sorts of things and really advancing the popularity of the game. So for me, being in the Hall of Fame with those guys, I just really felt that I didn't earn that place like they did.

But then I also felt blessed in the sense that it's really not anything I received personally. It was a result of great coaches like Coach LeBeau, and honestly maybe one of the greatest runs of any defense in the NFL for my 12 years in the NFL. We were the No. 1 defense or a Super Bowl defense over half the time, about seven seasons. It's more a tribute to my teammates. The way that Coach LeBeau had taught defense was everybody has their role and it takes 11 guys to play great team defense, and we were not really big on individual statistics, other than the fact that statistics will show the story of how well we did collectively as a team. That's the other part that's really humbling, and I'm blessed that I'm able to pay tribute to my teammates with the Pittsburgh Steelers.

LOGAN: I get sporadic texts from him. I would just say, "Hey buddy, thinking about you." It might be a day or two later and he comes back with, "Hey man, love you." If he doesn't text back, that's cool, too. I've come to accept that. Whenever we have something going on at the field, one of the reunions, everybody's wondering if Troy's coming back, but no one's really expecting him.

The last time I saw Troy, he and his wife were doing a charity event through the program that I work for. They had tickets. I didn't let him know I was coming. I went and saw him and Theodore and he was like, "Bro!" He pulled me to the side and we sat down and talked for 30, 40 minutes. I said, "Don't you have to get back?" And he said, "Oh, man, I wanted to catch up with you." I was kind of surprised we sat down and talked for that long. But that's Troy. He was in the moment.

I told Troy that when I took my family to tour Liverpool's empty football stadium, we also toured Beatles sights in the city and that at night we ran into another pillar of the British Invasion, Ray Davies, the founder of the Kinks.

"The Kings?" Troy asked.

No, the Kinks. They did "Lola."

"Is that the song Eric Clapton did?"

No, that was "Layla."

"Oh. Was he nice?"

He was extremely nice.

And this made Polamalu smile

ACKNOWLEDGMENTS

Cool Papa Bell had as much to do with this book as Shelley Polamalu. Shelley, of course, raised Troy from the age of nine. She invited me to meet her family and friends as I drove through Oregon in 2007 for my previous book, Steeler Nation.

She unwittingly started the process for this book. I returned in 2011 for more extensive interviews as Shelley became my go-to for family names and historical details that are so important in a book which turned out to be more comprehensive than expected.

I've always wanted to write a biography, probably because I love to read biographies. I want to learn the subtle details of successful people, and details are so important to athletes.

The writing gig kicked up back in the early 1980s. I was an Information Systems major as a sophomore at Robert Morris College, where I took a class in business writing. The professor had us read about the Soviet grain embargo and asked us to write a paper on it.

I couldn't understand the book, much less write a paper, and I wasn't the only one. The professor returned our papers the next day with disgust. But he needed us to learn how to write something, anything, so he told us to write whatever we wanted. I wrote about Cool Papa Bell, the great center fielder in the Negro leagues.

The next day, the professor – and I wish I could remember his name – passed 30-some copies to everyone in class. He handed them out in his other classes, too. He called it "a chocolate chip cookie packed with chocolate chips."

I was shocked and a bit puffed up. So when I transferred to my next school, as a junior, I joined the University of Pitt-Greensburg school paper. I just wanted to grab an easy grade because I was still pursuing some kind of computer-information-business-make-real-money degree at Pitt, but I made the mistake of arguing about football with someone before class. That someone turned out to be the returning editor, and he nominated me as the next sports editor.

Forty years later I'm wondering what could I have been thinking?

It's almost a prerequisite to make self-deprecating remarks in this field, but what you really need are teachers. I had three: the first stoked my interest, the second taught me fundamentals and discipline, and the third provided polish.

The first was Pittsburgh poetry goddess Judy Vollmer. She was the head of the newspaper at Pitt-Greensburg and gave me the belief that I could write and thereby sparked my interest, so I became an English Writing major.

My second teacher was Vic Ketchman. He hired me while I was still at Pitt, and he said, "I don't want any of that English Writing shit. I want who, what, when, where, why and how."

Vic had covered the Steelers through the 1970s and 1980s, so he's seen the good and the bad of the football spectrum and consistently won national awards that honored our small paper in Westmoreland County. He left in 1994 to work for the Jacksonville Jaguars and authored the world famous internet column "Ask Vic." That's when I moved up to cover the Pittsburgh Steelers.

On that beat I met my third teacher, Bob Labriola, my editor the past 25 years at Steelers Digest. He was similar to Vic with the discipline, but he wanted more creativity. He actually wanted "that English Writing shit." He was like the Douglas High basketball coach who begged Troy to shoot more.

Well, yeah, you're going to get more creativity, but, Bob, I'm not a natural shooter.

"Do it anyway," he said.

Bob provided the polish necessary to stick in this field, and the result is this book that's in your lap.

Ed Bouchette wasn't so much a teacher as he was a mentor. He was the first to approach me at Three Rivers Stadium leading up to the draft of 1995. He showed that the biggest and best guys are usually the most comfortable in their skin. He just wanted to see if I had any questions about this new beat. Ed was always there to answer questions.

So, anyway, those were my teachers/mentors. They contributed to this book as much as any of the teammates, coaches and friends of Troy Polamalu who returned calls and talked for hours.

I want to thank the University of Southern California for allowing me on campus to research its library and interview Keneti Polamalu back in 2011.

USC also sent photos of Troy after Troy had given them the OK that, while he wouldn't be contributing to the book, he didn't mind it being written.

I also thank Burt Lauten of the Steelers for facilitating my interview with Mike Tomlin and for authorizing photos for use here. Burt's No. 2, Angela Tegnelia, lost her father in 2020 and her well-being has been on everyone's mind. She deserves a special shout out for working through a difficult time.

I also want to thank the Steelers' alumni relations manager, Lynn Molyneaux, for working so hard and enthusiastically in helping me procure other interviews which were so important to this book.

My team was outstanding. It was just a magic mixture that came together without reason. I sought out Alan Paul to edit this book because I enjoyed his last two books – One Way Out and Texas Flood – so much that I stole his writing style. He's Pittsburgh-raised and a Steelers fan, so he was happy to hear I was doing a book on Troy Polamalu. I then realized he would be perfect as the editor, and he was.

Pamela Diana designed this beautiful book. She proved saintly as I would often call to ask that a block of text be moved, or changed, only to call back the next day and ask her to change it back.

Keeping this A Team rolling was my technological advisor, Tim Beck. He runs Computer Medix in Irwin, Pa. He's there for me every July when I bring him my laptop for a pre-season tweak. I showed up a little early in 2020 and Tim was excited about the project and helped preserve it.

It was a massive collaboration. I was merely the guy pulling it all together. I'm convinced that I was assigned this task by the universe. I'm convinced God wanted to evolve the species by providing this blueprint biography of a great athlete who did everything the right way and for the right reasons.

So, for everyone out there who inspired and helped with this book, you were part of that universal calling. It had to be done.

And now it is.

REFERENCE LIST/NOTES

1: MIKE MILLER'S WAR (*WE'LL SEE)

1. Chapter title derived from the movie *Charlie Wilson's War*, featuring "We'll see" fable told by actor Philip Seymour Hoffman.

2. La Canfora, Jason (2014, Sept. 14). Colorado Pro Day. *CBS Sports NFL Insider*.

3. Ron Lippock with the interview tip on my old friend Mike Miller.

2: DESCENDED FROM ROYALTY

1. Chapter-heading quote from March 18, 2020, tweet by Ryan Clark's DB Precision.

2. Mazza Hillier, Gina (2006, August). The Vertical Game of Football. *Point of Light* magazine (Vol. 12, Issue 48).

3. Corbett, Jim (2006, Feb. 15). Polamalu's sudden impact revolutionizing safety position. *USA Today Sports Weekly*.

4. Whicker, Mark (2001, Dec. 18). Polamalu is USC's expert on discipline. *Orange County Register*.

5. Kamp, David (2006, September). Troy Story. *GQ*.

6. Henry, Don (1995, Nov. 25). Aumua leaves gang problems behind. *El Paso Times*.

7. Ruck, Rob (2018). *Tropic Of Football*. The New Press.

8. Silverstein (2006, Feb. 1). "... smoked a cigarette." *Milwaukee Journal Sentinel*.

3: ONCE A TROJAN, ALWAYS A TROJAN

1. Whicker, Mark (2001, Dec. 18). Polamalu is USC's expert on discipline. *Orange County Register*.

2. Jenkins, Lee (2005, Jan. 20). Polamalu Dances With Fire. *Black And Gold World blogspot*.

3. Lesneck, David (2006, Feb. 5). Libby's Neil Fuller coached the Pittsburgh Steelers' defensive star in high school. *Daily Inter Lake*.

4. Douglas High football quotes and statistics courtesy *The News-Review of Roseburg*, Oregon.

5. Neighbor, Fritz (2011, Feb. 5). Libby's Fuller remembers Troy Polamalu before The Hair. *Missoulian*.

6. Myers, Justin (2020, Feb.). With guest Troy Polamalu. *The Bridge Podcast*, NBC Sports Northwest.

4: LEGACY STORIES

1. Klima, John (2009, Jan. 29). Polamalu spurned Braves to follow football. *Yahoo Sports.*

5: HERE COMES THE SUN

1. Florence, Mal (1982, Oct. 22). USC's Jackson Is Working Overtime. *Los Angeles Times.*

2. Baker, Chris (1981, Oct. 9). Mater Dei's Pola, a Name to Remember. *Los Angeles Times.*

3. Matsude, Darryl (1982, March 29). This Coach May be Taking Wrong Path. *Los Angeles Times.*

4. Hamilton, Tom (1984, Aug. 22). Trojan's Pola Learns to Expect Unexpected. *Los Angeles Times.*

5. Burlison, Frank (1999, Feb. 4). Trojans have that California look. *The Orange County Register.*

6: NEXT THING YOU KNOW, TROY'S TAKING THE BALL

1. Whicker, Mark (2001, Dec. 18). Polamalu is USC's expert on discipline. *The Orange County Register.*

2. "highlight reel" (1999, Oct. 9). Trojans Defeated in the Desert. *Associated Press.*

3. "teeth-rattling" – Joe Starkey (2003, Oct. 1). USC safety lays it all on the line. *Pittsburgh Tribune-Review.*

7: LET THEM SAY I LIVED IN THE TIME OF POLAMALU

1. Chapter title altered from a line in the movie *Troy*, "Let them say I lived in the time of Achilles."

2. Klein, Gary (2012, Oct. 12). USC's Khaled Holmes knows tragedy and heroism. *Los Angeles Times.*

3. Re: Alex Holmes (2000, Nov. 6). USC's Renaissance Man. *USCtrojans.com*

4. "Thank God ..." (2002). Keneti Polamalu, RB coach. *USC media guide,* page 82.

5. "I used the time to think ..." (2002). Troy Polamalu. *USC media guide.*

6. Bisheff, Steve (2000, Aug. 28). Trojans defense's creed is speed. *The Orange County Register.*

7. Harmonson, Todd (2001, Aug. 22). Amazing Antuan Simmons is ready again to lead Trojans' backfield. *The Orange County Register.*

8. Harmonson, Todd (2000, Oct. 29). USC's effort a bad copy. *The Orange County Register.*

9. Harmonson, Todd (2000, Nov. 24). Rumor mill wears on assistants. *The Orange County Register.*

10. Harmonson, Todd (2000, Nov. 29). Garrett steps in as the interim coach. *The Orange County Register.*

11. Harmonson, Todd and Jenkins, Lee (2002, Nov. 30). Top 10 notes. *The Orange County Register.*

8: ROCK YOURSELF A LITTLE HARDER

1. Chapter title from the Josh Ritter song "Girl in the War" the line "Paul said to Peter, 'You've got to rock yourself a little harder.'"

2. USC baseball story told to Myers, Justin (2020, Feb.). With guest Troy Polamalu. *The Bridge Podcast,* NBC Sports Northwest.

3. Dienhart, Tom (2001, Jan. 1). Carroll's hiring is another mistake for troubled USC. *The Sporting News.*

4. Drehs, Wayne (2001). Chow brings new ideas to home of Student Body Right. *ESPN.com.*

5. Hackett's "military approach" ... told to Myers, Justin (2020, Feb.). With guest Troy Polamalu. *The Bridge Podcast,* NBC Sports Northwest.

6. Kamp, David (2006, September). Troy Story. GQ, page 408.

7. Harmonson, Todd (2001, Aug. 29). Family ties: Pola and Polamalu glad to get a chance to make amends. *The Orange County Register.*

8. Harmonson, Todd (2001, Aug 25). Leinart Catching on Fast. *The Orange County Register.*

9. Bortstein, Larry and Harmonson, Todd (2001, Sept. 2). USC defense figures out small problem. *The Orange County Register.*

10. Bisheff, Steve (2001, Sept. 9). Snyder gives USC a lesson. *The Orange County Register.*

11. Harmonson, Todd (2001, Sept. 9). USC Notes. *The Orange County Register.*

12. Harmonson, Todd (2001, Sept. 11). USC's Allmond waits or decision. *The Orange County Register.*

13. Plaschke, Bill (2002, Dec. 28). In The Name of His Father. Appeared in *South Florida Sun-Sentinel.*

14. SC Playbook (2002, Aug. 27). Malaefou MacKenzie's future. Courtesy of *The Orange County Register.*

15. Coyne, Tom (2001, Oct. 20). Trojan Football falls to Irish. *Associated Press.*

16. Harmonson, Todd (2001, Oct. 23). Carroll, assistant take punt disaster blame. *The Orange County Register.*

17. Carr, Janis and Harmonson, Todd (2001, Nov. 4). Special teams play special. *The Orange County Register.*

18. Harmonson, Todd (2001, Nov. 29). Polamalu earns All-America recognition. *The Orange County Register.*

9: CONQUEST

1. Kamp, David (2006, September). Troy Story. *GQ*, page 408.

2. Whicker, Mark (2001, Dec. 18). Polamalu is USC's expert on discipline. *The Orange County Register.*

3. Harmonson, Todd (2002, Aug. 16). USC's Polamalu hurt in collision. *The Orange County Register.*

4. Robinson, Alan (2006, Feb. 2). Matt Leinart from story "Polamalu a contradicting storm of big hits." *Associated Press.*

5. Hoffman, Leslie (2007, September). Pete Carroll from story "Renaissance Man." *WHIRL* Magazine.

6. Harmonson, Todd (2002, Aug. 20). Setting up the Heisman race. *The Orange County Register.*

7. Harmonson, Todd (2002, Aug. 10). Palmer: I haven't done anything. *The Orange County Register.*

8. Jenkins, Lee (2002, Aug. 24). Ranking the teams. *The Orange County Register.*

9. "It wasn't different ..." told to Myers, Justin (2020, Feb.). With guest Troy Polamalu. *The Bridge Podcast,* NBC Sports Northwest.

10. Whicker, Mark (2002, Sept. 3). The Trojans' defense settles down in second half. *The Orange County Register.*

11. Harmonson, Todd (2002, Sept. 15). 40-3. *The Orange County Register.*

12. Harmonson, Todd (2002, Sept. 19). Wildcats remember Polamalu's personal foul. *The Orange County Register.*

13. Harmonson, Todd (2002, Oct. 3). Carroll's calling. *The Orange County Register.*

14. Harmonson, Todd (2002, Aug. 31. Palmer on Troy in "Full speed ahead." The Orange County Register.

15. Harmonson, Todd (2002, Oct. 6). Defensive woes a Troy story. *The Orange County Register.*

16. DiPaola, Jerry (2004, Nov. 17). Polamalu brings a lot to the table. *Pittsburgh Tribune-Review.*

17. Harmonson, Todd (2002, Oct. 25). Incentive plan for Polamalu. *The Orange County Register.*

18. Harmonson, Todd (2002, Nov. 6). Ankle sprain frustrates Polamalu. *The Orange County Register.*

19. Harmonson, Todd (2002, Nov. 10). Polamalu takes of the safety. *The Orange County Register.*

20. Harmonson, Todd and Jenkins, Lee (2002, Nov. 30). First and Ten. *The Orange County Register.*

21. Bisheff, Steve (2002, Nov. 26). A time to give thanks ... for Polamalu. *The Orange County Register.*

22. Bisheff, Steve (2002, Dec. 1). Palmer turns game into trophy dash. *The Orange County Register.*

23. Harmonson, Todd and Zupke, Curtis (2002, Dec. 1). Legend of Troy grows. *The Orange County Register.*

24. Harmonson, Todd (2003, Jan. 3). Polamalu never got untracked. *The Orange County Register.*

25. Harmonson, Todd (2003, Jan. 3). Fantastic Finish. *The Orange County Register.*

10: MASTER OF NONE

1. Merrill Hoge (2006, April). On rookie Troy Polamalu standing still, interview with *WDVE.*

12: CELLULOID HEROES

1. Chapter headline derived from The Kinks' song "Celluloid Heroes" in honor of Troy Polamalu's study habits, the Steelers 15-1 record, and the Patriots' cheating.

2. Mazza Hillier, Gina (2006, August). The Vertical Game of Football. *Point of Light* magazine (Vol. 12, Issue 48).

3. Darren Perry to Lippock, Ron. Interview on Bengals game. *Steelers Takeaways.*

4. "We have their signs." One-on-one interview with Marc Edwards at youth soccer tournament c. 2014.

13: SERENITY, NOW

1. Chapter headline with punctuation change from Episode 3 of Seinfeld Season 9, character George Costanza's exhortations of Serenity Now!

2. Hoffman, Leslie (2007, September). Troy and Theodora's marriage information from "Renaissance Man." *WHIRL* Magazine.

3. "For a football player ..." told to Myers, Justin (2020, Feb.). With guest Troy Polamalu. *The Bridge Podcast*, NBC Sports Northwest.

4. Lippock, Ron. Interview with Chris Hope on close team. *Steelers Takeaways*.

14: REDEMPTION SONG

1. Chapter headline is the title of a popular song by Bob Marley and the Wailers, Troy Polamalu's favorite band at the time (2005).

2. "Pack your bags for Denver" a tribute to Steelers radio analyst Tunch Ilkin's commentary during the final turbulent moments of the Steelers-Colts playoff game in 2006.

3. Leverone, Bill (2006, Sept. 1). "He held up his ring finger ..." *The Sporting News*.

15: GOING HOME

1. Corbett, Jim (2006, Feb. 15). Polamalu's sudden impact revolutionizes safety position (John Lynch interview). *USA Today Sports Weekly*.

16: HOPE IS LOST

1. Kamp, David (2006, September). Troy Story. *GQ*, page 409.

2. Cook, Ron (2006, Nov. 20). Polamalu's play on a higher level. *Pittsburgh Post-Gazette*.

3. Lippock, Ron. Interview with Jovon Johnson. *Steelers Takeaways*.

17: STATE OF GRACE

1. "... he stole a Bible ..." Kamp, David (2006, September). Troy Story. *GQ*, page 408.

2. Crouse, Karen (2011, Jan. 12) A Defensive Anchor Walks a Spiritual Path. *New York Times*.

3. "... learned the Greek language ..." Mazza Hillier, Gina (2006, August). The Vertical Game of Football. *Point of Light* magazine (Vol. 12, Issue 48).

4. Troy Polamalu on religion - Kamp, David (2006, September). Troy Story. *GQ*.

20: CALL DOWN THE THUNDER

1. "You called down the thunder, well now you got it!" From the movie *Tombstone*.

2l: SUPER BOWL 43

1. Marvin Lewis interview at the Senior Bowl in Mobile, Alabama; yes, sadly, where the author watched the AFCCG.

2. Gil Brandt interview (2009, Jan. 30). Sirius radio.

3. "Oh, that Jamaican food." (2020, Jan. 31). YouTube interview with Troy Polamalu. *USA Today Sports.*

24: HE'S NOT SUPERMAN, HE'S TROY

1. Kerry Collins to Wyatt, Jim (2015, April 10). Titans Won't Forget Troy Polamalu. *The Tennessean.*

25: SWEETNESS

1. Chapter headline is the nickname of the late Chicago Bears Hall of Famer Walter Payton, the childhood hero of Troy Polamalu. Payton wore No. 34.

2. Gabe Sewell to Ruck, Rob (2018). *Tropic of Football.* The New Press.

28: BOLT FROM THE BLUE

1. Loni Fangupo to Lippock, Ron. *Steelers Takeaways.*

2. Solotaroff, Paul (2011, August). James Harrison: Confessions of an NFL Hitman. *Men's Journal.*

3. "LeBeau did calm him down ..." (2015, April 9). Troy Polamalu's retirement interview.

4. Rodney Harrison to Pittsburgh's 93.7 The Fan (2011, Oct. 26).

5. Jim Nantz to Krause, David (2012, March 13). Tomlin told Nantz he feared Tim Tebow big play in OT. *The Denver Post.*

29: COMMIT ALL YOUR ATROCITIES AT ONCE

1. Chapter headline merges Machiavelli quotes: "... one may call those atrocities that are committed at a stroke ..." and "Do all the harm you must at one and the same time." *The Prince.*

2. David Gilreath to Lippock, Ron. *Steelers Takeaways.*

30: WOE TO THE MONK WHO BECOMES FAMOUS

1. Chapter headline taken from the book *Mountain of Silence* in a quote from the hermit Paisios: "Woe to the monk who becomes famous. He can never find peace of mind. People will begin to weave all sorts of stories about him that are often not true."

3I: THE LAST RIDE

1. Ryan Clark on Steelers smoking marijuana (2014, Feb. 6) *First Take*. ESPN.

2. Rice, Grantland (1924, Oct. 18). The Four Horsemen. *New York Herald Tribune*.

32: A LOSS IN THE FORCE

1. Troy Polamalu one-on-one interview (2014, April 9).

2. Brian Billick to Bill Cowher on NFL Network.

3. End-of-chapter questions based on *The Last Dance*, a 2020 ESPN documentary on Michael Jordan.